THE WAY
FURROW
THE FORGE

JOSEMARÍA ESCRIVÁ

THE WAY
FURROW
THE FORGE

Scepter

This edition is published in the United States by SCEPTER PUBLISHERS, INC. PO Box 211, New York NY 10018-0004. http://www.scepterpublishers.org

© 1939 *Camino*; 1986 *Surco*; 1988 *Forja*.
by SCRIPTOR, S.A. (MADRID)

ISBN: 1889334723
Second printing, March 2008

CONTENTS

FURROW

THE FORGE

THE FORCE

EDITOR'S NOTE

There are books which have to be read with urgency because of the need to be up to date. There are also classic books which are read more peacefully and those which are referred to time and again because they deal with solid and permanent references. To that last category belongs— as experience has sufficiently demonstrated—THE WAY, FURROW and THE FORGE. The intention of the author Saint Josemaría Escrivá was, according to the words of Monsignor Alvaro del Portillo, 'to encourage and to facilitate personal prayer.'[1] The spirit behind every page of these books is oriented towards that end. Its formal structure, the division into chapters and the brief points, contribute to the author's intentions.

In combining the three titles in one volume—homogeneous in their contents but complementing one another with the variety and richness of the themes—this publisher has fulfilled an old desire and complied with a

[1] Foreword of Furrow, p. 258

request from its readers. This volume not only offers the advantage of combining the three volumes which are now acknowledged as classics of Christian spirituality, but also provides combined indices which simultaneously refer to each one of them. To unify the presentation of the analytical index, the subject titles of FURROW and THE FORGE were followed. Consequently, this has enriched the index of THE WAY.

We are confident that this publication will be a practical and effective instrument in the hands of those who already have discovered, in each separate work, a help in their personal encounter with God.

THE AUTHOR

Saint Josemaría Escrivá was born in Barbastro, in northern Spain, on January 9, 1902. At the age of 15 or 16, he began to feel the first intimations that God was calling him and he decided to become a priest. He started his ecclesiastical studies in the Seminary of Logroño in 1918, and later, in 1920, in that of St Francis de Paula in Saragossa, where from 1922 he was a superior or tutor. In 1923, he began to study Civil Law in the University of Saragossa, with the permission of his ecclesiastical superiors. These studies did not interfere with his theological studies. He was ordained deacon on December 20, 1924 and became a priest on March 28, 1925.

He began his work as a priest in the village of Perdiguera, within the diocese of Saragossa, and afterwards in Saragossa itself. In the spring of 1927, with the permission of the Archbishop of Saragossa, he moved to the Spanish capital Madrid and there carried out abundant priestly work among all kinds of people, devoting attention also to the poor and destitute in the outlying districts of the city, and especially to the in-

curably sick and the dying in the hospitals. He worked as chaplain to the Patronato de Enfermos (Foundation for the Sick), a welfare organization run by the Apostolic Sisters of the Sacred Heart. He also taught at a university academy, and continued his studies for a doctorate in Civil Law, which at that time could only be obtained from the University of Madrid.

On October 2, 1928, God made him see clearly what up to then he had only inklings of; and Saint Josemaría Escrivá founded Opus Dei (in English, the Work of God). Under God's continuing guidance, on February 14, 1930, he understood that he must open up the apostolic work of Opus Dei to women also. As a result, a new path was opening up in the Church, to promote, among people of all social classes, the search for holiness and the practice of the apostolate, through the sanctification of ordinary work, in the midst of the world and without changing one's state in life.

From October 2, 1928, the Founder of Opus Dei directed his energies to the mission God had entrusted to him, with great apostolic zeal for all souls. In 1934, he was appointed Rector of the Patronato de Santa Isabel (St Elizabeth Foundation). During the Spanish Civil War, at times putting his life at risk, he carried out his priestly ministry in Madrid and, subsequently, in the northern city of Burgos. Already in those years, Saint Josemaría Escrivá experienced harsh and sustained opposition, which he bore calmly and with a supernatural outlook.

On February 14, 1943, he founded the Priestly Society of the Holy Cross, which is inseparably united to Opus Dei and which, as well as opening up the possibility of ordaining lay members of Opus Dei to the priesthood and incardinating them for the service of the Work, would later on also enable priests who are incardinated in dioceses to share the spirituality and asceticism of Opus Dei, seeking holiness in the exercise of their ministerial duties, while remaining exclusively under their respective Ordinaries.

In 1946, he took up residence in Rome, which was to be his home for the rest of his life. From there, he stimulated and guided the development of Opus Dei throughout the world, using all his energies to give to the men and women of Opus Dei a solid formation in doctrine, ascetical spirit and apostolate. At the time of his death, Opus Dei had more than 60,000 members from 80 different nationalities.

Saint Escrivá was a Consultor to the Pontifical Commission for the authentic interpretation of the Code of Canon Law, and to the Sacred Congregation for Seminaries and Universities. He was a Domestic Prelate and an honorary Academician of the Pontifical Roman Academy of Theology. He was also the Chancellor of the Universities of Navarre (in Spain) and Piura (in Peru).

Saint Josemaría Escrivá died on June 26, 1975. For years, he had been offering his life for the Church and for the Pope. He was buried in the Crypt of the church of Our Lady of Peace in Rome. Msgr. Alvaro del Portillo (1914-1994), who for many years had been his closest collaborator, was unanimously elected to succeed him. The present Prelate of Opus Dei is Msgr. Javier Echevarria, who also worked for several decades with Saint Josemaría Escrivá and with his first successor, Msgr. del Portillo. Opus Dei, which from its inception had had the approval of the diocesan authorities and from 1943, also the appositio manuum *and subsequently the approval of the Holy See, was established as a Personal Prelature by his holiness Pope John Paul II on November 28, 1982. This was the canonical formula foreseen and desired by Saint Josemaría Escrivá.*

The reputation for holiness which the Founder of Opus Dei enjoyed in his lifetime has spread after his death to the far corners of the earth, as can be seen from countless spiritual and material favors attributed to his interces-sion; among them, a number of cures which are medically inexplicable. Many letters from all the continents, and among them those of 69 Cardinals and nearly 1300 Bish-ops (more than a third of the episcopate worldwide), were written requesting the Pope to open the Cause of Beatifi-cation and Canonization of Msgr. Escrivá. The Congrega-tion for the Causes of Saints gave its nihil obstat *for the opening of the Cause on January 30, 1981 and this was ratified by Pope John Paul II on February 5, 1981.*

Between 1981 and 1986, two processes took place, one in Rome and the other in Madrid, to gather information on the life and virtues of Msgr. Escrivá. Following the results of these two processes and accepting the favorable opinions of the congress of theological consultors and the Commission of Cardinals and Bishops, members of the Congregation for the Causes of Saints, the Holy Father, on April 9, 1990, declared the heroicity of the virtues of Msgr. Escrivá, who thus received the title of Venerable. On July 6, 1991, the Pope commanded the publication of a Decree declaring the miraculous nature of a cure attributed to the intercession of the Venerable Josemaría Escrivá. This act completed the juridical stages for the beatification of the Founder of Opus Dei, which was celebrated in Rome on May 17, 1992 in a solemn ceremony presided over by his holiness Pope John Paul II in St Peter's Square. Josemaría Escrivá was canonized on October 6, 2002.

From May 21, 1992, the body of Saint Josemaría rests in the altar of the Prelatic Church of Our Lady of Peace, in the central offices of the Prelature of Opus Dei. It is accompanied constantly by the prayers and thanksgiving of many people from all over the world who have been brought closer to God, attracted by the example and teachings of the founder of Opus Dei and by the devotion of those who turn to his intercession.

Among his published writings, apart from the theological and legal study La Abadesa de las Huelgas, *there are books of spirituality which have been translated into numerous languages:* The Way, Holy Rosary, Christ is Passing By, Friends of God, The Way of the Cross, Loving the Church, Furrow, The Forge *(the last five titles have been published posthumously). Another book, which brings together press interviews, is entitled* Conversations with Msgr. Escrivá.

THE WAY

THE WAY

PROLOGUE OF THE AUTHOR

Read these counsels slowly.
Pause to meditate on these thoughts.
They are things that I whisper in your
ear—confiding them—as a friend, as a
brother, as a father.
And they are being heard by God.
I won't tell you anything new.
I will only stir your memory,
so that some thought will arise
and strike you;
and so you will better your life
and set out along ways of prayer
and of Love.
And in the end you will be
a more worthy soul.

CHARACTER

1 Don't let your life be sterile. Be useful. Blaze a trail. Shine forth with the light of your faith and of your love.

With your apostolic life wipe out the slimy and filthy mark left by the impure sowers of hatred. And light up all the ways of the earth with the fire of Christ that you carry in your heart.

2 May your behavior and your conversation be such that everyone who sees or hears you can say: This man reads the life of Jesus Christ.

3 Maturity. Stop making faces and acting up like a child! Your bearing ought to reflect the peace and order in your soul.

4 Don't say, "That's the way I am—it's my character." It's your *lack* of character. *Esto vir!*—Be a man!

5 Get used to saying No.

6 Turn your back on the deceiver when he whispers in your ear, "Why complicate your life?"

7 Don't have a "small town" outlook. Enlarge your heart until it becomes universal—"catholic."
   Don't fly like a barnyard hen when you can soar like an eagle.

8 Serenity. Why lose your temper if by losing it you offend God, you trouble your neighbor, you give yourself a bad time... and in the end you have to set things aright anyway?

9 What you have just said, say it in another tone, without anger, and what you say will have more force... and above all, you won't offend God.

10 Never reprimand anyone while you feel provoked over a fault that has been committed. Wait until the next day, or even longer. Then make your remonstrance calmly and with a purified intention. You'll gain more with an affectionate word than you ever would from three hours of quarreling. Control your temper.

11 Will-power. Energy. Example. What has to be done is done... without wavering... without worrying about what others think...

Otherwise, Cisneros* would not have been Cisneros; nor Teresa of Ahumada, St Teresa; nor Iñigo of Loyola, St Ignatius.

God and daring! *"Regnare Christum volumus!"*—"We want Christ to reign!"

12 Let obstacles only make you bigger. The grace of our Lord will not be lacking: *"inter medium montium pertransibunt aquae!"*—"through the very midst of the mountains the waters shall pass." You will pass through mountains!

What does it matter that you have to curtail your activity for the moment, if later, like a spring which has been compressed, you'll advance much farther than you ever dreamed?

13 Get rid of those useless thoughts which are at best a waste of time.

*Cisneros (1436-1517): Spanish Cardinal, Regent of the Throne of Spain and Confessor of Queen Isabella the Catholic. Cardinal Cisneros started the reform of the Church in Spain, anticipating what years later the Council of Trent would start for all Christendom. His courage and strength of character were widely known.

14   Don't waste your energy and your time—which belong to God—throwing stones at the dogs that bark at you on the way. Ignore them.

15   Don't put off your work until tomorrow.

16   Give in? Be just commonplace? You, a sheep-like follower? You were born to be a leader!

Among us there is no place for the lukewarm. Humble yourself and Christ will kindle in you again the fire of love.

17   Don't succumb to that disease of character whose symptoms are a general lack of seriousness, unsteadiness in action and speech, foolishness—in a word, frivolity.

And that frivolity, mind you, which makes your plans so void—"so filled with emptiness"—will make of you a lifeless and useless dummy, unless you react in time—not tomorrow, but now!

18   You go on being worldly, frivolous and giddy because you are a coward. What is it, if not cowardice, to refuse to face yourself?

19   Will-power. A very important quality. Don't disregard the little things, which are really never futile or trivial. For by the constant practice of repeated self-denial in little things, with God's grace you will increase in strength and manliness of character. In that way you'll first become master of yourself, and then a guide and a leader: to compel, to urge, to draw others with your example and with your word and with your knowledge and with your power.

20 You clash with the character of one person or another... It has to be that way—you are not a dollar bill to be liked by everyone.

Besides, without those clashes which arise in dealing with your neighbors, how could you ever lose the sharp corners, the edges—imperfections and defects of your character—and acquire the order, the smoothness and the firm mildness of charity, of perfection?

If your character and that of those around you were soft and sweet like marshmallows, you would never become a saint.

21 Excuses. You'll never lack them if you want to avoid your duties. What a lot of rationalizing!

Don't stop to think about excuses. Get rid of them and do what you should.

22 Be firm! Be strong! Be a man! And then... be an angel!

23   You say you can't do more? Couldn't it be... that you can't do less?

24   You are ambitious: for knowledge... for leadership. You want to be daring.
   Good. Fine. But let it be for Christ, for Love.

25   Don't argue. Arguments usually bring no light because the light is smothered by emotion.

26   Matrimony is a holy sacrament. When the time comes for you to receive it, ask your spiritual director or your confessor to suggest an appropriate book. Then you'll be better prepared to bear worthily the burdens of a home.

27   Do you laugh because I tell you that you have a "vocation to marriage"? Well, you have just that—a vocation.
   Commend yourself to St Raphael that he may keep you pure, as he did Tobias, until the end of the way.

28   Marriage is for the rank and file, not for the officers of Christ's army. For, unlike food, which is necessary for every individual, procreation is necessary only for the species, and individuals can dispense with it.

A desire to have children? Behind us we shall leave children—many children... and a lasting trail of light, if we sacrifice the selfishness of the flesh.

29 The limited and pitiful happiness of the selfish man, who withdraws into his shell, his ivory tower... is not difficult to attain in this world. But that happiness of the selfish is not lasting.

For this false semblance of heaven are you going to forsake the Joy of Glory without end?

30 You're shrewd. But don't tell me you are young. Youth gives all it can—it gives itself without reserve.

31 Selfish! You... always looking out for yourself.

You seem unable to feel the brotherhood of Christ. In others you don't see brothers; you see stepping-stones.

I can foresee your complete failure. And when you are down, you'll expect others to treat you with the charity you're unwilling to show them.

32 You'll never be a leader if you see others only as stepping-stones to get ahead. You'll be a leader if you are ambitious for the salvation of all souls.

You can't live with your back turned on everyone; you have to be eager to make others happy.

33   You never want "to get to the bottom of things." At times, because of politeness. Other times—most times—because you fear hurting yourself. Sometimes again, because you fear hurting others. But always because of fear!

With that fear of digging for the truth you'll never be a man of good judgment.

34   Don't be afraid of the truth, even though the truth may mean your death.

35   There are many pretty terms I don't like: you call cowardice "prudence". Your "prudence" gives an opportunity to those enemies of God, without any ideas in their heads, to pass themselves off as scholars, and so reach positions that they never should attain.

36   Yes, that abuse *can* be eradicated. It's a lack of character to let it continue as something hopeless—without any possible remedy.

Don't evade your duty. Do it in a forthright way, even though others may not.

37   You have, as they say, "the gift of gab". But in spite of all your talk, you can't get me to justify—by calling it "providential"—what has no justification.

38 Can it be true (I just can't believe it!) that on earth there are no men—only bellies?

39 "Pray that I may never be satisfied with what is easy," you say. I've already prayed. Now it is up to you to carry out that fine resolution.

40 Faith, joy, optimism. But not the folly of closing your eyes to reality.

41 What a sublime way of carrying on with your empty follies, and what a way of getting somewhere in the world: rising, always rising simply by "weighing little," by having nothing inside—neither in your head nor in your heart!

42 Why those variations in your character? When are you going to apply your will to something? Drop that craze for laying cornerstones, and finish at least one of your projects.

43 Don't be so touchy. The least thing offends you. People have to weigh their words to talk to you even about the most trivial matter.

Don't feel hurt if I tell you that you are... unbearable. Unless you change, you'll never be of any use.

44 Use the polite excuse that christian charity and good manners require. But then... keep on going with holy shamelessness, without stopping until you have reached the summit in the fulfillment of your duty.

45 Why feel hurt by the unjust things people say of you? You would be even worse, if God ever left you.
      Keep on doing good, and shrug your shoulders.

46 Don't you think that equality, as many people understand it, is synonymous with injustice?

47 That pose and those important airs don't fit you well. It's obvious that they're false. At least, try not to use them either with God, or with your director, or with your brothers; and then there will be between them and you one barrier less.

48 You lack character. What a mania for interfering in everything! You are bent on being the salt of every dish. And—you won't mind if I speak clearly—you haven't the qualities of salt: you can't be dissolved and pass unnoticed, as salt does.
      You lack a spirit of sacrifice. And you abound in a spirit of curiosity and ostentation.

49 Keep quiet. Don't be "babyish," a caricature of a child, a tattle-tale, a trouble-maker, a squealer. With your stories and tales you have chilled the warm glow of charity; you couldn't have done more harm. And if by any chance you—your wagging tongue—have shaken down the strong walls of other people's perseverance, your own perseverance ceases to be a grace of God. It has become a treacherous instrument of the enemy.

50 You're curious and inquisitive, prying and nosey. Aren't you ashamed that even in your defects you are not much of a man? Be a man, and instead of poking into other people's lives, get to know what you really are yourself.

51 Your manly spirit—simple and straightforward—is crushed when you find yourself entangled in gossip and scandalous talk. You don't understand how it could happen and you never wished to be involved in it anyway. Suffer the humiliation that such talk causes you and let the experience urge you to greater discretion.

52 When you must judge others, why put in your criticism the bitterness of your own failures?

53 That critical spirit—granted you mean well—should never be directed toward the apostolate in which you work nor toward your brothers. In your supernatural undertakings that critical spirit—forgive me for saying it—can do a lot of harm. For when you get involved in judging the work of others, you are not doing anything constructive. Really you have no right to judge, even if you have the highest possible motives, as I admit. And with your negative attitude you hold up the progress of others.

"Then," you ask worriedly, "my critical spirit, which is the keynote of my character...?"

Listen. I'll set your mind at ease. Take pen and paper. Write down simply and confidently—yes, and briefly— what is worrying you. Give the note to your superior, and don't think any more about it. He is in charge and has the grace of state. He will file the note... or will throw it in the wastebasket. And since your criticism is not gossip and you do it for the highest motives, it's all the same to you.

54   Conform? It is a word found only in the vocabulary of those ("You might as well conform," they say) who have no will to fight—the lazy, the cunning, the cowardly—because they know they are defeated before they start.

55   Man, listen! Even though you may be like a child—and you really are one in the eyes of God—be a little less naive: don't put your brothers "on the spot" before strangers.

DIRECTION

56 The "stuff" of saints. That's what is said about some people—that they have the stuff of saints. But apart from the fact that saints are not made of "stuff," having "stuff" is not sufficient.

A great spirit of obedience to a director and a great readiness to correspond to grace are required. For if you don't allow God's grace and your director to do their work, the sculptured image of Christ, into which the saintly man is shaped, will never appear.

And that "stuff" of which we have been speaking will be only a rough, unshaped log fit for the fire—for a good fire if it is good "stuff".

57 Get to know the Holy Spirit, the Great Unknown, the one who has to sanctify you.

Don't forget that you are a temple of God. The Paraclete is in the center of your soul: listen to him and follow his inspirations with docility.

58   Don't hinder the work of the Paraclete. Be united to Christ in order to purify yourself, and together with him experience the insults, the spit, the blows and the thorns... Experience with him the weight of the cross, the nails tearing your flesh, and the agony of a forsaken death... And enter into the pierced side of our Lord Jesus until you find secure shelter in his wounded heart.

59   It's good for you to know this doctrine, which is always sound: your own spirit is a bad advisor, a poor pilot to steer your soul through the squalls and storms and across the reefs of the interior life.

That's why it is the will of God that the command of the ship be entrusted to a master who, with his light and knowledge, can guide us to a safe port.

60   You wouldn't think of building a good house to live in here on earth without an architect. How can you ever hope, without a director, to build the castle of your sanctification in order to live forever in heaven?

61   When a layman sets himself up as an arbiter of morals, he frequently errs; laymen can only be disciples.

62   A director—you need one, in order to offer yourself, to surrender yourself... by obedience. You need a director who understands your apostolate, who knows what God wants. Such a one will effectively help to forward the work of the Holy Spirit in your soul without taking you from your place, filling you with peace and teaching you how your work can be fruitful.

63 You think you are really somebody: your studies— your research, your publications; your social position— your name; your political accomplishments—the offices you hold; your wealth; your age... no longer a child!

Precisely because of all this, you—more than others— need a director for your soul.

64 Don't hide those suggestions of the devil from your director. When you confide them to him, your victory brings you more grace from God. Moreover, you now have the gift of counsel and the prayers of your spiritual father to help you keep right on conquering.

65 Why do you hesitate to know yourself and to let your director know you as you really are?

You'll have won a great battle if you lose the fear of letting yourself be known.

66 A priest—whoever he may be—is always another Christ.

67 Though you know it well, I want to remind you again that a Priest is "another Christ", and that the Holy

Spirit has said, *"Nolite tangere Christos meos"*—"Do not touch my Christs."

68 *Presbyter*—priest—etymologically means an elderly man. If old age deserves reverence think how much more you ought to revere a priest.

69 What a lack of refinement—and what a lack of respect—to play a trick on a priest, whoever he may be, under any circumstances!

70 I insist: those tricks or jokes about a priest, in spite of what may seem to you to be attenuating circumstances, always are at least vulgar, a lack of good manners.

71 How we should admire purity in the priesthood! It is its treasure. No tyrant will ever be able to wrest this crown from the Church.

72 Don't ever make a priest run the risk of losing his dignity. It is a virtue which, without pompousness, he simply must have.

How hard that young priest—a friend of ours—prayed for it: "Lord, grant me... eighty years of dignity!"

You too should pray for it for all priests, and you'll have done something good.

73 It hurt you—like a dagger in your heart—to hear people say you had spoken badly of those priests. And I'm glad it hurt, for now I'm quite sure you have the right spirit!

74 To love God and not to revere the priest... This is not possible.

75 Like the good sons of Noah, cover the weaknesses you may see in your father, the priest, with a cloak of charity.

76 If you don't have a plan of life, you'll never have order.

77 You told me that to tie yourself to a plan of life, to a schedule, would be so monotonous!

And I answered, "It is monotonous because you lack Love."

78 If you don't get up at a set hour, you'll never fulfill your plan of life.

79 Virtue without order? Strange virtue!

80 With order, your time will be multiplied, and you will be able to give more glory to God by doing more work in his service.

PRAYER

81   Action is worthless without prayer; prayer is worth more with sacrifice.

82   First, prayer; then, atonement; in the third place— very much "in the third place"—action.

83   Prayer is the foundation of the spiritual edifice. Prayer is all-powerful.

84   *"Domine, doce nos orare."*—"Lord, teach us to pray!"

And our Lord answered, "When you pray, say: *Pater noster, qui es in coelis...*"—"Our Father, who art in heaven..."

How can we fail to appreciate the value of vocal prayer!

85 Slowly. Think about what you're saying, who is saying it and to whom. Because talking fast, without pausing for reflection, is only noise—the clatter of tin cans.

Along with St Teresa I'll tell you that, however much you move your lips, I do not call it prayer.

86 Your prayer ought to be liturgical. Would that you were given to reciting the psalms and prayers of the missal instead of private or special prayers!

87 "Not by bread alone does man live, but by every word that comes forth from the mouth of God," said our Lord. Bread and the word! The host and prayer.

Without these you won't live a supernatural life.

88 You seek the friendship of those who, with their conversation and affection, with their company, help you to bear more easily the exile of this world—although sometimes those friends fail you. I don't see anything wrong with that.

But how is it that you do not seek everyday, more eagerly, the company, the conversation of that great friend who will never fail you?

89 "Mary has chosen the better part," we read in the holy Gospel. There she is, drinking in the words of the

Master. Apparently idle, she is praying and loving. Afterwards she accompanies Jesus in his preaching through
towns and villages.

Without prayer, how difficult it is to accompany him!

90 You don't know how to pray? Put yourself in the
presence of God, and as soon as you have said, "Lord,
I don't know how to pray!" you can be sure you've
already begun.

91 You wrote to me: "To pray is to talk with God. But
about what?" About what? About him, and yourself: joys,
sorrows, successes and failures, great ambitions, daily
worries—even your weaknesses! And acts of thanksgiving and petitions—and love and reparation.

In short, to get to know him and to get to know
yourself—"to get acquainted!"

92 *"Et in meditatione mea exardescit ignis."*—"And
in my meditation a fire shall flame out." That is why you
go to pray: to become a bonfire, a living flame giving heat
and light.

So, when you are not able to go on, when you feel
that your fire is dying out, if you cannot throw on it sweet-
smelling logs, throw on the branches and twigs of short
vocal prayers and ejaculations, to keep the bonfire burning. And you will not have wasted your time.

93   You see yourself so poor and weak that you recognize you are unworthy of having God listen to you. But, what about the merits of Mary? And the wounds of your Lord? And... Aren't you a child of God?

Besides, he listens to you, *"quoniam bonus..., quoniam in saeculum misericordia eius,"*—"for he is good, and his mercy endures forever."

94   He has become so small—you see: an infant!—so that you can come close to him with confidence.

95   *"In te, Domine, speravi"*—"In Thee, O Lord, have I hoped." And together with human means I prayed and took my cross. And my hope was not in vain, nor will it ever be. *"Non confundar in aeternum"*—Let me never be confounded."

96   It is Jesus who speaks: "Amen I say to you, ask and it shall be given to you, seek and you shall find, knock and it shall be opened to you."

Pray! In what human venture can you have greater guarantee of success?

97   You don't know what to say to our Lord in prayer. Nothing comes to you and yet you would like to ask his advice about many things.

Look: take some notes during the day of the things you want to think about in the presence of God. And then go with those notes to pray.

98 After the prayer of priests and of consecrated virgins, the prayer most pleasing to God is that of children and of the sick.

99 When you go to pray, let this be a firm resolution: Don't prolong your prayer just because you find consolation in it, nor curtail it just because you find it dry.

100 Don't tell Jesus you want consolation in prayer. But if he gives it to you, thank him.

Tell him always that what you want is perseverance.

101 Persevere in prayer. Persevere, even when your efforts seem sterile. Prayer is always fruitful.

102 Your mind is sluggish and won't work. You struggle to coordinate your ideas in the presence of our Lord, but it's useless: a complete fog!

Don't force yourself, and don't worry either. Listen closely: it is the hour for your heart.

103 Those words that struck you when you were praying: engrave them in your memory and recite them slowly many times during the day.

104 *"Pernoctans in oratione Dei"*—"He spent the whole night in prayer to God," says St Luke of our Lord.

And you? How many times have you persevered like that?

Well, then...

105 If you don't keep in touch with Christ in prayer and in the bread, how can you make him known to others?

106 You wrote, and I well understand: "Every day I spend my 'little time' in prayer. If it weren't for that...!"

107 Sanctity without prayer? I don't believe in such sanctity.

108 Following the words of another writer, I'll tell you that your apostolic life is worth only as much as your prayer.

109 If you're not a man of prayer, I don't believe in the sincerity of your intentions when you say that you work for Christ.

110 You told me once that you feel like a broken clock that strikes at the wrong time; you're cold, dry and arid at the time of your prayer. And, on the other hand, when you least expect it, on the street, in your everyday tasks, in the midst of the noise and hustle of the city or in the concentrated calm of your professional work, you find yourself praying... At the wrong time? Possibly; but don't let those chimes of your clock go to waste. The Spirit breathes where he pleases.

111 I had to laugh at the impatience of your prayer. You were telling him, "I don't want to grow old, Jesus... To have to wait so long to see you! By then, perhaps, I won't have my heart so inflamed as it is now. 'Then' seems too late. Now, my union would be more gallant, because I love you with a youthful love."

112 I like to see you live that "ambitious reparation" —"for the world!" you said.

Good. But first of all reparation for the members of your spiritual family, for your relatives, for the people of your own country.

113 You were telling him: "Don't trust me, Jesus. But I, ...I do trust you. I abandon myself in your arms; there I leave all I have—my weaknesses!" And I think it's a very good prayer.

114 The prayer of a Christian is never a monologue.

115 "Minutes of silence." Leave silence for those whose hearts are dry.

We Catholics, children of God, speak with our Father who is in heaven.

116 Don't neglect your spiritual reading. Reading has made many saints.

117 "By reading," you wrote me, "I build up a store of fuel. It seems a lifeless pile, but I often find that my mind spontaneously draws from it material which fills my prayer with life and inflames my thanksgiving after communion."

HOLY PURITY

118 Holy purity is granted by God when it is asked for with humility.

119 How beautiful is holy purity! But it is not holy, not pleasing to God, if we separate it from charity. Charity is the seed that will grow and yield savory fruit when it is moistened with the waters of purity. Without charity, purity is fruitless and its sterile waters turn the soul into a swamp, a stagnant marsh, from which rises the stench of pride.

120 "Purity?" they ask. And they smile. They are the ones who go on to marriage with worn-out bodies and disillusioned souls.

I promise you a book—God willing—that could be entitled: *Celibacy, Matrimony and Purity.*

121   There is need for a crusade of manliness and purity to counteract and nullify the savage work of those who think man is a beast.

And that crusade is *your* work.

122   Many live like angels in the middle of the world. You,... why not you?

123   When you decide firmly to lead a clean life, chastity will not be a burden on you: it will be a crown of triumph.

124   You, a doctor-apostle, wrote to me: "We all know from experience that we can be chaste, living vigilantly, frequenting the sacraments and stamping out the first sparks of passion before the fire gets started."

"And it is precisely among the chaste where the most clean-cut men from every point of view are found. And among the impure abound the timid, the selfish, the hypocritical and the cruel—all characters of little manliness."

125   I wish—you told me—that John, the young apostle, would take me into his confidence and give me advice, and would encourage me to acquire purity of heart.

If you really want it, tell him so: you'll feel encouraged, and you'll receive advice.

126 Gluttony is the forerunner of impurity.

127 Don't try to reason with concupiscence. Scorn it.

128 Decency and modesty are "little brothers" of purity.

129 Without holy purity you can't persevere in the apostolate.

130 O Jesus, remove that unclean scab of sensual corruption that covers my heart, so that I can feel and readily follow the breath of the Paraclete in my soul.

131 Never talk of impure things or events, not even to deplore them. Look, it's a subject that sticks more than tar. Change the conversation, or if that's not possible, continue, but speaking of the need and beauty of holy purity—a virtue of the men who know what their souls are worth.

132 Don't be such a coward as to be "brave." Flee!

133 Saints are not abnormal cases to be studied by a modernistic doctor.

They were—they are—normal, with flesh like yours. And they conquered.

134 "Even if flesh is dressed in silk..." That's what I'll tell you when I see you waver in a temptation that hides its impurity under the name of art, science... or charity!

With the words of an old proverb I'll tell you, "Even if flesh is dressed in silk, it's still flesh."

135 If you only knew what you are worth!... It is St Paul who tells you: You have been bought "*pretio magno*"—"at a great price."

And he adds: "*glorificate et portate Deum in corpore vestro*"—"glorify God and bear him in your body."

136 When you have sought the company of a sensual satisfaction, what loneliness afterwards!

137 And to think that for the satisfaction of a moment, which left bitter dregs within you, you've lost "the way"!

138 "*Infelix ego homo!, quis me liberabit de corpore mortis huius?*"—"Unhappy man that I am, who will deliver me from this body of death?" Thus cried St Paul. Courage! He too had to fight.

139 At the time of temptation think of the love that awaits you in heaven: foster the virtue of hope—it's not a lack of generosity.

140 No matter what happens, don't worry as long as you don't consent. For only the will can open the door of the heart and let that corruption in.

141 You seem to hear a voice within you saying, "That religious prejudice...!" And then the eloquent defense of all the weaknesses of our poor fallen flesh: "Its rights!"

When this happens to you, tell the enemy that there is a natural law, and a law of God, and God!... and also hell.

142 *"Domine!"*—"Lord!" *"si vis, potes me mundare."* —"If you will, you can make me clean."

What a beautiful prayer for you to say often, with the faith of the poor leper, when there happens to you what God and you and I know may happen. You won't have to wait long to hear the Master's reply: *"Volo, mundare!"* —"I will! Be made clean!"

143 To defend his purity, St Francis of Assisi rolled in the snow, St Benedict threw himself into a thornbush, St Bernard plunged into an icy pond...

You... what have *you* done?

144 The spotless purity of John's whole life makes him strong facing the cross. The rest of the Apostles flee from Golgotha. He, with the Mother of Christ, remains.

Don't forget that purity strengthens and invigorates your character.

145 The battle front in Madrid. A score of officers in noble and cheerful camaraderie. A song is heard, then another, and another...

That young lieutenant with the brown moustache only heard the first one:

> "I do not like
> divided hearts;
> and if I give mine,
> I give it whole."

"What resistance to give my heart whole!" And a prayer flowed forth in a calm, broad stream.

HEART

146 You give me the impression you are carrying your heart in your hands, as if you were offering goods for sale. Who wants it? If it doesn't appeal to anyone, you'll decide to give it to God.

Do you think that's how the saints acted?

147 Creatures for you? Creatures for God. If for you, let them be yours for his sake.

148 Why stoop to drink from the puddles of worldly consolations if you can satisfy your thirst with waters that spring up into life everlasting?

149 Detach yourself from creatures until you are stripped of them. For the devil, says Pope St Gregory, has nothing of his own in this world, and he goes into battle naked. If you are "clothed" when you fight with him, you'll soon be pulled down to the ground, because he will have something to grab on to.

150 It's as if your angel were saying to you, "You have your heart so full of human attachments"... Is that what you want your guardian to watch over?

151 Detachment. How hard it is! How I wish that I were fastened only by three nails and had no more feeling in my flesh than the cross!

152 Don't you sense that more peace and more union await you when you have corresponded to that extraordinary grace that requires complete detachment?

Struggle for him to please him, but strengthen your hope.

153 Go, generously and like a child ask him, "What are you going to give me when you ask 'this' of me?"

154 You're afraid of becoming distant and cold with everyone—you want so much to be detached!

Get rid of that fear. If you belong to Christ—completely to Christ—he will give you fire, light and warmth for all men.

155 Jesus is never satisfied "sharing". He wants all.

156 You don't want to submit yourself to the will of God... and instead you adapt yourself to the will of anybody and everybody.

157 Don't twist things around! If God gives himself to you, why are you so attached to creatures?

158 Now it's tears! It hurts, doesn't it? Of course, man! That's what it was meant to do.

159 Your heart weakens and you reach out for something on earth to support you. Good, but take care that what you grasp to stop you from falling doesn't become a dead weight that will drag you down, a chain that will enslave you.

160 Tell me, tell me: This... is it a friendship or a chain?

161 You squander your tenderness. And I tell you: "Charity toward your neighbor, yes: always." But listen closely, apostolic soul: that feeling which our Lord himself has placed in your heart is Christ's and Christ's alone.

Besides, when you opened one of the locks of your heart—which needs at least seven locks—isn't it true that more than once a cloud of doubt remained over your soul? And you asked yourself, worried in spite of the purity of your intentions, "Haven't I gone too far in my outward show of affection?"

162 Put your heart aside. Duty comes first. But, when fulfilling your duty, put your heart into it. It helps.

163 "If your right eye scandalizes you, pluck it out and cast it from you!" Poor heart... that's what scandalizes you!

Grasp it, hold it tight in your hands—and don't give it any consolation. And, when it asks for consolation, full of noble compassion say to it slowly, as if confiding, "My heart... heart on the cross, heart on the cross!"

164 How goes your heart?... Don't be worried. The saints—who were perfectly ordinary, normal beings like you and me—also felt those natural inclinations. And if they had not felt them, their *supernatural* reaction of keeping their heart—body and soul—for God, instead of giving it to creatures, would have had little merit.

That's why, once the way has been seen, the weakness of the heart should be no obstacle for a soul filled with determination and completely in Love.

165 You, who for an earthly love have endured so many degradations, do you really believe that you love

Christ when you are not willing to suffer—for him!—that humiliation?

166   You write me: "Father, I have... a 'toothache' in my heart." I won't laugh, because I realize that you need a good dentist to make a few extractions.

If only you'd let him!...

167   "Oh, if only I had broken it off at the start!" you said to me. May you never have to repeat that belated exclamation.

168   "It made me laugh to hear you speak of the 'account' our Lord will demand of you. No, for you he will not be a judge—in the harsh sense of the word. He will simply be Jesus." These words, written by a holy bishop, have consoled more than one troubled heart and could very well console yours.

169   Suffering overwhelms you because you take it like a coward. Meet it bravely, with a christian spirit, and you will esteem it like a treasure.

170   How clear the way! How obvious the obstacles! What good weapons to overcome them! And yet, how many times you go astray and how many times you stumble! Isn't it true?

That fine thread—a chain, a chain forged of iron—
which you and I know about and which you don't want
to break: that is what draws you from the way and makes
you stumble and even fall.

What are you waiting for? Cut it... and advance.

171 Love... is well worth any love!

MORTIFICATION

172 Unless you mortify yourself you'll never be a prayerful soul.

173 The appropriate word you left unsaid; the joke you didn't tell; the cheerful smile for those who bother you; that silence when you're unjustly accused; your kind conversation with people you find boring and tactless; the daily effort to overlook one irritating detail or another in those who live with you... this, with perseverance, is indeed solid interior mortification.

174 Don't say, "That person bothers me." Think: "That person sanctifies me."

175 No ideal becomes a reality without sacrifice. Deny yourself. It is so beautiful to be a victim!

176 How many times you resolve to serve God in something and then have to content yourself—you are so weak—with offering him that frustrated feeling, the feeling of having failed to keep that easy resolution!

177 Don't miss a chance to "give in". It's hard—but how pleasing in the eyes of God!

178 Whenever you see a poor, wooden cross, alone, uncared-for, worthless... and without a corpus, don't forget that that cross is *your* cross— the everyday hidden cross, unattractive and unconsoling—the cross that is waiting for the corpus it lacks: and that corpus must be you.

179 Choose mortifications that don't mortify others.

180 Where there is no mortification, there is no virtue.

181 Interior mortification. I don't believe in your interior mortification if I see that you despise mortification of the senses—that you don't practice it.

182 In our poor present life, let us drink to the last drop from the chalice of pain. What does it matter to suffer for ten, twenty, fifty years, if afterwards there is heaven forever, forever... forever!

And above all—even better than for the sake of the reward, *propter retributionem*—what does suffering matter if we accept it to console, to please God our Lord, with a spirit of reparation, united with him on his cross—in a word, if we suffer for Love?...

183 The eyes! Through them much wickedness enters into the soul. How many experiences like David's!

If you guard your eyes, you'll be assured of guarding your heart.

184 Why should you look around you, if you carry "your world" within you?

185 The world admires only the spectacular sacrifice, because it does not realize the value of the sacrifice that is hidden and silent.

186 We must give ourselves in everything, we must deny ourselves in everything. Our sacrifice must be a holocaust.

187 Paradox: To live one must die.

188 Remember that the heart is a traitor. Keep it locked with seven bolts.

189 Everything that doesn't lead you to God is an obstacle. Tear it out and cast it far from you.

190 A soul whose immediate superior was bad tempered and irritable was moved by God to say, "Thank you, my God, for this truly divine treasure. Where would I find another to repay each kindness with a kick?"

191 Conquer yourself each day from the very first moment, getting up on the dot, at a set time, without granting a single minute to laziness.

If, with the help of God, you conquer yourself in that moment, you'll have accomplished a great deal for the rest of the day.

It's so discouraging to find yourself beaten in the first skirmish!

192 You always come out beaten. Resolve, each time, to work for the salvation of a particular soul, or his sanctification, or his vocation to the apostolate. If you do so, I'll be sure of your victory.

193 Don't be "namby pamby"! That's not the way I want you. It's time you get rid of that peculiar pity that you feel for yourself.

194 I'm going to tell you which are man's treasures on earth so you won't slight them: hunger, thirst, heat, cold, pain, dishonor, poverty, loneliness, betrayal, slander, prison...

195 It is true, whoever said it, that the soul and the body are two enemies that cannot be separated, and two friends that cannot get along.

196 The body must be given a little less than it needs. Otherwise it will turn traitor.

197 If they have witnessed your weaknesses and faults, does it matter if they witness your penance?

198 These are the savory fruits of the mortified soul: tolerance and understanding toward the defects of others; intolerance toward his own.

199 If the grain of wheat does not die, it remains unfruitful. Don't you want to be a grain of wheat, to die through mortification, and to yield stalks rich in grain? May Jesus bless your wheatfield!

200 You don't conquer yourself, you aren't mortified, because you are proud. You lead a life of penance? Remember: pride can exist with penance.

Furthermore: Your sorrow, after your falls, after your failures in generosity, is it really sorrow or is it the frustration of seeing yourself so small and weak?

How far you are from Jesus if you are not humble...
even if new roses blossom every day from your disciplines!

201 What a taste of gall and vinegar, or ash and
bitterness! What a dry mouth, coated and cracked! Yet
that physical feeling is nothing compared with the bad
taste in your soul.

The truth is that "more is being asked of you" and you
can't bring yourself to give it. Humble yourself! Would
that bitter taste still remain in your flesh and in your spirit
if you did all that you could?

202 You're going to punish yourself voluntarily for
your weakness and your lack of generosity? Good. But
let it be a reasonable penance imposed, as it were, on an
enemy who is at the same time your brother.

203 The happiness of us poor men, even when it has
supernatural motives, always leaves a bitter aftertaste.
What did you expect? Here on earth, suffering is the salt
of our life.

204 Many who would let themselves be nailed to a
cross before the astonished gaze of thousands of spectators,
won't bear the pinpricks of each day with a christian
spirit!

But think, which is the more heroic?

205 We were reading—you and I—the heroically ordinary life of that man of God. And we saw him struggle whole months and years (what an "accounting" he kept in his particular examination of conscience!); one day at breakfast he would win, the next day he'd lose..."I didn't take butter... I did take butter!" he would jot down.

May we too—you and I—live our... "drama" of the butter.

206 The heroic minute. It's time to get up, on the dot! Without hesitation, a supernatural thought and... up! The heroic minute; here you have a mortification that strengthens your will and does not weaken your body.

207 Give thanks, as for a very special favor, for that holy abhorrence that you feel toward yourself.

PENANCE

208 Blessed be pain. Loved be pain. Sanctified be pain... Glorified be pain!

209 A whole program for a good course in the "subject" of suffering has been given to us by the Apostle: *"spe gaudentes"*—"rejoicing in hope," *"in tribulatione patientes"*—"patient in tribulation," *"orationi instantes"*— "persevering in prayer."

210 Atonement: this is the path that leads to life.

211 Do penance: bury your negligences, offenses and sins in the deep pit dug by your humility. Thus does the farmer bury rotten fruit, dead twigs and fallen leaves at the foot of the tree that bore them. And what was unfruitful, even harmful, makes a real contribution to a new fertility.

Learn to draw from your falls a new impulse: from death, life.

212   That Christ you see is not Jesus. At best it is only the pitiful image that your blurred eyes are able to form...

Purify yourself. Make your sight cleaner with humility and penance. Then the pure light of love will not fail you. And you will have perfect vision. The image you see will really be his: Jesus himself.

213   Jesus suffers to carry out the will of the Father. And you, who also want to carry out the most holy will of God, following the steps of the Master, can you complain if you meet suffering on your way?

214   Say to your body: "I would rather keep you in slavery than be myself your slave."

215   What great fear people have of atonement! If what they do to please the world were done with purified intention for God, what saints many would be!

216   You are weeping? Don't be ashamed. Weep! Yes, for men also weep like you when they are alone and before God. At night, says King David, I bathe my bed with tears.

With those burning and manly tears, you can purify your past and supernaturalize your present life.

217   I want you to be happy on earth. But you won't be if you don't get rid of that fear of suffering. For as long as we are "wayfarers", it is precisely in suffering that our happiness lies.

218 How beautiful it is to give up this life for *the* life!

219 If you realize that those sufferings—physical or spiritual—are purification and merit, bless them.

220 "God give you health, brother." Doesn't this wish for physical well-being, with which some beggars demand or acknowledge alms, produce a bad taste in your mouth?

221 If we are generous in our voluntary atonement, Jesus will fill us with grace so that we can love the trials he sends us.

222 May your will exact from your senses—by means of atonement—what the other faculties deny your will in prayer.

223 How little penance is worth without constant mortification!

224 You are afraid of penance?... Of penance, which will help you to obtain life everlasting. Yet, do you see how men submit themselves to the thousand tortures of a painful surgical operation in order to preserve this poor present life?

225 Your worst enemy is yourself.

226 Treat your body with charity, but with no more charity than you would show toward a treacherous enemy.

227 If you realize that your body is your enemy, and an enemy of God's glory since it is an enemy of your sanctification, why do you treat it so softly?

228 "Have a good time," they said as usual. And the comment of a soul very close to God was, "What a limited wish!"

229 With you, Jesus, how joyful is pain and how bright is darkness!

230 You are suffering! Listen: "his" heart is no smaller than ours. You are suffering? That's for the best.

231 A strict fast is a penance most pleasing to God. But with one thing and another, we've all grown lax. There is no objection—on the contrary!—if, with your director's approval, you fast frequently.

232 Motives for penance? Atonement, reparation, petition, thanksgiving; as a means of progress—for you, for me, for all the rest, for your family, for your country, for the Church... And a thousand motives more.

233 Don't perform more penance than your director allows.

234 How we ennoble suffering by giving it its due place (atonement) in the economy of the spirit!

EXAMINATION
OF CONSCIENCE

235 Examination of conscience. A daily task. Book-keeping—never neglected by anyone in business.

And is there any business worth more than that of eternal life?

236 At the time of your examination beware of the devil that ties your tongue.

237 Examine yourself: slowly, with courage. Isn't it true that your bad temper and your sadness—both without cause, without apparent cause—are due to your lack of determination in breaking the subtle but real snares laid for you—cunningly and attractively—by your concupiscence?

238   The general examination is a weapon of defense. The particular, of attack. The first is the shield. The second, the sword.

239   A glance at the past. To bewail it? No: that is useless. To learn: that is fruitful.

240   Ask for light. Insist on it... until the root is laid bare and you can get at it with your battle-axe: the particular examination.

241   In your particular examination you have to go straight toward the acquisition of a definite virtue or toward the rooting out of the defect which is dominating you.

242   How much, as a Christian, I owe God! My lack of correspondence to his grace in the face of that debt has made me weep with sorrow—the sorrow of love. "*Mea culpa!*"—"Through my fault!"

It is good that you acknowledge your debts, but don't forget how they are paid: with tears... and with works.

243   "*Qui fidelis est in minimo et in maiori fidelis est*"—"He who is faithful in a very little thing is faithful also in much." Words from St Luke that show you— examine yourself—why you have so often gone astray.

244   Wake up! Listen to what the Holy Spirit is saying to you: *"Si inimicus meus maledixisset mihi, sustinuissem utique"*—"If my enemy had reviled me I would verily have borne with it." But you...*"tu vero homo unanimis, dux meus, et notus meus, qui simul mecum dulces capiebas cibos"*—"you, my friend, my apostle, who sit at my table and take sweet food with me!"

245   During a retreat your examination should be much deeper and much longer than that usual nightly moment. Otherwise you miss a great chance to straighten things out.

246   Always end your examination with an act of love—sorrow of love: for yourself, for all the sins of mankind. And consider the fatherly care of God in removing obstacles in your way lest you should stumble.

RESOLUTIONS

247 Be specific. Don't let your resolutions be like fireworks that sparkle for an instant, only to leave as bitter reality a blackened, useless butt that is disgustedly thrown away.

248 You are so young! You seem to me like a ship beginning its voyage. That present slight deviation will in the end keep you from port, unless you correct it now.

249 Make few resolutions. Make specific resolutions. And fulfill them with the help of God.

250 I listened in silence as you said to me, "Yes, I want to be a saint"—although generally I have little respect for such a broad and vague assertion.

251 "Tomorrow!" Sometimes it is prudence; many times it is the adverb of the defeated.

252 Make this firm and determined resolution: to recall, when you receive honors and praise, everything that brings you shame and embarrassment.

The shame and embarrassment are yours; the praise and the glory are God's.

253 Conduct yourself well "now," without looking back on "yesterday" which is really gone, and without worrying about "tomorrow," which for you may never come.

254 Now! Return to your noble life now. Don't let yourself be fooled. "Now" is not too soon... nor too late.

255 Do you want me to tell you everything I think about "your way"?

Well, it's like this. If you really correspond to his call, you'll work for Christ like the best. If you become a man of prayer, you'll be given that correspondence I mentioned, and hungry for sacrifice, you'll seek the hardest tasks...

And you'll be happy here, and most happy hereafter— in the life.

256 That wound is painful. But it is well on its way to being healed. Be firm in your resolutions, and the pain will soon turn into joy and peace.

257 You drag along like a sandbag. You don't do your share. No wonder you are beginning to feel the first symptoms of lukewarmness. Wake up!

SCRUPLES

258 Get rid of those scruples that deprive you of peace. What robs you of your peace of soul cannot come from God.

When God comes to you, you will realize the truth of those greetings: My peace I give to you... My peace I leave with you... My peace be with you... And this peace you will feel even in the midst of tribulation.

259 Still those scruples! Talk simply and clearly with your director.

Obey... and don't belittle the most loving heart of our Lord.

260 Sadness, depression. I'm not surprised: it's the cloud of dust raised by your fall. But... enough of it! Can't you see that the cloud has been borne far away by the breath of grace?

Moreover, your sadness—if you don't reject it—could very well be the cloak of your pride. Did you really think yourself perfect and sinless?

261 I forbid you to think any more about it. Instead, bless God, who has given life back to your soul.

262 Don't think any more about your fall. Besides overwhelming and crushing you under its weight, that recollection may easily be an occasion of future temptation.

Christ has forgiven you! Forget the "old man"—your former self.

263 Don't be disheartened. I have seen you struggle. Today's defeat is training for the final victory.

264 You've done well, even though you have fallen so low. You've done well, because you humbled yourself, because you straightened yourself out, because you filled yourself with hope—and that hope brought you back again to his Love.

Don't look so amazed: you've done well! You rose up from the ground. "*Surge*"—"Arise"—cried anew the mighty voice—"*et ambula*"—"and walk!" Now—to work.

PRESENCE OF GOD

265 Children. How they seek to behave worthily in the presence of their fathers!

And the children of kings, in the presence of their father, the king, how they seek to uphold the royal dignity!

And you... Don't you realize that you are always in the presence of the great king, God, your Father?

266 Never make a decision without stopping to consider the matter in the presence of God.

267 It's necessary to be convinced that God is always near us. Too often we live as though our Lord were somewhere far off—where the stars shine. We fail to realize that he is also by our side—always.

For he is a loving Father. He loves each one of us more than all the mothers in the world can love their children, helping us and inspiring us, blessing... and forgiving.

How often we've erased the frowns from our parents' brows, telling them after some prank, "I won't do it again!" Maybe that same day we fall again... And our father, with feigned harshness in his voice and a serious face, reproves us, while at the same time his heart is softened because he knows our weakness: "Poor boy," he thinks, "How hard he tries to behave well!"

We have to be completely convinced, realizing it to the full, that our Lord, who is close to us and in heaven, is a Father, and very much *our* Father.

268 Make it a habit to raise your heart to God, in acts of thanksgiving, many times a day. Because he gives you this and that... Because someone has despised you... Because you don't have what you need, or because you do have it.

And because he made his Mother, who is also your Mother, so beautiful. Because he created the sun and the moon and this animal or that plant. Because he made that man eloquent and you he left slow of speech...

Thank him for everything, because everything is good.

269 Don't be so blind or so thoughtless that you fail to "go into" each tabernacle when you glimpse the walls or the steeple of each house of our Lord. He is waiting for you.

Don't be so blind or so thoughtless that you fail to say at least an ejaculation to Mary Immaculate, whenever you go past a place where you know Christ is being offended.

270 As you make your usual way through the city streets, aren't you happy when you discover another tabernacle?

271 Said a prayerful soul: In intentions, may Jesus be our end; in affections, our love; in speech, our theme; in actions, our model.

272 Make use of those holy "human devices" I've recommended to keep you from losing the presence of God: ejaculations, acts of love and reparation, spiritual communions, "glances" at a picture of our Lady.

273 Alone! You are *not* alone. We are keeping you close company from afar. Besides abiding in your soul in grace is the Holy Spirit—God with you!—giving a supernatural tone to all your thoughts, desires and works.

274 "Father," said that big fellow, a good student at the Central* (I wonder what has become of him), "I was

---

*The Central: how the University of Madrid was called at the time *The Way* was written.

thinking of what you told me—that I'm a son of God!—
and I found myself walking along the street, head up, chin
out, and a feeling of pride inside... a son of God!"

With sure conscience I advised him to foster that
"pride."

275   I don't doubt your good intentions. I know you
act in the presence of God. But—and there is a "but"!—
your actions are witnessed or may be witnessed by men
who judge by human standards... And you must set a
good example for them.

276   If you accustom yourself, at least once a week,
to seek union with Mary in order to go to Jesus, you will
have more presence of God.

277   You ask me, "Why that wooden cross?" And I
quote from a letter: "As I raise my eyes from the micro-
scope, my sight comes to rest on the cross—black and
empty. That cross without a corpus is a symbol; it has a
meaning others won't see. And I, tired out and on the
point of abandoning my work, once again bring my eyes
close to the lens and continue. For that lonely cross is
calling for a pair of shoulders to bear it."

278   Live in the presence of God and you will have
supernatural life.

SUPERNATURAL LIFE

279 People see only the flat surface. Their vision is two-dimensional and fixed to the ground.

When you live a supernatural life, God will give you the third-dimension: height, and with it, perspective, weight and volume.

280 If you lose the supernatural meaning of your life, your charity will be philanthropy; your purity, decency; your mortification, stupidity; your discipline, a lash; and all your works, fruitless.

281 Silence is the doorkeeper of the interior life.

282 Paradox: Sanctity is more attainable than learning, but it is easier to be a scholar than to be a saint.

283   A little diversion! You've got to have a change! So you open your eyes wide to let in images of things, or you squint because you're nearsighted!

Close them altogether! Have interior life, and you'll see the wonders of a better world, a new world with undreamed-of color and perspective... and you'll draw close to God. You'll feel your weaknesses; and you'll become more Godlike... with a godliness that will make you more of a brother to your fellowmen by bringing you closer to your Father.

284   Aspiration: that I be good, and everyone else be better than I!

285   Conversion is a matter of a moment. Sanctification is the work of a lifetime.

286   There is nothing better in the world than to be in the grace of God.

287   Purity of intention: You'll have it always, if you seek ever and in all things to please only God.

288   Enter into the wounds of Christ crucified. There you will learn to guard your senses, you will have interior life, and you will continually offer to the Father the sufferings of our Lord and those of Mary, in payment of your debts and the debts of all men.

289 Your holy impatience to serve God doesn't displease him. But it will be barren if it is not accompanied by an effective improvement in your daily conduct.

290 To reform. Every day a little. This has to be your constant task if you really want to become a saint.

291 You have the obligation to sanctify yourself. Yes, even you. Who thinks this is the exclusive concern of priests and religious?

To everyone, without exception, our Lord said: "Be perfect, as my heavenly Father is perfect."

292 Your interior life has to be just that: to begin... and to begin again.

293 In your interior life, have you taken the time to consider the beauty of *serving* with actual willingness?

294 The plants were hidden under the snow. And the farmer, the owner of the land, remarked with satisfaction: "Now they're growing on the inside."

I thought of you, of your forced inactivity... Tell me, are you also growing on the inside?

295 If you are not master of yourself—even if you're powerful—acting the master is to me something laughable and to be pitied.

296 It is hard to read in the holy Gospel that question of Pilate's: "Whom do you wish that I release to you, Barabbas or Jesus, who is called the Christ?" But it is more painful to hear the answer: "Barabbas!"

And it is more terrible still when I realize that very often—when I have wandered away—I, too, have said, "Barabbas!" And I've added, "Christ?... *Crucifige eum!*— Crucify him!"

297 All that worries you for the moment is only of passing importance. What is of absolute importance is that you be happy... that you be saved!

298 New lights! What joy you feel that God has let you find "it's really true!"

Take advantage of the occasion. It is the moment to break into a hymn of thanksgiving. And it is also the moment to dust the odd corners of your soul, to get out of your rut, to put more of the supernatural into your work, to avoid a possible scandal to your neighbor.

In a word: let your gratitude be shown in some specific resolution.

299 Christ died for you. You... what should you do for Christ?

300 Your personal experience—that dejection, that restlessness, that bitterness—brings to life the truth of those words of Jesus: No one can serve two masters!

MORE ABOUT
INTERIOR LIFE

301 I'll tell you a secret, an open secret: these world crises are crises of saints.

God wants a handful of men "of his own" in every human activity. Then... *"pax Christi in regno Christi"*— "the peace of Christ in the kingdom of Christ."

302 Your crucifix: As a Christian you should always carry a crucifix with you. Place it on your desk. Kiss it before you go to bed and when you wake up. And when your poor body rebels against your soul, kiss your crucifix!

303 Don't be afraid to call our Lord by his name— Jesus—and to tell him that you love him.

304   Each day try to find a few minutes of that blessed solitude you need so much to keep your interior life going.

305   You wrote me: "Simplicity is the salt of perfection. And that's what I lack. I want to acquire it, with his help and with yours."

You'll lack neither his help nor mine. Use the means.

306   "The life of man upon earth is warfare." So said Job many centuries ago.

There are still some easygoing individuals unaware of this fact.

307   That supernatural way of conducting yourself is real military strategy. You carry on the war—the daily battles of your interior life—in positions far from the main walls of your fortress.

And the enemy comes to meet you there: in your small mortification, in your daily prayer, in your orderly work, in your plan of life. And only with difficulty does he get close to the otherwise easily-scaled battlements of your citadel. And if he does, he arrives exhausted.

308   You write and I quote: "My joy and my peace. I can never have real happiness if I have no peace. And what is peace? Peace is something intimately associated with war. Peace is the result of victory. Peace demands of me a constant struggle. Without that struggle, I'll never be able to have peace."

309 Consider what depths of mercy lie in the justice of God! For, according to human justice, he who pleads guilty is punished, but in the divine court, he is pardoned.

Blessed be the holy sacrament of penance!

310 *"Induimini dominum Iesum Christum"*—"Put on the Lord Jesus Christ," says St Paul to the Romans. It is in the sacrament of penance that you and I put on Jesus Christ and his merits.

311 War! "War has a supernatural end that the world is unaware of," you tell me, "because war has been for us..."

War is the greatest obstacle to the easy way. But in the end we have to love it, as the religious should love his disciplines.

312 The power of your name, Lord! As a heading to my letter I had written, as I usually do, "May Jesus watch over you."

Then came the reply: "That 'May Jesus watch over you!' of your letter has already helped me out of more than one tight corner. May he also watch over all of you."

313 "Now that our Lord is helping me with his usual generosity, I will try to correspond by bettering my ways." So you told me. And I had nothing to add.

314 I wrote to you and said: "I'm relying on you. You'll see what we can do...!" What could we do, except rely on him!

315 A missionary. You dream of being a missionary. You vibrate like a Xavier, longing to conquer an empire for Christ—Japan, China, India, Russia; the peoples of North Europe, or of America, or Africa, or Australia!

Foster that fire in your heart, that hunger for souls. But don't forget that you're more of a missionary obeying. Geographically far away from those apostolic fields, you work both here and there. Don't you feel your arm tired—like Xavier's!—after administering baptism to so many?

316 You tell me: "Yes, I want to!" Good. But do you "want to" as a miser wants his gold, as a mother wants her child, as a worldling wants honors, or as a poor sensualist wants his pleasure?

No? Then you don't "want to!"

317 What zeal men put into their earthly affairs! Dreaming of honors, striving for riches, bent on sensuality!

Men and women, rich and poor, old and middle-aged and young and even children: all of them alike.

When you and I put the same zeal into the affairs of our souls, then we'll have a living and working faith. And there will be no obstacle that we cannot overcome in our apostolic works.

318 To you who like sports, the words of the Apostle should really make sense: *"Nescitis quod ii qui in stadio currunt omnes quidem currunt, sed unus accipit bravium? Sic currite ut comprehendatis"*—"Do you not know that those who run in the race, all indeed run, but one receives the prize? So run as to obtain it."

319 Withdraw into yourself. Seek God within you and listen to him.

320 Foster those noble thoughts, those incipient holy desires... A single spark can start a conflagration.

321 Apostolic soul, that intimacy between Jesus and you—so close to him for so many years! Doesn't it mean anything to you?

322 It's true that I always call our tabernacle Bethany. Become a friend of the Master's friends—Lazarus, Martha,

Mary—and then you will ask me no more why I call our tabernacle Bethany.

323   You know that there are "counsels of the Gospel". To follow them is a refinement of love.

They say it is the way of the few. At times I feel that it could be the way of many.

324   *"Quia hic homo coepit aedificare et non potuit consummare!"*—"This man began to build and was not able to finish!" A sad commentary which need never be made about you, if you don't wish it to be. For you possess everything necessary to crown the edifice of your sanctification: the grace of God and your own will.

LUKEWARMNESS

325 Fight against the softness that makes you lazy and careless in your spiritual life. Remember that it might well be the beginning of tepidity... and, in the words of the Scripture, God will vomit out the lukewarm.

326 It hurts me to see you place yourself in danger of tepidity when you don't go straight toward perfection within your state in life.

Say with me: I don't want to be lukewarm! *"Confige timore tuo carnes meas!"*—"Pierce my flesh with your fear!" Grant me, my God, a filial fear that will stir me up!

327 I already know that you avoid mortal sins. You want to be saved! But you are not worried about that constant and deliberate falling into venial sins, even though in each case you feel God's call to conquer yourself.

It is your lukewarmness that makes you so badly disposed.

328   What little love for God you have when you give in without a fight because it's not a grave sin!

329   Venial sins do great harm to the soul. That's why our Lord says in the *Canticle of Canticles*: "*capite nobis vulpes parvulas, quae demoliuntur vineas*"—"catch the little foxes that destroy the vines."

330   How sad you make me feel when you are not sorry for your venial sins! For, until you are, you cannot begin to have true interior life.

331   You are tepid if you carry out listlessly and reluctantly those things that have to do with our Lord; if deliberately or "shrewdly" you look for some way of lessening your duties; if you think only of yourself and of your comfort; if your conversation is idle and vain; if you don't abhor venial sin; if you act from human motives.

STUDY

332   There is no excuse for those who could be scholars and are not.

333   Study. Obedience. *Non multa, sed multum*—not many things, but well.

334   You pray, you mortify yourself, you labor at a thousand apostolic activities... but you don't study. You are useless then, unless you change your ways.

Study—any professional development—is a serious obligation for us.

335   An hour of study, for a modern apostle, is an hour of prayer.

336   If you are to serve God with your mind, to study is a grave obligation for you.

337 You frequent the sacraments, you pray, you are chaste, but you don't study. Don't tell me you're good; you're only "goodish."

338 Formerly, when human knowledge—science—was very limited, it seemed quite feasible for a single scholar to defend and vindicate our holy faith.

Today, with the extension and the intensity of modern science, the apologists have to divide the work among themselves, if they wish to defend the Church scientifically in all fields.

You... cannot shirk this responsibility.

339 Books. Don't buy them without advice from a Catholic who has real knowledge and discernment. It's so easy to buy something useless or harmful.

How often a man thinks he is carrying a book under his arm, and it turns out to be a load of trash!

340 Study. Study in earnest. If you are to be salt and light, you need knowledge, capability.

Or do you imagine that an idle and lazy life will entitle you to receive infused knowledge?

341 It's good for you to put such determination into your study, as long as you put the same determination into acquiring interior life.

342 Don't forget that before teaching one must act. "*Coepit facere et docere,*" the holy Scripture says of Jesus Christ: "He began to do and to teach."

First, action: so that you and I may learn.

343 Work! When you are engrossed in professional work, the life of your soul will improve, and you'll become more of a man for you'll get rid of that "carping spirit" that consumes you.

344 Teacher: your undeniable keenness to know and practise the best methods of helping your students acquire earthly knowledge is good. But be equally keen to know and practise christian asceticism, which is the only method of helping them and yourself to be better.

345 Culture, culture! Good! Don't let anyone get ahead of us in striving for it and possessing it.

But remember that culture is a means, not an end.

346 Student: form in yourself a solid and active piety; be outstanding in study; have strong desires for a professional apostolate. And with that vigor in your religious and scientific training, I promise you rapid and far-reaching developments.

347   You worry only about building up your culture.
But what you really need to build up is your soul. Then
you will work as you should—for Christ.

   In order that he may reign in the world, it is necessary
to have people of prestige who with their eyes fixed on
heaven, dedicate themselves to all human activities, and
through those activities exercise quietly—and effectively
—an apostolate of a professional character.

348   Your indolence, your carelessness, your laziness
are really cowardice and sloth—so your conscience
continually tells—but they are not "the way".

349   Don't be upset when you state an orthodox opinion
and the malice of whoever heard you caused him to be
scandalized. For his scandal is pharisaical.

350   In addition to being a good Christian, it's not
enough to be a scholar. If you don't correct your rudeness,
if you make your zeal and your knowledge incompatible
with good manners, I don't see how you can ever become
a saint. And, even if you are a scholar—in spite of being
a scholar—you should be tied to a stall, like a mule.

351   With that self-satisfied air you're becoming an
unbearable and repulsive character. You're making a fool
of yourself, and what is worse, you're diminishing the
effect of your work as an apostle.

Don't forget that even the mediocre can sin by being too scholarly.

352 Your very inexperience leads you to presumption, vanity and to all that you imagine gives you an air of importance.

Correct yourself, please! Foolish and all, you may come to occupy a post of responsibility (it's happened more than once), and if you're not convinced of your lack of ability, you will refuse to listen to those who have the gift of counsel. And it's frightening to think of the harm your mismanagement will do.

353 Nonsectarianism. Neutrality. Those old myths that always try to seem new.

Have you ever bothered to think how absurd it is to leave one's catholicism aside on entering a university, or a professional association, or a scholarly meeting, or Congress, as if you were checking your hat at the door?

354 Make good use of your time. Don't forget the fig tree cursed by our Lord. And it was doing something: sprouting leaves. Like you...

Don't tell me you have excuses. It availed the fig tree little, relates the evangelist, that it was not the season for figs when our Lord came to it to look for them.

And barren it remained forever.

355   People engaged in worldly business say that time is money. That means little to me. For us who are engaged in the business of souls, time is glory!

356   I don't understand how you can call yourself a Christian and lead such an idle, useless life. Have you forgotten Christ's life of toil?

357   "All the sins," so you said, "seem to be waiting for the first idle moment. Really, idleness itself must be a sin!"

Whoever gives himself to work for Christ cannot expect to have a free moment, for even to rest is not to do nothing: it is to relax with activities that require less effort.

358   To be idle is something inconceivable in a man who has apostolic spirit.

359   Add a supernatural motive to your ordinary professional work and you will have sanctified it.

FORMING THE SPIRIT

360 How frankly you laughed when I advised you to put your youthful years under the protection of St Raphael, "so that he'll lead you, as he did young Tobias, to a holy marriage, with a girl who is good and pretty—and rich," I added jokingly.

And then how thoughtful you became, when I went on to advise you to put yourself also under the patronage of that youthful apostle John, in case God were to ask more of you.

361 For you who complain to yourself that they treat you harshly and who feel the contrast between this harshness and the conduct of those of your own blood, I copy these lines from the letter of an army doctor:

"Toward the sick there can be the cold and efficient attitude of an honest doctor, which is objective and useful to the patient, or the weeping tenderness of a family. What would happen at a first-aid station during a battle, when the stream of wounded begins to pour in, if around each stretcher there stood a family? One might as well go over to the enemy."

362   I have no need of miracles. There are more than enough in the Scriptures. But I do need the fulfillment of your duty, your correspondence to grace.

363   You're disheartened, crestfallen. Men have just taught you a lesson! They thought you didn't really need their help and so they made you plenty of empty promises. The possibility that they might have to help you with hard cash—just a few pennies—turned their friendship into indifference.

Trust only in God and those united with you through him.

364   Ah, if you would only resolve to serve God *seriously*, with the same earnestness that you put into serving your ambitions, your vanities, your sensuality...

365   If you feel an impulse to be a leader, this should be your aim: to be the last among your brothers and the first among all others.

366   Let's see: do you feel slighted because so-and-so enjoys more confidence with certain persons he knew before or to whom he feels more attracted by temperament, profession, or character?

All right, but among your own, carefully avoid even the appearance of any particularly close friendship.

367 The choicest morsel, if eaten by a pig, turns—to put it bluntly—into pig's meat!

Let us be angels, so as to dignify the ideas we assimilate.

Let us at least be men and convert our food into strong, fine muscles or perhaps into a powerful brain, capable of understanding and adoring God.

But, let us not be beasts, like so many, so very many!

368 You're bored? That's because you keep your senses awake and your soul asleep.

369 The charity of Jesus Christ will often lead you to make concessions—a noble yielding. And the charity of Jesus Christ will often lead you to stand fast. That too is very noble.

370 If you're not bad, and yet you seem to be, then you're a fool. And that foolishness—a cause of scandal—is even worse than being bad.

371 When you see people of doubtful professional reputation acting as leaders at public activities of a religious nature, don't you feel the urge to whisper in their ears: "Please, would you mind being just a little less Catholic!"

372 If you have an official position, you have certain rights and also certain duties which go with it.

You stray from your apostolic way if the occasion—or the excuse—of a work of zeal makes you leave the duties of your office unfulfilled. For you will lose your professional prestige, which is exactly your "bait" as a fisher of men.

373 I like your apostolic motto: "Work without resting."

374 Why that rushing around? Don't tell me it's activity: It's confusion!

375 Dissipation. You slake your senses and faculties at whatever puddle you meet on the way. And then you experience the results: unsettled purpose, scattered attention, deadened will, aroused concupiscence.

Subject yourself again seriously to a plan that will make you lead a christian life. Otherwise you'll never do anything worthwhile.

376 "Environment is such an influence," you've told me. And I have had to answer: No doubt. That's why you have to be formed in such a way that you can carry your own environment about with you in a natural manner, and so give your own tone to the society in which you live.

And then, when you've acquired this spirit, I'm sure you'll tell me with all the amazement of the early disciples as they contemplated the first fruits of the miracles performed by their hands in Christ's name: "How great is our influence on our environment!"

377 And how shall I acquire "our formation" and how shall I keep "our spirit"? By being faithful to the specific "norms" that your director gave you, and explained to you, and made you love. Be faithful to them and you'll be an apostle.

378 Don't be a pessimist. Don't you realize that everything that happens or can happen is for the best?

Optimism will be a necessary consequence of your faith.

379 Naturalness. Let your christian spirit—your salt and your light—be manifested spontaneously, without anything odd or foolish. Always carry with you your spirit of simplicity.

380 "And in a pagan or in a worldly atmosphere, when my life clashes with its surroundings, won't my naturalness seem artificial?" you ask me.

And I reply: Undoubtedly your life will clash with theirs; and that contrast—because you're confirming your faith with works—is exactly the naturalness I ask of you.

381 Don't worry if people say you have too much *esprit de corps*. What do they want? A delicate instrument that breaks to pieces the moment it is grasped?

382 When I made you a present of that *Life of Jesus*, I wrote in it this inscription: "May you seek Christ. May you find Christ. May you love Christ."

These are three very distinct steps. Have you at least tried to live the first one?

383 If they see you weaken—you, the leader—it is no wonder their obedience wavers.

384 Confusion. I knew you were unsure of the rightness of your judgment. And, so that you might understand me, I wrote you: "The devil has a very ugly face, and since he's so smart he won't risk our seeing his horns. He never makes a direct attack. That's why he so often comes in the disguise of nobleness and even of spirituality!"

385 Our Lord says: "A new commandment I give you: that you love one another. By this shall all men know that you are my disciples."

And St Paul: "Bear each other's burdens, and thus you shall fulfill the law of Christ."

I have nothing to add.

386 Don't forget, my son, that for you there is but one evil on earth: sin. You must fear it and avoid it with the grace of God.

YOUR SANCTITY

387 The plane of the sanctity our Lord asks of us is determined by these three points: holy steadfastness, holy forcefulness and holy shamelessness.

388 Holy shamelessness is one thing, and worldly boldness quite another.

389 Holy shamelessness is characteristic of the life of childhood. A little child doesn't worry about anything. He makes no effort to hide his weaknesses, his natural weaknesses, even though everyone is watching him.

Shamelessness, carried to the supernatural life, suggests this train of reasoning: praise, contempt; admiration, scorn; honor, dishonor; health, illness; riches, poverty; beauty, ugliness... Well, all right, does it matter?

390 Laugh at ridicule. Scorn whatever may be said. See and feel God in yourself and in your surroundings. Thus you will soon acquire the holy shamelessness you need in order to live, paradoxically, with the refinement of a christian gentleman.

391 If you have holy shamelessness, you won't be bothered by the thought of what people have said or what they will say.

392 Convince yourself that ridicule does not exist for those who are doing what is best.

393 A man—a gentleman—ready to compromise would condemn Jesus to death again.

394 Compromising is a sure sign of not possessing the truth. When a man yields in matters of ideals, of honor or of faith, that man is without ideals, without honor, and without faith.

395 That man of God, an old campaigner, argued like this: So I won't yield an inch. And why should I, if I am convinced of the truth of my ideals? You, on the other hand, are very ready to compromise. Would you agree that two and two are three and a half? No? Not even for friendship's sake would you yield in such a little thing.

It's simply because, for the first time, you feel convinced that you possess the truth... and you've come over to my side!

396 Holy steadfastness is not intolerance.

397 Be steadfast in doctrine and in conduct, but pliant in manner: a powerful blacksmith's hammer wrapped in a quilted covering.

Be steadfast, but don't be obstinate.

398 Steadfastness is not simply intransigence: it is "holy intransigence".

Don't forget that there also exists a "holy forcefulness".

399 If, to save an earthly life, it is praiseworthy to use force to keep a man from committing suicide, are we not allowed to use the same coercion—"holy coercion"—in order to save the Lives (with a capital) of so many who are stupidly bent on killing their souls?

400 How many crimes are committed in the name of justice! If you were a dealer in guns and someone paid you for one so that he might use it to kill your mother, would you sell it to him? And yet, wasn't he ready to pay you a just price for it?

Professor, journalist, politician, diplomat: meditate.

401   God and daring! Daring is not imprudence. Daring is not recklessness.

402   Don't ask Jesus to forgive only your own faults: don't love him with *your* heart alone.

Console him for every offense that has been, is, and will be done to him. Love him with all the strength of all the hearts of all the men who have loved him most.

Be daring: tell him you are carried away with more love than Mary Magdalene, more than Teresa and little Therese, more carried away than Augustine and Dominic and Francis, more than Ignatius and Xavier.

403   Be more daring still, and whenever you need anything, mindful always of the "*Fiat*"—"Your will be done"—don't ask, tell him: "Jesus, I want this or that". For that's the way children ask.

404   You say you've failed! We *never* fail. You placed your confidence wholly in God. And you did not neglect any human means.

Convince yourself of this truth: your success—this time—was to fail. Give thanks to our Lord, and try again!

405   So you've failed? You—be convinced of it—can never fail.

You haven't failed; you've acquired experience. Forward!

406 That was a failure, a disaster, because you lost your spirit. You know well that as long as we act for supernatural motives, the outcome (victory? defeat? Bah!) has only one name: success.

407 Let's not confuse the rights of the office with personal rights. The former can never be renounced.

408 Sanctimony is to sanctity what "piosity" is to piety: its caricature.

409 Remember that even if your virtues seem saintly, they're worth nothing if they are not united to the ordinary christian virtues.

That would be like adorning yourself with splendid jewels over your underclothes.

410 May your virtue not be noisy.

411 Many false apostles, in spite of themselves, do good to the masses, to the people, through the very power of the doctrine of Jesus which they preach—even though they don't practise it.

But this good does not compensate for the enormous and very real harm they do by killing the souls of leaders, of apostles, who turn away in disgust from those who don't practise what they preach.

That's why such men and women, if they are not willing to live an upright life, should never push themselves forward as leaders.

412 May the fire of your love not be a will-ó-the-wisp, a vain fire, an illusion—an illusion of fire, which neither enkindles what it touches nor gives any heat.

413 The "*non serviam*"—"I will not serve"—of Satan has been too fruitful. Don't you feel the generous impulse to say every day, with desires for prayer and deeds, a *serviam*—"I will serve you, I will be faithful!"—surpassing in fruitfulness that cry of rebellion?

414 How pathetic: a "man of God" who has fallen away! But how much more pathetic: a "man of God" who is lukewarm and worldly!

415 Don't worry too much about what the world calls victories or defeats. How often the "victor" ends up defeated!

416 "*Sine me nihil potestis facere!*"—"Without me you can do nothing!" New light—new *splendor*—for my eyes, from the eternal light, the holy Gospel.

Now should I be surprised at all of "my" foolishness?

Let me put Jesus into everything that is mine; then there will be no foolishness in my conduct. And if I would speak correctly, I would talk no more of what is "mine", but of what is "ours".

LOVE OF GOD

417 The only real love is God's love!

418 The secret that ennobles the humblest things, even the most humiliating, is to love.

419 Children... the sick... As you write these words, don't you feel tempted to write them with capitals?

The reason is that in little children and in the sick a soul in love sees him!

420 How little a life is to offer to God!

421 A friend is a treasure. Well... you have a friend! For where your treasure is, there is your heart.

422 Jesus is your Friend—*the* friend —with a human heart, like yours, with most loving eyes that wept for Lazarus.

And as much as he loved Lazarus, he loves you...

423 My God, I love you, but... oh, teach me to love!

424 To punish for the sake of Love: this is the secret that raises to a supernatural plane any punishment imposed on those who deserve it.

For the love of God, who has been offended, let punishment serve as atonement. For the love of our neighbor, for the sake of God, may punishment never be revenge, but a healing medicine.

425 To realize that you love me so much, my God, and yet I haven't lost my mind!

426 In Christ we have every ideal: for he is King, he is Love, he is God.

427 Lord, may I have balance and measure in everything—except in Love.

428 If Love, even human love, gives so many consolations here, what will Love be in heaven?

429 Everything done for the sake of Love acquires greatness and beauty.

430 Jesus, may I be the last in everything... and the first in Love.

431 Don't fear God's justice. It is no less admirable and no less lovable than his mercy. Both are proofs of his love.

432 Consider what is most beautiful and most noble on earth, what pleases the mind and the other faculties, and what delights the flesh and the senses. Consider the world, and the other worlds that shine in the night—the whole universe.

And this, along with all the satisfied follies of the heart, is worth nothing, *is* nothing and less than nothing, compared with this God of mine!—of yours! Infinite treasure, most beautiful pearl... humbled, become a slave, reduced to nothingness in the form of a servant in the stable where he willed to be born... in Joseph's workshop, in his passion and in his ignominious death, and in the frenzy of Love—the blessed eucharist.

433 Live by Love and you will conquer always—even when you are defeated—in the Navas* and the Lepantos** of your interior life.

*The Navas of Tolosa: famous battle that occurred in 1212 in southern Spain, won by armies of the Christian kingdoms of the Iberian Peninsula over the Moslems of Andalusia and northern Africa.

**Lepanto: naval battle that took place in the Mediterranean Sea in 1571 between a Turkish and a Christian squadron. It was won by the Christian fleet.

434   Let your heart overflow in effusions of love and gratitude as you consider how the grace of God saves you each day from the snares the enemy sets in your path.

435   *"Timor Domini sanctus"*—"The fear of the Lord is holy." This fear is a son's veneration for his Father— never a servile fear. For God, your Father, is not a tyrant.

436   Sorrow of love—because he is good; because he is your friend, who gave his life for you; because everything good you have is his, because you have offended him so much, ...because he has forgiven you. He! Forgiven *you*!

Weep, my son, with sorrow of love.

437   If one of my fellow men had died to save me from death...

God died. And I remain indifferent.

438   Mad! Yes, I saw you (in the bishop's chapel, you thought you were alone) as you left a kiss on each newly-consecrated chalice and paten, so that he might find it there when for the first time he would "come down" to those eucharistic vessels.

439   Don't forget that sorrow is the touchstone of Love.

CHARITY

440 When you have finished your work, do your brother's, helping him, for the sake of Christ, with such finesse and naturalness that no one—not even he—will realize that you are doing more than in justice you ought.

This, indeed, is virtue befitting a son of God!

441 You are hurt by your neighbor's lack of charity toward you. Think how God must be hurt by your lack of charity—of love—toward him!

442 Never think badly of anyone, not even if the words or conduct of the person in question give you good grounds for doing so.

443 Don't make negative criticism. If you can't praise, say nothing.

444 Never speak badly of your brother, not even when you have plenty of reasons for doing so. Go first to the tabernacle, and then go to the priest, your father, and also tell him what is bothering you.

And to no one else.

445 Gossip is trash that soils and hinders the apostolate. It goes against charity, takes away strength, takes away peace, and makes one lose his union with God.

446 If you have so many defects, why are you surprised to find defects in others?

447 After seeing how many people waste their lives (without a break: gab, gab, gab—and with all the consequences!), I can better appreciate how necessary and lovable silence is.

And I can well understand, Lord, why you will make us account for every idle word.

448 Talking comes easier than doing. You who have that cutting tongue—like a hatchet—have you ever tried, by chance, to do *well* what others, according to your "authoritative" opinion, do less well?

449 This is what that really is: grumbling, gossiping, tale-bearing, scandal-mongering, back-biting. Or even slander? Or viciousness?

When those who are not supposed to sit in judgment do so, they very easily end up as gossiping old maids.

450 How the injustice of the "just" offends God, how it harms many souls—and how it can sanctify others!

451 Let us be slow to judge. Each one sees things from his own point of view and with his own mind, with all its limitations, through eyes that are often dimmed and clouded by passion.

Moreover, like so many of those modern artists, some people have an outlook which is so subjective and so unhealthy that they make a few random strokes and assure us that these represent our portrait, our conduct. Of what little worth are the judgments of men!

Don't judge without sifting your judgment in prayer.

452 Force yourself, if necessary, always to forgive those who offend you, from the very first moment. For the greatest injury or offense you can suffer from them is nothing compared to what God has forgiven you.

453 Back-biting? Then you are losing the right spirit, and if you don't learn to check your tongue, each word will be one more step toward the exit from that apostolic undertaking in which you work.

454 Don't judge without having heard both sides. Even persons who think themselves virtuous very easily forget this elementary rule of prudence.

455 Can you know what damage you do throwing stones with your eyes blindfolded?

Neither do you know—because you're blinded by thoughtlessness or passion—the harm you produce, at times very great, dropping uncharitable comments that to you seem trifling.

456 To criticize, to destroy, is not difficult; the clumsiest laborer knows how to drive his pick into the noble and finely-hewn stone of a cathedral.

To construct—that is what requires the skill of a master.

457 Who are you to judge the rightness of a superior's decision? Don't you see that he has more basis for judging than you? He has more experience; he has more upright, experienced and impartial advisers; and above all, he has more grace, a special grace, the grace of his state, which is the light and the powerful aid of God.

458 Those clashes with the world's selfishness will make you appreciate much more the fraternal charity of your brother-apostles.

459 Your charity is presumptuous. From afar, you attract; you have light. From nearby, you repel; you lack warmth. What a pity!

460 "*Frater qui adiuvatur a fratre quasi civitas firma.*"—"A brother who is helped by his brother is like a strong city."

Think for a moment and make up your mind to live that brotherhood I've always recommended to you.

461 If I don't see you practice that blessed brotherly spirit that I preach to you constantly, I'll remind you of those loving words of St John: "*Filioli mei, non diligamus verbo neque lingua, sed opere et veritate*"—"My dear children, let us love not in word, neither with the tongue but in deed and in truth."

462 The power of charity! If you live that blessed brotherly spirit, your mutual weakness will also be a support to keep you upright in the fulfillment of duty—just as in a house of cards, one card supports the other.

463 Charity consists not so much in giving as in understanding. That's why you should seek an excuse for your neighbor—there are always excuses—if yours is the duty to judge.

464   You know that that person's soul is in danger? From afar, with your life of union, you can give him effective help. Help him, then, and don't worry.

465   I think it is all right for you to feel concern for your brothers—there is no better proof of your mutual love. Take care, however, to keep your worries from degenerating into anxiety.

466   "Generally," you write me, "people are not too generous with their money. Plenty of talk, noisy enthusiasm, promises, plans. But at the moment of sacrifice, few come forward to lend a hand. And if they do, it has to be with trimmings attached—a dance, a raffle, a movie, a show—or an announcement and subscription-list in the newspapers."

It's a sad state of affairs, but it has its exceptions. May you, too, be one of those who give alms without letting their left hand know what their right hand is doing.

467   Books. I put my hand out, like one of Christ's beggars, and I asked for books—books that are nourishment for the Roman, Catholic, and apostolic minds of many university students.

I put my hand out, like one of Christ's beggars, and each time had it brushed aside!

Why can't people understand, Jesus, the profound christian charity of this alms, more effective than a gift of the finest bread?

468 You were exceedingly naive. How few really practise charity! Being charitable doesn't mean giving away old clothes or copper pennies... And you tell me your tale of woe and disillusionment.

Only one idea occurs to me: let us—you and I—give and give ourselves unstintingly. And we'll keep those who come in contact with us from going through the same sad experience.

469 "Greet all the saints. All the saints send you greetings. To all the saints who are at Ephesus. To all the saints in Christ Jesus who are at Philippi." What a moving name—saints!—the early Christians used to address one another!

Learn how to treat your brothers.

THE MEANS

470 The means? They're the same as those of Peter and Paul, of Dominic and Francis, of Ignatius and Xavier: the cross and the Gospel.

Do they seem little to you, perhaps?

471 In apostolic undertakings it's very good—it's a duty—to consider what means the world has to offer you $(2 + 2 = 4)$. But don't forget—ever—that your calculations must fortunately include another term: God $+ 2 + 2...$

472 Serve your God straightforwardly; be faithful to him, and don't worry about anything else. For it's a great truth that if you "seek first the kingdom of God and his justice, all other things"—material things, the means—"will be given you besides". He will provide them for you.

473 Cast away that despair produced by the realization of your weakness. It's true: financially you are a zero, and socially another zero, and another in virtues, and another in talent...

But to the left of these zeros is Christ... And what an immeasurable figure it turns out to be!

474 So you are a nobody. And others have done wonders—are still doing them—through organization, through the press, through promotion. And they have all the means, while you have none. Well, then, just remember Ignatius. Ignorant among the doctors of Alcala; poor, penniless, among the students of Paris; persecuted, slandered...

That's the way: love, and have faith, and... suffer! Your love and your faith and your cross are the unfailing means to make effective and to perpetuate the ardent desires for apostolate that you bear in your heart.

475 You realize you are weak. And so, indeed, you are. In spite of all that—rather, because of it—God has sought you. He always uses inadequate instruments so that the work may be seen to be his.

From you he asks only docility.

476 When you *really* give yourself to God, no difficulty will be able to shake your optimism.

477 Why do you neglect those corners in your heart? As long as you don't give yourself completely, you can't expect to win others.

What a poor instrument you are!

478 But, surely—at this stage—you don't mean to tell me you need the approval, the favor, the encouragement of the powerful, to go on doing what God wants?

The powerful are often changeable, and you have to be constant. Be grateful if they help you, but go your way if they show you contempt.

479 Don't let it bother you. The "prudent" have always called the works of God madness.

Onward! Be daring!

480 Do you see? That cable—strand upon strand, many of them woven tightly together—is strong enough to lift enormous weights.

You and your brothers, with wills united to carry out God's will, can overcome all obstacles.

481 When you seek only God, and want to forward a work of zeal, you can very well practise that principle stated by a good friend of ours. "Spend all you ought, though you owe all you spend."

482 What does it matter if the whole world with all
its power is against you? Forward!

Repeat the words of the psalm: "The Lord is my light
and my salvation; whom shall I fear?... *Si consistant
adversum me castra, non timebit cor meum*—If armies in
camp should stand together against me, my heart shall not
fear."

483 Courage! You can! Don't you see what God's
grace did to that sleepy, cowardly Peter, who had denied
him... to that fierce, relentless Paul, who had persecuted
him?

484 Be an instrument of gold or of steel, of platinum
or of iron—big or small, delicate or rough. They're all
useful. Each serves its own purpose. Who would dare say
that the carpenter's saw is any less useful than the surgeon's
scalpel?

Your duty is to be an instrument.

485 Well, so what? Unless your motive is hidden
pride (you think you're perfect), I don't understand how
you can give up that work for souls just because God's
fire which first attracted you, besides giving the light and
warmth that aroused your enthusiasm, should also at times
produce the smoke that results from the weakness of the
instrument!

486 Work. It's there. The instruments can't be left to grow rusty. There are also "norms" to avoid the mildew and the rust. Just put them into practice.

487 Don't worry about the financial difficulties in store for your apostolic undertaking. Have greater confidence in God; do all that your human means permit, and you'll see how soon money ceases to be a difficulty!

488 Don't let the lack of "instruments" stop your work. Begin as well as you can. As time passes, the function will create the organ. Some instruments formerly worthless, will become suitable. The rest can undergo a surgical operation, even though it be painful (there were no better "surgeons" than the saints!) and the work will go on.

489 A keen and living faith. A faith like Peter's. When you have it—our Lord has said so—you will move mountains, humanly insuperable obstacles that rise up against your apostolic undertakings.

490 An upright heart and good will. With these, and your mind intent on carrying out what God wants, you will see your dreams of Love come true and your hunger for souls satisfied.

491 *"Nonne hic est fabri filius? Nonne hic est faber, filius Mariae?"*—"Is not this the carpenter's son? Is not this the carpenter, the son of Mary?

This, said of Jesus, may very well be said of you, with a bit of amazement and a bit of mockery, when you *really* decide to carry out the will of God, to be an instrument: "But isn't this the one...?"

Say nothing, and let your works confirm your mission.

OUR LADY

492   The love of our Mother will be the breath that kindles into a living flame the embers of virtue that are hidden under the ashes of your indifference.

493   Love our Lady. And she will obtain abundant grace to help you con-quer in your daily struggle. And the enemy will gain nothing by those perversities that seem to boil up continually within you, trying to engulf in their fragrant corruption the high ideals, those sublime commands that Christ himself has placed in your heart. *"Serviam!"*—"I will serve!"

494   Be Mary's, and you will be ours.

495   To Jesus we always go, and to him we always return, through Mary.

496 How men like to be reminded of their relationship with distinguished figures in literature, in politics, in the armed forces, in the Church!

Sing to Mary Immaculate, reminding her:

Hail Mary, daughter of God the Father! Hail Mary, Mother of God the Son! Hail Mary, Spouse of God the Holy Spirit! Greater than you—no one but God!

497 Say to her: Mother of mine—yours, because you are hers on many counts—may your love bind me to your Son's cross; may I not lack the faith, nor the courage, nor the daring, to carry out the will of our Jesus.

498 All the sins of your life seem to be rising up against you. Don't give up hope! On the contrary, call your holy mother Mary, with the faith and abandonment of a child. She will bring peace to your soul.

499 Mary most holy, Mother of God, passes unnoticed, just as one more among the women of her town.

Learn from her how to live with "naturalness."

500 Wear on your breast the holy scapular of Carmel. There are many excellent Marian devotions, but few are as deep-rooted among the faithful and so richly blessed by the popes. Besides, how motherly is the sabbatine privilege!

501 When you were asked which image of our Lady aroused your devotion most, and you answered with the air of long experience, "all of them", I realized that you are a good son. That's why you are equally moved— "they make me fall in love," you said— by all the pictures of your Mother.

502 Mary, teacher of prayer. See how she asks her Son at Cana. And how she insists, confidently, perseveringly... And how she succeeds.

Learn.

503 The loneliness of Mary. Alone! She weeps, forsakenly.

You and I should keep Our Lady company, and weep also: for Jesus has been fastened to the wood, with nails, our miseries.

504 The holy Virgin Mary, Mother of fair love, will bring relief to your heart, when it feels as if it's made of flesh, if you have recourse to her with confidence.

505 Love of our Lady is proof of a good spirit, in works and in individuals.

Don't trust the undertaking that lacks this characteristic.

506   Our Lady of sorrows. When you contemplate her, look into her heart: she is a Mother with two sons, face to face: him... and you.

507   What humility, that of my holy Mother Mary! She's not to be seen amidst the palms of Jerusalem, nor—except that first one at Cana—at the hour of the great miracles.

But she doesn't flee from the degradation of Golgotha: there she stands, *"juxta crucem Iesu"*—"by the cross of Jesus"—his Mother.

508   Marvel at the courage of Mary—at the foot of the cross, in the greatest of human sorrow (there is no sorrow like hers) filled with fortitude.

And ask her for that same fortitude, so that you, too, will know how to remain close to the cross.

509   Mary, teacher of the sacrifice that is hidden and silent.

See her, nearly always in the background, cooperating with her Son: she knows and remains silent.

510   See the simplicity? *"Ecce ancilla!"*—"Behold the handmaid!" And the Word was made flesh.

That's how the saints worked: without any outward show. And if there was any, it was in spite of themselves.

511   *"Ne timeas, Maria!"*—"Do not be afraid, Mary!"
—Our Lady was troubled at the presence of the archangel!

And I want to throw away those safeguards of modesty
that are the shield of my purity!

512   O Mother, Mother! With that word of yours, *"Fiat"*
—"Be it done"—you have made us brothers of God and
heirs to his glory. Blessed are you!

513   Before, by yourself, you couldn't. Now, you've
turned to our Lady, and with her, how easy!

514   Have confidence. Return. Invoke our Lady and
you'll be faithful.

515   So your strength is failing you? Why don't you
tell your Mother about it: *"consolatrix afflictorum, auxilium
christianorum..., Spes nostra, Regina apostolorum"*—
"comforter of the afflicted, help of Christians..., our Hope,
Queen of apostles!"

516   Mother! Call her with a loud voice. She is listening
to you; she sees you in danger, perhaps, and she—your
holy mother Mary—offers you, along with the grace of
her son, the refuge of her arms, the tenderness of her
embrace... and you will find yourself with added strength
for the new battle.

THE CHURCH

517 *"Et unam, sanctam, catholicam et apostolicam Ecclesiam!"* I can well understand that pause of yours as you pray, savoring the words: "I believe in the Church, one, holy, catholic and apostolic."

518 What joy to be able to say with all the fervor of my soul: I love my Mother, the holy Church!

519 *"Serviam!"*—"I will serve!" That cry is your determination to serve the Church of God faithfully, even at the cost of fortune, of honor and of life.

520 Catholic, apostolic, Roman! I want you to be very Roman, ever anxious to make your "pilgrimage" to Rome *"videre Petrum"*—"to see Peter."

521 How good Christ was to leave the sacraments to his Church! They are a remedy for all our needs.

Venerate them and be very grateful, both to our Lord and to his Church.

522   Show veneration and respect for the holy liturgy of the Church and for its ceremonies. Observe them faithfully. Don't you see that, for us poor humans, even what is greatest and most noble enters through the senses?

523   The Church sings, it has been said, because just speaking would not satisfy its desires for prayer. You, as a Christian—and a chosen Christian—should learn to sing the liturgical chant.

524   "Let's burst into song!" said a soul in love, after seeing the wonders that our Lord was working through his ministry.

And the same advice I give to you: Sing! Let your grateful enthusiasm for your God overflow into joyous song.

525   To be "Catholic" means to love our country, and to let nobody surpass us in that love. And at the same time, it means to hold as our own the noble aspirations of all the other lands. How many glories of France are glories of mine! And in the same way, many things that make Germans proud—and Italians, British, Americans and Asians and Africans—are also sources of pride to me.

Catholic! A great heart, an open mind.

526 If you don't have the highest reverence for the priesthood and for the religious state, you certainly don't love God's Church.

527 That woman in the house of Simon the leper in Bethany, anointing the Master's head with precious ointment, reminds us of the duty to be generous in the worship of God.

All the richness, majesty and beauty possible would still seem too little to me.

And against those who attack the richness of sacred vessels, of vestments and altars, we hear the praise given by Jesus: *"opus enim bonum operata est in me"*—"She has done me a good turn."

HOLY MASS

528 A very important characteristic of the apostolic man is his love for the Mass.

529 "The Mass is long," you say, and I reply: "Because your love is short."

530 Many Christians take their time and have leisure enough in their social life (no hurry here). They are leisurely, too, in their professional activities, at table and recreation (no hurry here either). But isn't it strange how those same Christians find themselves in such a rush and want to hurry the priest, in their anxiety to shorten the time devoted to the most holy sacrifice of the altar?

531 "Treat him well for me, treat him well," said a certain elderly bishop with tears in his eyes to the priests he had just ordained.

Lord, I wish I had the voice and the authority to cry out in the same way to the ears and the hearts of many, many Christians!

532 How that saintly young priest, who was found worthy of martyrdom, wept at the foot of the altar as he thought of a soul who had come to receive Christ in the state of mortal sin!

Is that how you offer him reparation?

533 The humility of Jesus: in Bethlehem, in Nazareth, on Calvary. But still more humiliation and more self-abasement in the most sacred host—more than in the stable, more than in Nazareth, more than on the cross.

That is why I must love the Mass so! (*Our* Mass, Jesus.)

534 Receiving communion every day for so many years! Anybody else would be a saint by now—you told me—and I... I'm always the same!

Son, I replied, keep up your daily communion, and think: What would I be if I hadn't received?

535 Communion, union, communication, intimacy: Word, bread, love.

536 Receive. It's not a lack of respect. Receive today precisely when you have just got over that "bit of trouble".

Have you forgotten what Jesus said? It is not those who are well but those who are sick who need the physician.

537 When you approach the tabernacle remember that *he* has been waiting for you for twenty centuries.

538 There he is: King of Kings and Lord of Lords, hidden in the bread.

To this extreme has he humbled himself for love of you.

539 He's here on earth for *you*. Don't think it's reverence to stay away from communion, if you are prepared to receive. The only irreverence is to receive him unworthily.

540 What a source of grace there is in spiritual communion! Practise it frequently and you'll have greater presence of God and closer union with him in all your actions.

541 Piety has its own good manners. Learn them. It's a shame to see those "pious" people who don't know how to assist at Mass—even those who hear it daily—nor how to bless themselves (they make some weird gestures very hurriedly), nor how to bend their knee before the tabernacle (their ridiculous genuflections seem a mockery), nor how to bow their heads reverently before an image of our Lady.

542 Don't put up those mass-produced statues for public devotion. I prefer a rough, wrought-iron figure of Christ to those colored, plaster statues that look as if they were made of sugar candy.

543 You saw me celebrate holy Mass on a plain altar without any decoration behind it. The crucifix was large, the candlesticks heavy, with thick candles of graded height, sloping up toward the cross.

The frontal, the liturgical color of the day; a sweeping chasuble; the chalice, rich, simple in its lines, with a broad cup. We had no electric light, nor did we miss it.

And you found it difficult to leave the oratory. You felt at home there. Do you see how we are led to God, brought close to him, by the liturgy of the Catholic Church?

COMMUNION
OF THE SAINTS

544 The communion of the saints. How shall I explain it to you? You know what blood transfusions can do for the body? Well, that's what the communion of the saints does for the soul.

545 Live a special communion of the saints, and at the moment of interior struggle, as well as during the long hours of your work, each of you will feel the joy and the strength of not being alone.

546 Son, how well you live the communion of the saints when you wrote: "Yesterday I 'felt' that you were praying for me!"

547 Someone else who knows of this "communication" of supernatural riches told me: "That letter did me a world of good: I could feel everyone's prayers behind it... and I very much need to be prayed for."

548　If you feel the communion of the saints—if you live it—you'll gladly be a man of penance. And you will realize that penance is "*gaudium, etsi laboriosum*"—"joy in spite of hardship," and you will feel yourself "allied" to all the penitent souls that have been, that are, and that ever will be.

549　You will find it easier to do your duty if you think of how many brothers are helping you, and of the help you fail to give them when you are not faithful.

550　"*Ideo omnia sustineo propter electos*"—"I bear all things for the sake of the elect," "*ut et ipsi salutem consequantur*"—"that they also may obtain the salvation," "*quae est in Christo Iesu*"—"that is in Christ Jesus."

What a good way to live the communion of the saints! Ask our Lord to give you that spirit of St Paul.

DEVOTIONS

551 Flee from routine as from the devil himself. The great means to avoid falling into that abyss, the grave of true piety, is the constant presence of God.

552 Have only a few private devotions, but be constant in them.

553 Don't forget your childhood prayers, learned perhaps from your mother's lips. Say them each day with simplicity, as you did then.

554 Don't omit your visits to the blessed sacrament. After saying your usual prayer tell Jesus, really present in the tabernacle, about the cares and worries of your day. And he will give you light and courage for your life as a Christian.

555   How truly lovable is the sacred humanity of our God! Having placed yourself in the most holy wound of your Lord's right hand, you asked me: "If one of Christ's wounds cleans, heals, soothes, strengthens, kindles, and enraptures, what wouldn't the five do as they lie open on the cross?"

556   The way of the cross. Here indeed is a strong and fruitful devotion! May you make it a habit to go over those fourteen points of our Lord's passion and death each Friday. I assure you that you'll gain strength for the whole week.

557   Christmas devotions. I don't frown when I see you making the imitation mountains of the crib, and placing the simple clay figures around the manger. You have never seemed more a man to me than now, when you are so like a child.

558   The holy Rosary is a powerful weapon. Use it with confidence and you'll be amazed at the results.

559   St Joseph, a father to Christ, is also your father and your lord. Have recourse to him.

560   St Joseph, our father and lord, is a teacher of the interior life. Put yourself under his patronage and you'll feel the effect of his power.

561 Speaking of St Joseph in her autobiography, St Teresa writes: "Whoever fails to find a master to teach him how to pray should choose this glorious saint for a master; and he will not go astray." This advice comes from an experienced soul. Follow it.

562 Have confidence in your guardian angel. Treat him as a very dear friend—that's what he is—and he will do a thousand services for you in the ordinary affairs of each day.

563 Win over the guardian angel of the one you want to draw to your apostolate. He is always a great "accomplice".

564 If you would remember the presence of your guardian angel and those of your neighbors, you would avoid many of the foolish things you let slip into your conversation.

565 You seem amazed because your guardian angel has done so many obvious favors for you. But you shouldn't be: that's why our Lord has placed him at your side.

566 You say there are many occasions of going astray in such surroundings? That's true, but aren't there any guardian angels as well?

567   Turn to your guardian angel at the moment of trial; he will protect you from the devil and bring you holy inspirations.

568   How joyfully the holy guardian angels must have obeyed that soul who said to them: "Holy angels, I call upon you, like the spouse of the Canticle of Canticles, '*ut nuntietis ei quia amore langueo*'—'to tell him that I am dying with love.' "

569   I know you will be glad to have this prayer to the holy guardian angels of our tabernacles:

O angelic spirits, who guard our tabernacles, wherein lies the adorable treasure of the holy eucharist, defend it from profanation and preserve it for our love.

570   Drink at the clear fountain of the *Acts of the Apostles*. In the twelfth chapter, Peter is freed from prison by the ministry of angels and comes to the house of Mark's mother. Those inside don't want to believe the servant girl when she tells them Peter is at the door. "*Angelus eius est!*"—"It's his angel!" they say.

See on what intimate terms the early Christians were with their guardian angels.

And what about you?

571   The holy souls in purgatory. Out of charity, out of justice, and out of an excusable selfishness (they have such power with God!) remember them often in your sacrifices and in your prayers.

Whenever you speak of them, may you be able to say, "My good friends, the souls in purgatory."

572   You ask me why I always recommend so insistently the daily use of holy water. I could give you many reasons. This one of the saint of Avila would surely suffice for you: "From nothing do evil spirits flee more, never to return, than from holy water."

573   Thank you, my God, for placing in my heart such love for the pope.

574   Who told you it's not manly to make novenas? These devotions can be very manly if it is a man who does them, in a spirit of prayer and penance.

FAITH

575 There are some who pass through life as through a tunnel: they fail to realize the splendor and the security and the warmth of the sun of faith.

576 With what infamous lucidity does Satan argue against our Catholic faith!

But, let's tell him always, without entering into debate: I am a child of the Church.

577 You feel yourself with gigantic faith. He who gives you that faith will give you the means.

578 It is St Paul who tells you, apostolic soul: *"Iustus ex fide vivit"*—"He who is just lives by faith."

How is it that you're letting that fire die down?

579 Faith. It's a pity to see how frequently many Christians have it on their lips and yet how sparingly they put it into their actions.

You would think it a virtue to be preached only, and not one to be practised.

580 Humbly ask God to increase your faith. Then, with new lights, you'll see clearly the difference between the world's paths and your way as an apostle.

581 How humbly and simply the evangelists relate incidents that show up the weak and wavering faith of the apostles!

This is to keep you and me from giving up the hope of some day achieving the strong and unshakeable faith that those same apostles had later.

582 How beautiful is our Catholic faith! It provides a solution for all our anxieties; it gives peace to the mind and fills the heart with hope.

583 I'm not miracle-minded. As I've told you, I can find more than enough miracles in the holy Gospel to confirm my faith.

But I can't help pitying those Christians, many of them pious people, "apostles" even, who smile when people speak of extraordinary ways, superna-tural events. I feel the urge to tell them: Yes, this is still the age of miracles. We, too, would work them if we had enough faith!

584 Stir up the fire of your faith! Christ is not a figure of the past. He is not a memory lost in history.

He lives! "*Iesus Christus heri et hodie: ipse et in saecula!*" As St Paul says "Jesus Christ is the same yesterday and today—yes, and forever!"

585 "*Si habueritis fidem, sicut granum sinapis!*"—"If you have faith like a grain of mustard seed...!"

What promises are contained in this exclamation of the Master!

586 God is always the same. It is men of faith that are needed: then there will be a renewal of the wonders we read of in the holy Scriptures.

"*Ecce non est abbreviata manus Domini*"—"The hand of God the Lord"—his power—"has not grown weaker!"

587 They have no faith, but they do have superstitions. We laughed, and at the same time we're sorry, when that tough character became alarmed at the sight of a black cat or at hearing a certain word which of itself meant nothing but for him was a bad omen.

588 *"Omnia possibilia sunt credenti"*—"All things are possible for him who believes." The words are Christ's. How is it that you don't say to him with the apostles: *"Adauge nobis fidem!"*—"Increase my faith!"

HUMILITY

589 When you hear the plaudits of triumph, let there also sound in your ears the laughter you provoked with your failures.

590 Don't aspire to be like the gilded weather vane on top of a great building. However much it may glitter, however high it may be, it adds nothing to the firmness of the structure.

Rather be like an old stone block hidden in the foundations, under the ground where no one can see you. Because of you, the house will not fall.

591 The more I am exalted, my Jesus, the more you must humble me in my heart, showing me what I've been and what I'll be if you forsake me.

592 Don't forget that you are just a trash can. So if by any chance the divine gardener should lay his hands on you, and scrub and clean you, and fill you with magnificent flowers, neither the scent nor the colors that beautify your ugliness should make you proud.

Humble yourself: don't you know that you are a trash can?

593 The day you see yourself as you are, you will think it natural to be despised by others.

594 You're not humble when you humble yourself, but when you are humbled by others and you bear it for Christ.

595 If you really knew yourself, you would rejoice at being despised, and your heart would weep in the face of honors and praise.

596 Don't feel hurt when others see your faults. What should really distress you is the offense against God and the scandal you may give.

Apart from that, may you be known for what you are and be despised. Don't be sorry if you are nothing, because then Jesus will have to put everything into you.

597 If you were to obey the impulse of your heart and the dictates of reason, you would always lie flat on the ground, prostrate, a vile worm, ugly and miserable in the sight of that God who puts up with so much from you!

598 How great is the value of humility! *"Quia respexit humilitatem..."*—"Because he has regarded the lowliness..." It is not of her faith, nor of her charity, nor of her immaculate purity that our Mother speaks in the house of Zachary. Her joyful hymn sings:

"Because he has regarded the lowliness of his handmaid, behold: henceforth all generations shall call me blessed."

599 You are dust, fallen and dirty. Even though the breath of the Holy Spirit should lift you above all earthly things and make you shine like gold—your misery reflecting in those heights the sovereign rays of the Sun of Justice—don't forget the lowliness of your state.

An instant of pride would cast you back to the ground; and having been light, you would again become dirt.

600 You,... proud? About what?

601 Pride? Why? Before long (maybe years, maybe days) you'll be a heap of rotting flesh, worms, foul-smelling fluids, your shroud in filthy shreds...and no one on earth will remember you.

602 For all your learning, all your fame, all your eloquence and power, if you're not humble, you're worth nothing. Cut out that ego that dominates you so completely —root it out. God will help you. And then you'll be able to begin to work for Christ in the lowest place in his army of apostles.

603 That false humility is laziness. Such a "humble-ness" leads you to give up rights that really are duties.

604 Humbly acknowledge your weakness. Then you can say with the Apostle: "*Cum enim infirmor, tunc potens sum*"—"For when I am weak, then I am strong."

605 "Father, how can you stand such filth?" you asked me after a contrite confession.

I said nothing, thinking that if your humility makes you feel like that—like filth, a heap of filth!—then we may yet turn all your weakness into something really great.

606 See how humble our Jesus is: a donkey was his throne in Jerusalem!

607 Humility is one of the good ways to achieve interior peace. He has said so: "Learn of me, for I am meek and humble of heart, and you will find rest for your souls."

608 It's not lack of humility to be aware of your soul's progress. That way you can thank God for it.

But don't forget that you are a beggar, wearing a good suit... on loan.

609 Self-knowledge leads us by the hand, as it were, to humility.

610 Your firm defense of the spirit and norms of the apostolate in which you work should never falter through false humility. That firmness is not pride: it's the cardinal virtue of fortitude.

611 It was because of pride. You thought you were already capable of everything—all by yourself. But then he left you for a moment and you fell—headlong.

Be humble, and his extraordinary aid will not fail you.

612 Get rid of those proud thoughts! You are but the brush in the hand of the artist, and nothing more.

Tell me, what is a brush good for if it doesn't let the artist do his work?

613 So that you'll be humble—you, who are so self-satisfied and empty—it's enough to consider these words of Isaias: You're a drop of water or dew that falls on the earth and is scarcely seen.

OBEDIENCE

614 In apostolic work there is no such thing as a trifling disobedience.

615 Temper your will. Strengthen your will. With God's grace, let it be like a sword of steel.

Only by being strong-willed can you know how not to be so in order to obey.

616 With that slowness, with that passivity, with that reluctance to obey, what damage you do to the apostolate and what satisfaction you give the enemy!

617 Obey, as an instrument obeys in the hands of the artist—not stopping to consider the why and the wherefore of what it is doing. Be sure that you'll never be directed to do anything that isn't good and for the greater glory of God.

618   The enemy: "Will you obey, even in this ridiculous little detail?"

You with God's grace: "I will obey, even in this *heroic* little detail!"

619   Initiative. You must have it in your apostolate, within the limits of your instructions.

If your projects exceed those limits or if you're in doubt, consult your superior, without telling anyone else your thoughts.

Never forget: You are only an agent.

620   If obedience doesn't give you peace, it's because you're proud.

621   What a pity if the one in charge doesn't give you good example! But is it only for his personal qualities that you obey? Or do you in your selfishness interpret St Paul's *"obedite praepositis vestris"*—"Obey your superiors" with an addition of your own: "Always provided they have virtues to my own taste?"

622   How well you understand obedience when you write: "Always to obey is to be a martyr without dying!"

623 You've been told to do something that seems difficult and useless. Do it. And you'll see that it's easy and fruitful.

624 Hierarchy: Each piece in its place. What would be left of a Velazquez painting if each color were to go out of its place, each thread of the canvas were to break apart, each piece of the wooden frame were to separate itself from the others?

625 Your obedience is not worthy of the name unless you are ready to abandon your most flourishing work whenever someone with authority so commands.

626 Isn't it true, Lord, that you were greatly consoled by the child-like remark of that man who, disconcerted by having to obey in something unpleasant and repulsive, whispered to you: "Jesus, may I put on a good face!"

627 Yours should be a silent obedience. That tongue!

628 Right now, when you are finding it hard to obey, remember your Lord, *"factus obediens usque ad mortem, mortem autem crucis"*—"obedient unto death, even to death on the cross!"

629   Oh, the power of obedience! The lake of Genesareth had denied its fishes to Peter's nets. A whole night in vain.

Then, obedient, he lowered his net again into the water and they caught *"piscium multitudinem copiosam"*—"a great number of fishes."

Believe me, the miracle is repeated every day.

POVERTY

630 Don't forget it: he has most who needs least. Don't create needs for yourself.

631 Detach yourself from the goods of this world. Love and practice poverty of spirit: be content with what is sufficient for leading a simple and temperate life.

Otherwise, you'll never be an apostle.

632 True poverty is not to lack things but to be detached, to give up voluntarily one's dominion over them.

That's why some poor people are really rich... and vice versa.

633 As a man of God, put the same effort into scorning riches that men of the world put into possessing them.

634   What an attachment to the things of the world!
But soon they will slip from your grasp, for the rich man
cannot carry his riches with him to the grave.

635   You don't have the spirit of poverty if you don't
select for yourself what is worst, when you are able to
choose in such a way that it will not be noticed.

636   *"Divitiae, si affluant, nolite cor apponere"*—"If
riches abound, set not your heart upon them." Strive,
rather, to use them generously—and, if necessary,
heroically.
    Be poor of spirit.

637   You don't love poverty if you don't love what
poverty brings with it.

638   What holy resources poverty has!
    Do you remember? It was a time of financial stress in
your apostolic undertaking. You had given without stint
down to the last penny. Then that priest of God said to
you: "I, too, will give you all I have." You knelt and you
heard, "May the blessing of almighty God, the Father, the
Son and the Holy Spirit, descend upon you and remain
with you forever!"
    You are still convinced that you were well paid.

DISCRETION

639 Remain silent, and you will never regret it. Speak, and you often will.

640 How can you dare ask others to keep your secret, when that very request is a sign that you aren't able to keep it yourself?

641 Discretion is neither mystery nor secrecy. It is simply naturalness.

642 Discretion is... "fineness of spirit". Don't you feel annoyed and uncomfortable deep down inside when the affairs of your family, honorable and ordinary, emerge from the warmth of the home into the indifference or curiosity of the public gaze?

643 Be slow to reveal the intimate details of your apostolate. Don't you see that the world in its selfishness will fail to understand?

644 Be silent! Don't forget that your ideal is like a newly-lit flame. A single breath might be enough to put it out in your heart.

645 How fruitful is silence! All the energy you lose through your failures in discretion is energy taken from the effectiveness of your work.

Be discreet.

646 If you were more discreet, you would not have to complain within yourself about the bad taste left by so many of your conversations.

647 Don't seek to be "understood". That lack of understanding is providential: so that your sacrifice may pass unnoticed.

648 If you hold your tongue, you'll gain greater effectiveness in your apostolic undertakings (so many people let their strength slip through their mouths!) and you'll avoid many dangers of vainglory.

649 Always display! You ask me for pictures, charts and statistics.

I won't send you what you ask, because (though I respect the opposite opinion) I would then think I had acted with a view to making good on earth, and where I want to make good is in heaven.

650 There are many people, holy people, who don't understand your way. Don't strive to make them understand. It would be a waste of time and would give rise to indiscretions.

651 "What gives life to roots and branches is the sap, which always works on the inside."

Your friend who wrote those words knew you were nobly ambitious. And he showed you the way: discretion and sacrifice—"working on the inside!"

652 Discretion, a virtue of the few.

Who slandered women by saying that discretion is not a woman's virtue? How many men—yes, red-blooded men—have yet to learn!

653 What an example of discretion the Mother of God has given us! Not even to St Joseph does she communicate the mystery.

Ask our Lady for the discretion you lack.

654 Bitterness has sharpened your tongue. Be silent!

655 I cannot overemphasize the importance of discretion.

If it isn't the blade of your sword, at least it's the hilt.

656 Always remain silent when you feel indignation surge up within you—even when you have reason to be angry.

For in spite of your discretion, you always say more than you want to in such moments.

JOY

657 True virtue is not sad and repulsive, but pleasantly joyful.

658 If things go well let's rejoice, blessing God, who makes them prosper. And if they go wrong? Let's rejoice, blessing God, who allows us to share the sweetness of his cross.

659 The cheerfulness you should have is not the kind we might call physiological—like that of a healthy animal. Rather, it is the supernatural happiness that comes from the abandonment of everything, including yourself, into the loving arms of our Father God.

660 If you're an apostle you should never feel discouraged. There is no obstacle that you cannot overcome.
    Then why are you sad?

661 Long faces, coarse manners, a ridiculous appearance, a repelling air. Is that how you hope to inspire others to follow Christ?

662 You are unhappy? Think: there must be an obstacle between God and me. You will seldom be wrong.

663 You ask me to suggest a cure for your sadness. I'll give you a prescription from an expert adviser, the apostle St James:

"Tristatus aliquis vestrum?"—"Are you sad, my son?" *"Oret!"*—"Pray!" Try it and you will see.

664 Don't be sad. Let your outlook be more... "ours"— more christian.

665 I want you always to be happy, for cheerfulness is an essential part of your way.

Pray that the same supernatural joy may be granted to us all.

666 *"Laetetur cor quaerentium Dominum"*—"Let the hearts of them rejoice who seek the Lord."

There you have light to help you discover the reasons for your sadness.

OTHER VIRTUES

667 Acts of faith, hope and love are valves which provide an outlet for the fire of those souls who live the life of God.

668 Do everything unselfishly, for pure love, as if there were neither reward nor punishment. But in your heart foster the glorious hope of heaven.

669 It's good that you serve God as a son, without payment—generously. But don't worry if at times you think of the reward.

670 Jesus says: "Everyone who has left house or brothers or sisters or father or mother or wife or children or lands, for my name's sake, shall receive a hundredfold and shall possess life everlasting."

Try to find anyone on earth who repays with such generosity!

671 "Jesus remains silent."—*"Iesus autem tacebat."* Why do you speak, to console yourself or to explain yourself?

Say nothing. Seek joy in contempt: you'll always receive less than you deserve. Can you, by any chance, ask: *"Quid enim mali feci?"*—"What evil have I done?"

672 You can be sure you're a man of God if you suffer injustice gladly and in silence.

673 What a beautiful answer was given by a certain venerable man to his young friend who complained of an injustice he had suffered: "Does it hurt you?" he asked. "Then, don't desire to be good!"

674 Never give your opinion if you're not asked for it, even though you may think it is the best one.

675 It's true that he was a sinner. But don't pass so final a judgment. Have pity in your heart and don't forget that he may yet be an Augustine, while you remain just another mediocrity.

676 All the things of this world are no more than dirt. Place them in a heap under your feet and you'll be so much nearer to heaven.

677   Gold, silver, jewels: dirt, piles of manure.

Delights, sensual pleasures, satisfactions of the appetites: like a beast, like a mule, like a hog, like a cock, like a bull...

Honors, distinctions, titles: things of air, puffs of pride, lies, nothingness.

678   Don't set your heart on things here below. Such love is selfish. A few short hours after God calls you into his presence, those you love will recoil from you in horror and revulsion.

Elsewhere is the love that endures.

679   Gluttony is an ugly vice. Don't you feel a bit amused and even a bit disgusted when you see a group of distinguished gentlemen seated solemnly around a table, stuffing fatty foods into their digestive tubes with an air of ritual, as if the whole thing were an end in itself?

680   Don't talk about food at the table. That's a lack of refinement unworthy of you. Speak about noble things—of the mind, of the soul—and you'll have dignified this duty.

681   The day you leave the table without having made some small mortification, you will have eaten like a pagan.

682 Ordinarily you eat more than you need. And the natural result, a heavy fullness and discomfort, benumbs your mind and renders you unfit to savor supernatural treasures.

What a fine virtue temperance is, even by earthly standards!

683 I see you, christian gentleman (that's what you say you are), kissing an image, muttering some vocal prayer, crying out against those who attack the Church of God, even frequenting the holy sacraments.

But I don't see you making a sacrifice, nor avoiding certain conversations of a worldly nature (I could with justice have used another adjective!), nor being generous toward those in need (including that same Church of God!), nor putting up with a failing in one of your brothers, nor checking your pride for the sake of the common good, nor getting rid of that tight cloak of selfishness, nor... so many other things!

Yes, I see you... But I don't see you... And yet, you say you are a christian gentleman! What a poor idea you have of Christ!

684 So your talents, your personality, your qualities are being wasted. So you're not allowed to take full advantage of them.

Meditate well on these words of a spiritual writer: "The incense offered to God is not wasted. Our Lord is more honored by the immolation of your talents than by their vain use."

TRIBULATIONS

685 The storm of persecution is good. What is lost? You can't lose something if it's already lost.

When the whole tree is not torn up by the roots—and there is no wind or hurricane that can uproot the tree of the Church—only the dry branches fall. And it is best that they fall.

686 All right: that person has behaved badly toward you. But, haven't you behaved worse toward God?

687 Jesus: wherever you have passed not a heart has remained indifferent. You are either loved or hated.

When an apostolic man follows you, carrying out his duty, is it surprising—if he is another Christ!—that he should provoke similar murmurs of aversion or of love?

688   Once again, they've been talking, they've written
—in favor, against; with good, and with not so good will;
insinuations and slanders, panegyrics and plaudits; hits
and misses...

Fool, big fool! As long as you keep going straight
toward your target—head and heart intoxicated with God—
why care about the clamor of the wind or the chirping
of the cricket, or the bellowing, or the grunting, or the
neighing?

Besides, it's inevitable; don't try to install doors in
open air.

689   Tongues have been wagging and you've suffered
rebuffs that hurt you, and all the more because you were
not expecting them.

Your supernatural reaction should be to pardon—and
even to *ask* for pardon!—and to take advantage of the
experience to detach yourself from creatures.

690   When you meet with suffering, contempt, ...the
cross, your thoughts should be: what is this compared to
what I deserve?

691   Are you suffering some great tribulation? Do you
have reverses? Say very slowly, as if savoring the words,
this powerful and manly prayer:

"May the most just and most lovable will of God be done, be fulfilled, be praised and eternally exalted above all things. Amen. Amen."

I assure you that you'll find peace.

692   You suffer in this present life, which is only a dream, and a short one at that. Rejoice, because your Father God loves you so much, and if you put no obstacles in his way, after this bad dream he will give you a good awakening.

693   It hurt you not to have been thanked for that favor. Answer me these two questions: Are you so grateful toward Christ Jesus? Did you really do that favor in the hope of being thanked for it on earth?

694   I don't know why you're amazed: the enemies of Christ were never very reasonable.

When Lazarus was raised from the dead, you might have thought they would yield and confess the divinity of Jesus. But no! "Let us kill him who gives life!" they said.

It's the same today.

695   In the moments of struggle and tribulation, when perhaps the "good" fill your way with obstacles, lift up your apostolic heart: listen to Jesus as he speaks of the grain of mustard seed and of the leaven, and say to him: *"Edissere nobis parabolam"*—"Explain the parable to me."

And you'll feel the joy of contemplating the victory to come: the birds of the air under the shelter of your apostolate, now only in its beginnings, and the whole of the meal leavened.

696   If you accept tribulation with a faint heart, you lose your joy and your peace, and you run the risk of not deriving any spiritual profit from that trial.

697   Public events have led you to prefer a voluntary confinement, which is worse perhaps, because of the circumstances, than the confinement of a prison. You've suffered an eclipse of your personality.

On all sides you feel yourself hemmed in: selfishness, curiosity, misunderstanding, gossip. Well, so what? Have you forgotten your very free will and that power of yours as a "child"? The absence of leaves and flowers (of external action) does not exclude the growth and activity of the roots (interior life).

Work: things will change and you'll yield more fruit than before—and it will be more savory.

698   So you've been hauled over the coals? Don't follow the advice of pride and lose your temper. Think:

how charitable they are toward me! The things they've left unsaid!

699 Cross, toil, tribulation: such will be your lot as long as you live. That was the way Christ followed, and the disciple is not above his Master.

700 Agreed: there is a lot of external pressure, which excuses you in part. But there is also complicity within (take a good look), and there I see no excuse.

701 Have you not heard the parable of the vine and the branches from the lips of the Master? Console yourself: He demands much of you, for you are the branch that bears fruit. And he must prune you, *"ut fructum plus afferas"*—"so that you'll yield more fruit."

Of course that cutting—that pruning—hurts. But, afterwards, how luxuriant the growth, how fruitful your works!

702 You are upset. Look: happen what may in your interior life or in the world around you, never forget that the importance of events or of people is very relative. Take things calmly. Let time pass. And then, as you view persons and events dispassionately and from afar, you'll acquire the perspective that will enable you to see each thing in its proper place and in its true proportion.

If you do this, you'll be more objective and you'll be spared many a cause of anxiety.

703 A bad night in a bad inn. That's how St Teresa of Jesus is said to have described this earthly life. It's a good comparison, isn't it?

704 A visit to a famous monastery. A certain foreign lady was deeply moved on seeing the poverty of the place: "You lead a very hard life, don't you?" And the pleased monk merely replied, as if speaking to himself, "Just what you asked for, isn't it so? Now that you have it, don't let it go."

These words, which I joyfully heard that holy man say, I can only repeat to you with sorrow when you tell me you're not happy.

705 Worry? Never! That's to lose your peace.

706 Physical collapse. You are worn out... Stop that exterior activity. Rest. Consult a doctor. Obey, and don't worry.

You'll soon return to your normal life and, if you're faithful, you'll improve your apostolate.

INTERIOR STRUGGLE

707   Don't be troubled if, as you consider the marvels of the supernatural world, you hear that other voice—the intimate, insinuating voice of the "old man".

It's "the body of death" that cries out for its lost privileges. God's grace is sufficient for you: be faithful and you will conquer.

708   The world, the devil and the flesh are a band of adventurers who take advantage of the weakness of that savage you have within you. In exchange for the poor bauble of pleasure, which is worth nothing, they want you to hand over to them the pure gold and the pearls, the diamonds and the rubies, drenched in the living and redeeming blood of your God—the price and the treasure of your eternity.

709   Do you hear these words? "In another state in life, in another place, in another position or occupation, you would do much more good. Talent isn't needed for what you are doing."

Well, listen to me: Wherever you have been placed, you please God, ...and what you've just been thinking is clearly a suggestion of the devil.

710   You are worried and sad because your communions are cold and barren. Tell me, when you approach the sacrament, do you seek yourself or do you seek Jesus? If you seek yourself, there is reason indeed to be sad. But if you seek Christ—as you ought—could you want a surer sign than the cross to know you've found him?

711   Another fall... and what a fall! Despair? No! Humble yourself and through Mary, your Mother, have recourse to the merciful love of Jesus. A *miserere*—"have mercy on me"—and lift up your heart! And now, begin again.

712   How low you have fallen this time! Begin the foundations from down there. Be humble. "*Cor contritum et humiliatum, Deus, non despicies.*"—"A contrite and humbled heart, O God, you will not despise."

713   You haven't set yourself against God. Your falls are due to weakness. All right, but those weaknesses are so frequent! You don't know how to avoid them, so that, even if you don't want me to consider you bad, I'll have to consider you both bad and stupid.

714   Yours is a desire without desire, as long as you don't put firmly aside the occasion of falling. Don't fool yourself telling me you're weak. You're a coward, which is not the same thing.

715   That confusion in your spirit, the temptation that envelops you, is like a blindfold over the eyes of your soul.

You are in the dark. Don't insist on walking by yourself, for by yourself you will fall. Go to your Director—to your superior—and he will make you hear once again those words of Raphael the Archangel to Tobias:

"Forti animo esto, in proximo est ut a Deo cureris."

"Take comfort; before long God will heal you." Be obedient and the scales, the blindfold, will fall from your eyes and God will fill you with grace and peace.

716   "I don't know how to conquer myself!" you write me despondently. And I answer: But have you really tried to use the means?

717   Blessed be the hardships of this earth! Poverty, tears, hatred, injustice, dishonor... You can endure all things in him who strengthens you.

718 You suffer and you want to bear it in silence. It doesn't matter if you complain—it's the natural reaction of our poor flesh—as long as your will wants, now and always, only what God wants.

719 Never despair. Lazarus was dead and decaying: "*iam foetet, quatriduanus est enim*"—"by now he will smell; this is the fourth day," Martha told Jesus.

If you hear the inspiration of God and follow it— "*Lazare, veni foras!*"—"Lazarus, come forth!—you will return to Life.

720 It's hard! Yes, I know. But, forward! No one receives the reward—and what a reward!—except those who fight bravely.

721 If your spiritual edifice is tottering, or if everything seems to be up in the air, ...lean on filial confidence in Jesus and Mary; it's the firm and steady rock on which you should have built from the beginning.

722 This time the trial has been long. Perhaps—and without the perhaps—you haven't borne it well so far, for you were still seeking human consolations. But your Father God has torn them out by the roots so as to leave you no other refuge but him.

723 So you couldn't care less? Don't try to fool yourself. This very moment, if I were to ask you about persons and activities, in which for God's love you put your soul, I know that you would answer me eagerly, with the interest of one speaking of what is his own.

It's not true that you don't care. It's just that you're not tireless, and that you need more time for yourself: time that will also be for your work, since, after all, you are the instrument.

724 You tell me that in your heart you have fire and water, cold and heat, empty passions and God: one candle lit to St Michael and another to the devil.

Calm yourself. As long as you are willing to fight there are not two candles burning in your heart. There is only one: the archangel's.

725 The enemy nearly always works like that on the souls who are going to resist him: hypocritically, quietly, using spiritual motives, trying not to attract attention. And then, when there seems to be no way out (though there is), he comes brazenly, trying to bring on a despair like that of Judas—despair without repentance.

726 After losing those human consolations you have been left with a feeling of loneliness, as if you were hanging by a thin thread over the emptiness of a black abyss. And your cries, your shouts for help, seem to go unheard by anybody.

The truth is you deserve to be so forlorn. Be humble; don't seek yourself; don't seek your own satisfaction. Love the cross—to bear it is little—and our Lord will hear your prayer. And in time, calm will be restored to your senses. And your heart will heal, and you will have peace.

727 Your flesh is tender and raw. That's how you are. Everything seems to make you suffer in your mind and in your senses. And everything is a temptation to you...

Be humble—I insist. You will see how quickly all this passes. The pain will turn into joy, and the temptation into firm purpose.

But meanwhile, strengthen your faith; fill yourself with hope; and make constant acts of love, even though you think they come only from your lips.

728 All our fortitude is on loan.

729 Each day, O my God, I am less sure of myself and more sure of you!

730 If you don't leave him, he won't leave you.

731 Depend on Jesus for everything. You have nothing, are worth nothing, are capable of nothing. He will act, if you abandon yourself to him.

732 O Jesus! I rest in you.

733 Trust always in your God. He does not lose battles.

LAST THINGS

734 "This is your hour and the power of darkness." So, the sinner has his hour then? Yes... and God his eternity!

735 If you're an apostle, death will be a good friend who helps you on your way.

736 Have you seen the dead leaves fall in the sad autumn twilight? So fall souls each day into eternity. One day, the falling leaf will be you.

737 Haven't you heard the mournful tone with which the worldly complain that "each day that passes is a step nearer death"?

It is. And I tell you: rejoice, apostolic soul, for each day that passes brings you closer to Life.

738   For others, death is a stumbling block, a source of terror. For us, death—Life—is an encouragement and a stimulus.

For them it is the end; for us, the beginning.

739   Don't be afraid of death. Accept it from this day on, generously... when God wills it, how God wills it, where God wills it. Believe me, it will come at the time, in the place and in the way that are best—sent by your Father God. May our sister death be welcome!

740   What part of the world would collapse if I were missing, if I were to die?

741   Do you see how the corpse of a loved one disintegrates in foul and reeking fluids? Well, that is the body beautiful! Contemplate it and draw your own conclusions.

742   Those paintings by Valdez Leal,* with so much distinguished heap of decaying flesh—bishops, noblemen, all in rank corruption—surely they must move you.

What then do you say of the Duke of Gandia's** cry: "No more will I serve a lord whom I can lose through death!"?

---

*Valdéz Leal: A Spanish painter famous for his pictures of the dead.
**Duke of Gandia: Later St Francis Borgia.

743 You talk of dying "heroically". Don't you think that it is more heroic to die unnoticed, in a good bed, like a bourgeois, ...but to die of Love?

744 You—if you are an apostle—will not have to die. You will move to a new house, that's all.

745 "He shall come to judge the living and the dead." Thus we say in the Creed. May you never lose sight of that judgment and of that justice and... of that judge.

746 Doesn't your soul burn with the desire to make your Father God happy when he has to judge you?

747 There is a great tendency among worldly souls to think of God's mercy, and so they are emboldened to persist in their follies.

It's true that God our Lord is infinitely merciful, but he is also infinitely just; and there is a judgment, and he is the judge.

748 Courage. Don't you know that St Paul tells the Corinthians that "each one will receive his own wages according to his works"?

749 There is a hell. A trite enough statement, you think. I will repeat it, then: there is a hell!

Echo it, at the right moment, in the ears of one friend, and another, and another.

750 Listen to me, you who are up to your neck in science: your science cannot deny the reality of diabolic activities. My Mother, the holy Church, for many years— and it is also a praiseworthy private devotion—required the priests each day at the foot of the altar to invoke St Michael, "*contra nequitiam et insidias diaboli*"—"against the wickedness and snares of the devil."

751 Heaven: "The eye has not seen, nor the ear heard, neither has it entered into the heart of man what things God has prepared for them who love him."

Don't these revelations of the Apostle spur you on to fight?

752 Always. Forever! Words brought to our lips by the human desire to prolong—to make eternal—what is pleasant.

Lying words, on earth, where everything must end.

753 The things of this earth are continually passing away: hardly has pleasure begun when it is already ended.

THE WILL OF GOD

754 This is the key to open the door and enter the kingdom of heaven: "*qui facit voluntatem Patris mei qui in coelis est, ipse intrabit in regnum coelorum*"—"he who does the will of my Father, he shall enter!"

755 Many great things depend—don't forget it—on whether you and I live our lives as God wants.

756 We are stones—blocks of stone—that can move, can feel, that have completely free wills.

God himself is the stonecutter who chips off the edges, shaping and modifying us as he desires, with blows of the hammer and chisel.

Let us not try to draw aside, let us not try to evade his will, for in any case we won't be able to avoid the blows. We will suffer all the more, and uselessly. Instead of polished stone suitable for building, we will be a shapeless heap of gravel that people will trample on contemptuously.

757   Resignation?... Conformity? *Love* the will of God!

758   The wholehearted acceptance of the will of God is the sure way of finding joy and peace: happiness in the cross. It's then we realize that Christ's yoke is sweet and that his burden is not heavy.

759   Peace, peace, you tell me. Peace is... for men of *good* will.

760   Here is a thought that brings peace and that the Holy Spirit provides ready-made for those who seek the will of God: *"Dominus regit me, et nihil mihi deerit"*— "The Lord rules me, and I shall want nothing."

What can upset a soul who sincerely repeats these words?

761   Free man, subject yourself to a voluntary servitude, so that Jesus won't have to say of you what we are told he said to St Teresa of others: "Teresa, I was willing. But men were not."

762   An act of complete correspondence to the will of God: Is that what you want, Lord?... Then it's what I want also!

763 Don't hesitate: let your lips pronounce a heartfelt *"Fiat"*—"be it done!" That will be the crowning of your sacrifice.

764 The closer an apostle is to God, the more universal his desires. His heart expands and takes in everybody and everything in its longing to lay the universe at the feet of Jesus.

765 So much do I love your will, my God, that I wouldn't accept heaven itself against your will—if such an absurdity could be.

766 Abandonment to the will of God is the secret of happiness on earth. Say, then: *"meus cibus est, ut faciam voluntatem eius"*—"my food is to do his will."

767 This abandonment is exactly what you need so as never to lose your peace again.

768 *"Gaudium cum pace"*—"joy with peace"—the unfailing and savory fruit of abandonment.

769 Holy indifference is not coldness of heart, as the heart of Jesus was not cold.

770 You're not less happy with too little than with too much.

771 God exalts those who carry out his will in the very same things in which he humbled them.

772 Ask yourself many times during the day: Am I doing at this moment what I ought to be doing?

773 Jesus, whatever you *want*, I love!

774 Steps: to be resigned to the will of God; to conform to the will of God; to want the will of God; to love the will of God.

775 Lord, if it is your will, turn my poor flesh into a crucifix.

776 Don't fall into a vicious circle. You are thinking: when this is settled one way or another, I'll be very generous with my God.

Can't you see that Jesus is waiting for you to be generous without any reservation, so that he can settle things far better than you imagine?

A firm resolution, as a logical consequence: in each moment of each day I will try generously to carry out the will of God.

777 Your own will, your own judgment: that's what upsets you.

778 It takes only a second. Before starting anything ask yourself: What does God want of me in this?

Then, with divine grace, do it!

THE GLORY OF GOD

779 It's good to give glory to God, without seeking a foretaste (wife, children, honors...) of that glory which we will enjoy fully with him in the eternal life...

Besides, he is generous. He returns a hundredfold; and this is true even of children. Many deprive themselves of children for the sake of his glory, and they have thousands of children of their spirit—children, as we are children of our Father in heaven.

780 *"Deo omnis gloria"*—"All glory to God." It is an emphatic confession of our nothingness. He, Jesus, is everything. We, without him, are worth nothing: Nothing.

Our vainglory would be just that: vain glory; it would be sacrilegious theft; the "I" should not appear anywhere.

781 Without me you can do nothing, our Lord has told us. And he has said it so that you and I won't credit

ourselves with successes that are his. "*Sine me, nihil!*"—
"Without me, nothing!"

782 How can you dare use that spark of the divine
intelligence—your mind—in any way other than in giving
glory to your Lord?

783 If life didn't have as its aim to give glory to God,
it would be detestable—even more, loathsome.

784 Give "all" the glory to God. With your will aided
by grace, "squeeze" out each one of your actions, so that
nothing remains in them that smacks of human pride, of
self-complacency.

785 "*Deus meus es tu, et confitebor tibi: Deus meus
es tu, et exaltabo te.*"—"You are my God and I will praise
you; you are my God and I will exalt you." A beautiful
program for an apostle of your caliber.

786 May no attachment bind you to earth except the
most divine desire of giving glory to Christ and, through
him and with him and in him, to the Father and to the
Holy Spirit.

787 Rectify, purify your intention! What a shame if
your victory turns out worthless because you acted from
human motives.

788 Purity of intention. The suggestions of pride and the impulses of the flesh are not difficult to recognize... And you fight, and with grace, you conquer.

But the motives that inspire you, even in your holiest actions, don't seem clear. And deep down inside you hear a voice which makes you aware of your human motives...so that your soul is subtly haunted by the disturbing thought that you are not acting as you should—for pure love, solely and exclusively to give God all his glory.

React at once each time and say: "Lord, for myself I want nothing. All for your glory and for Love."

789 There is no doubt that you have purified your intentions well when you have said: from this moment on I renounce all human gratitude and reward.

WINNING
NEW APOSTLES

790 Don't you long to shout to those youths who are bustling around you: Fools! Leave those worldly things that shackle the heart and very often degrade it... Leave all that and come with us in search of Love!

791 You lack drive. That's why you sway so few. You don't seem very convinced of what you gain by giving up the things of the earth for Christ.

Remember: "A hundredfold and life everlasting!" Would you call that a poor bargain?

792 *"Duc in altum."*—"Put out into the deep." Cast aside the pessimism that makes a coward of you. *"Et laxate retia vestra in capturam"*—"And lower your nets for a catch."

Don't you see that, as Peter said, "*in nomine tuo, laxabo rete*"—"at your word I will lower the net," you can say, "Jesus, in your name I will seek souls!"

793 Winning new apostles. It's the unmistakable sign of true zeal.

794 To sow. The sower went out... Scatter the seed, apostolic soul. The wind of grace will bear it away if the furrow where it falls is not worthy... Sow, and be certain that the seed will take root and bear fruit.

795 By good example good seed is sown; and charity compels us all to sow.

796 Yours is only a small love if you are not zealous for the salvation of all souls. Yours is only a poor love if you are not eager to inflame other apostles with your madness.

797 You know that your way is not clear, and that by not following Jesus closely you remain with that clouded vision.

Then, what are you waiting for to make up your mind?

798 Reasons? What reasons could the poor Ignatius have given to the wise Xavier?

799   What amazes you seems quite natural to me: God has sought you out right in the midst of your work.

That is how he sought the first, Peter and Andrew, John and James, beside their nets, and Matthew, sitting in the custom-house.

And—wonder of wonders—Paul, in his eagerness to destroy the seeds of christianity!

800   The harvest indeed is great, but the laborers are few. "*Rogate ergo!*"—"Pray therefore the Lord of the harvest to send forth laborers into his vineyard."

Prayer is the most effective means of winning other apostles.

801   Through the world still echoes that divine cry: "I have come to cast fire upon the earth, and what will I but that it be kindled?" And you see: it has nearly all died out...

Don't you want to spread the blaze?

802   There is a brilliant man whom you long to draw to your apostolate; there is another, a man of great influence; and a third, full of prudence and virtue.

Pray, offer sacrifices, and work on them with your word and example. They don't come! Don't lose your peace: it's because they are not needed.

Do you think there were no brilliant and influential and prudent and virtuous contemporaries of Peter outside the apostolate of the first twelve?

803 I've been told that you have the knack of drawing souls to your way.

It's a gift to thank God for: to be an instrument for seeking instruments!

804 Help me to cry: Jesus, souls! Apostolic souls! They are for you, for your glory.

You'll see how in the end he will hear us.

805 Listen, where you are... mightn't there be one... or two, who could understand us well?

806 Tell him—yes, *that one*—that I need fifty men who love Jesus Christ above all things.

807 You tell me of a certain friend of yours that he frequents the sacraments, that he is clean-living and a good student... but that he won't respond. When you speak to him of sacrifice and apostolate, he grows sad and tries to avoid you.

Don't let it worry you. It's not a failure of your zeal. It is, to the letter, the scene related by the evangelist: "If you want to be perfect, go, sell what you have and give to the poor" (sacrifice), "and come, follow me" (apostolate).

The young man also "*abiit tristis*"—"went away sad." He was not willing to correspond to grace.

808 "Some good news: a new 'madman' for the 'asylum'." ...And all is excitement in the "fisherman's" letter.

May God make your nets really effective!

809 Winning others. Who does not hunger to perpetuate his apostolate?

810 That burning desire to win fellow-apostles is a sure sign of your dedication.

811 Do you remember? Night was falling as you and I began our prayer. From close by came the murmur of water. And, through the stillness of the Castilian city, we also seemed to hear voices of people from many lands, crying to us in anguish that they do not yet know Christ.

Unashamedly you kissed your crucifix and you asked him to make you an apostle of apostles.

812 I can understand that you love your country and your people so much and that still, in spite of these ties, you long for the moment when you will cross lands and seas—far away—for your heart is consumed by the thought of the harvest.

LITTLE THINGS

813 Do everything for love. In that way there will be no little things: everything will be big. Perseverance in the little things for love is heroism.

814 A little act, done for love, is worth so much!

815 Do you really want to be a saint? Carry out the little duty of each moment: do what you ought and put yourself into what you are doing.

816 You have mistaken the way if you scorn the little things.

817 "Great" holiness consists in carrying out the "little" duties of each moment.

818 Great souls pay much attention to little things.

819 Because you have been "*in pauca fidelis*"—
"faithful in the little things"—enter into the joy of your
Lord. The words are Christ's. "*In pauca fidelis!...*" Now
will you disdain little things, if heaven itself is promised
to those who keep them?

820 Don't judge by the smallness of the beginnings.
My attention was once drawn to the fact that there is no
difference in size between seeds that produce annual plants
and those that will grow into ageless trees.

821 Don't forget that on earth every big thing has had
a small beginning. What is born big is monstrous and
dies.

822 You tell me: when the chance comes to do
something great, then...! Then? Are you seriously trying
to convince me—and to convince yourself—that you will
be able to win in the supernatural olympics without daily
preparation, without training?

823 Have you seen how that imposing building was
constructed? One brick after another. Thousands. But,
one by one. And bags and bags of cement, one by one.
And stone upon stone, each of them insignificant compared
with the massive whole. And beams of steel, and men
working, hour after hour, day after day...

Did you see how that imposing building was constructed?... By dint of little things!

824 Have you noticed how human love consists of little things? Well, divine love also consists of little things.

825 Persevere in the exact fulfillment of the obligations of the moment. That work—humble, monotonous, small —is prayer expressed in action, which prepares you to receive the grace of that other work—great and broad and deep—of which you dream.

826 Everything in which we poor little men take part— even sanctity—is a fabric of small trifles which, depending upon one's intention, can form a splendid tapestry of heroism or of degradation, of virtue or of sin.

The epic legends always related extraordinary adventures, but never fail to mix them with homely details about the hero. May you always attach great importance— faithfully—to the little things.

827 Have you ever stopped to consider the enormous sum that many small amounts can come to?

828 It's been a hard experience, but don't forget the lesson. Your big cowardices of the moment correspond— it's very plain—to your little cowardices of each day.

You "have not been able" to conquer in the big things, because you "did not want" to conquer in the little ones.

829 Didn't you see the light in Jesus' eyes when the poor widow left her alms in the temple?

Give him what you can: the merit is not in whether it is big or small, but in the intention with which you give it.

830 Don't be a fool! It's true that at most you play the part of a small bolt in that great undertaking of Christ's.

But do you know what happens when a bolt is not tight enough or when it works itself out of place? Bigger parts also work loose or gears are damaged or broken.

The whole work is slowed up. Perhaps the whole machine will be rendered useless.

What a big thing it is to be a little bolt!

TACTICS

831 Among those around you, apostolic soul, you are the stone fallen into the lake. With your word and example produce a first ripple... and it will produce another... and then another, and another... each time wider.

Now do you understand the greatness of your mission?

832 How anxious people are to get out of place! Think what would happen if each bone and each muscle of the human body wanted to occupy some position other than its own.

There is no other reason for the world's discontent. Continue where you are, my son; right where you are... how much you'll be able to work for the true kingdom of our Lord!

833 Leaders! Strengthen your will so that God will make a leader of you.

Don't you see how evil secret societies work? They've never won over the masses. In their dens they form a number of demon-men who set to work agitating and stirring up the multitudes, making them go wild, so that they will follow them over the precipice, into every excess... and into hell. They spread an accursed seed.

If you wish, you will spread God's word, which is a thousand times blessed and can never fail. If you're generous, if you correspond, with your personal sanctification you can bring about the sanctification of others, the kingdom of Christ, the *"Omnes cum Petro ad Jesum per Mariam"*—"All with Peter to Jesus through Mary."

834 Is there any greater madness than scattering the golden wheat over the ground to let it rot? But without that generous madness there would be no harvest.

Son, how do you stand in regard to generosity?

835 You long to glitter like a star, to shine like a light from high in the heavens?

Better to burn like a torch, hidden, setting fire to all you touch. That's your apostolate; that's why you are on earth.

836 To serve as a loud-speaker for the enemy is the height of idiocy. And if the enemy is an enemy of God, it's a great sin. That's why, in the professional field, I'll never praise the knowledge of those who use it as a rostrum for attacking the Church.

837   Rush, rush, rush! Hustle and bustle! Feverish activity! The mad urge to dash about. Amazing material structures...

On the spiritual level... shams, illusions: flimsy backdrops, cheesecloth scenery, painted cardboard... Hustle and bustle! And a lot of people running hither and thither.

It is because they work thinking only of "today"; their vision is limited to "the present". But you must see things with the eyes of eternity, "keeping in the present" what has passed and what has yet to come.

Calmness. Peace. Intense life within you. Without that wild hurry. Without that mad urge for change. From your own place in life, like a powerful generator of spiritual energy, you will give light and vigor to ever so many without losing your own vitality and your own light.

838   Have no enemies. Have only friends: friends on the right—if they have done or have wished to do you good; and on the left—if they have harmed or tried to harm you.

839   Never go into details of "your" apostolate unless it be for someone else's benefit.

840 May your special dedication pass unnoticed, as for thirty years did that of Jesus.

841 Joseph of Arimathea and Nicodemus visit Jesus secretly in ordinary times and in the time of triumph.

But they are courageous in the face of authority, declaring their love for Christ *audacter*—"boldly"—in the time of cowardice. Learn.

842 Don't worry if "you are known" by your works. It's the good odor of Christ. Moreover as long as you always work exclusively for him, you can rejoice at the fulfillment of those words of the Scripture: "That they may see your good works and give glory to your Father in heaven."

843 "*Non manifeste, sed quasi in occulto*"—"Not publicly, but as if he would keep himself hidden": thus goes Jesus to the feast of Tabernacles.

Thus will he go on the way to Emmaus with Cleophas and his companion. Thus will he be seen after his resurrection by Mary of Magdala.

And thus will he appear—"*non tamen cognoverunt discipuli quia Iesus est*"—"the disciples did not know it was Jesus"—at the miraculous draught of fishes, as St John tells us.

And more hidden still, through love for men, is he in the host.

844 Raise magnificent buildings? Construct sumptuous palaces? Let others raise them. Let others construct them.

Souls! Let us give life to souls—for those buildings and for those palaces!

What fine dwellings are being prepared for us!

845 How you made me laugh, and how you made me think, with that trite remark of yours: I'm all for first things first.

846 Agreed: you do better work with that friendly chat or that heart-to-heart conversation than with making speeches—spectacle! display!—in public before thousands of people.

Nevertheless, when speeches have to be made, make them.

847 The efforts of each one of you individually have little effect. But if you're united by the charity of Christ you'll be amazed at their effectiveness.

848 You want to be a martyr. I'll place a martyrdom within your reach: to be an apostle and not call yourself an apostle, to be a missionary—with a mission—and not call yourself a missionary, to be a man of God and to seem a man of the world: to pass unnoticed!

849 Come on! Ridicule him! Tell him he's behind the times: it's incredible that there are still people who insist on regarding the stagecoach as a good means of transportation. That's for those who dig up musty, old fashioned "Voltairianisms" or discredited liberal ideas of the nineteenth century.

850 What conversations! What vulgarity and what dirt! And you have to associate with them, in the office, in the university, in the operating room...in the world.

If you ask them kindly to shut up, they laugh at you. If you look annoyed, they persist. If you leave them, they continue.

The solution is this: first, pray for them and offer up some sacrifice; then face them like a man and make use of the "strong-language apostolate". When I see you I'll tell you—privately—some useful expressions.

851 Let's channel the "providential imprudence" of youth.

SPIRITUAL CHILDHOOD

852 Try to know the "way of spiritual childhood" without forcing yourself to follow this path. Let the Holy Spirit work in you.

853 The way of childhood. Abandonment. Spiritual childhood. All this is not utter nonsense, but a sturdy and solid christian life.

854 In the spiritual life of childhood the things which the "children" say or do are never puerile or childish.

855 Spiritual childhood is not spiritual foolishness or softness; it is a sane and forceful way which, due to its difficult easiness, the soul must begin and then continue, led by the hand of God.

856   Spiritual childhood demands submission of the mind, which is harder than submission of the will. In order to subject our mind we need not only God's grace, but a continual exercise of our will as well, denying the intellect over and over again, just as it says "no" to the flesh. And so we have the paradox that whoever wants to follow this "little way" in order to become a child, needs to add strength and manliness to his will.

857   To be little. The great daring is always that of children. Who cries for the moon? Who won't stop at danger to get what he wants?

Put in such a child a great deal of God's grace, the desire to do God's will, a great love for Jesus and all the human knowledge he is capable of acquiring, and you'll have a likeness of the apostles of today just as God undoubtedly wants them.

858   Be a child. Even more than you are. But don't stay in the show-off age: have you ever seen anything sillier than a little lad acting like a "big fellow" or a grown man acting like a baby?

A child, with God: and because of that, very much a man in everything else. Ah! and drop those bad habits of a whimpering lap dog.

859 Sometimes we feel the urge to act as little children. What we do then has a wonderful value in God's eyes and, as long as we don't let routine creep in, our "little" works will indeed be fruitful, just as love is always fruitful.

860 Before God, who is eternal, you are a smaller child than, in your sight, a two-year-old toddler.

And besides being a child, you are a child of God. Don't forget it.

861 Child, set yourself on fire with desires to make up for the excesses of your adult life.

862 Foolish child, the day you hide some part of your soul from your director, you will have ceased to be a child, for you will have lost your simplicity.

863 Child, when you really are one, you will be all-powerful.

864 Being a child, you'll have no cares; children quickly forget what troubles them and return to their usual games. With abandonment, therefore, you won't have to worry, for you will rest in the Father.

865 Child, each day offer him... even your frailties.

866 Good child, offer him the work of those neighbors of yours who don't know him; offer him the natural joy of those poor little ones who are brought up in godless schools.

867 Children have nothing of their own; everything belongs to their parents... And your Father always knows very well how to manage the household.

868 Be little, very little. Don't be more than two years old, three at the most. For older children are little rascals who already want to deceive their parents with unbelievable lies.

This is because they have the *fomes*, the inclination to evil, the prelude to sin, but still lack the real experience of evil which will teach them the "science" of sinning and show them how to cover the falseness of their deceits with an appearance of truth.

They have lost their simplicity, and without simplicity it is impossible to be a child before God.

869 But child, why do you insist on walking on stilts?

870 Don't try to be older. A child, always a child, even when you are dying of old age. When a child stumbles and falls, nobody is surprised, and his father promptly picks him up.

When the person who stumbles and falls is older, the immediate reaction is one of laughter. Sometimes, after this first impulse, the laughter gives way to pity. But older people have to get up by themselves.

Your sad experience is that each day is full of stumbles and falls. What would become of you if you were not continually more of a child?

Don't try to be older. Be a child, and when you stumble, may your Father God pick you up by the hand.

871 Child, abandonment demands docility.

872 Don't forget that our Lord has a predilection for little children and for those who become as little children.

873 Paradoxes of a little soul. When Jesus sends you what the world calls good luck, feel sorrow in your heart at the thought of his goodness and of your wickedness. When Jesus sends you what people consider bad luck, rejoice in your heart, for he always gives you what is best. This is the beautiful moment to love the cross.

874 Daring child, cry out: What love was that of Teresa! What zeal was that of Xavier! What an extraordinary man was St Paul! Ah, Jesus, well I... I love you more than Paul, Xavier and Teresa!

LIFE OF CHILDHOOD

875 Don't forget, silly child, that love has made you almighty.

876 Child, don't lose your loving habit of "storming" tabernacles.

877 When I call you "good child" don't think that I imagine you bashful or timid. If you are not manly and normal, instead of being an apostle you will be a caricature that causes laughter.

878 Good child, say to Jesus many times each day: I love you, I love you, I love you...

879 When you feel oppressed by your weaknesses don't let yourself be sad. Glory in your infirmities, like St Paul, for children can imitate their elders without fear of ridicule.

880 Don't let your defects and imperfections nor even your more serious falls, take you away from God. A weak child, if he is wise, tries to keep near his Father.

881 Don't worry if you become annoyed doing those little things he asks of you. You'll come to smile.

Have you never seen a father testing his simple child? How reluctantly the child gives his father the candy he had in his hand! But he gives it: love has conquered.

882 When you want to do things well, really well, it's then you do them worse. Humble yourself before Jesus, saying to him: Don't you see how I do everything wrong? Well, if you don't help me very much, I'll do it all even worse!

Take pity on your child: You see, I want to write a big page each day in the book of my life. But, I'm so clumsy, that if the Master doesn't guide my hand, instead of graceful strokes my pen leaves behind blots and scratches, that can't be shown to anyone.

From now on, Jesus, the writing will always be done by both of us together.

883 I realize, my love, that my clumsiness is so great..., so great that even when I wish to caress I cause pain. Refine the manners of my soul: within the sturdy manliness of this life of childhood, give me—I want you to give me—the gentleness and affection that children show toward their parents in their intimate outpourings of love.

884 You are full of weaknesses. Every day you see them more clearly. But don't let them frighten you. He well knows you can't yield more fruit.

Your involuntary falls—those of a child—show your Father God that he must take more care, and your Mother Mary that she must never let you go from her loving hand. Each day, as our Lord picks you up from the ground, take advantage of it, embrace him with all your strength and lay your wearied head on his open breast so that you'll be carried away by the beating of his most loving heart.

885 One pinprick. And another. And another. Suffer them, man! Don't you see you are so little that in your life—in your way—you can offer him only those little crosses?

Besides, look: one cross upon another—one pinprick after another—what a huge pile!

Finally, child, you will have learned to do one really big thing: to love.

886 When a child-like soul tells our Lord of his desires to be forgiven, he can be sure that he will soon see those desires fulfilled. Jesus will tear away from that soul the filthy tail that it drags in punishment for its past offenses.

He will remove the dead weight, that residue from all its impurities, which keeps it tied to the ground. He will cast far away all the earthly ballast of that child's heart, so that he may rise up, even to the majesty of God to be dissolved in that living flame of love.

887 That discouragement produced by your repeated lack of generosity, by your relapses, by your falls—perhaps only apparent—often makes you feel as if you had broken something of exceptional value: your sanctification.

Don't be worried: bring to your supernatural life the wise way simple children have of resolving such a conflict.

They have broken—nearly always through frailty—an object that is dear to their father. They're sorry, perhaps they shed tears, but they go to seek consolation from the owner of what has been damaged through their awkwardness; and their father forgets the value—great though it may be—of the broken object and, filled with tenderness, he not only pardons, but consoles and encourages the little one. Learn.

888 Let your prayer be manly. To be a child does not mean to be effeminate.

889 For the person who loves Jesus, prayer—even prayer without consolation—is the sweetness that always puts an end to all sorrow: he goes to pray with the eagerness of a child going to the sugar bowl after taking a bitter dose of medicine.

890   You are distracted in prayer. Try to avoid distractions, but don't worry if in spite of everything you're still distracted.

Don't you see how in ordinary life even the most considerate children play with everything around them, and often pay no attention to what their father says? This does not imply a lack of love, or respect: it's the weakness and littleness proper to a child.

Look then: you are a child before God.

891   When you pray keep the distracting ideas moving, just as if you were a policeman on traffic duty; that's why you have the energetic will-power your life of childhood has given you. But now and then you may retain some such thought for a while to commend to God those who inopportunely have come to your mind.

And then, on your way again, ...and so, until the time is up. When you pray like this, though you may feel you are wasting time, rejoice and believe that you have succeeded in pleasing Jesus.

892   How good it is to be a child! When a man asks a favor, his request must be backed by an account of his achievements.

When it is a child who asks—since children have no achievements—it is enough for him to say: I am a son of such and such a man.

Ah, Lord—tell him with all your soul—I am a child of God!

893 To persevere. A child knocking at a door, knocks once, twice... many times,... and loud and long—shamelessly! And the anger of whoever comes to open is dispelled by the simplicity of the disturbing little creature. So you with God.

894 Have you seen the gratitude of little children? Imitate them, saying to Jesus when things are favorable and when they aren't, "How good you are! How good!"

Those words, said with deep feeling, are part of the way of childhood; and they will lead you to peace, with a measure of tears and laughter, but without any measure of Love.

895 Work tires you physically and leaves you unable to pray. But you're always in the presence of your Father. If you can't speak to him, look at him every now and then like a little child... and he'll smile at you.

896 You think there is something wrong because, in your thanksgiving after communion, the first thing you find yourself doing, without being able to help it, is asking: Jesus, give me this; Jesus, this soul; Jesus, that undertaking?

Don't worry, and don't try to force yourself; when the father is good and the child is simple and fearless, haven't you seen how the little lad puts his hand into his father's pocket, looking for candy, before greeting him with a kiss? Well then...

897 Our will, strengthened by grace, is all-powerful before God. Thus as we travel on a streetcar for instance, if in view of so many offenses against our Lord we say to Jesus with an efficient will: "My God, I would like to make an act of love and of reparation for each turn of the wheels carrying me," then in that very instant in Jesus' eyes, we have really loved him and atoned just as we desired.

Such "nonsense" is not pushing spiritual childhood too far: it's the eternal dialogue between the innocent child and the father doting on his son: "Tell me, how much do you love me?" and the little lad pipes out, "A mil-lion mil-lion ti-mes!"

898 If you live the "life of childhood," you should have the sweet-tooth of a child, a "spiritual sweet-tooth"! Like those "of your age", think of the good things your Mother keeps for you.

And do so, many times a day. It's a matter of a moment: Mary... Jesus... the tabernacle... communion... love... suffering... the holy souls in purgatory... those who are fighting: the pope, the priests... the faithful... your soul... the souls of your people... the guardian angels... the sinners...

899 How hard that little mortification is! You struggle. It seems as if someone were saying to you: Why must you be so faithful to your plan of life, to the clock? Look: have you noticed how easily little children are fooled? They don't want to take bitter medicine, but "Come on!" they are told, "This little spoonful for Daddy, and this one for Granny." And so on, until they've had the full dose.

Do the same: fifteen minutes more mortification for the souls in purgatory; five minutes more for your parents; another five for your brothers in the apostolate... And so on, until the allotted time is up.

Your mortification done in this way is worth so much!

900 You're not alone. Suffer tribulation cheerfully. It's true, poor child, that you don't feel your Mother's hand in yours. But have you never seen the mothers of this earth, with their arms outstretched, following their little ones when, without anyone's help, they venture to take their first shaky steps? You're not alone: Mary is beside you.

901   Jesus, even if I should die for Love, I could never repay you for the grace you have showered on me in making me little.

CALLING

902 Why don't you give yourself to God once and for all, ...really, ...*now!*

903 If you see your way clearly, follow it. Why don't you shake off the cowardice that holds you back?

904 "Go, preach the gospel... I will be with you." Jesus has said this, and he has said it to you.

905 Patriotic fervor—which is praiseworthy—leads many men to give their lives in service, even in a "crusade". Don't forget that Christ, too, has "crusaders" and people chosen for this service.

906 *"Et regni eius non erit finis"*—"His kingdom will have no end."

Doesn't it fill you with joy to work for a kingdom like that?

907 *"Nesciebatis quia in his quae Patris mei sunt oportet me esse?"*—"Did you not know that I must be about my Father's business?"

This reply was made by Jesus the Youth. And the reply was to a mother like his Mother, who had been seeking him for three days, believing him to be lost. It is a reply that has as a complement those words of Christ recorded by St Matthew: "He that loves his father or his mother more than me is not worthy of me."

908 It is oversimplicity on your part to judge the value of apostolic undertakings by what you can see of them. With that standard you would have to prefer a ton of coal to a handful of diamonds.

909 Now that you have given yourself to him, ask him for a new life—a "seal"—to strengthen the genuiness of your mission as a man of God.

910 Your ideal, your vocation: it's madness. And your friends, your brothers: they're crazy. Haven't you heard that cry deep down within you sometimes? Answer firmly that you are grateful to God for the honor of being one of those "lunatics".

911 You write me: "The great longing we all have to see our work get ahead and spread seems to turn into impatience. When will it get under way? When will it break through? When will we see the world ours?"

And you add: "The longing won't be useless if we use it in pestering and 'coercing' God with prayers. Then we will have made excellent use of our time."

912 I can understand how you are suffering when, in the midst of that forced inactivity, you consider the work still to be done. Your heart would break the bounds of the universe, and yet it has to adapt itself to... an insignificant routine job.

But, for what occasion are we saving the "*Fiat*"— "Your will be done?"

913 Don't doubt it: your vocation is the greatest grace our Lord could have given you. Thank him for it.

914 How pitiful are those crowds—high and low and middle-class—without an ideal! They give the impression that they do not know they have souls: they are a flock, a drove, a herd.

Jesus, only with the help of your merciful love, will we turn the flock into a legion, the drove into an army, and from the herd of swine draw, purified, those who no longer wish to be unclean.

915   The works of God are not a lever, nor a stepping stone.

916   Lord, make us crazy with a contagious craziness that will draw many to your apostolate.

917   *"Nonne cor nostrum ardens erat in nobis, dum loqueretur in via?"*—"Was not our heart burning within us, while he spoke to us on the way?"

If you are an apostle, these words of the disciples of Emmaus should rise spontaneously to the lips of your professional companions when they meet you along the ways of their lives.

918   Go to the apostolate to give everything, and not to seek anything of this world.

919   By calling you to be an apostle, our Lord has reminded you, so that you will never forget it, that you are a child of God.

920   Each one of you must try to be an apostle of apostles.

921   You are salt, apostolic soul. *"Bonum est sal"*— "Salt is good," one reads in the holy Gospel, *"si autem sal evanuerit"*—"but if the salt loses its strength," it is good for nothing, neither for the soil nor for the manure; it is cast out as useless.

You are salt, apostolic soul. But if you lose your strength...

922 My son, if you love your apostolate, be certain that you love God.

923 The day that you really "get the feel" of your apostolate, that apostolate will serve you as a shield to withstand all the attacks of your enemies on this earth and in hell.

924 Pray always for perseverance for yourself and for your companions in the apostolate. Our adversary, the devil, knows only too well that you are his great enemies, ...and when he sees a fall in your ranks, how pleased he is!

925 Just as observant religious are eager to know how the first of their order or congregation lived, so as to have their model to follow, so you too—christian layman— should seek to know and imitate the lives of those disciples of Jesus who knew Peter and Paul and John, and all but witnessed the death and resurrection of the Master.

926 You asked me and so I answer you: your perfection consists in living perfectly in the place, occupation and position in which God, through those in authority, has assigned to you.

927 Pray for one another. One is wavering?... And another?...

Keep on praying, without losing your peace. Some are leaving? Some are being lost?... Our Lord has you all numbered from eternity!

928 You are right. "The peak," you write me, "dominates the country for miles around, and yet there is not a single plain to be seen: just one mountain after another. At times the landscape seems to level out, but then the mist rises and reveals another range that had been hidden."

So it is, so it must be, with the horizon of your apostolate: the world has to be crossed. But there are no roads made for you. You yourselves will make the way through the mountains, beating it out by your own footsteps.

THE APOSTLE

929 The cross on your breast? Good. But the cross on your shoulders, the cross in your flesh, the cross in your mind. Thus will you live for Christ, with Christ and in Christ; only thus will you be an apostle.

930 Apostolic soul, first take care of yourself. Our Lord has said through St Matthew: Many will say to me on the day of judgment: "Lord, Lord, did we not prophesy in your name, and cast out devils in your name, and work many miracles in your name?" Then I will declare to them: "I never knew you. Depart from me, you workers of iniquity."

Let it not be, says St Paul, that I who have preached to others should myself be rejected.

931 St Ignatius, with his military genius, gives us a picture of the devil calling up innumerable demons and scattering them through nations, states, cities and villages after a "sermon" in which he exhorts them to fasten their chains and fetters on the world, leaving no one unbound.

You've told me that you want to be a leader... and what good is a leader in chains?

932   Look: the apostles, for all their evident and undeniable weaknesses, were sincere, simple... transparent.

You, too, have evident and undeniable weaknesses. May you not lack simplicity.

933   There is a story of a soul who, on saying to our Lord in prayer, "Jesus, I love you", heard this reply from heaven: "Deeds are love—not sweet words."

Think if you also could deserve this gentle reproach.

934   Apostolic zeal is a divine madness I want you to have, and it has these symptoms: hunger to know the Master; constant concern for souls; perseverance that nothing can shake.

935   Don't rest on your laurels. If, humanly speaking, that attitude is neither comfortable nor becoming, how will it be when—as now—the laurels are not really yours, but God's?

936 You have come to the apostolate to submit, to annihilate yourself, not to impose your own personal viewpoints.

937 Never be men or women generous in action and sparing in prayer.

938 Try to live in such a way that you can voluntarily deprive yourself of the comfort and ease you wouldn't approve of in the life of another man of God.

Remember, you are the grain of wheat of which the Gospel speaks. If you don't bury yourself and die, there will be no harvest.

939 Be men and women of the world, but don't be worldly men and women.

940 Let us not forget that unity is a symptom of life; disunion is decay, a sure sign of being a corpse.

941 Obedience, the sure way. Blind obedience to your superior, the way of sanctity. Obedience in your apostolate, the only way: for, in a work of God, the spirit must be to obey or to leave.

942 Bear in mind, my son, that you're not just a soul who has joined other souls in order to do a good thing.

That's a lot, but it's still little. You are the apostle, carrying out an imperative command of Christ.

943 Be careful that in dealing with other people you don't make them feel like someone who once exclaimed (and not without reason), "I'm fed up with these righteous characters!"

944 You must inspire others with love of God and zeal for souls, so that they in turn will set on fire many more who are at a third plane, who will in their turn spread the flame to their associates.

What a lot of spiritual calories you need! And what a tremendous responsibility if you let yourself grow cold! And—I don't even want to think of it—what a terrible crime if you were to set a bad example!

945 You are badly disposed if you listen to the word of God with a critical spirit.

946 If you want to give yourselves to God in the world, more important than being scholars (women need not be scholars: it's enough for them to be prudent),* you

---

*At the time this book was written, very few women in Spain attended universities. Nevertheless, even then the author encouraged the young women with whom he was in contact to pursue university studies if they felt called to do so.

must be spiritual, closely united to our Lord through prayer. You must wear an invisible cloak that will cover every single one of your senses and faculties: praying, praying, praying; atoning, atoning, atoning.

947 You were amazed that I should approve of the lack of uniformity in the apostolate in which you work. And I said to you:

Unity and variety. You have to be different from one another, as the saints in heaven are different, each having his own personal and very special characteristics. But also, you have to be as identical as the saints, who would not be saints if each of them had not identified himself with Christ.

948 Feel and live that fraternal spirit, favored son of God, but without familiarities.

949 To aspire to positions of responsibility in any apostolic undertaking is a useless thing in this life and a danger for the next.

If it's what God wants, you'll be called. And then you ought to accept. But don't forget that wherever you are, you can and you must sanctify yourself, for that is why you are there.

950 If you are working for Christ and imagine that a position of responsibility is anything but a burden, what disillusionment awaits you!

951 To be in charge of an apostolic undertaking means being ready to suffer everything, from everybody, with infinite charity.

952 In apostolic work there can be no forgiveness for disobedience, nor for insincerity. Remember, simplicity is not imprudence, nor indiscretion.

953 You are obliged to pray and sacrifice yourself for the person and intentions of whoever is in charge of your apostolic undertaking. If you are remiss in fulfilling this duty, you make me think that you lack enthusiasm for your way.

954 Be extremely respectful to your superior, whenever he consults you and you have to oppose his opinions. And never contradict him in the presence of others who are subject to him, even though he may be wrong.

955 In your apostolic undertaking don't fear the enemies "outside", however great their power. This is the enemy most to be feared: your lack of filial spirit and your lack of fraternal spirit.

956 I well understand that you are amused by the slights you receive—even though they may come from influential enemies—as long as you can feel united to your God and your brothers in the apostolate. Slighted? So what!

957 I frequently compare apostolic work with an engine: gears, pistons, valves, bolts.

Well, charity—your charity—is the lubricant.

958 Get rid of that self-satisfied air that keeps the souls around you isolated from your soul. Listen to them and speak with simplicity. Only thus will your work as an apostle expand and be fruitful.

959 Contempt and persecution are blessed signs of divine favor, but there is no proof and sign of favor more beautiful than this: to pass unnoticed.

THE APOSTOLATE

960 Just as the clamor of the ocean is made up of the noise of each of the waves, so the sanctity of your apostolate is made up of the personal virtues of each one of you.

961 It is necessary that you be a "man of God", a man of interior life, a man of prayer and of sacrifice. Your apostolate must be the overflow of your life "within".

962 Unity. Unity and submission. What do I want with the loose parts of a clock—even though they are finely wrought—if they can't tell me the time?

963 Don't form "cliques" within your work. That would belittle the apostolate: for if, in the end, the "clique" got control of a universal undertaking, how quickly that universal undertaking would be reduced to a clique itself!

964   "There are so many ways!" you told me dejectedly. There need to be many, so that each soul can find its own in that wonderful variety.

Bewildered? Make your choice once and for all: and the confusion will turn into certainty.

965   Rejoice when you see others working in a good apostolate. And ask God to grant them abundant grace and correspondence to that grace.

Then, you, on your way. Convince yourself that for you—yours is the only way.

966   You show a bad spirit if it hurts you to see others work for Christ without regard for what you are doing. Remember this passage in St Mark: "Master, we saw a man who was not one of our followers casting out devils in your name, and we forbade him." "Do not forbid him," Jesus replied, "because there is no one who shall work a miracle in my name, and forthwith be able to speak ill of me. For he who is not against you, is for you."

967   It's useless to busy yourself in so many external works if you lack Love. It's like sewing with a needle and no thread.

What a pity if in the end you had carried out *your* apostolate and not *his* apostolate!

968 Joyfully I bless you, my son, for that faith in your mission as an apostle which inspired you to write: "There's no doubt about it; the future is certain, perhaps in spite of us. But it's essential that we should be one with the head—*ut omnes unum sint!*—'that all may be one!'— through prayer and through sacrifice."

969 Those who pray and suffer, leaving action for others, will not shine here on earth; but what a radiant crown they will wear in the kingdom of life! Blessed be the "apostolate of suffering"!

970 It is true that I have called your discreet apostolate a "quiet and effective mission". And I have nothing to add.

971 I think so highly of your devotion to the early Christians that I will do all I can to foster it, so that you— like them—will work each day with greater enthusiasm for that effective apostolate of discretion and confidence.

972 When you practise your "apostolate of discretion and confidence," don't tell me that you don't know what to say. For with the psalmist, I will remind you: "*Dominus dabit verbum evangelizantibus virtute multa*"—"the Lord placed on his apostles' lips words filled with efficacy."

973   Those words whispered at the proper time in the ear of your wavering friend; that helpful conversation you manage to start at the right moment; the ready advice that improves his studies; and the discreet indiscretion by which you open for him unsuspected horizons for his zeal—all that is the "apostolate of friendship".

974   "The apostolate of the dinner table!" It is the old hospitality of the patriarchs, together with the fraternal warmth of Bethany. When we practise it, can we not picture Jesus there, presiding as in the house of Lazarus?

975   It is urgent that we strive to rechristianize popular celebrations and customs. It is urgent that public amusements should no longer be left to face the dilemma of being either over-pious or pagan.

Ask God to provide laborers for this much-needed work which could be called the 'entertainment apostolate'.

976   You praised very highly the "letter-writing apostolate". You said: "I don't always find words when it comes to putting down things that might be useful to the friend I am writing. But when I begin, I tell my guardian angel that all I hope from my letter is that it may do some good. And even though I may write only nonsense, no one can take from me—or from my friend—the time I have spent praying for what I know he needs the most."

977 "The letter came on days that were sad—for no reason—and it cheered me up immensely to read and see how the others were working." And another: "Your letters and news of my brothers help me like a happy dream in the midst of the practical realities." And another: "How wonderful it is to receive those letters and know I am a friend of such friends!" And so another, and a thousand more like it: "I received a letter from 'X' and I was ashamed to think of my lack of spirit compared with his."

Now, what do you say of the effectiveness of the "letter writing apostolate"?

978 *"Venite post me, et faciam vos fieri piscatores hominum."*—"Come, follow me, and I will make you fishers of men." Not without reason does our Lord use these words: men—like fish—have to be caught by the head.

What an evangelical depth there is in the intellectual apostolate!

979 It is human nature to have little appreciation for what costs but little. That is why I recommended to you the "apostolate of not giving".

Never fail to claim what is fairly and justly due to you from the practice of your profession, even if your profession is the instrument of your apostolate.

980   Have we not a right to take with us on our journeys some woman, a sister in Jesus Christ, to help us, as do the other apostles, and the brethren of the Lord and Peter himself?

That is what St Paul says in his first epistle to the Corinthians. We cannot disdain the cooperation of women in the apostolate.

981   "And it came to pass afterwards," we read in the eighth chapter of St Luke, "that he was journeying through towns and villages preaching and proclaiming the good news of the kingdom of God. And with him were the twelve, and certain women who had been cured of evil spirits and infirmities: Mary, who is called Magdalene, from whom seven devils had gone out, and Joanna, the wife of Chuza, Herod's steward, and Susanna, and many others, who used to provide for him out of their means."

I copy these words. And I pray God that if some woman reads me, she may be filled with a holy and fruitful envy.

982   Woman is stronger than man and more faithful in the hour of trial: Mary Magdalene and Mary Cleophas and Salome.

With a group of valiant women like these, closely united to our sorrowful Mother, what work for souls could be done in the world!

PERSEVERANCE

983 To begin is for everyone, to persevere is for saints.

May your perseverance not be a blind consequence of the first impulse, the effect of inertia; may it be a reflective perseverance.

984 Say to him, "*ecce ego quia vocasti me!*"—"Here I am, for you did call me!"

985 You strayed from the way and did not return because you were ashamed. It would be more logical if you were ashamed not to return.

986 "The truth is," you tell me, "that it's not necessary for me to be a hero or to go to ridiculous extremes in order to persevere when I am forced to be isolated."

And you add: "As long as I fulfill the 'norms' you gave me, I won't worry about the snares and pitfalls of my environment; to fear such trifles—that is what I would be afraid of."

Wonderful.

987   Foster and preserve that most noble ideal just born within you. Consider how many flowers blossom in the spring and how few are those that develop fruit.

988   Discouragement is the enemy of your persevarance. If you don't fight against discouragement, you will become pessimistic first and lukewarm afterwards. Be an optimist.

989   Come, now! After saying so often, "The cross, Lord, the cross," it is obvious you wanted a cross to your own taste.

990   Perseverance that nothing can shake. You lack it. Ask it of our Lord and do what you can to obtain it; for perseverance is a great safeguard against your ever turning from the fruitful way you have chosen.

991   You cannot "climb". It's not surprising: that fall! Persevere and you will "climb". Remember what a spiritual writer has said: your poor soul is like a bird whose wings are caked with mud.

You need suns of heaven and personal efforts—small and constant—to root out those inclinations, those vain fancies, that depression—that mud clinging to your wings.

And you will be free. If you persevere, you will "climb".

992   Give thanks to God who helped you, and rejoice over your victory. What a deep joy you feel in your soul after having corresponded to grace.

993   You reason well... coldly: how many motives for abandoning the task! And some of them are apparently conclusive.

I see without any doubt that you have reasons—but you are not right.

994   "My enthusiasm is gone," you wrote me. Yours has to be a work not of enthusiasm, but of Love, conscious of duty—which means self-denial.

995   Unshakable: that is what you must be. If your perseverance wavers because of other people's weaknesses or because of your own, I cannot but form a poor opinion of your ideal.

Make up your mind once and for all.

996   You have a poor idea of your way, if lack of enthusiasm makes you think you have lost it! It is only the moment of testing: that is why you have been deprived of all sensible consolations.

997 Absence, isolation: trials for your perseverance. Holy Mass, prayer, sacraments, sacrifices, communion of the saints: weapons to conquer in the trial.

998 O blessed perseverance of the donkey that turns the waterwheel! Always the same pace. Always around the same circle. One day after another, every day the same.

Without that, there would be no ripeness in the fruit, nor blossom in the orchard, nor scent of flowers in the garden.

Carry this thought to your interior life.

999 And what is the secret of perseverance? Love. Fall in Love, and you will not leave him.

FURROW

FOREWORD

In 1950 the Servant of God Josemaría Escrivá had already promised to meet his readers again in a new book—*Furrow*. In the preface to the seventh Spanish edition of *The Way* he wrote, "I hope to let you have it in a few months' time".[1] What the Founder of Opus Dei wanted then has become a reality now, on the eleventh anniversary of his going to Heaven.

Furrow could really have been brought out many years ago. Monsignor Escrivá was on the point of sending it to the printers on several occasions, but as the old Castillian proverb says: "You can't ring the bells and walk in the procession at the same time". He was prevented from making that last revision of the manuscript with leisure by his intense foundational work, his attention to the task of governance at the head of Opus, his wide pastoral work with so many souls and his many other duties in service of the Church. *Furrow* had been finished, however, for some time, including the titles for the chapters into which it was divided. All that needed doing was to arrange the

---

[1] J. Escrivá de Balaguer, *Camino*, seventh ed. Rialp, Madrid 1950.

various entries in numerical order and to make a final stylistic revision.

The Way is a book that has sold more than three million copies and has been translated into more than thirty languages. Like it, *Furrow* is the fruit of Monsignor Escrivá's interior life and experience with souls. It was written with the intention of encouraging personal prayer and making it easier. Because of its approach and style, then, it cannot be classified as a systematic theological treatise, though its rich and deep spirituality does contain profound theology.

Furrow is directed to the whole Christian person— body and soul, nature and grace—and not only to the mind. That is why its source is not reflection alone, but Christian life itself. It reflects the waves of movement and rest, of spiritual energy and of peace, which the action of the Holy Spirit had impressed in the soul of the Servant of God and of those around him. *Spiritus, ubi vult, spirat*, the Spirit breathes where it wills[2], and brings with it a depth and harmony of life which cannot be equalled, which cannot—and should not—be confined by the narrow limits of a merely man-made structure.

There lies the reason for the approach of this book. Monsignor Escrivá never wished—in any field, much less in the things of God—to make a suit of clothes first and

---

[2] Jn 3:8.

then fit the child in by force. Out of respect for the freedom of God and the freedom of men, he preferred to be an attentive observer, to be able to recognize the gifts of God, to learn first and only then to teach. I heard him say so often, when he arrived in a new country, or when he got together with a new group of people, "I have come here to learn"; and he did learn. He learned from God and from souls, and he transformed his capacity to learn into a constant process of teaching for those of us who were around him.

With the considerations he makes in this book, drawn from his wide experience of souls, the Founder of Opus Dei displays before us a series of qualities which should shine in the life of all Christians: generosity, daring, sincerity, naturalness, loyalty, friendship, purity, a sense of responsibility... Just by reading the table of contents we can discover the full scope of human perfection—"the virtues of man" (Preface)—which Monsignor Escrivá discovers in Jesus Christ, "perfect God and perfect Man".[3]

Jesus is the complete model of the human ideal of a Christian, for "Christ the Redeemer fully reveals man to man himself".[4] Let the words of the author of *Furrow* serve as a summary of these virtues as he gives thanks to Our Lord for having decided to become "perfect Man,

[3] The *Athanasian Creed*.
[4] John Paul II, Encyclical *Redemptor hominis*, March 4, 1979, 10.

with a Heart which loved and is most lovable; which
loved unto death and suffered; which was filled with joy
and sorrow; which delighted in the things of men and
showed us the way to Heaven; which subjected itself
heroically to duty and acted with mercy; which watched
over the poor and the rich and cared for sinners and the
just" (813).

What appears in these pages is Christian life itself, in
which—at Christ's pace—the divine and the human are
interwoven, not confused, and yet kept in perfect union.
"But do not forget that these considerations of mine,
though they may seem very human to you, must be priestly
as well, since I have written them for you and for myself—
and I have put them into practice too—before God"
(Preface). They are the human virtues of a Christian, and
precisely for that reason they appear fully developed; they
delineate the character of the mature man or woman, who
has the maturity that belongs to a child of God, who
knows that his Father is close by: "We should make no
mistake. God is no shadowy or distant being who created us
then abandoned us; nor is he a master who goes away and
does not return. (...) God is here with us, really present,
living. He sees and hears us, he guides us, and knows our
smallest deeds, our most hidden intentions" (658).

Thus, Monsignor Escrivá presents the virtues in the
light of man's divine destiny. The chapter "Beyond Death"
gives the reader this perspective; it frees him from an

exclusively human way of thinking and anchors him to another—an eternal way (cf. 879). The Christian human virtues are thereby placed far above the merely natural virtues: they are "the virtues of the children of God". Awareness of his divine filiation must permeate the whole life of a Christian, who finds in God the strength and the motive for striving to be better, even humanly better: "Once you were pessimistic, hesitant and apathetic. Now you are completely transformed: you feel courageous, optimistic and self-confident, because you have made up your mind, at last, to rely on God alone" (426).

Another example of how Christian human virtues have divine roots is found in suffering. Confronted by the sorrows of this world, Christian fortitude cannot be confused with a stoic acceptance of adversity, for—with one's sights on Christ's Cross—it becomes the source of supernatural life, because "the great Christian revolution has been to convert pain into fruitful suffering and to turn a bad thing into something good" (887). Monsignor Escrivá knows how to discover God's action in suffering, both in this life—"Allow yourself to be cut, gratefully, because God has taken you in his hands as if you were a diamond" (235)—and after death: "Purgatory shows God's great mercy and washes away the defects of those who wish to become one with him" (889).

The human virtues never appear as if they were an addition to a Christian existence. Together with the supernatural virtues and the gifts of the Holy Spirit, they form the framework of the daily life of the children of God. Grace penetrates nature to its roots, to heal it and divinize it. If, as a result of original sin, human nature cannot reach its fullness without grace, it is no less true that grace should not be thought of as juxtaposed to nature, acting on its margin. On the contrary, grace makes nature achieve its greatest perfection so that it can then be made divine. Monsignor Escrivá cannot conceive how one could live in a divine manner without being very human, for this is the first victory of grace. That is why he gives such importance to the human virtues. For if they were absent they would lead to the failure of Christian life itself: "There are many Christians who follow Christ and are astonished by his divinity, but forget him as Man. And they fail in the practice of supernatural virtues despite all the external paraphernalia of piety, because they do nothing to acquire human virtues" (652). This deep human sense of the Christian life was always present in the preaching and writings of the Founder of Opus Dei. He did not like disembodied 'spiritualities', for he would say that the Lord has made us human beings, not angels, and we should behave as human beings.

Monsignor Escrivá's teaching brings together the human and the divine aspects of Christian perfection. That must be so when the Catholic doctrine on the Incarnate Word is known in depth and when it is loved, and lived, passionately. The practical and vital consequences of that joyful reality are clearly drawn in *Furrow*. The author has sketched in outline the life and work of a Christian in the midst of the world, fully committed to the noble aspirations that move other men, and at the same time totally directed towards God. The resulting portrait is most attractive. A Christian has "a calm and balanced character" (417), and that is why he knows how to play the notes "used in ordinary life, the ones people normally hear" (440). He is endowed with "inflexible will, deep faith and an ardent piety" (417), and he places at the service of others the qualities he possesses (cf. 422). His universal mentality shows the following characteristics: "A breadth of vision and a deepening insight into the things that remain alive and unchanged in Catholic orthodoxy; a proper and healthy desire, which should never be frivolous, to present anew the standard teachings of traditional thought in philosophy and the interpretation of history; a careful awareness of trends in science and contemporary thought; and a positive and open attitude towards the current changes in society and in ways of living" (428).

In clear contrast with this portrait, Monsignor Escrivá also sketches the characteristic features of the frivolous man, lacking in true virtues, who is like a reed moved by the wind[5] of his own fancies or comfort. His typical

[5]Cf. Mt 11:7

excuse is: "I don't want to commit myself to anything" (539); and his existence takes place in the most desolate emptiness. Such frivolity, from a Christian point of view, can be given other names too: "calculation, tepidity, easy-goingness, lack of idealism and mediocrity" (541).

The prescription of a remedy follows the diagnosis of the illness. "Nothing perfects our personality so much as correspondence with grace" (443). He then proposes a very sound and practical piece of advice: "Try to imitate the Virgin Mary and you will be a complete man and woman" (443). Next to Jesus, a Christian always discovers his Mother, Holy Mary, and always goes to her for all his needs: to imitate her, to get to know her, to avail himself of her powerful intercession. It is most significant that all the chapters of *Furrow* should end with some thought related to the Blessed Virgin. Every Christian effort to grow in virtue leads to identification with Jesus Christ, and there is no surer or more direct way for this than devotion to Our Lady. It is as if I can still hear the voice of the Servant of God, on one of the first occasions I met him, joyfully explaining to me that "one always goes and returns to Jesus through Mary".

ALVARO DEL PORTILLO
ROME, JUNE 26, 1986

PROLOGUE OF THE AUTHOR

My reader and friend,
let me help your soul
contemplate the virtues of man,
for grace works upon nature.
But do not forget
that these considerations of mine,
though they may seem very human to you,
must be priestly as well,
since I have written them
for you and for myself
—and I have put them into practice too—
before God.
I ask Our Lord
that these pages
may be of use for us.
May we profit by them
and be moved by them
so that in our lives
our deeds may leave behind
a deep and fertile furrow.

GENEROSITY

1   There are many Christians who are persuaded that the Redemption will be completed in all environments of the world, and that there have to be some souls—they do not know which ones—who will contribute to carrying it out with Christ. But they see this in terms of centuries, many centuries. It would be an eternity, if it were to take place at the rate of their self-giving.

That was the way you thought, until they came to "wake you up".

2   Self-giving is the first step along the road of sacrifice, joy, love, union with God. And thus, a whole life is filled with a holy madness which makes us encounter happiness where human logic would only see denial, suffering, pain.

3   "Pray", you said, "that I may be generous, that I may progress, and be able to change in such a way that one day I may be useful in something".

Good. But what means are you using so that these resolutions can be effective?

4   You often ask yourself why souls who have had the great fortune of knowing the true Jesus ever since their childhood hesitate so much in responding with the best they have: their life, their family, their ideals.

Look: you are bound to show yourself very grateful to the Lord, precisely because you have received it *all* in one go. Just as it would strike a blind man if he suddenly recovered his sight, while it does not even occur to others to give thanks because they see.

But that is not enough. You have to help those around you, daily, to behave with gratitude for their being sons of God. If you don't, don't tell me you are grateful.

5   Meditate upon this slowly: I am asked for very little compared to how much I am being given.

6   As you never seem to manage to set off, consider what a brother of yours wrote to me: "It takes an effort, but once you have 'made up your mind', how you gasp with happiness when you find yourself firmly on your way!"

7   "These days", you were saying, "have been the happiest in my life". And I answered you without hesitation:

that is because you *have lived* with a little more self-giving than usual.

8   The Lord's calling—vocation—always presents itself like this: "If any man would come after me, let him deny himself and take up his cross daily and follow me". Yes: a vocation demands self-denial, sacrifice. But how pleasant that sacrifice turns out to be—*gaudium cum pace*, joy and peace—if that self-giving is complete.

9   When they talked to him about committing himself personally, his reaction was to reason in the following manner: "If I did, I could do that..., I would have to do this other..."

The answer he got was: "Here, we don't bargain with the Lord. The law of God, the invitation of the Lord, is something you either take or leave, just as it is. You need to make up your mind: go forward, fully decided and without holding back; otherwise, go away. *Qui non est mecum...* —whoever is not with Me, is against Me".

10   There is only one step between lack of generosity and lukewarmness.

11   I am copying this example of cowardice from a letter so that you will not imitate it: "I am certainly grateful to you for keeping me in mind, because I need many prayers. But I would also be grateful if, when you ask Our Lord to make me an *apostle*, you would not insist on asking him to make me surrender my freedom".

12   That acquaintance of yours, very intelligent, well off, a good man, used to say: "You have to do what the law says, but within limits, doing what is strictly necessary, without going too far".

And he would add: "You shouldn't sin, of course, but there is no need to give up everything".

How sad it is to see men who are mean, calculating, incapable of making any sacrifice, of giving themselves wholeheartedly to a noble ideal.

13   More should be asked of you, because you can give more and you should give more. Think about it.

14   "It's very difficult", you exclaim, disheartened.

Listen, if you make an effort, with the grace of God that is enough. Put your own interests to one side, you will serve others for God, and you will come to the aid of the Church in the field where the battles are being fought today: in the street, in the factory, in the workshop, in the university, in the office, in your own surroundings, amongst your family and friends.

15   You wrote to me saying: "In the end, it's the same as ever, a great lack of generosity. What a pity, what a

shame, to find the way and then allow a few—inevitable—
clouds of dust to obscure the goal!"

Don't be annoyed if I tell you that you are the only
one to blame: struggle courageously against yourself. The
means you have are more than enough.

16   If your selfishness leads you away from the ordinary
desire for the holy and healthy well-being of mankind,
if you count the cost or if you are not moved by the
wretched material or moral condition of your neighbor,
you force me to reproach you strongly, so that you can
do something about it. If you do not feel a holy fraternity
with your fellowmen, and you live on the margin of the
great Christian family, you are just a poor foundling.

17   The summit? For a soul which has surrendered
itself, everything becomes a summit to conquer. Every
day it discovers new goals, because it does not know how,
or want, to limit the love of God.

18   The more generous you are for God, the happier
you will be.

19   One often feels tempted to reserve a bit of time for
oneself alone.

Learn once and for all to remedy such meanness, by
putting things right immediately.

20   You were one of those "all or nothing" types. And as you could do nothing..., what a disgrace!

Begin to fight with humility, to light up that poor self-giving of yours, which is so mean, until it becomes "all" effective.

21   Those of us who have dedicated ourselves to God have lost nothing.

22   I would like to speak into the ear of so many men and women: giving up one's children to the service of God is not a sacrifice: it is an honor and a joy.

23   A time of hard trial arrived and he came to you grief-stricken.

Do you remember? For him—the friend who used to give you his "prudent" advice—your behavior was only a utopia, the result of deformed ideas, manipulation of wills, and... other "cleverness" of that type.

"This self-giving to the Lord", he would assert, "is an abnormal excitement of the religious sentiment". And with his faulty reasoning, he thought that between your family and you a stranger had entered: Christ.

Now he has understood what you told him so often: Christ never separates souls.

24 Here is an urgent task: to stir up the conscience of believers and non-believers, to gather together men of good will, who are willing to help and to provide the material instruments which are needed for the work with souls.

25 He shows a great deal of enthusiasm and understanding. But when he realizes that it refers to *him*, and that it is *he* who has to contribute in earnest, he slinks away like a coward.

It reminds me of those who, during moments of grave danger, used to shout with false courage: War! War! But they did not want to give any money or to enrol to defend their country.

26 It is sad to see what some people understand by almsgiving: a few pennies or some old clothes. They seem not to have read the Gospel.

Don't be over-cautious: help people to acquire sufficient faith and fortitude to be ready to deny themselves generously, in this life, what they need.

To those who lag behind, explain that it is neither very noble nor very agreeable, even from an earthly point of view, to wait for the last moment, when they will be obliged to take nothing with them.

27   "Whoever lends anything, never gets it back; if he does get it back, it will never be the full amount; and if so, it won't be exactly right; but if it is exactly right, he'll be an enemy for life".

Well then?... Give, without counting the cost, and always for God. In this way you will live, even humanly speaking, closer to the rest of humanity, and you will make your contribution and the number of the ungrateful will be less.

28   I saw a blush on the face of that simple man; he was almost in tears. He had contributed generously to good works, giving honest money which he himself had earned, and then he heard that "good people" had called his actions dishonest.

With the candidness of a beginner in these battles of God, he murmured: "They see that I make a sacrifice... and they still sacrifice me!"

I talked to him slowly: he kissed my crucifix, and his natural indignation was changed into peace and joy.

29   Don't you have that mad desire to give yourself more completely, more *irrevocably*?

30   How ridiculous is the attitude of us poor little human beings when we deny the Lord such trifles again and again! As time goes by, and we begin to see things in their true perspective, then shame and sorrow are born.

31 *Aure audietis, et non intelligetis: et videntes videbitis, et non perspicietis.* These are the clear words of the Holy Spirit: they hear with their own ears, and they do not understand; they see with their own eyes, but they do not perceive.

Why worry if some, although they *see* the apostolate and they know how great it is, still do not give themselves to it? Pray in peace, and persevere along your way. If they don't want to set out, there will be others!

32 Ever since you said *Yes*, time has broadened your horizons, giving them new and brighter colors and making them more beautiful every day. But you have to continue saying *Yes*.

33 The Blessed Virgin Mary, Teacher of unlimited self-giving. Do you remember? It was in praise of her that Jesus Christ said: "Whoever fulfills the Will of my Father, he—she—is my mother!..."

Ask of this good Mother that her answer, with the generosity it shows, may grow stronger in your soul—with the strength of love and liberation. *Ecce ancilla Domini*—behold the handmaid of the Lord.

HUMAN RESPECT

34   When the defense of truth is at stake, how can one desire neither to displease God nor to clash with one's surroundings? These two things are opposed: it is either the one or the other! The sacrifice has to be a holocaust where everything is burned up, even the thought: "what will they say?", even what we call our reputation.

35   How clearly I see now that "holy shamelessness" is rooted, very deeply, in the Gospel. Fulfill the Will of God, mindful of Jesus falsely accused, Jesus spat upon and buffeted, Jesus brought before the shabby courts of men..., Jesus silent! A resolution: bow your head when insulted, and persevere in the godly undertaking with which the merciful Love of Our Lord has wished to entrust us, even though you know that humiliations will no doubt follow.

36   It is terrible how much harm we can do if we allow ourselves to be carried away by the fear or the shame of being seen as Christians in ordinary life.

37   There are some people who, when they speak about God or the apostolate, seem to feel the need to apologize. Perhaps it is because they have not discovered the value of human virtues, but, on the other hand, have been greatly deformed spiritually, and are too cowardly.

38   It is no use trying to please everyone. There will always be people who disagree, who complain. The way popular wisdom sums it up is: "What is good for the sheep is bad for the wolves".

39   Don't behave like someone frightened by an enemy whose only strength is his *aggressive voice*.

40   You understand the work that is being carried out..., you have nothing against it(!). But you are very careful not to take part in it, and even more careful to ensure that others do not see or suspect you are lending a hand.

You told me that you were afraid that people might think you are better than you are! Is it not rather that you are afraid God and men might ask you to be more consistent?

41 He seemed to be totally determined. But, when he took up his pen to break with his girl friend, his indecision and lack of courage got the better of him: it was all very human and understandable, people said. According to some, it seems human love is not among the things which one has to leave behind in order to follow Jesus Christ totally, when he asks you.

42 Some people make mistakes through weakness— on account of the fragile clay we are all made of—but retain the Church's doctrine in its integrity.

They are the ones who, with the grace of God, display heroic courage and humility in acknowledging their mistakes and defending the truth firmly.

43 Some call faith and trust in God being imprudent and rash.

44 It is madness to trust in God...! And is it not greater madness to trust in oneself, or in other men?

45 You wrote to tell me that you have at last gone to confession and that you experienced the humiliation of having to open the sewer—that is what you say—of your life to "a man".

When will you get rid of that feeling of vain self-esteem? You will then go to confession happy to show yourself as you are to "that man", who being anointed, is another Christ—Christ himself—and gives you absolution, God's forgiveness.

46 May we have the courage always to act in public in accordance with our holy faith.

47 "We cannot be sectarian", they told me with an air of reasonableness, referring to the way the Church's doctrine remains firm.

Afterwards, when I let them see that whoever is in possession of the truth cannot be sectarian, they realized their mistake.

48 If you want to see how ridiculous it is to take fashion as the way to behave, just look at old portraits.

49 I am glad that you love processions, and all the external practices of our Holy Mother the Church, so as to render God the worship due to him..., and that you really put yourself into them!

50 *Ego palam locutus sum mundo.* I have preached openly before the whole world, was the answer Jesus gave to Caiphas when the time had come for him to give his Life for us.

And yet there are Christians who are afraid to show *palam*—openly—veneration for Our Lord.

51 When the apostles fled, and the enraged mob made themselves hoarse shouting angrily at Jesus, the Holy Virgin Mary followed close behind her Son through the streets of Jerusalem. She did not draw back when the crowd cried out, nor did she leave Our Redeemer alone when each person, anonymous in that crowd, was in his cowardice emboldened to ill-treat Christ.

Call upon her with all your strength: *Virgo fidelis!*, Virgin most faithful!, and ask her that those of us who call ourselves God's friends may truly be so at all times.

CHEERFULNESS

52 Nobody is happy on earth until he decides not to be. This is the way the path goes: suffering—in Christian terms—the Cross; God's Will, Love; happiness here and, afterwards, eternally.

53 *Servite Domino in laetitia!*—I will serve God cheerfully. With a cheerfulness that is a consequence of my Faith, of my Hope, and of my Love—and that will last forever. For, as the Apostle assures us, *Dominus prope est!*—the Lord follows me closely. I shall walk with him, therefore, quite confidently, for the Lord is my Father, and with his help I shall fulfill his most lovable Will, even if I find it hard.

54 A piece of advice on which I have insisted repeatedly: be cheerful, always cheerful. It is for those to be sad who do not consider themselves to be sons of God.

55 I am trying to do everything to help my younger brothers find the way *easy* as you asked us. There are so many joys to be found in "having it tough".

56 Another man of faith wrote to me: "When you have to be on your own, you can notice clearly the help of your brothers. Now, when it comes to my mind that I have to put up with everything 'all alone', I often think that, if it weren't for that 'company we keep from afar'— the holy Communion of Saints—I would not be able to preserve this optimism which fills my heart".

57 Don't forget that sometimes one needs to have smiling faces around.

58 "You are all so cheerful, and one doesn't expect that", I heard someone comment.

Christ's enemies never tire of using the diabolical ploy of spreading the rumor that the people who give themselves to God are all wrapped up in themselves. And, unfortunately, some of those who wish to be *good*, echo those words, with their *sad virtues*.

We give you thanks, Lord, because you have chosen to count on our cheerful, happy lives to erase that false caricature.

I also ask you that we may not forget it.

59 May no one read sadness or sorrow in your face, when you spread in the world around you the sweet smell of your sacrifice: the children of God should always be sowers of peace and joy.

60 The cheerfulness of a man of God, of a woman of God, has to overflow: it has to be calm, contagious, attractive...; in a few words, it has to be so supernatural, and natural, so infectious that it may bring others to follow Christian ways.

61 "Happy?"—The question made me think.

Words have not yet been invented to express all that one feels—in the heart and in the will—when one knows oneself to be a son of God.

62 Christmas time. You write: "Together with the holy expectation of Mary and Joseph, I also await the Child, impatiently. How happy I shall feel at Bethlehem! I have a feeling that I won't be able to contain this joy without bounds. Yes! but, with him, I also want to be born anew". I hope you really mean what you say!

63 A sincere resolution: to make the way lovable for others and easy, since life brings enough bitterness with it already.

64   What a wonderful thing to convert unbelievers, to gain souls!...

Well, it is as pleasing, and even more pleasing to God, to avoid their being lost.

65   Once again you had gone back to your old follies! And afterwards, when you returned, you didn't feel very cheerful, because you lacked humility.

It seems as if you obstinately refuse to learn from the second part of the parable of the prodigal son, and you still feel attached to the wretched happiness of the pig-swill. With your pride wounded by your weakness, you have not made up your mind to ask for pardon, and you have not realized that, if you humble yourself, the joyful welcome of your Father God awaits you, with a feast to mark your return and your new beginning.

66   It is true: we are worth nothing, we are nothing, we can do nothing, we have nothing. And, at the same time, in the midst of our daily struggle, obstacles, and temptations are not lacking. But the *joy* of your brothers will banish all difficulties, as soon as you are back with them, because you will see them firmly relying on him: *Quia tu es Deus fortitudo mea*—because you, Lord, are our strength.

67 The scene of the parable is being repeated: it is the same as with those people who were invited to the wedding feast. Some are afraid, others have their own concerns, many...make up stories or give silly excuses.

They put up resistance. That is why they feel the way they do: fed up, all in a muddle, listless, bored, bitter. And yet how easy it is to accept the divine invitation at every moment, and live a happy life, full of joy!

68 It is all too easy to say: "I'm useless; nothing turns out right for me—for us". Apart from not being true, that pessimism masks a great deal of laziness. There are things you do well, and things you do badly. Fill yourself with joy and with hope on account of the former; and face up to the latter—without losing heart—in order to put things right; and they will work out.

69 "Father, following your advice, I laugh at my weaknesses—without forgetting that I can't give in—and then I feel much happier.

But when I am silly enough to become sad, it seems to me that I am losing the way".

70 You asked me if I had a cross to bear. And I answered, "Yes, we always have to bear the Cross". But it is a glorious Cross, a divine seal, the authentic guarantee of our being children of God. That is why, with the Cross, we always travel happily on our way.

71   You feel happier. But this time it is a fidgety sort of happiness, a bit impatient. With it comes the clear feeling that something is being wrested from you as a sacrifice.

Listen to me carefully: here on earth there is no perfect happiness. That is why, now, immediately, without complaining or feeling a victim, you should offer yourself as an oblation to God, with total and absolute self-surrender.

72   You are enjoying a few days of great happiness, and your soul seems to be filled with light and color. And, funnily enough, the motives for your joy, are the same ones that at other times disheartened you!

It is always the same: it all depends on the point of view. *Laetetur cor quaerentium Dominum*!—when you seek the Lord, your heart always overflows with happiness.

73   There are men who have no faith, who are sad and hesitant because of the emptiness of their existence, and exposed like weathercocks to "changeable" circumstances. How different that is from our trusting life as Christians, which is cheerful, firm, and solid, because we know and are absolutely convinced of our supernatural destiny!

74 You are not happy because you make everything revolve around yourself as if you were always the center: you have a stomach-ache, or you are tired, or they have said this or that...

Have you ever tried thinking about him, and through him, about others?

75 The Apostle calls a Christian, *miles*—a soldier.

Thus it is that in this holy and Christian war of love and peace for the happiness of all souls, there are, in God's ranks, tired, hungry soldiers, covered in wounds... but happy. For they bear in their hearts the sure light of victory.

76 "I am sending you, Father, the resolution always to smile: with a heart that is happy even if it is wounded".

I think it is a splendid resolution. I pray that you may keep it.

77 Sometimes you feel that you are beginning to lose heart and that everything is getting on top of you. This kills your good desires, and you can hardly manage to overcome this feeling even by making acts of hope. Never mind: this is a good time to ask God for more grace. Then, go on! Renew your joy for the struggle, even though you might lose the odd skirmish.

78   You don't feel like doing anything and there is nothing you look forward to. It is like a dark cloud. Showers of sadness fell, and you experienced a strong sensation of being hemmed in. And, to crown it all, a despondency set in, which grew out of a more or less objective fact: you have been struggling for so many years..., and you are still so far behind, so far.

All this is necessary, and God has things in hand. In order to attain *gaudium cum pace*—true peace and joy, we have to add to the conviction of our divine filiation, which fills us with optimism, the acknowledgment of our own personal weakness.

79   You have become younger! You notice, in fact, that getting to know God better has made you regain in a short time the simple and happy age of your youth, including the security and joy—without any childishness— of spiritual childhood... You look around, and you realize that the same thing has happened to others: the years since they met with the Lord have gone by and, having reached maturity, they are strengthened with a permanent youth and happiness. Although they are no longer young, they are youthful and happy!

This reality of the interior life attracts, confirms and wins over souls. Give thanks for it daily *ad Deum qui laetificat iuventutem*—to God who fills your youth with joy.

80 You will not lack the grace of God. Therefore, if you respond to it, you will be sure to win.

Victory depends on you: your strength and drive—together with that grace—are reason enough for you to have the optimism of one who knows victory is assured.

81 Perhaps yesterday you were one of those people whose ideals have gone sour, who are defrauded in their human ambitions. Today, now that God has entered into your life—thank you, my God!—you laugh and sing and carry your smile, your Love and your happiness wherever you go.

82 There are many who feel unhappy, just because they have too much of everything. Christians, if they really behave as God's children, will suffer discomfort, heat, tiredness, cold... But they will never lack joy, because that—all that—is ordained or permitted by him who is the source of true happiness.

83 Faced by all those men without faith, without hope; by minds desperately near the boarders of anguish, seeking for a meaning in their life, you found your purpose: him!

This discovery will permanently inject a new happiness into your existence, it will transform you, and present you with an immense daily hoard of beautiful things of which you were unaware, and which show you the joyful expanse of that broad path that leads you to God.

84 Your steadfastness in faith, purity and the way God has marked out for you is the measure of your happiness on earth.

85 Give thanks to God that you are happy, with a deep joy which has no need to be expressed aloud.

86 With God, I thought, every day seems more attractive. I can see "little bits" at a time. One day I notice some wonderful detail; on another, I discover a sight I had not seen before... At this rate, it is impossible to say what will happen next.

Then, I noticed that he was reassuring me: "Your happiness will grow greater every day, for you will be drawn deeper and deeper into that divine adventure, into that great *complication* with which you have become involved. And you will realize that I will never abandon you".

87 Happiness is a consequence of self-surrender. It is re-affirmed every time you turn the water-wheel.

88 Now that you have given yourself to God your happiness cannot be taken away. But you must feel a great concern and desire for everyone to share in your joy!

89   All the things that are now worrying you can be put into a smile which shows your love of God.

90   Optimism? Yes, always! Even when things seem to turn out badly: perhaps that is the time to break into a song, with a *Gloria*, because you have sought refuge in him, and nothing but good can come to you from him.

91   Hope does not mean beginning to see the light, but trusting with one's eyes closed that the Lord possesses the light fully, and lives in its clarity. He is the Light.

92   Every Christian has the duty to bring peace and joy to his own surroundings on earth. This cheerful crusade of manliness will move even shrivelled or rotten hearts, and raise them to God.

93   If you cut any hint of envy out at the roots, and if you sincerely rejoice in other people's success, you will not lose your cheerfulness.

94   That friend of mine came up to me: "They tell me you are in love". I was very surprised and the only thing I could think to ask was where he got that news.

He said that he could read it in my eyes, which shone with joy.

95   What must the cheerful way that Jesus looked upon people have been like? It must have been the same which shone from the eyes of his Mother who could not contain her joy—*Magnificat anima mea Dominum*!—and her soul glorified the Lord while she carried him within her and by her side.

Oh, Mother!: May we, like you, rejoice to be with him and to hold him.

DARING

96   Don't be narrow-minded men or women who are immature, short-sighted, and incapable of embracing our supernatural Christian outlook as children of God. God and daring!

97   Daring is not imprudence, or unreflective bravado, or simple pluck.

Daring is fortitude, a cardinal virtue, a requirement of the soul's life.

98   You made up your mind after reflection, rather than with any burning enthusiasm. Although you would have very much liked to feel it, there was no room for sentiment: you gave yourself to God when you were convinced that he wanted you.

And, since then, you have *felt* no serious doubts; rather you experience a calm and peaceful joy, which sometimes overflows. It is thus that God rewards the daring feats of Love.

99 I read a proverb which is very popular in some countries: "God owns the world, but he rents it out to the brave", and it made me think.

What are you waiting for?

100 I am not the apostle I should be. I am...too timid.

Could it not be that you are fainthearted, because your love is so small? It is time to change!

101 The difficulties you have met have made you shrink back, and you have become "prudent, moderate, and objective".

Remember that you have always despised those terms, when they became synonyms for cowardly, fainthearted, and comfort-seeking.

102 Fear? That is only for those who know they are acting badly. For you, never.

103 There are a great number of Christians who would be apostles..., if they were not afraid.

They are the same people who then complain, because the Lord—they say!—has abandoned them. How do *they* treat God?

104 There are many of us; with the help of God, we can reach everywhere, they exclaim enthusiastically.

Why does fear hold you back then? With divine grace, you can become a saint, which is what matters.

105 When you feel your conscience gnawing at you for not having carried out something good, it is a sign that the Lord did not want it to be omitted.

Just so. Moreover, you can be sure that you *could* have done it, with the grace of God.

106 Let us not forget it: when fulfilling the divine Will, you can get over obstacles, or under them..., or you can go round them. But..., they can be overcome!

107 When one is working to extend an apostolic undertaking, "no" must never be taken for a final answer: you have to try again!

108 You are too "cautious" and not very "supernatural" and that is why you are a bit too clever: don't start inventing your own "snags" and trying to solve them all.

Perhaps the person you speak to is less "clever" or maybe more generous than you are, and as he can count on God, he won't raise so many objections.

109 There are some ways of acting that are so careful that, in a word, they are just pusillanimous.

110 Rest assured: when you work for God, there are no difficulties that cannot be overcome, nor discouragements that will make you abandon the task, nor failures worthy of the name, however unfruitful the results may seem.

111 Your faith is not operative enough; it seems that you are over-pious, rather than a man who is struggling to be a saint.

112 Be calm! Be daring!

With these virtues you must rout the fifth column of people who are lukewarm, who are cowards or traitors.

113 You assured me that you wanted to fight without respite, and now you come to me with a long face.

Look, even humanly speaking, it is good not to find it all done for you, with no hitches. Something—a lot!—depends on you. Otherwise, how could you *become* a saint?

114 You won't commit yourself to working in that supernatural enterprise, because—you say—you are afraid of not knowing how to please, or of making some unfortunate mistake. If you thought more about God, those excuses would disappear.

115 Sometimes I think that a few enemies of God and his Church live off the fear of many good people, and I am filled with shame.

116 As we talked, he assured me that he never wanted to leave the hut where he lived, because he preferred to count the beams of "his" shack rather than the stars in heaven.

There are many like him who are incapable of leaving their own petty things so as to raise their eyes to heaven: it is time they acquired a loftier vision!

117 I understand the supernatural and human joy of one man who had the good fortune of being in the vanguard of the divine sowing.

"It is wonderful to be the only one, to stir up a whole city and its surroundings", he would often say, fully convinced.

Don't wait until you can count on more means, or until others come: souls have need of you today, now.

118 Be daring in your prayer, and the Lord will turn you from a pessimist into an optimist; from being timid, to being daring, from being feeble-spirited to being a man of faith, an apostle!

119 Those problems which used to overwhelm you and seemed like enormous mountains disappeared completely. They were solved in a divine way, as when Our Lord commanded the winds and the waters to be calm.

And to think that you still doubted!

120 "Don't help the Holy Spirit so much!", a friend of mine said, jokingly, but sounding very scared.

I answered: I think we "help him" very little.

121 When I see so much cowardice, so much false prudence..., in both men and women, I burn with the desire to ask them: Are faith and trust only to be preached, then? Not practised?

122 You find yourself in a position which seems rather strange: on the one hand, you feel fainthearted, as you look inward; on the other, sure, encouraged, as you look upwards.

Don't worry: it is a sign that you are beginning to know yourself better and—more importantly!—that you are beginning to know him better.

123 Do you see? With him you could do it. Why are you surprised?

Be convinced: there is nothing to be surprised about. If you trust in God—really trust—things work out easily. And, what is more, you always go further than you imagined you could.

124 Do you want to be daring in a holy way, so that God may act through you? Have recourse to Mary, and she will accompany you along the path of humility, so that, when faced by what to the human mind is impossible, you may be able to answer with a *fiat!*—be it done!, which unites the earth to Heaven.

THE STRUGGLE

125   Not all of us can become rich, wise, famous...
Yet, all of us—yes, *all of us*—are called to be saints.

126   Being faithful to God demands a struggle. And
it means close combat, man to man—the old man against
the man of God—in one small thing after another, without
giving in.

127   The test, I don't deny it, proves to be very hard:
you have to go uphill, "against the grain".

What is my advice? That you must say: *omnia in
bonum*, everything that happens, "everything that happens
to me", is for my own good... Therefore the right conclusion
is to accept, as a pleasant reality, what seems so hard to
you.

128 Today it is not enough for men and women to be good. Moreover, whoever is content to be nearly good, is not good enough. It is necessary to be "revolutionary".

Faced by hedonism, faced by the pagan and materialistic wares that we are being offered, Christ wants objectors!— rebels of Love!

129 Whoever really wants to achieve sanctity, takes no breaks or holidays.

130 Some behave, throughout their lives, as though Our Lord had only talked of self-giving and upright behavior to those who did not find it hard—they don't exist!— or to those who don't need to fight.

They forget that Jesus said, for all: the Kingdom of heaven is won by violence, by the holy battle of every moment.

131 What eagerness many show for reform!

Would it not be better for us all to reform ourselves, each one of us, so as to fulfill faithfully what is laid down?

132 You wade into temptations, you put yourself in danger, you fool around with your sight and with your imagination, you chat about...stupidities. And then you are anxious that doubts, scruples, confusion, sadness, and discouragement might assail you.

You must admit that you are not very consistent.

133   After initial enthusiasm, the doubts, hesitations, and anxieties have begun. You are worried about your studies, your family, your financial situation, and, above all, the thought that you are not up to it, that perhaps you are of no use, that you lack experience in life.

I will give you a sure means of overcoming such fears, which are temptations coming from the devil or from your lack of generosity! *Despise them*: remove those recollections from your memory. The Master already poignantly preached this twenty centuries ago: "No one who looks behind him..."

134   We have to instill in our souls a true horror for sin. Lord—say it with a contrite heart—may I never offend you again!

But don't be frightened when you become aware of the burden of your poor body and of human passions: it would be silly and childishly naive to find out now that "this" exists. Your wretchedness is not an obstacle but a spur for you to become more united to God and seek him constantly, because he purifies us.

135 If your imagination bubbles over with thoughts about yourself and creates fanciful situations and circumstances which would not normally find a place in your way, then these will foolishly distract you. They will dampen your ardor and separate you from the presence of God. This is vanity.

If your imagination revolves around others, you will easily fall into the defect of passing judgment when this is not your responsibility. You will interpret their behavior not at all objectively but in a mean way. This is rash judgment.

If your imagination concerns itself with your own talents and ways of speaking, or with the general admiration that you inspire in others, then you will be in danger of losing your rectitude of intention, and of providing fodder for your pride.

Generally, letting your imagination loose is a waste of time, and, if it is not controlled, it opens the door to a whole string of voluntary temptations.

Do not leave off the practice of interior mortification for even a single day!

136 Do not be so stupidly naive as to think you have to go through temptations to be sure that you are firm in your vocation. It would be like asking someone to stop your heart to prove that you want to live.

137 Do not enter into dialogue with temptation. Allow me to repeat it: have the courage to run away and the moral strength not to dally with your weakness or wonder how far you can go. Break off, with no concessions!

138 You have no excuse whatsoever. You have only yourself to blame. If you are aware—and you know it well enough—that going along that path, reading those things, keeping that company, can bring you to a precipice, why do you persist in thinking that perhaps it is a short cut which will help you to develop or which makes your personality more mature?

You must change your plan radically, even though it demands an effort and means fewer amusements at your disposal. It is high time you behaved as a responsible person.

139 The irresponsibility of so many men and women, who make no effort to avoid deliberate venial sins, pains Our Lord very much. It's normal, they think, and they seek to excuse themselves by saying that we all fall at those stumbling blocks!

Listen carefully: most of that mob, which condemned Christ and put him to death, also began by shouting—just as the others did—by going to the Garden of Olives—just like the rest of them.

In the end, still carried along by what "everyone" was doing, they did not know how to draw back or did not want to..., and they crucified Jesus!

Now, after twenty centuries, we still have not learned.

140 Ups and downs. You have many, too many, ups and downs.

The reason is clear: till now, you have led an easy life, and you are reluctant to admit that there is an obvious gap between "wanting" and "giving oneself".

141 As, sooner or later, you are surely bound to stumble upon the evidence of your own personal wretchedness, I wish to forewarn you about some of the temptations which the devil will suggest to you and which you should reject straight away. These include the thought that God has forgotten about you, that your call to the apostolate is in vain, and that the weight of sorrow and of the sins of the world are greater than your strength as an apostle.

None of this is true!

142 If you are really fighting, you need to make an examination of conscience.

Take care of the daily examination: find out if you feel the sorrow of Love, for not getting to know Our Lord as you should.

143 In the same way that many go to see *first stones* being laid, without bothering about whether the works then begun will ever be finished, sinners deceive themselves with their "last times".

144 When it is a matter of "breaking off"—never forget it—the "last time" has to be the one before, the one that has already happened...

145 I advise you to try to return sometime...to the beginning of your *first conversion*, which, if it is not becoming like children, is very much like it. In the spiritual life you have to let yourself be led with complete trust, single-mindedly and without fear. You have to speak with absolute clarity about what you have in your mind and in your soul.

146 How are you going to get out of that state of lukewarmness and lamentable languor if you do not make use of the means? You struggle very little, and when you make an effort, you do so as if annoyed and uneasy. You even hope that your feeble efforts will produce no results, so that you can then justify yourself and you will not have to make demands on yourself and others will not ask any more of you.

It is your own will you are following, not God's. If you don't change in earnest you will neither be happy nor able to obtain the peace you now lack.

Humble yourself before God, and try really to want to.

147 It is such a waste of time and such a human way of looking at things, when everything is reduced to tactics, as if the secret of being effective lay there.

They forget that God's *tactics* are charity, the Love without limits: thus it was that he bridged the unbridgeable gap that man, through sin, opens up between Heaven and earth.

148 Apply a *savage* of sincerity to your examination of conscience; that is to say, be courageous. It is the same as when you look at yourself in the mirror to know where you have hurt yourself or where the dirt is or where your blemishes are, so that you can get rid of them.

149 I must warn you against a ploy of *satan*—yes, without a capital, because he deserves no more— who tries to make use of the most ordinary circumstances, to turn us away, slightly or greatly, from the way that leads us to God.

If you are struggling, and even more if you are really struggling, you should not be surprised at feeling tired or at times having to "go against the grain", without any spiritual or human consolation. See what someone wrote to me some time ago, and which I kept for those who naively consider that grace does away with nature: "Father, for a few days now I have been feeling tremendous lazy and lacking in enthusiasm for fulfilling the plan of life. I have to force myself to do everything, and I have very little taste for it. Pray for me so that this crisis may soon pass, for it makes me suffer a lot to think it could make me turn from my way".

I answered only: did you not know that Love demands sacrifice? Read the words of the master slowly: "Whoever does not take up his Cross *cotidie*—every day—is not worthy of Me." And further on: "I will not leave you orphans…" Our Lord allows that dryness of yours, which you find so hard, so that you may love him more, so that you may trust only in him, so that you may co-redeem with the Cross, so that you may meet him.

150 "The devil doesn't seem to be very clever", you told me. "I can't understand how he can be so stupid: he always uses the same deceits, the same falsehoods…"

You are absolutely right. But we men are less clever, and we do not learn from the experience of others… And satan counts on all that in order to tempt us.

151 I once heard of a curious thing that happens in great battles. Although victory may be certain beforehand, because of the superiority in numbers and equipment, later, in the heat of combat, there are times when defeat threatens through the weakness of one flank. Then peremptory orders come from the high command, and where the flank was in difficulties the breach is stemmed.

I thought about you and me. With God, who does not lose battles, we will always be the victors. That is why in the struggle for sanctity, if you feel lacking in strength, you should listen to the commands, do what you are told, let yourself be helped—for he does not fail.

152 You opened your heart sincerely to your Director, speaking in the presence of God..., and it was marvellous to see how you yourself were finding the proper answers to your evasive attempts. Let us love spiritual direction.

153 I will grant that you behave properly... But, allow me to speak sincerely. You must admit that you are doing things in such a leisurely way that, apart from not being entirely happy, you remain very far from holiness.

That is why I ask: Do you really behave properly? Could it be that you have a mistaken idea of what is proper?

154 If you fool around, are inwardly frivolous and outwardly hesitant when faced with temptation, wanting and not wanting, it will be impossible for you to advance in the interior life.

155 I have always thought that many mean by "tomorrow" or "later", a resistance to grace.

156 Another paradox of the spiritual way: the soul which has less need to reform its behavior is the more anxious to do so, and does not stop until it has succeeded. And the contrary is also true.

157 You sometimes invent "problems", because you do not go to the root of your behavior.

All you need is a determined change of attack: to fulfill your duty loyally and be faithful to the indications that you have been given in spiritual direction.

158 You have become more keenly aware of the urgency, of the single ideal of being a saint; and you have gone into battle daily with no hesitation, convinced that you have to root out bravely any symptom of being fond of comfort.

Later, while talking to Our Lord in your prayer you understood that fighting is a synonym for Love, and you asked for a greater Love, with no fear of the struggle awaiting you, since you would be fighting for him, with him and in him.

159 Complications?... Be sincere, and acknowledge that you prefer to be the slave of some selfish whim of yours, rather than serve God or that soul. Admit it!

160 *Beatus vir qui suffert tentationem...* Blessed is the man who suffers temptation because, after he has been tested, he will receive the crown of Life.

Is your heart filled with joy when you realize that this interior sport is a source of peace which can never be exhausted?

161 *Nunc coepi!*—now I begin! This is the cry of a soul in love which, at every moment, whether it has been faithful or lacking in generosity, renews its desire to serve—to love!—God with a wholehearted loyalty.

162 It really did hurt you deeply when you were told that what you were looking for was not your conversion, but a container for your wretchedness. In that way you would be able to carry on comfortably—but with a taste of bitterness—bearing that sorry load.

163 You don't know whether it is physical depression or a sort of interior tiredness that has come over you, or both at the same time. You fight without fighting, without the desire of an authentic positive improvement, to transmit the joy and love of Christ to souls.

I wish to remind you of the clear words of the Holy Spirit: only those who fight *legitime*, genuinely, in spite of everything, will be crowned.

164 I could behave better, show more decision and spread around more enthusiasm...Why don't I?

Because—forgive my frankness—you are a fool. The devil knows full well that one of the worst-guarded doors of the soul is that of human foolishness: vanity. That is where he attacks with all his might: pseudo-sentimental memories, the hysterical form of a black-sheep complex, the unfounded impression of a lack of freedom...

What are you waiting for in order to follow the Master's injunction: Watch and pray, for you know not the day nor the hour?

165 You told me with a boasting but uncertain swagger that some go up and others go down... And others, like yourself!, are just idling.

Your indolence saddened me, and I added: idlers are made to shift by those going up; and—normally with greater vigor—also by those going down. Consider what an uncomfortable attitude you are adopting!

The holy bishop of Hippo already pointed it out: not to go forward is to go back.

166 In your life, there are two things that do not fit together: your head and your heart.

Your intelligence—enlightened by faith—shows you the way clearly. It can also point out the difference between following that way heroically or stupidly. Above all, it places before you the divine greatness and beauty of the undertakings the Trinity leaves in our hands.

Your feelings, on the other hand, become attached to everything you despise, even while you consider it despicable. It seems as if a thousand trifles were awaiting the least opportunity, and as soon as your poor will is weakened, through physical tiredness or lack of supernatural outlook, those little things flock together and pile up in your imagination, until they form a mountain that oppresses and discourages you. Things such as the rough edges of your work, your resistance to obedience; the lack of proper means; the false attractions of an easy life; greater or smaller but repugnant temptations; bouts of sensuality; tiredness; the bitter taste of spiritual mediocrity... And sometimes also fear; fear because you know God wants you to be a saint, and you are not a saint.

Allow me to talk to you bluntly. You have more than enough "reasons" to turn back, and you lack the resolution to correspond to the grace that he grants you, since he has called you to be another Christ, *ipse Christus*!—Christ himself. You have forgotten the Lord's admonition to the Apostle: "My grace is enough for you", which is confirmation that, if you want to, you can.

167 Make up the time you have lost resting on the laurels of your self-complacency, and thinking what a good person you are, as if it were enough just to keep going, without stealing or killing.

Speed up the pace of your piety and your work: you still have such a long way to go: Live happily with everyone, even with those who annoy you, and make an effort to love—to serve!—those whom you despised before.

168 You revealed your past wounds—full of pus— in Confession. And the priest dealt with your soul like a good doctor, like a conscientious doctor. He made an incision where he had to, and would not let the wound heal over until everything had been cleaned out. Be grateful.

169 Tackling serious matters with a sporting spirit gives very good results. Perhaps I have lost several games? Very well, but—if I persevere—in the end I shall win.

170 Change now, when you still feel young. How difficult it is to put things right when the soul has aged.

171 *Felix culpa!*, sings the Church. Blessed be your mistake—I whisper in your ear—if it has prompted you not to sin again, and if it has also made you understand and help your neighbor better, for he is of no worse mettle than you.

172 "Is it possible", you ask after having rejected the temptation, "is it possible, Lord, that I could be... so bad?"

173 I am going to summarize your clinical history: here I fall and there I get up. The latter is what matters. So continue with that interior struggle, even though you go at the pace of the tortoise. Forward! You know well, my son, where you can end up, if you don't fight: one depth leads to another and another.

174 You are ashamed, before God, and before the others. You have discovered filth within yourself both old and renewed: there is no evil instinct or tendency that you do not feel under your skin. And you also carry a cloud of uncertainty in your heart. Furthermore, temptation arises when you least want it or expect it, when your will is weakened by tiredness.

You no longer know whether it humiliates you, although it hurts you to see yourself like this. But let it hurt you because of him, and for Love of him. This contrition of love will help you to remain vigilant, for the fight will last as long as we live.

175 You are consumed by the desire to confirm once more the self-dedication you made some time ago: remembering that you are a son of God and living like one too.

Put your many weaknesses and infidelities in the Lord's hands. For that is also the only way to lessen their weight.

176 Renewal is not relaxation.

177 Days on retreat. Recollection in order to know God, to know yourself and thus to make progress. A necessary time for discovering where and how you should change your life. What should I do? What should I avoid?

178 There should be no repetition of what happened last year.

"How did the retreat go?" you were asked. And you answered: "We had a very good rest"...

179 Days of silence and of intense grace... Prayer face to face with God...

I broke out into thanksgiving, on seeing those people, mature in years and experience, who opened out to the touch of grace. They responded like children, eagerly grasping the chance to convert their lives, even now, into something useful, which would make up for all the times they have gone astray and for all their lost opportunities.

Recalling that scene, I put it to you: do not neglect your struggle in the interior life.

180 *Auxilium christianorum!*—Help of Christians, says the litany of Loreto with confidence. Have you tried to repeat that aspiration in time of difficulty? If you do it with faith, with the tenderness of a daughter or a son, you will discover the power of the intercession of your Holy Mother Mary, who will lead you to victory.

FISHERS OF MEN

181 We could see, while we talked, the lands of that continent. A light was enkindled in your eyes, your soul was filled with impatience, and, thinking about those peoples, you said: Could it be possible that on the other side of those seas, the grace of God is rendered ineffective?

You then answered your own question: In his infinite goodness, he wishes to use docile instruments.

182 What compassion you feel for them!... You would like to cry out to them that they are wasting their time... Why are they so blind, and why can't they perceive what you—a miserable creature—have seen? Why don't they go for the best?

Pray and mortify yourself. Then you have the duty to wake them up, one by one, explaining to them—also one by one—that they, like you, can find a divine way, without leaving the place they occupy in society.

183 You began in good heart. But little by little your spirit has shrunk... And you are going to end up in your own poor shell, if you continue to let your horizons become smaller and smaller.

You have to allow your heart to expand more and more, with real hunger for the apostolate. Out of a hundred souls we are interested in a hundred.

184 Thank the Lord for the paternal and maternal tenderness he continues to show for you.

You always had those dreams of great adventures, and you have committed yourself to a wonderful enterprise..., which leads you to holiness.

I repeat: thank God for this by leading an apostolic life.

185 When you launch out into the apostolate, be convinced that it is always a question of making people happy, very happy: Truth is inseparable from true joy.

186 People from different countries, different races, and very different backgrounds and professions... When you speak to them about God, you become aware of the human and supernatural value of your vocation as an apostle. It is as if you are re-living, in its total reality, the miracle of the first preaching of Our Lord's disciples. Each person hears in his own language phrases spoken in a strange tongue which open up new ways. And in your mind you can see that scene, taking on a new life, in which "Parthians, Medes, and Elamites" have come to God joyfully.

187 Listen to me carefully and echo my words: Christianity is Love; getting to know God is a most positive experience; concern for others—the apostolate—is not an extra luxury, the task of a few.

Now that you know this, fill yourself with joy, because your life has acquired a completely different meaning; an act in consequence.

188 Naturalness, sincerity, and cheerfulness are indispensable conditions for the apostle to attract people.

189 The way Jesus called the first twelve could not have been simpler: "Come and follow me".

There is one consideration that fits you like a glove, since you are always looking for excuses not to keep on with your task. The human knowledge of those first apostles was very poor, and yet what an impact they made on those who listened to them!

Never forget this: it is he who continues to do the work through each one of us.

190 Vocations to the apostolate are sent by God. But you must not cease to make use of the means: prayer, mortification, study or work, friendship, supernatural outlook..., interior life!

191 When I speak to you about "apostolate of friendship", I mean a *personal* friendship, self-sacrificing, and sincere: face to face, heart to heart.

192 In the apostolate of friendship and trust, the first step has to be understanding, service,—and holy intransigence in doctrine.

193 Those who have met Christ cannot shut themselves in their own little world: how sad such a limitation would be! They must open out like a fan in order to reach all souls. Each one has to create—and widen—a circle of friends, whom he can influence with his professional prestige, with his behavior, with his friendship, so that Christ may exercise his influence by means of that professional prestige, that behavior, that friendship.

194 You have to be a live ember that sets fire to whatever it touches. And, when your surroundings are incapable of catching fire, you have to raise their spiritual temperature.

If not, you are wasting time miserably, and wasting the time of those around you.

195 When there is zeal for souls, good people can always be found, fertile soil can always be discovered. There is no excuse!

196 Rest assured, there are many people there who can understand your way. There are also souls who, whether they know it or not, are looking for Christ and have not found him. But "How can they hear about him, if nobody tells them?"

197 Don't tell me that you care for your interior life, if you are not carrying out an intense and ceaseless apostolate. The Lord—whom you assure me you are close to—wishes all men to be saved.

198 He told you that this way is very hard. And, on hearing it, you heartily agreed, remembering that bit about the Cross being a sure sign of the true way... But your friend noticed only the rough part of the road, without bringing to mind Jesus' promise: "My yoke is sweet".

Remind him about it, because—perhaps when he realizes it—he will give himself.

199 He hasn't got the time?—So much the better. Christ is interested precisely in those who do not have the time.

200 When you consider how many people do not take advantage of a wonderful opportunity, but allow Jesus to pass by, think: where does this clear calling which was so providential, and showed me my way, come from?

Meditate upon this every day: an apostle has always to be another Christ, Christ himself.

201 Don't be surprised and don't be cowed because he has reproached you with having placed him face to face with Christ, nor because he may have added, indignantly: "Now I can't live in peace unless I make up my mind".

Pray for him.—It would be useless to try to calm him down. What may have happened is that some previous cause for concern, the voice of his own conscience, has now come to the fore.

202 Are they scandalized because you have talked about their giving themselves to God to people who had never thought about that problem?—Well, what does it matter, if you have the vocation of being an apostle of apostles?

203 You don't get through to people because you speak a different "language". I advise you to be natural.

The trouble is that artificial formation of yours!

204 Do you hesitate to launch yourself into speaking about God, about a Christian life, about vocation,... because you do not want to cause suffering? You forget that it is not you who are doing the calling, it is he: *Ego scio quos elegerim*—I know well those I have chosen.

Moreover, I should not like to think that behind this false respect lurked a spirit of comfort or lukewarmness. At this stage, do you still prefer poor human friendship to the friendship of God?

205 You have spoken to one person and another, and yet another, because you are consumed by zeal for souls.

One took fright; another consulted a "prudent" man, who guided him badly... You must persevere, and no one afterwards will be able to excuse himself by saying *Quia nemo nos conduxit*—nobody has called us.

206 I understand your holy impatience, but at the same time you must realize that there are some who need to think things over and others who will respond all in good time. Wait for them with open arms. Add the spice of abundant prayer and mortification to your holy impatience. They will be more youthful and generous when they come. They will have got rid of their *bourgeois* approach, and they will be all the more courageous.

Think how God is waiting for them!

207 An indispensable requirement in the apostolate is faith, which is often shown by constancy in speaking about God, even though the fruits are slow to appear.

If we persevere and carry on in the firm conviction that the Lord wills it, signs of a Christian revolution will appear around you, everywhere. Some will follow the call, others will take their interior life seriously, and others—the weakest—will at least be forewarned.

208 Days of real excitement: three more people!

The words of Jesus are being fulfilled: "My Father's name has been glorified if you yield abundant fruit and prove yourselves my disciples".

209 You made me smile, because I know what you meant when you said: I am enthusiastic about the possibility of going to new lands and opening a breach there, perhaps very far away... I would like to find out if there are men on the moon...

Ask the Lord to increase that apostolic zeal of yours.

210 At times, seeing those souls asleep, one feels an enormous desire to shout at them, to make them take notice, to wake them up from that terrible torpor they have fallen into. It is so sad to see them walk like a blind man hitting out with his stick, without finding the way!

I can well understand how the tears of Jesus over Jerusalem sprang from his perfect charity.

211 Dig further every day into the apostolic depths of your Christian vocation. He unfurled a banner to be followed twenty centuries ago, for you and me to proclaim aloud to men. It is indeed meant for all those who have a sincere heart and are capable of loving... What clearer invitations do you need than these: *Ignem veni mittere in terram*—I have come to bring fire to the earth, and the thought of those two thousand five hundred million souls who still do not know Christ!

212 *Hominem non habeo*—I have no one to help me. This, unfortunately, could be said by many who are spiritually sick and paralytic, who could be useful—and should be useful.

Lord: may I never remain indifferent to souls.

213 Ask with me for a new Pentecost, which will once again set the world alight.

214 "If any man comes to me without hating his father and mother and wife and children and brothers and sisters, yes, and his own life too, he can be no disciple of mine".

Every day I see more clearly, Lord, that family ties, if they do not pass through your most lovable Heart, are, for some, a permanent souce of the cross; for others they are a cause of more or less direct temptation against perseverance; for others again, the reason why they are totally ineffective; and, for all, a dead weight which impedes their total surrender.

215 The ploughshare that breaks up the earth and opens up the furrow sees neither the seed nor the harvest.

216 When you made up your mind, you would discover something new every day. Do you remember how it used to be when you constantly asked yourself: "How should this be done?"... But you then kept on experiencing doubts or disappointments...

Now you always find an exact answer which is clear and fully reasoned. And, when you listen to the answers you get to your often childish questions, you think: "Jesus must have looked after the first Twelve like this".

217 Vocations, Lord, more vocations! It doesn't matter whether I did the sowing or someone else—it was you, Jesus, who sowed the seed with our hands. All I know is that you have promised that the fruit will ripen; *et fructus vester maneat*—and your fruit will endure.

218 Be honest. If there are people who tell you that you have been trying "to catch them", admit that this is what you want to do. But there is no need for them to worry! Because, if they haven't got a vocation—if he does not call them—they won't come; and if they have, what a shame for them to end up like the rich young man in the Gospel: alone and sad.

219 As an apostle you have a great and beautiful task. You find yourself at the place where grace and the freedom of each soul meet. You are also present at that most solemn occasion in the life of some men: their encounter with Christ!

220 It seems as if you have been individually picked, he said.

And that is right!

221 Be sure of this: you need to be fully formed to face the rush of people that is going to press upon us with a specific and urgent question: "Well then, what must I do?"

222 Here is a recipe to make your apostolic spirit effective: make definite plans, not for the whole week but for the day ahead, for this moment and the next.

223   Christ expects a lot from your work. But you will have to look for souls, as the Good Shepherd went after the hundredth sheep: without waiting to be called. Then make use of your friends to do good to others. Tell each one of them that nobody can feel at ease with a spiritual life which, after filling him, does not overflow with apostolic zeal.

224   It is no use wasting your time with "your own silly little concerns" when there are so many souls awaiting you.

225   Doctrinal apostolate: that will always be your apostolate.

226   The marvel of Pentecost consecrates all the different ways: it can never be understood as monopoly or the appreciation of only one way to the detriment of the others.

Pentecost provides an unlimited variety of tongues, of methods, of forms of meeting God: not violent uniformity.

227   You wrote: A young fellow, who was going North, joined our group. He was a miner. He sang well and joined in with us. I prayed for him until he arrived at his station. When he got off, he said: "I'd have loved to continue the journey with you!"

I was immediately reminded of that *mane nobiscum*—stay with us, Lord! And I asked him again with faith that others might "see him" in each one of us, as companions along "his way".

228 The masses have been going off down "the road of a justified discontentment" and continue to do so.

It hurts...but, how many we have caused to be disaffected among those who are spiritually or materially in need!

Christ may once more be set among the poor and the humble: it is precisely with them that he prefers to be!

229 Teacher: may you be eager to make your pupils understand quickly what has cost you hours of study to see clearly.

230 The wish to *teach* and to *teach from the heart* creates in pupils a gratitude which is a suitable soil for the apostolate.

231 I like the motto: "Let each wayfarer follow his way", the road God has marked out for him, to be followed faithfully, lovingly, even though it is hard.

232 What an extraordinary lesson each one of the teachings of the New Testament contains. The Master, before ascending to the right hand of the Father, told the disciples: "Go and preach to all nations", and they had remained full of peace. But they still had doubts: they did not know what to do, and they gathered around Mary, Queen of Apostles, so as to become zealous preachers of the Truth which will save the world.

SUFFERING

233 You spoke about the scenes in the life of Jesus which moved you most: when he met men in the flesh..., when he brought peace and health to those whose bodies and souls were racked with pain... You were inspired— you went on—seeing him cure leprosy, restore sight to the blind, heal the paralytic at the pool: the poor beggar forgotten by everybody. You are able to contemplate him as he was, so profoundly human, so close at hand!

Well..., Jesus continues being the same as then.

234 You asked Our Lord to let you suffer a little for him. But when suffering comes in such a normal, human form—family difficulties and problems... or those thousand awkward things of ordinary life—you find it hard to see Christ behind it. Open your hands willingly to those nails... and your sorrow will be turned into joy.

235 Don't complain if you suffer. It is the prized and valued stone that is polished.

Does it hurt? Allow yourself to be cut, gratefully, because God has taken you in his hands as if you were a diamond. An ordinary pebble is not worked on like that.

236 Those who flee like cowards from suffering have something to meditate upon when they see the enthusiasm with which other souls embrace pain.

There are many men and women who know how to suffer in a Christian way. Let us follow their example.

237 You complain?—And you tell me you have reason to complain: One pinprick after another!...

But do you not realize that it is silly to be surprised at finding thorns among roses?

238 Let me continue, as I have always done, to speak to you confidentially. For not to have the heart to talk about my own sufferings it is enough to have a Crucifix in front of me... And I don't mind adding that I have suffered a lot, though always cheerfully.

239 Are you misunderstood? He was the Truth and the Light, but not even those close to him understood him. As I have asked you so often before, remember Our Lord's words: "The disciple is not greater than his Master".

240 For a son of God, contradictions and calumnies are what wounds received on the battlefield are for a soldier.

241 They say this and that about you... But what does your good name matter?

In any case don't feel ashamed or sorry for yourself, but for them: for those who ill-treat you.

242 Sometimes they didn't want to understand: it is as if they were blind... But sometimes it has been you who did not manage to make yourself understood properly. You must change that.

243 It is not enough to be right. You have to know how to prove it so that others will be willing to recognize the truth.

However, state the truth whenever necessary, without bothering about "what they will say".

244 If you frequent the Master's school, you will not be surprised at also having put to up with the misunderstandings of so very many people who could help you a great deal if only they made the effort to be a bit more understanding.

245   You have not ill-treated him physically... But you have ignored him so often; you have looked at him with indifference, as if he were a stranger.

Isn't that harm enough!

246   Without wanting to, persecutors sanctify... But woe to these "sanctifiers!"

247   On earth, one is very often rewarded with calumny.

248   There are souls who seem bent on inventing sufferings, on torturing themselves with their imagination.

Afterwards, when objective sorrows and contradictions come their way, they do not know how to be like the Most Holy Virgin at the foot of the cross with her eyes fixed on her Son.

249   Sacrifice, sacrifice! It is true that to follow Jesus Christ is to carry the Cross—he has said so. But I do not like to hear souls who love our Lord speak so much about crosses and renunciations, because where there is Love, it is a willing sacrifice—though it remains hard—and the cross is the Holy Cross.

A soul which knows how to love and give itself in this way, is filled with peace and joy. Therefore, why insist on "sacrifice", as if you were seeking consolation, if Christ's Cross—which is your life—makes you happy?

250 One could get rid of so much neurosis and hysteria if people were taught—together with Christian doctrine—really to live as Christians: loving God and knowing how to accept contradictions as a blessing from his hand!

251 Do not pass by a neighbor's affliction with indifference. That person—a relative, a friend, a colleague... someone you don't know—is your brother.

Remember the Gospel story you have heard so often with sadness: not even the relatives of Jesus trusted him.—Make sure the scene is not repeated.

252 Imagine that on earth there was only God and you.

Thus it will be easier to suffer humiliations. And, in the end, you will do the things God wants and in the way he wants.

253 That sick person, consumed by a zeal for souls, said: "Sometimes the body protests and complains, but I also try to transform 'those moans' into smiles, because then they become very effective".

254 An incurable illness restricted his movements. And yet he cheerfully assured me: "The illness suits me well and I love it more all the time. If they gave me the choice, I would be born again this way a hundred times!"

255 Jesus came to the Cross, after having prepared himself for thirty-three years, all his life!

His disciples, if they really want to imitate him, have to convert their existence into a co-redemption of Love, with their own active and passive self-denial.

256 The Cross is present in everything, and it comes when one least expects it. But don't forget that, normally, the Cross comes when you start to be effective.

257 The Lord, the Eternal Priest, always blesses with the Cross.

258 *Cor Mariae perdolentis, miserere nobis*!—Invoke the Heart of Holy Mary, with the purpose and determination of uniting yourself to her sorrow, in reparation for your sins and the sins of men of all times.

And pray to her—for every soul—that her sorrow may increase in us our aversion from sin, and that we may be able to love the physical or moral contradictions of each day as a means of expiation.

HUMILITY

259 *Prayer* is the humility of the man who acknowledges his profound wretchedness and the greatness of God. He addresses and adores God as one who expects everything from him and nothing from himself.

Faith is the humility of the mind which renounces its own judgment and surrenders to the verdict and authority of the Church.

Obedience is the humility of the will which subjects itself to the will of another, for God's sake.

Chastity is the humility of the flesh, which subjects itself to the spirit.

Exterior *mortification* is the humility of the senses.

Penance is the humility of all the passions, immolated to the Lord.

Humility is truth on the road of the ascetic struggle.

260 It is a great thing to know oneself to be nothing before God, because that is how things are.

261 "Learn from me, for I am meek and humble of heart..." The humility of Jesus!... What a lesson for you who are a poor earthenware vessel. He—always merciful—has raised you up, and made the light of the sun of grace shine upon your baseness, which has now been freely exalted. And you, how often you have covered your pride under a cloak of dignity or justice...! And how many chances to learn from the Master you have wasted by not knowing how to supernaturalize them!

262 Those periods of depression, because you see your defects or because others discover them, have no foundation...

Ask for true humility.

263 Allow me to remind you that among other evident signs of a lack of humility are:

— Thinking that what you do or say is better than what others do or say;

— Always wanting to get your own way;

— Arguing when you are not right or—when you are—insisting stubbornly or with bad manners;

— Giving your opinion without being asked for it, when charity does not demand you to do so;

— Despising the point of view of others;

— Not being aware that all the gifts and qualities you have are on loan;

— Not acknowledging that you are unworthy of all
honor or esteem, even the ground you are treading
on or the things you own;

— Mentioning yourself as an example in conversation;

— Speaking badly about yourself, so that they may
form a good opinion of you, or contradict you;

— Making excuses when rebuked;

— Hiding some humiliating faults from your director,
so that he may not lose the good opinion he has of
you;

— Hearing praise with satisfaction, or being glad that
others have spoken well of you;

— Being hurt that others are held in greater esteem
than you;

— Refusing to carry out menial tasks;

— Seeking or wanting to be singled out;

— Letting drop words of self-praise in conversation,
or words that might show your honesty, your wit
or skill, your professional prestige...;

— Being ashamed of not having certain possessions...

264 To be humble does not mean to feel anxiety or
fear.

265 Let us flee from the false humility which is called
comfort-seeking.

266 It is Peter who speaks: Lord, do you wash my feet? Jesus answers: You do not understand what I am doing now; you will understand it later. Peter insists: You will never wash my feet. And Jesus explains: If I do not wash your feet, you will have no part with me. Simon Peter surrenders: Lord, not only my feet, but also my hands and my head.

Faced by the call to total self-giving, complete, and without any hesitation, we often oppose it with false modesty like Peter's... May we also be men with a heart like the Apostle's! Peter allows no one to love Jesus more than he does. That love leads us to reply thus: Here I am! Wash me, head, hands, and feet! Purify me completely, for I want to give myself to you without holding anything back.

267 I copy for you from a letter: "I am enchanted by evangelical humility. But I rebel against the timid and thoughtless way some Christians shrink away. They discredit the Church. That atheist author must have had them in mind when he wrote that Christian morality is the morality of slaves". In fact we are servants: servants raised to the rank of children of God, who do not wish to behave as if enslaved by their passions.

268 If you are convinced of your "poor quality"—if you know yourself—you will react to events supernaturally. Joy and peace will take a firmer root in your soul, in the face of humiliations, being despised, calumnies...

In these cases, after saying *fiat*—Lord, whatever you want—you should think: "Is that all he said? He obviously does not know me, otherwise he wouldn't have left it at that".

Being convinced that you deserve worse treatment, you will feel grateful to that person, and rejoice at what might have made somebody else suffer.

269 The higher a statue is raised, the harder and more dangerous the impact when it falls.

270 Go to spiritual direction with greater humility each time. And go punctually, for that is also humility.

See yourself—and you will not be mistaken, because God speaks to you there—as a very sincere little child who is being taught to speak, to read, to know the names of flowers and birds, to experience joys and sorrows, to notice the ground he is treading on.

271 "I am still a poor creature", you tell me.

But once, when you realized it, you felt very bad about it! Now, without getting used to it or giving in to it, you are starting to make a habit of smiling, and of beginning your fight again with growing joy.

272 If you are sensible and humble, you will have realized that one never stops learning. This happens in every field; even the wisest will always have something to learn, until the end of their lives; if they don't, they cease to be wise.

273 Dear Jesus: if I have to be an apostle, you will need to make me very humble.

Everything the sun touches is bathed in light. Lord, fill me with your clarity, make me share in your divinity so that I may identify my will with your adorable Will and become the instrument you wish me to be. Give me the madness of the humiliation you underwent, which led you to be born poor, to work in obscurity, to the shame of dying sewn with nails to a piece of wood, to your self-effacement in the Blessed Sacrament.

May I know myself: may I know myself and know you. I will then never lose sight of my nothingness.

274 Only the stupid are obstinate: the very stupid are very obstinate.

275 Do not forget that in human affairs other people may also be right: they see the same question as you, but from a different point of view, under another light, with other shades, with other contours.

Only in faith and morals is there an indisputable standard: that of our Mother the Church.

276 How good it is to know how to put things right with yourself. And how few people learn that art!

277 Rather than commit a fault against charity, give in, offer no resistance, whenever you have the chance. Show the humility of the grass, which yields without needing to know whose foot is stepping on it.

278 To be converted you must climb via humility, along the path of self-abasement.

279 You said: "the *self* has to be decapitated...". But it's hard, isn't it?

280 One often has to force oneself, to humble oneself and say repeatedly to the Lord in earnest, *Serviam*!—I will serve you.

281 *Memento, homo, quia pulvis es...* —remember, man, that you are dust... If you are dust, why should you find it irksome to be trodden upon?

282 The path of humility takes you everywhere... but above all to Heaven.

283 A sure way to be humble is to contemplate how, even without talents, fame or fortune, we can be effective instruments if we go to the Holy Spirit so that he may grant us his gifts.

The apostles, though they had been taught by Jesus for three years, fled in terror from the enemies of Christ. But after Pentecost they let themselves be flogged and imprisoned, and ended up giving their lives in witness to their faith.

284 It is true that nobody can be certain of his perseverance... But that uncertainty is another reason for humility and an obvious proof of our freedom.

285 Although you don't amount to much, God has made use of you, and he continues to make use of you to perform fruitful works for his glory.

Don't put on airs. Think what would an instrument of iron or steel say about itself, when a craftsman uses it to set golden jewelry with precious stones?

286 What is of more value: a pound weight of gold or a pound of copper?... And yet in many cases copper is more useful and better than gold.

287 Your vocation—God's calling—is to direct, to draw others, to serve, to lead. If through a false or ill-conceived humility you isolate yourself, all huddled up in a corner, you are failing in your duty to be a divine instrument.

288 When the Lord makes use of you to pour his grace into souls remember that you are only the wrapping round the gift, the paper that is torn up and thrown away.

289 *Quia respexit humilitatem ancillae suae*—because he has looked graciously upon the lowliness of his handmaid...

I am more convinced every day that authentic humility is the supernatural basis for all virtues!

Talk to Our Lady, so that she may train us to walk along that path.

CITIZENSHIP

290 The world awaits us. Yes, we love the world passionately because God has taught us to: *Sic Deus dilexit mundum...* —God so loved the world. And we love it because it is there that we fight our battles in a most beautiful war of charity, so that everyone may find the peace that Christ has come to establish.

291 The Lord has shown us this refinement of Love: he has let us conquer the world for him.

He is always so humble that he has wished to limit himself to making it possible... To us he has granted the easiest and most agreeable part: taking action and gaining the victory.

292 The world... "That is our field!" you said, after directing your eyes and thoughts to heaven, with all the assurance of the farmer who walks through his own ripe corn. *Regnare Christum volumus*!—we want him to reign over this earth of his!

293   "It is a time of hope, and I live off this treasure. It is not just a phrase, Father", you tell me, "it is a reality".

Well then..., bring the whole world, all the human values which attract you so very strongly—friendship, the arts, science, philosophy, theology, sport, nature, culture, souls—bring all of this within that hope: the hope of Christ.

294   That pleasant but insubstantial enchantment of the world is there all the time. You are attracted by the color and smell of the flowers by the wayside, by the birds of the air; by all creatures.

My poor son: it is quite reasonable. For, if you were not fascinated by it all, what sacrifice would you be able to offer Our Lord?

295   Your Christian vocation requires you to be in God and, at the same time, to be concerned with the things of the earth, using them objectively, just as they are: to give them back to him.

296   It seems incredible that one could be so happy in this world, where so many are bent on leading sad lives because they follow their own selfishness, as if everything came to an end down here.

Don't you be one of them, rectify your intention all the time.

297 The world is cold and seems to be asleep. You often look upon it, from your vantage point, with a glance that would set it on fire. Lord, may it awaken!

Channel your bursts of impatience and be sure that if we know how to keep our own lives well lit, we shall set every corner of the world alight, and the way it all looks will change.

298 When I ask you always to be faithful in the service of God and souls, it is not an easy enthusiasm I am looking for. It is the enthusiasm you can acquire in the world when you see how much there is to be done everywhere.

299 A good son of God has to be very human. But not to such an extent that he becomes uncouth and bad-mannered.

300 It is difficult to make one's mark through quiet work and the proper fulfillment of our duties as citizens, so that later one can demand one's rights and place them in the service of the Church and of society.

It is difficult, but it is very effective.

301 It is not true that there is opposition between being a good Catholic and serving civil society faithfully. In the same way there is no reason why the Church and the State should clash when they proceed with the lawful exercise of their respective authorities, in fulfillment of the mission God has entrusted to them

Those who affirm the contrary are liars, yes, liars! They are the same people who honor a false liberty, and ask us Catholics "to do them the favor" of going back to the catacombs.

302 Your task as a Christian citizen is to help see Christ's love and freedom preside over all aspects of modern life: culture and the economy, work and rest, family life and social relations.

303 A son of God cannot entertain class prejudice, for he is interested in the problems of all men. And he tries to help solve them with the justice and charity of Our Redeemer.

The Apostle already pointed it out when he wrote that the Lord is no respecter of persons. I have not hesitated to translate his words thus: there is only one race of men, the race of the children of God.

304 Worldly men go out of their way to make souls lose God as soon as possible; and then, make them lose the world. They do not love this world of ours—they exploit it by trampling over others.

I hope you too do not fall victim to this double swindle.

305 Some people feel embittered all the time. Everything makes them uneasy. They go to sleep with a physical obsession: that this sleep, the only possible escape, is not going to last very long. They wake up with the unwelcome and disheartening feeling that they now have another day in front of them.

Many have forgotten that the Lord has placed us in the world on our way to eternal happiness. They do not realize that only those who walk on earth with the joy of the children of God will be able to attain it.

306 Show people through your behavior as a Christian citizen the difference between living sadly and living cheerfully; between being timid and being daring; between acting cautiously, with duplicity—hypocritically—and acting as men of simplicity and integrity. In a word, between being worldly and being children of God.

307 A fundamental error against which you must be on guard is to think that the noble and just customs and needs of your times and environment cannot be directed and accommodated to the holiness of the moral teaching of Jesus Christ.

Notice that I have specified that the customs and needs should be "noble and just". If they are not, they lack the right to be adopted by citizens.

308 Religion cannot be separated from life, either in theory or in daily reality.

309 Far away on the horizon heaven seems to meet the earth. Do not forget that where heaven and earth really meet is in the heart of a child of God.

310 We cannot simply fold our arms when a subtle persecution condemns the Church to die of starvation, putting it outside the sphere of public life, and above all obstructing its part in education, culture, and family life.

These are not our rights; they are God's rights. He has entrusted them to us Catholics so that we may exercise them!

311 Many things, whether they be material, technical, economic, social, political or cultural, when left to themselves, or left in the hands of those who lack the light of the faith, become formidable obstacles to the supernatural life. They form a sort of closed shop which is hostile to the Church.

You, as a Christian and, perhaps, as a research worker, writer, scientist, politician or laborer, have the duty to sanctify those things. Remember that the whole universe—as the Apostle says—is groaning as in the pangs of labor, awaiting the liberation of the children of God.

312 You should not want to make the world into a convent, because this would be a disorder. But don't convert the Church into some earthly faction either, because that would be tantamount to committing treason.

313 How sad it is to have the mentality of a Roman Emperor, and not to understand the freedom other citizens enjoy in the things God has left to the free choice of men.

314 "Who said that to reach sanctity you need to seek refuge in a cell or on a solitary mountain?" That was what a good family man asked himself in amazement, and he added: "If that were so, it would not be the people who would be holy, but the cell, or the mountain. It seems they have forgotten that Our Lord expressly told each and every one of us: be holy as my heavenly Father is holy".

My only comment was: "Our Lord, besides wanting us to be saints, grants each one of us the relevant graces".

315 Love your own country: it is a Christian virtue to be patriotic. But if patriotism becomes nationalism, which leads you to look at other people, at other countries, with indifference, with scorn, without Christian charity and justice, then it is a sin.

316 It is not patriotism to justify crimes or to deny the rights of other peoples.

317 The Apostle wrote that "there is no more Gentile and Jew, no more circumcised and uncircumcised; no one is barbarian or Scythian, no one is a slave or a free man; there is nothing but Christ in any of us".

Those words are as valid today as they were then. Before the Lord there is no difference of nation, race, class, state... Each one of us has been born in Christ to be a new creature, a son of God. We are all brothers, and we have to behave fraternally towards one another.

318 Many years ago now, I saw most clearly a truth which will always be valid: the whole web of society needs to live anew and spread the eternal truths of the Gospel, since it has departed from Christian faith and morals. Children of God at the very heart of that society, of the world, have to let their virtues shine out like lamps in the darkness—*quasi lucernae lucentes in caliginoso loco*.

319 The perennial vitality of the Catholic Church ensures that the truth and spirit of Christ do not become remote from the different needs of the times.

320 To follow in Christ's footsteps, today's apostle does not need to reform anything, but even less has he to take no part in the contemporary affairs going on around him. He has only to act as the first Christians did, and give life to his environment.

321 You live in the midst of the world and you are just another citizen living in contact with men who say they are good or bad. You must always want to give other people the happiness you enjoy as a Christian.

322 A decree went out from the Emperor Augustus, enjoining that all the inhabitants of Israel should be registered. Mary and Joseph made their way to Bethlehem. Has it ever occurred to you that the Lord made use of the prompt acceptance of a law to fulfill his prophecy?

Love and respect the ways of behaving by which you may live in amity with other people. Have no doubt, either, that your loyal submission to duty can be the means for others to discover Christian integrity, which is the fruit of divine love, and to find God.

SINCERITY

323 Anyone who hides a temptation from his director shares a secret with the devil. He has become a friend of the enemy.

324 The dust thrown up by your fall blinds and disorients you, and you have thoughts which rob you of your peace.

Have you sought relief in tears by the side of Our Lord, and in confident conversation with a brother?

325 If you are sincere with God, with your director, and your fellowmen, I shall be certain of your perseverance.

326 Do you want to know how to be frank and simple? Listen to these words of Peter and meditate upon them: *Domine, Tu omnia nosti...* —Lord, you know all things!

327 "What shall I say?", you asked when you began to open up your soul. And with a sure conscience, I answered: "In the first place say what you would not like to be known".

328 The defects you see in others are perhaps your own. *Si oculus tuus fuerit simplex...* —If your eye is clear, the whole of the body will be lit up; whereas if the eye is diseased, the whole of the body will be in darkness.

Moreover: "How is it that you can see the speck of dust in your brother's eye, and are not aware of the beam that is in your own"?

Examine yourself.

329 We all need to be aware of our lack of objectivity whenever we judge our own conduct. You too.

330 I agree, you are saying *nearly* all the truth... Therefore you are not truthful.

331 You complain..., and I go on with holy intransigence: you complain..., because this time I have put my finger where it hurts.

332 You understood what sincerity is when you wrote to me: "I am trying to form the habit of calling things by their proper names and, above all, of not looking for words for what does not exist".

333 Think about this carefully: being transparent lies more in not hiding things rather than in wanting things to be seen. It is a matter of allowing the objects lying at the bottom of a glass to be perceived, and not trying to make the air visible.

334 Let us always act in the presence of God in such a way that we never have to hide anything from men.

335 Your worries are at an end. You have discovered that being sincere with the director sorts out all complications with admirable ease.

336 How mistaken parents, teachers, directors can be, when they demand absolute sincerity and then, when they are told the whole truth, are frightened.

337 You were reading in that dictionary the synonyms for insincere: "two-faced, surreptitious, evasive, disingenuous, sly". As you closed the book, you asked the Lord that nobody should ever be able to apply those adjectives to you, and you resolved to improve much more in this supernatural and human virtue of sincerity.

338 *Abyssus, abyssum invocat...* —one depth makes answer to another, as I have already reminded you. It is the exact description of how liars, hypocrites, renegades, and traitors behave. As they are disgusted with their own behavior, they hide their misdeeds from others and go from bad to worse, creating an abyss between themselves and their neighbor.

339 The liturgy rejoices with the song: *Tota pulchra es Maria, et macula originalis non est in te!* You are all fair, O Mary, without original sin! In her there is not the slightest shadow of duplicity. I pray daily to our Mother that we may be able to open our souls in spiritual direction and the light of grace may shine in all our behavior.

Mary will obtain for us the courage to be sincere, if we ask her for it, so that we may come closer to the Most Blessed Trinity.

LOYALTY

340 A consequence of loyalty is your assurance that you are walking along the right road, without being unsettled or confused. You are also strengthened in this additional certainty: that good sense and happiness exist.

See whether this is fulfilled in every instant of your life.

341 You told me that God sometimes fills you with light for a while and sometimes does not.

I reminded you, firmly, that the Lord is always infinitely good. That is why those moments of light are enough to help you carry on; but the times when you see no light are good for you too, and make you more faithful.

342 The salt of the earth. Our Lord said that his disciples—you and I also—are the salt of the earth: to render immune to infection, to prevent corruption, to season the world.

But he also added: *Quod si sal evanuerit...* —if the salt itself becomes tasteless, it will be cast out and trampled underfoot by men.

On seeing the many things happening which we lament, can you now find an explanation for what you could not explain before?

343 That passage of the Second Epistle to Timothy makes me shudder, when the Apostle laments that Demas has fallen in love with this present world and gone to Thessalonica. For a trifle, and for fear of persecution, this man, whom Saint Paul had quoted in other epistles as being among the saints, had betrayed the divine enterprise.

I shudder when I realize how little I am: and it leads me to demand from myself faithfulness to the Lord even in events that might seem to be indifferent—for if they do not help me to be more united to him, I do not want them.

344 I thought the comment of loyalty you had written to me was very appropriate to all those moments in history which the devil makes it his business to repeat: "I carry with me every day in my heart, in my mind, and on my lips, an aspiration: *Rome*".

345 What a great discovery! Something you barely half-understood turned out to be very clear when you had to explain it to others.

You had to speak very gently with someone, who was disheartened because he felt useless and did not want to be a burden to anyone. You understood then better than ever why I always talk to you about being little donkeys turning the water-wheel: carrying on faithfully, with large blinkers which prevent us personally seeing or tasting the results—the flowers, the fruit, the freshness of the garden—confident about the effectiveness of our fidelity.

346 Loyalty demands a real hunger for formation, because you are moved by a sincere love and you do not wish to run the risk of spreading or of defending, through ignorance, principles or attitudes which are very far from being in accordance with the truth.

347 "I would like", you write, "my loyalty and perseverance to be so solid and so eternal, and my service so vigilant and loving, that you could be pleased with me, and I could provide a bit of solace for you".

And I answer: may God confirm you in your resolution, so that we may provide help and solace for him.

348   It is true that some who become enthusiastic leave later on. Don't worry: they are the needle God makes use of to draw the thread through the cloth.

Oh, and pray for them, because perhaps one can manage to get them to keep giving an impulse to others.

349   For you who are wavering, I copy from a letter: "From now on I *may* continue to be the same inept instrument as ever. But in spite of that, I have changed my way of defining and solving the problem of my life, because there is in me a firm desire to persevere... forever!"

You must never doubt that he never fails.

350   Your life is service, but always with stalwart loyalty, laying down no conditions. Only thus shall we be able to give the Lord what he expects.

351   I shall never share the idea, either in the ascetical or the juridical field, of those who think and live as if serving the Church were equivalent to climbing to the top.

352   It hurts you to see that some use the technique of speaking about the Cross of Christ, only so as to climb and obtain positions. They are the same people who consider nothing they see as clean if it does not coincide with their own particular standards.

All the more reason, then, for you to persevere in the rectitude of your intentions, and to ask the Master to grant you the strength to repeat: *Non mea voluntas, sed tua fiat!*—Lord, may I fulfill your Holy Will with love.

353 Every day you must grow in loyalty towards the Church, the Pope, and the Holy See... with a love that should be always more theological.

354 You have a great desire truly to love the Church: and all the greater, when you see that those who wish to make her appear ugly are more active. This seems very natural to me: because the Church is your Mother.

355 Sooner or later, those who do not wish to understand that the faith demands service to the Church and to souls, invert the terms, and end up by having the Church and souls serving their own personal ends.

356 May you never fall into the error of identifying the Mystical Body of Christ with a particular personal or public attitude of any of its members.

And may you never let other people with less formation fall into that error.

Now you realize the importance of your integrity, of your loyalty!

357 I cannot understand you when you talk about matters of morals and of faith and you tell me that you are an independent Catholic.

From whom are you independent? That false independence is equivalent to leaving the way of Christ.

358 You must never give in with regard to the doctrine of the Church. When an alloy is made, the better metal is debased.

Furthermore, that treasure is not yours, and—as the Gospel says—the Owner may ask you to render an account when you least expect it.

359 I have to agree with you that there are practising Catholics who even seem devout in the eyes of others and are perhaps sincerely convinced, yet are naively serving the enemies of the Church.

Into their very homes, under various names, invariably wrongly used—ecumenism, pluralism, democracy—has insinuated itself the worst adversary—ignorance.

360 Although it seems a paradox, those who call themselves sons of the Church may often be precisely those who sow greater confusion.

361 You are tired of fighting. You are weary of an environment characterized by lack of loyalty. Everyone rushes upon the man who has fallen, to trample on him!

I do not know why you are surprised. The same thing happened to Christ himself, but he did not pull back, because he had come precisely to save the sick and those who did not understand him.

362 The disloyal are eager that those who are loyal should remain inactive.

363 Flee from sectarianism, which is opposed to loyal collaboration.

364 True unity cannot be promoted by making new divisions. Even less can it come about when its promoters wish to gain control and take over from lawful authority.

365 You became very thoughtful when you heard me say: I want the blood of my Mother the Church to run in my veins; not Alexander's, or Charlemagne's, or that of the Seven Sages of Greece.

366 To persevere is to persist in love, *per Ipsum et cum Ipso et in Ipso...* Indeed we can also interpret this as: He himself, with me, for me, and in me.

367 Among Catholics it might perhaps be that some have little Christian spirit; or so it might seem to those who have dealings with them at some particular moment.

But if you were to be scandalized by this fact, you would show that you knew very little about human wretchedness and...about your own wretchedness. Furthermore, it is neither just nor loyal to use the example of the weaknesses of a few to speak ill of Christ and his Church.

368 It is true that we, the children of God, ought not to serve the Lord in order to be noticed. But we should not mind being seen, much less should we cease to fulfil our duty because we are seen!

369 Twenty centuries have gone by, and every day the scene is repeated: they continue to judge, to scourge and crucify the Master... And many Catholics, with their behavior and with their words, continue to shout: Him? I don't know him!

I would like to go around everywhere, reminding many, confidentially, that God is merciful, but he is also very just! That is why he declared: "I too will disown whoever disowns me before men".

370 I have always thought that lack of loyalty out of human respect is lack of love—and a lack of personality.

371 Turn your eyes towards the Blessed Virgin and see how she practices the virtue of loyalty. When Elizabeth needs her, the Gospel says that she went *cum festinatione*, —joyfully making haste. Learn from her!

DISCIPLINE

372 Obey with docility—but intelligently too, with love and a sense of responsibility which has nothing to do with judging those who govern and direct you.

373 In the apostolate, obey without paying attention to the human qualities of whoever it is asks you to do something, or to the way he asks you. Otherwise it is no virtue at all.

There are many kinds of crosses: some have jewels or pearls or emeralds on them, some are lacquered or made of ivory. But some are made of wood like Our Lord's. All deserve the same veneration, for the Cross tells us about the sacrifice of God made Man. Apply this consideration to your obedience, without forgetting that he embraced the Wood of the Cross lovingly, without hesitation! There he obtained our Redemption.

Only after obeying, which is a sign of rectitude of intention, may you make fraternal correction with the required conditions, and reinforce unity by fulfilling the duty in question.

374 Obey with your lips, your heart, and your mind. It is not a man who is being obeyed, but God.

375 You do not love obedience if you do not really love whatever you have been asked to do, or if you do not really love whoever has asked you.

376 Some worries can be remedied immediately. Others, not so quickly. But they all are solved if we are faithful, if we obey, and carry out what has been proposed to us.

377 The Lord wants a definite apostolate from you, such as catching those one hundred and fifty-three big fish—not others—taken on the right-hand side of the boat.

And you asked me: How is it I know myself to be a fisher of men, can live in contact with many companions, and be able to distinguish towards whom I should direct my specific apostolate, but still catch nobody? Is it Love that is lacking? Do I lack interior life?

Listen to the answer from Peter's lips, on the occasion of that other miraculous draught: —"Master, we toiled all night and took nothing! But at your word I will let down the nets".

In the name of Jesus Christ, begin again. And being strengthened, rid yourself of that indolence!

378 Obey without so much useless brooding. Appearing sad or reluctant when asked to do something is a very considerable fault. But just to feel like this is not only no fault, but can in fact be the opportunity for a great victory, for crowning an act of heroic virtue.

I have not invented this. Remember the Gospel tells us that a father asked his two sons to do the same job. And Jesus rejoices in the one who, despite raising difficulties, does it! He rejoices because discipline is the fruit of Love.

379 Most acts of disobedience come from not knowing how to *listen* to what it is you are being asked to do, which in the end shows a lack of humility or of interest in serving.

380 Do you want to obey fully? Well then, listen carefully so that you may understand the extent and the spirit of what is being pointed out to you; and if you do not understand something, ask.

381 When will you be convinced that you have to obey? And you disobey if, instead of fulfilling your plan of life, you waste your time. You have to fill every minute with work, study, proselytism, interior life.

382 The Church, through care of the liturgy, makes us intuitively aware of the beauty of the mysteries of Religion and leads us to love them better. In a similar way, without being theatrical, we should behave with a certain attitude of deep respect—it may appear worldly—which may even be external, towards our director, through whose lips the Will of God is made known to us.

383 In governing, after considering the common good, one must realize that both in spiritual and in civil affairs it will be very rare for a law to displease nobody.

There is a popular saying: The rain never pleases everybody. Yet you can be sure that it is not a defect of the law, but an unjustified rebelliousness of pride and selfishness by a few.

384 Order, authority, discipline... They listen, if they do at all, with cynical smiles, claiming that they—both men and women—are defending their freedom.

They are the very people who later pretend that we should respect their erring ways or adapt to them; with their scurrilous protests, they do not understand that their behavior is not—it cannot be—accepted by the authentic freedom of the rest.

385 Those who direct spiritual tasks have to be concerned with all things human, so as to raise them to the supernatural order and make them Godlike.

If they cannot be made Godlike, do not be deceived: such "human" things are not human, they are "brutish", inappropriate for a rational creature.

386 Authority. This does not consist in the one above *yelling* at the one below, and he in turn to the one further down.

In such a way of behaving—a caricature of authority— apart from an evident lack of charity and of decent human standards, all that is achieved is that the one at the top becomes isolated from those who are governed, because he does not serve them: rather could it be said that he uses them.

387 Don't be one of those who let their own homes be badly managed but attempt to meddle in the management of other people's.

388 But do you really think you know it all just because you have been placed in authority?

Listen carefully: the good ruler *knows* that he can, that he *should*, learn from others.

389 Freedom of conscience: No! How many evils this lamentable error, which permits actions against the dictates that lie deepest in oneself, has brought about in nations and individuals.

Freedom "of consciences", yes: for it means the duty to follow that interior command... ah, but after receiving a serious formation!

390 To govern is not to mortify others.

391 Occupying as you do a post of government, I say, "Meditate on this: the strongest and most effective instruments, if they are not properly used, become dented, worn out, and useless".

392 Decisions of governance taken lightly or by someone on his own are always, or nearly always, influenced by a one-sided view of the problems.

However good your training or talents might be, you must listen to those who share with you that task of direction.

393 Never listen to anonymous accusations: it is the way villains behave.

394 In governing, consider this: you must take human material as it is and help it to improve while never despising it.

395 I think it is very good that you should try daily to increase the depth of your concern for those under you, for to feel surrounded and protected by the affectionate understanding of the one in charge can be the effective help which is needed by the people you have to serve by means of your governance.

396 How sad it is to see some people in positions of authority speaking and making judgments lightly, without studying the matter in hand. They make hard statements about persons or matters they know nothing about, even permitting certain *prejudices* which are the result of disloyalty!

397 If authority becomes dictatorial authoritarianism, and this situation is extended in time, historical continuity is lost. People without experience in government reach the top and the inexperienced and excitable young want to grab hold of the reins. How many evils and how many offenses against God—their own and those of others— are to be blamed on the ones who abuse authority so badly!

398 When he who commands is negative and distrustful, he will easily become tyrannical.

399 Try to be properly objective in your work of governance. Avoid the inclination common to those who tend to see rather—and sometimes only—what is not going well, the mistakes.

Be filled with joy and be assured that the Lord has granted to all the capacity to become holy precisely by fighting against their own defects.

400 Eagerness for novelty can lead to mismanagement.

You say we need new rules. But do you think the human body would be better with a different system of nerves and arteries?

401 How determined some people are to concentrate on mass behavior, to turn unity into amorphous uniformity and to drown freedom.

They seem to know nothing of the remarkable unity of the human body, which presents such a God-given variety in its members. Each one has its own function, yet contributes to the general health of the whole.

God does not want us all to be the same or to walk alike along exactly the same road.

402   People have to be taught how to work, but their preparation need not be overdone, for actually doing things is a way of learning too. They should accept in advance their unavoidable shortcomings—the best is the enemy of the good.

403   Never put your trust in organization alone.

404   The good shepherd does not need to terrorize the sheep. Such behavior befits bad rulers, and no one is very much surprised if they end up hated and alone.

405   Governing often consists in knowing how, with patience and affection, to *draw good* out of people.

406   Good governance knows how to be flexible when necessary, without falling into the mistake of not asking enough of people.

407   "As long as they don't make me sin!" said that poor man bravely when he had been almost ruined, in his private life and in his earthly and Christian ambitions, by powerful enemies.

Meditate upon this and learn to say: "As long as they don't make me sin!"

408   Not all citizens form part of the regular army. But in time of war everybody plays a part. And Our Lord said: "I have not come to bring peace, but war".

409   "I was a guerilla fighter", he wrote, "and I moved around the hills, shooting whenever I wanted. But I thought I had better become a soldier, because I realized that wars are won more easily by organized armies and well-disciplined armies. A poor guerilla fighter on his own cannot take whole cities, or conquer the world. I hung up my old musket—it was so out of date—and now I am better armed. At the same time, I know that I can no longer lie down in the hills, under the shade of a tree, and dream about winning the war all on my own".

Blessed be the discipline and blessed be the unity of our Holy Mother the Church!

410   I would say to many rebel Catholics that they fail in their duty if, instead of accepting the discipline and obedience due to lawful authority, they become a party, a small faction, sowers of discord, conspirators and gossips, promoters of stupid personal squabbles, weavers of a mesh of petty envies and difficulties.

411   A gentle wind is not the same as a hurricane. Anyone can resist the first: it is child's play, a parody of struggle.

Gladly you bore small contradictions, shortages, and little worries. And you enjoyed the interior peace of thinking: now I am really working for God, because here we have the Cross...

But now, my poor son, the hurricane has come, and you feel you are being shaken by a force that could uproot century-old trees. You feel this from without and within. But you must remain confident, for your Faith and your Love cannot be uprooted, nor can you be blown from your way, if you remain with the "head", if you maintain unity.

412 How easily you leave the plan of life unfinished, or do things so badly that it is worse than not doing them at all. Is that the way you mean to fall in love more each day with your way, and to pass on this love later to others?

413 Aspire to have no more than one right: that of fulfilling your duty.

414 Is the burden heavy? No, a thousand times no! Those obligations which you freely accepted are wings that raise you high above the vile mud of your passions.

Do the birds feel the weight of their wings? If you were to cut them off and put them on the scales you would see how heavy they are. But can a bird fly if they are taken away from it? It needs those wings and it does not notice their weight, for they lift it up above other creatures.

Your *wings* are heavy too. But if you did not have them you would fall into the filthiest mire.

415 "Mary kept all these things in her heart".

Discipline does not seem at all heavy when it goes together with a clean and sincere love. Even if it costs you a lot, it unites you to the Loved One.

PERSONALITY

416   The Lord needs strong and courageous souls who refuse to come to terms with mediocrity but will be able to enter all kinds of environments with a sure step.

417   A calm and balanced character, an inflexible will, deep faith, and an ardent piety: these are the indispensable characteristics of a son of God.

418   The Lord can raise children of Abraham from the very stones. But we must make sure that the stone is not crumbly, for though hard rock may be shapeless, it is easier to hew good stone for building from it.

419   An apostle must not remain at the level of the mediocre. God calls him to be fully human in his actions, and at the same time to reflect the freshness of eternal things. That is why the apostle has to be a soul who has undergone a long, patient, and heroic process of formation.

420 You say that you are discovering new things in yourself every day. I answer: you are now beginning to know yourself.

When you really love, you find new ways of loving even more.

421 It would be a very sad thing if anyone looking at the way Catholics in society behave, concluded that they were sheepish and easily imposed upon.

Never forget that our Master was, indeed is, *perfectus Homo*—perfect Man.

422 If the Lord has given you some natural quality or skill, you should not just enjoy it yourself or show off about it; you should use it charitably in the service of your neighbor.

And what better occasion than now will you find to serve, since you live with so many souls who share the same ideal as yourself?

423 Under the pressure and impact of a materialistic, pleasure-loving, faithless world, how can we demand and justify the freedom of not thinking as *they* do, and of not acting as *they do*?

A son of God has no need to ask for that freedom, because Christ won it for us once and for all. But he does need to defend it and practice it whatever the circumstance he finds himself in. Only thus will *they* understand that our freedom is not bound up in our surroundings.

424 Your relatives, colleagues, and friends have noticed the change, and realized that it is not a temporary phase, but that you are no longer the same.

Don't worry, carry on. *Vivit vero in me Christus*—it is now Christ that lives in me—that's what is happening.

425 You should respect those who are capable of saying *No* to you. And you should ask them to give you reasons for their refusal, so that you can learn—or put them right.

426 Once you were pessimistic, hesitant, and apathetic. Now you are completely transformed: you feel courageous, optimistic, and self-confident, because you have made up your mind, at last, to rely on God alone.

427 What a sorry state someone is in when he has marvellous human virtues but a total lack of supernatural outlook, because he will apply those virtues quite easily to his own selfish ends. Meditate upon this.

428 Since you want to acquire a Catholic or universal mentality, here are some characteristics you should aim at:

— a breadth of vision and a deepening insight into the things that remain alive and unchanged in Catholic orthodoxy;

— a proper and healthy desire, which should never be frivolous, to present anew the standard teachings of traditional thought in philosophy and the interpretation of history;

— a careful awareness of trends in science and contemporary thought;

— and a positive and open attitude towards the current changes in society and in ways of living.

429 You have to learn to disagree charitably with others—whenever the need arises—without becoming unpleasant.

430 With the grace of God and a solid formation you can make yourself understood in a backward environment. There, they would find it difficult to follow you if you lacked "the gift of tongues", the capacity to try and reach their understanding.

431 You should always be well-mannered towards everybody, especially towards those who present themselves as your adversaries (you should never have enemies) when you are trying to let them see their mistake.

432 You feel sorry for a spoilt child, don't you? Well then, don't look after yourself so well. Can't you see that you are going to get soft?

Moreover, you must know that the flowers with the sweetest scent are the wild flowers that have grown out in the open, through rain and drought.

433 He will go very far, they say. It is frightening to think of his future responsibility. He has never been known to perform an unselfish act or say a kind word or write anything fruitful. His life is entirely negative. He always gives the impression of being submerged in deep thought, although it is well known that he never cultivated any ideas worth thinking about. His face and manner have the gravity of a mule, and so he has the reputation of being prudent.

He will go very far; but, I ask myself, what will he be able to teach others? How and in what will he serve them if we do not help him to change?

434 The pedant interprets the simplicity and the humility of the wise man as ignorance.

435 Don't be one of those people who, when they receive an order, immediately begin to think about how to change it. They are said to have too much *personality*, but they cause disunity or ruin.

436   Experience, great knowledge of the world, being able to read between the lines, an exaggerated sharpness, a critical spirit. All those things, in your business and social relations, have led you too far, to such an extent that you have become a bit cynical. All that "excessive realism", which is a lack of supernatural spirit, has even invaded your interior life. Through failing to be simple, you have become cold and unfeeling.

437   At heart you are a good chap, but you fancy yourself as a Machiavelli. Remember that to enter into Heaven you have to be a good and honest man, not a tiresome intriguer.

438   That good humor of yours is admirable. But to take absolutely everything as a joke is, you must admit, going too far. But the real position is quite different. Since you do not have the will to take your own affairs seriously, you justify yourself by poking fun at others who are better than you.

439   I do not deny that you are clever. But your unreasonable vehemence leads you to act like a fool.

440   Yours is an unbalanced character. You are a broken keyboard. You play very well on the high notes and on the low notes, but no sound comes from the ones in the middle, the ones used in ordinary life, the ones people normally hear.

441 Take note from this: I told a certain learned, noble, and upright man, on a memorable occasion, that by defending a holy cause, which "good people" were attacking, a high post in his field was at stake—he was going to lose it. With a voice full of human and supernatural seriousness, despising the honors of this earth, he answered: "It is my soul that is at stake".

442 Diamonds are polished with diamonds, and souls with souls.

443 "A great sign appeared in Heaven: a woman adorned with the sun, with the moon under her feet, and a crown of twelve stars about her head." From this, you and I and everyone may be sure that nothing perfects our personality so much as correspondence with grace.

Try to imitate the Virgin Mary and you will be a complete man or woman.

PRAYER

444 Conscious of our duties, can we let a whole day go past without remembering we have a soul?

In our daily meditation, we have always to put things right lest we depart from the way.

445 If you abandon prayer you may at first live on spiritual reserves, and after that, by cheating.

446 Practise meditation for a fixed period and at a fixed time. Otherwise we would be putting our own convenience first; that would be a lack of mortification. And prayer without mortification is not at all effective.

447 You lack interior life: that is because you do not consider in your prayer other people's concerns and proselytism; because you do not make an effort to see things clearly, to make definite resolutions and fulfill

them; because you do not have a supernatural outlook in
your study, in your work, in your conversations, and your
dealings with others.

Are you living in the presence of God? For that is a
consequence and a manifestation of your prayer.

448 You haven't been praying? Why, because you
haven't had time? But you do have time. Furthermore,
what sort of works will you be able to do if you have not
meditated on them in the presence of the Lord, so as to
put them in order? Without that conversation with God,
how can you finish your daily work with perfection?
Look, it is as if you claimed you had no time to study
because you were too busy giving lessons. Without study
you cannot teach well.

Prayer has to come before everything. If you do not
understand this and put it into practice, don't tell me that
you have no time: it's simply that you do not want to pray.

449 Pray, and pray more. It may seem odd to say that
now when you are taking examinations and working
harder. But you need prayer, and not only the habitual
prayer as an exercise of devotion; you also need to pray
during odd moments, to pray between times, instead of
allowing your mind to wander on stupidities.

It does not matter if, in spite of your effort, you do not
manage to concentrate and be recollected. That meditation

may be of greater value than the one you made, with all ease, in the oratory.

450 Here is an effective custom for achieving presence of God: your first appointment every day should be with Jesus Christ.

451 Prayer is not the prerogative of monks; it is a Christian undertaking of men and women of the world who know themselves to be children of God.

452 Certainly, you have to follow your way: a man of action...with a contemplative vocation.

453 A Catholic, without prayer? It is the same as a soldier without arms.

454 Thank the Lord for the enormous gift he has granted you by making you understand that "only one thing is necessary." And along with that thanksgiving may no day go past without your offering a prayer of petition for those who as yet have no idea of this duty or do not understand it.

455 When they were *fishing* for you, you would ask yourself where they got that strength and fire which burned everything in sight. Now as you pray you realize

that this is the source that wells up within the true children
of God.

456   You belittle meditation. Might you not be afraid,
and so seek anonymity since you dare not speak with
Christ face to face?

You must see that there are many ways of *belittling*
meditation, even though you might say you are practising
it.

457   Prayer is a time for holy intimacies and firm
resolutions.

458   How much sense there was in the plea of a soul
who said: "Lord, don't abandon me; can't you see that
there is *another person* who is tugging at my feet?"

459   Will the Lord return and enkindle my soul? Your
head assures you that he will come and so, deep down,
does a faint sense of longing which is perhaps hope. On
the other hand, your heart and will (too much of the
former and too little of the latter) cast a paralyzing and
deadly melancholy over everything, like a sneer of bitter
mockery.

Listen to the promise of the Holy Spirit: "Within a very
short time, he who has to come will come and will not
delay. In the meantime, the just man lives by faith".

460 True prayer which absorbs the whole individual benefits not so much from the solitude of the desert as from interior recollection.

461 We prayed that evening right out in the country as night was falling. We must have looked rather peculiar to anyone who saw us and did not know what we were up to: sitting on the ground in silence, which was interrupted only by the reading of some points for meditation.

That prayer under the open sky, *hammering away* for everyone there with us, for the Church, for souls, was fruitful and pleasing to Heaven. Any place is fitting for that encounter with God.

462 I am glad that in your prayer you tend to go far: you contemplate lands different from the one in which you find yourself; before your eyes pass people of other races; you hear different tongues. It is like an echo of that commandment of Jesus, *Euntes docete omness gentes—* go, teach all nations.

To go ever further, you must enkindle that fire among those around you. Your dreams and ambitions will become reality: sooner, more, and better!

463 Your prayer will sometimes be intellectual; less often, it may be full of fervor; and, perhaps often, dry,

dry, dry. But what matters is that you, with the help of God are not disheartened.

Consider the sentry on duty. He does not know if the King or the Head of State is in the palace: he is not told what he might be doing, and generally the public figure does not know who is on guard.

It is not at all like that with our God. He lives where you live, he cares for you, and knows your innermost thoughts. Do not abandon the guard-duty of your prayer!

464 Look at the set of senseless reasons the enemy gives you for abandoning your prayer. "I have no time"—when you are constantly wasting it. "This is not for me". "My heart is dry..."

Prayer is not a question of what you say or feel , but of love. And you love when you try hard to say something to the Lord, even though you might not actually say anything.

465 "Just one minute of intense prayer is enough". Someone who never prayed must have said that.

Would someone in love think it enough to contemplate intensely the person they love for just a minute?

466 That ideal of fighting—and winning—Christ's battles can become a reality only by prayer and sacrifice, by Faith, and Love. Let us pray, then, and believe, and suffer, and Love!

467 Mortification is the drawbridge that enables us to enter the castle of prayer.

468 Do not be discouraged. However unworthy the person is, however imperfect the prayer turns out to be, if it is offered with humility and perseverance, God always hears it.

469 A penitent soul prayed: "Lord, I do not deserve to be heard, because I am wicked." But he added: "Yet... listen to me *quoniam bonus*—because you are good."

470 Our Lord sent out his disciples to preach, and when they came back he gathered them together and invited them to go with him to a desert place where they could rest. What marvellous things Jesus would ask them and tell them! Well, the Gospel is always relevant to the present day.

471 I understand perfectly when you write to me about your apostolate: "I am going to pray for three hours, studying Physics. It will be a bombardment so that another position, which is on the other side of the library table, *falls*—you have met him already when he came round here".

I remember how happy you were when you heard me say that prayer and work can easily go together.

472   The Communion of Saints: that young engineer understood it well when he told me: "Father, on such a day, at such a time, you were praying for me".

This is and will always be the first and most fundamental help that we can provide for souls: prayer.

473   Acquire the habit of saying vocal prayers in the morning, while you are dressing, like little children. You will have greater presence of God later during the day.

474   For those who use their intelligence and their study as a weapon, the Rosary is most effective. Because that apparently monotonous way of beseeching Our Lady as children do their Mother, can destroy every seed of vainglory and pride.

475   "Immaculate Virgin, I know very well that I am only a miserable wretch, and all I do is increase each day the number of my sins..." You told me the other day that was how you spoke to Our Mother.

And I was confident in advising you with assurance to pray the Holy Rosary. Blessed be that monotony of Hail Marys which purifies the monotony of your sins!

476 A sad way of not praying the Rosary is to leave it for the end of the day.

If you say it when going to bed, it will be done at best badly and with no meditation on the mysteries. It will be difficult then to avoid routine, which is what drowns true piety, the only piety worth the name.

477 The Rosary is said not with the lips alone, muttering Hail Marys one after the other. That is the way over-pious old men and women rattle them off. For a Christian, vocal prayer must spring from the heart, so that while the Rosary is said, the mind can enter into contemplation of each one of the mysteries.

478 You always leave the Rosary for later, and you end up not saying it at all because you are sleepy. If there is no other time, say it in the street without letting anybody notice it. It will, moreover, help you to have the presence of God.

479 "Pray for me," I said as I always do. And he answered in amazement: "But is something the matter?"

I had to explain that something is the matter or happens to us all the time; and I added that when prayer is lacking, "more and more weighty things are the matter".

480 Renew your acts of contrition during the day. You must realize that Jesus is being offended constantly, and unfortunately, these offenses are not being atoned for at the same rate.

That is why I have so often said: "Acts of contrition, the more the better!" Echo my words with your life and your advice.

481 The scene of the Annunciation is a very lovely one. How often we have meditated on this. Mary is recollected in prayer. She is using all her senses and her faculties to speak to God. It is in prayer that she comes to know the divine Will. And with prayer she makes it the life of her life. Do not forget the example of the Virgin Mary.

WORK

482 Work is man's original vocation. It is a blessing from God, and those who consider it a punishment are sadly mistaken.

The Lord, who is the best of fathers, placed the first man in Paradise *ut operaretur*, so that he would work.

483 To study, to work: these are inescapable duties for all Christians. They are means of defending ourselves from the enemies of the Church and of attracting, with our professional prestige, so many souls, who, being good, fight in isolation. They are the most fundamental weapons for whoever wants to be an apostle in the midst of the world.

484 I ask God that you may take as your model Jesus as an adolescent and as a young man, both when he disputed with the doctors in the temple and when he worked in Joseph's workshop.

485 Of Jesus' thirty-three years, thirty were spent in silence and obscurity, submission and work.

486 That big young man wrote to me saying: "My ideal is so great that only the sea could contain it". I answered: "And what about the Tabernacle, which is so 'small'; and the 'common' workshop of Nazareth?"

It is in the greatness of ordinary things that he awaits us!

487 Before God, no occupation is in itself great or small. Everything gains the value of the Love with which it is done.

488 Heroism at work is to be found in *finishing* each task.

489 Let me stress this point: it is in the simplicity of your ordinary work, in the monotonous details of each day, that you have to find the secret, which is hidden from so many, of something great and new: Love.

490 You say it helps you a lot to wonder how many businessmen have become saints since the time of the early Christians.

And you want to show that it is also possible today. The Lord will not abandon you in that effort.

491 You too have a professional vocation which *spurs* you on. Well, that *spur* is the hook to fish men.

Rectify your intention, then, and be sure you acquire all the professional prestige you can for the service of God and of souls. The Lord counts on this too.

492 To finish things you have to start them.

It seems a truism, but you so often lack that simple decision. And how satan rejoices in your ineffectiveness!

493 You cannot sanctify work which humanly speaking is slapdash, for we must not offer God badly-done jobs.

494 By neglecting small details you could work on and on without rest and yet live the life of a perfect idler.

495 You asked what you could offer the Lord. I don't have to think twice about the answer: offer the same things as before, but do them better, finishing them off with a loving touch that will lead you to think more about him and less about yourself.

496 Here is a mission for ordinary Christians which is heroic and will always be relevant to the present day: to carry out in a holy way all different kinds of occupations even those that might seem least promising.

497 Let us work. Let us work a lot and work well, without forgetting that prayer is our best weapon. That is why I will never tire of repeating that we have to be contemplative souls in the midst of the world, who try to convert their work into prayer.

498 You are writing to me in the kitchen, by the stove. It is early afternoon. It is cold. By your side, your younger sister—the last one to discover the divine folly of living her Christian vocation to the full—is peeling potatoes. To all appearances—you think—her work is the same as before. And yet, what a difference there is!

It is true: before she *only* peeled potatoes, now, she is sanctifying herself peeling potatoes.

499 You say that you are now beginning to understand what a *priestly soul* means. Don't be annoyed with me if I tell you that the facts show that you only realize it in theory. Every day the same thing happens to you: at night time, during the examination, it is all desire and resolutions; during the morning and afternoon at work, it is all objections and excuses.

Are you in this way living a "holy priesthood, to offer spiritual sacrifices, acceptable to God through Jesus Christ?"

500 When you started your ordinary work again, something like a groan of complaint escaped you: "It's always the same!"

And I told you: "Yes, it's always the same. But that ordinary job—which is the same one your fellow workers do—has to be a constant prayer for you. It has the same loveable words, but a different tune each day".

It is very much our mission to transform the prose of this life into poetry, into heroic verse.

501 We read in the Scriptures: *Stultorum infinitus est numerus*, the number of fools is infinite, and they seem to grow more every day. In all sorts of places, in the most unexpected situations, under the mantle of high office and respected positions—and even in the guise of virtue— you will have to put up with so much stupidity and so little good judgment.

But I do not understand how you can lose the supernatural view of life and give up caring. There is nothing you can do but put up with these situations, though your interior dispositions must be very poor if you put up with them for human motives.

If you do not help these people to find the right way by doing your work responsibly and finishing it well— by sanctifying it, that is—you will become like them, a fool. Either that or an accomplice.

502 You really do need to make an effort and put your shoulder to the wheel. For all that, you should put your professional interests in their place: they are only means to an end; they can never be regarded—in any way—as if they were the basic thing.

These attacks of *professionalitis* stop you being united with God!

503 Forgive my insistence: the instrument, the means, must not be made into an end. If a spade were to weigh a hundred-weight instead of what it should, the laborer would be unable to dig with it. He would use up all his energy humping it around, and the seed could not take root, for it would remain unused.

504 It has always been the same: however upright and blameless the behavior of someone at work may be, it can easily arouse rivalry, suspicion and envy. If you occupy a position of authority, remember that some people may have prejudices against a particular colleague, but that is not sufficient reason for getting rid of "the accused". It could be a sign, rather, that he would be useful in a greater enterprise.

505 Obstacles? Sometimes they may be present, but at times you just invent them out of cowardice or love of comfort. How cleverly the devil makes those excuses for not working look plausible! He knows full well that sloth is the mother of all vices.

506 You are untiring in your activity. But you fail to put order into it, so you do not have as much effect as you should. It reminds me of something I heard once from a very authoritative source. I happened to praise a subordinate in front of his superior. I said, "How hard he works!" "You ought to say", I was told, " 'How much he rushes around!' "

You are untiring in your activity, but it is all fruitless. How much you rush around...

507 You tried to belittle somebody else's work by mumbling. "He has only done his duty".

And I said. "Does that seem so little to you?" The Lord gives us the happiness of Heaven for doing our duty: *Euge serve bone et fidelis...intra in gaudium Domini tui*—Well done, good and faithful servant, enter into eternal joy!

508 The Lord has the right to be glorified by us "at every moment"—it is an obligation for each one of us. So if we waste time we are robbing God of his glory.

509 You know that the task is urgent, and that one minute given to comfort is time taken from glory of

God. Why, then, do you hesitate to make conscientious use of every moment?

Moreover, I ask you to think whether the minutes you have to spare throughout the day, which taken together come to hours, might not be prompted by your disorder and laziness.

510   Sadness and uneasiness grow in proportion to the time you waste. When you feel a holy impatience to use every minute you will be filled with joy and peace, because you will not be thinking about yourself.

511   What was I concerned about? I replied that I felt no concern, for I had concerns enough to keep me busy.

512   You are going through a critical stage. You feel a certain vague fear and find it difficult to adapt your plan of life. Your work seems to weigh you down, since twenty-four hours are not enough to do everything you ought to each day.

Have you tried following the Apostle's advice: "let all things be done decently and according to order"? That means, in the presence of God, with him, through him, and only for him.

513 When you parcel out your time, you need also to think how you can make use of the odd moments that become free at unforeseen times.

514 I have always seen rest as time set aside from daily tasks, never as days of idleness.

Rest means recuperation: to gain strength, form ideals, and make plans. In other words it means a change of occupation, so that you can come back later to give a new impetus to your daily job.

515 Now that you've got a lot to do, your "problems" have disappeared. Be honest: as you have made up your mind to work for him, you no longer have time to think about your own selfish interests.

516 Ejaculatory prayers do not hinder your work, just as the beating of your heart does not impede the movements of the body.

517 Sanctifying one's work is no fantastic dream, but the mission of every Christian—yours and mine.

That is what the lathe-worker had discovered, when he said: "I am overwhelmed with happiness when I think how true it is that while I am working at the lathe and singing—singing all the time, on the outside and on the inside—I can become a saint. How good God is!"

518   Your work has become disagreeable, especially when you see how little your colleagues love God and at the same time flee from grace and the good services you want to render them.

You have to try to make up for all that they leave out. You must give yourself to God in work too, as you have done up to now, and convert it into prayer that rises to Heaven for all mankind.

519   Working with cheerfulness is not the same as "working away merrily" with no depth, as if you were getting rid of a troublesome burden.

You must try not to lessen the value of your efforts through lack of attention or superficiality, so that in the end you are in danger of coming to God empty-handed.

520   Some people act out of prejudice in their work: on principle they trust nobody, and it goes without saying that they do not understand the need to seek to sanctify their job. If you mention it to them they tell you not to add another burden to their own work, which they put up with reluctantly as if they were supporting a heavy weight.

That is one of the battles of peace we have to win: to find God in our work and, with him and like him, serve others.

521 You are put off by difficulties, and you shrink back. Do you know what characterizes your behavior? Nothing but comfort, comfort, and more comfort.

You had said that you were ready to wear yourself out, unstintingly, yet you still seem to be at the level of an apprentice to heroism. It is time to act with more maturity.

522 As a student, you should dedicate yourself to your books with an apostolic spirit, and be convinced in your heart that one hour added to another already make up—even now—a spiritual sacrifice offered to God and profitable for all mankind, your country and your soul.

523 You have a warhorse called study. You resolve a thousand times to make good use of your time, yet you are distracted by the merest thing. Sometimes you get annoyed at yourself, because of your lack of willpower, even though you begin again every day.

Have you tried offering up your study for specific apostolic intentions?

524 It is easier to bustle about than to study, but it is also less effective.

525 If you know that study is apostolate, but limit yourself to studying just enough to get by, it is clear that your interior life is going badly.

If you are so careless you will lose the right spirit. Just like the worker in the parable who cunningly hid the talent he had received, you may, if you do not put things right, exclude yourself from God's friendship, and be stuck in the mire of your comfort-seeking calculations.

526 You must study…, but that is not enough.

What do those who kill themselves working to feed their self-esteem achieve? Or those who have nothing else in mind but assuring peace of mind for a few years ahead?

One has to study—to gain the world and conquer it for God. Then we can raise the level of our efforts: we can try to turn the work we do into an encounter with the Lord and the foundation to support those who will follow our way in the future.

In this way, study will become prayer.

527 I have seen many people live heroic lives for God without leaving their own place of work, and I have come to this conclusion: for a Catholic work is not just a matter of fulfilling a duty—it is to love, to excel oneself gladly in duty and in sacrifice.

528 When you come to understand that ideal of fraternal work for Christ, you will feel better, more secure, and as happy as one can be in this world, which so many are bent on making distorted and bitter by following their own selfish aims alone.

529 Sanctity is made up of heroic acts. Therefore, in our work we are asked for the heroism of *finishing* properly the tasks committed to us, day after day, even though they are the same tasks. If we don't, then we do not want to be saints.

530 I was convinced by that priest who is a friend of ours. He was talking about his apostolic work, and he assured me that there are no tasks of little importance. Hidden under this garden covered in roses, he said, is the silent effort of so many souls who with their work and prayer, their prayer and work, have won from Heaven abundant showers of grace, which makes everything fertile.

531 Place on your desk, in your room, in your wallet, a picture of Our Lady, and look at it when you begin your work, while you are doing it, and when you finish it. She will obtain, I can assure you, the strength for you to turn your task into a loving dialogue with God.

FRIVOLITY

532 When one thinks clearly about the poor things of this world, and compares them with the riches of life with Christ there is only one plain word, I can't help thinking, for the road that people choose: stupidity, stupidity, stupidity.

It is not just that most of us men make mistakes. There is something much worse about us: we are complete and utter fools.

533 It is sad that you do not want to remain hidden as a foundation stone and support the building. But to become a stumbling block for others? I think that is villainous!

534 Do not be scandalized because there are bad Christians who are active but do not practice. The Lord, says the Apostle, "will render to every man according to his works"; to you for yours, and to me, for mine.

If you and I make up our minds to behave well to begin with, there will be two fewer scoundrels in the world for a start.

535 If you do not fight against being frivolous, your head will be like a junk shop: you will only be storing up impossible ideals, false hopes, and...old rubbish.

536 You are very independent-minded. If you made use of this in a supernatural way, it would help you to become a great Christian. But the way you use it just makes you very free and easy.

537 You take everything so lightly that I am reminded of the old story. The cry went up: "There is a lion coming!" And the naturalist answered: "Why tell me? I catch butterflies".

538 A terrible person is one who is ignorant but at the same time works tirelessly.

Take care that even when you are old and decrepit, you keep on wanting to be better trained.

539 This is the excuse of a frivolous and selfish man: "I don't want to commit myself to anything".

540 You neither want to be an evil man nor a good one. And so, limping on both legs, you will have mistaken your way and filled your life with emptiness.

541 *In medio virtus*—Virtue is to be found in the mean, the wise saying goes, warning us against extremism. But do not make the mistake of turning that advice into a euphemism for your own comfort, calculation, tepidity, easy-goingness, lack of idealism, and mediocrity.

Meditate on these words of Sacred Scripture: "Would that you were cold or hot. But because you are lukewarm, and neither cold nor hot, I will vomit you out of my mouth".

542 You never reach the kernel of things. You always concern yourself with accidentals. Allow me to repeat what Sacred Scripture says: you have only "spoken in the wind".

543 Don't behave like those people who after hearing a sermon, instead of applying the doctrine to themselves, they think: that would suit So-and-so very well.

544   Sometimes people think there is no malice in slander. It is the hypothesis, they say, by which ignorance explains what it does not know or understand, so as to appear well-informed.

But it is doubly evil: as ignorance and as a lie.

545   Do not speak so irresponsibly. Don't you realize that as soon as you throw the first stone others—anonymously—will organize a full-scale stoning?

546   Is it you who are creating that atmosphere of discontent among those around you? Forgive me then for having to tell you that, apart from being bad, you are plain stupid.

547   When some misfortune or mistake occurs, it is poor satisfaction to be able to say: "I knew it would happen".

It would mean that you are unconcerned with the troubles of your neighbor, for you should have sought a remedy if it was in your power to do so.

548   There are many ways of sowing confusion. It is enough, for instance, to speak of the exception as if it were the general rule.

549 You say you are a Catholic. That is why I feel so sorry for you when I see that your convictions lack the solidity needed to let you practice Catholicism in action, without introducing reservations or compartmentalizing your life.

550 It would be laughable, if it were not so sad, to see the naivete with which you accept—through superficiality, ignorance, or an inferiority complex—the most transparent nonsense.

551 People who are stupid, unscrupulous, or hypocritical, think that the others are just the same. And—this is the real pity—they treat them as if they were.

552 It would be bad if you were to waste your time, which is not yours but God's and is meant for his glory. But if on top of that you make others waste it, you both diminish your own standing and defraud God more of the glory you owe him.

553 You lack the maturity and composure appropriate for those who make their way through this life with the certainty of an ideal, of a goal. Ask the Blessed Virgin to teach you how to praise God with your whole heart, without distractions of any kind.

NATURALNESS

554 The risen Christ: the greatest of miracles was seen by only a few—by those who needed to see. Naturalness is the signature of divine enterprises.

555 When one works wholly and exclusively for the glory of God one does everything with naturalness, like someone who is in a hurry and will not be delayed by "making a great show of things". In this way one does not lose the unique and incomparable company of the Lord.

556 Why, you asked indignantly, should the surroundings in which the apostolate has to be carried out and the things used to do it be ugly, dirty—and complicated? And you added: "It would take no more effort to do it well!"

I thought your indignation very reasonable. And I pondered how Jesus talked to everyone and attracted them all: poor and rich, wise and ignorant, cheerful and sad, young and old. How lovable and natural—supernatural —is his figure.

557 To be effective you must be natural. What can one expect of a brush—even in the hands of a great painter—if it is wrapped in a silk cover?

558 Saints always make other people feel *uncomfortable*.

559 Saints, abnormal? The time has come to do away with the prejudice.

We have to teach, with the supernatural naturalness of Christian asceticism, that not even mystical phenomena mean abnormality. These phenomena have their own naturalness, just as other psychological or physiological things have theirs.

560 I talked to you about the horizon which opens up before our eyes and of the road we have to follow. "I have no objections", you said, as if surprised at not having any.

Engrave this deeply on your mind: there is no reason why there should be!

561 Avoid that ridiculous adulation which, perhaps unconsciously, you pay to the person in charge, so that you automatically echo his opinions on points of no consequence.

At the same time, you must be much more careful not to keep on showing up his defects as if they were amusing details or to become too familiar, detracting from his authority. Take care too not to render the sad service of letting the bad practice grow of turning something bad into a bit of a joke.

562 You are creating an artificial climate around yourself, characterized by suspicion and a lack of trust. For when you speak, you give the impression of someone playing chess: you say each word thinking four moves ahead.

Notice that the Gospel, when describing the wary and hypocritical character of the scribes and Pharisees, relates that they asked Jesus questions and put certain problems to him *ut caperent eum in sermone*—to twist his words. Flee from such behavior.

563 Naturalness has nothing to do with rusticity, or being shabby, or doing things poorly, or being bad-mannered.

Some people are determined to reduce the service of God to working in the world of miserable and—forgive the expression—*lousy* poverty. Such work is and will always be admirable; but if we stop there, apart from abandoning the vast majority of souls, what should we do when we have brought them out of their need—ignore them?

564 You are unworthy, are you? Well, try to become worthy. And let that be the end of it.

565 How you long to be extraordinary. The trouble with such an ambition is how very vulgar it is.

566 "Blessed are you for believing", said Elizabeth to our Mother. Union with God, supernatural virtue, always brings with it the attractive practice of human virtues: Mary brought joy to her cousin's home, because she *brought* Christ.

TRUTHFULNESS

567 You were praying before a crucifix, and you made this resolution: it is better to suffer for the truth, than for truth to suffer because of me.

568 So often it seems impossible for the truth to be true, above all because it always has to be lived consistently.

569 If you are annoyed at being told the truth, then... why do you ask?

Is it perhaps that you want to be answered with your own "truth" so your errant ways can be justified?

570 You say that you have a great respect for the truth. Is that why you always place yourself at such a *respectful* distance from it?

571 Don't behave like a fool. No one is ever a fanatic for wanting to know better every day, and love more, and defend with greater conviction the truth he has to know, love, and defend.

On the other hand—I say this without fear—those who oppose this reasonable behavior in the name of a false liberty become sectarian.

572 It is as easy now as it was at the time of Jesus Christ to say *No*, to deny or to put to one side the truth of faith. You who call yourself a Catholic have to start from *Yes*.

Later after some study, you will be able to explain the reasons for your certainty, and that there is no contradiction—there can be none—between Truth and science, between Truth and life.

573 Do not deviate from the way, even though you have to live with people who are full of prejudices. Do not abandon the task as if you thought the basis of arguments or the meaning of words were fixed by their behavior or by their assertions.

Do try to get them to understand you, but if you don't manage it, carry on anyway.

574 You will find people who, because of their dull stubbornness, will be very difficult to convince. But, apart from those cases, it is worthwhile clearing up discrepancies, and clearing them up with all the patience that might be needed.

575 Some people listen—and want to listen—to nothing but the words they carry in their own heads.

576 The understanding that so many people demand of others is that everyone should join their party.

577 I cannot believe in your truthfulness if you feel no uneasiness—a disagreeable uneasiness too—when you countenance the smallest and most harmless lie. It is far from being small or harmless for it is an offense against God.

578 Why do you look about you and listen and read and talk with such a mean intention, and why do you try to gather up the "bad things" to be found, not in the intention of others, but only in your own soul?

579 For the reader who lacks an upright intention the honesty of the writer is hard to find.

580   The sectarian sees only sectarianism in all the activities of others. He measures his neighbor by the narrowness of his own mind.

581   I felt pity for that man in office. He suspected that there might have been some problems, which are, after all, to be expected in life, yet he was taken aback and annoyed when he was told about them. He preferred to remain ignorant of them, to live in the shadow or twilight of his vision, to that he might remain at ease.

I advised him to face up to these things openly and clearly, so that in this very way they could be got rid of. I assured him that then he would truly live in peace.

You must not solve problems, your own or those of others, by ignoring them; this would be nothing short of laziness and comfort-seeking, which would open the door to the action of the devil.

582   Have you fulfilled your duty? Have you had a right intention? You have? Then do not worry if there are twisted people who discover evil which only exists in their own minds.

583   Inquisitive people asked you whether you judged that decision of yours, which they considered indifferent, to be good or bad.

And, with a sure conscience, you answered: "I know only two things: that my intention is honest and that I know how much it cost me". And you added: God is the reason and the purpose of my life, that is why I am convinced that nothing can be indifferent.

584 You explained your ideals and your sure, firm conduct as a Catholic, and he seemed to accept and understand your way. But afterwards you were left doubting whether he might not have smothered his understanding under his not very well-ordered habits.

Seek him out again, and explain to him that one accepts truth in order to live by it or try to live by it.

585 "Who are they to want to try things out first? Why do they have to be mistrustful?" you ask me. Look, tell them this from me: they should mistrust their own wretchedness. And then you must continue along your own way in peace.

586 You feel sorry for them. With a complete lack of honesty they throw stones and pretend they haven't done so.

Listen to what the Holy Spirit has to say about them: "The forgers of error shall be confused and put to shame;

they will all be covered in ignominy". It is a judgement which will be inexorably fulfilled.

587 You say that many people libel and slander that apostolic enterprise? Well, as soon as you proclaim the truth, there will at least be one person who is not criticizing.

588 In the most beautiful and promising field of wheat it is easy to weed out cartloads of charlock, poppies and couchgrass.

Throughout history, the most upright and responsible people have been the object of volumes of malice. Think, too, how much has been said and written against Our Lord Jesus Christ.

I advise you—just as with the field of grain—to collect the golden ripe ears of wheat: the real truth.

589 You assured me that you want to have a clean conscience, so do not forget that to pick up a calumny without denying it is to become a refuse-collector.

590 You call it open-mindedness to admit easily any assertion against a person without hearing what he has to say. This propensity of yours is not precisely justice— even less is it charity.

591 A calumny sometimes causes harm to those who suffer it. But it truly dishonors those who invent it and spread it. And afterwards they carry a weight in the depth of their souls.

592 "Why do many people spread slander?", you ask in distress. Some do so through error, fanaticism or malice. But most of them pass on the story through inertia, superficiality, and ignorance.

That is why, I insist again: when you cannot praise, and there is no need to speak, keep quiet!

593 When the victim of the slander suffers in silence, "the executioners" are relentless in their bold cowardice.

Distrust those categorical assertions if those who utter them have made no attempt, or have preferred not to speak with the person concerned.

594 There are many ways of holding an investigation. With a bit of malice, by listening to slanders, ten large volumes can be compiled against any honest person or worthy enterprise. There will be more if that person or enterprise works effectively. And even more if that effectiveness is apostolic.

It is sorry work for the investigators, but more pitiful still is the attitude adopted by those who are ready to echo such wicked and superficial assertions.

595 "These people", he said sadly, "do not have the mind of Christ, but the mask of Christ". That is why they lack Christian judgment, cannot grasp the truth, and yield no fruit.

We, the sons of God, must not forget that the Master said: "Whoever listens to you, listens to me…" That is why we have to try to be Christ: never a caricature of him.

596 In this case, as in so many others, people are doing various things and all think they are right. But God is guiding them, that is to say, over and above their own particular ideas, God's inscrutable and most lovable Providence will win through in the end.

Allow yourself, therefore, to be *guided* by the Lord, without opposing his plans, even though they might go against your "basic assumptions".

597 It is painful to see that some people are less concerned with learning and taking possession of the treasures acquired by science than they are in spending their time tailoring them to their own taste through a more or less arbitrary process. But being aware of this must lead you to redouble your effort to go more deeply into the truth.

598 It is easier to write against people carrying out research, or against those who make new discoveries in science or technology, than to do the research oneself. But we should not allow those "critics" to pretend at the same time to set themselves up as absolute lords of wisdom who can govern the opinions of the ignorant.

599 "I just don't see that, it is not at all obvious", he said in response to the certain statements of the others. And the obvious thing was his own ignorance.

600 You are afraid of hurting people, of creating divisions, and appearing intolerant..., and you are giving in on positions and points (though you assure me they are not serious) which have fateful consequences for many.

Forgive my sincerity: through your behavior, you are falling into just the stupid and harmful intolerance that you were concerned to avoid: that of not allowing the truth to be proclaimed.

601 God in his infinite and perfect justice and mercy treats with the same love, but in an unequal way, his unequal children.

That is why equality does not mean using the same measure for everybody.

602 You speak a half-truth which is open to so many interpretations that it can really be called... a lie.

603   Doubt, whether it concerns the field of knowledge or the good name of others, is a plant that is easily sown but very difficult to root out.

604   You remind me of Pilate: *Quod scripsi, scripsi!*— what I have written shall not be changed—after he had allowed the most horrible of crimes. You may be immovable, but you ought to have adopted that attitude before, not afterwards!

605   It is a virtue to act in accordance with one's resolutions. But if in the course of time the facts change, one must also act accordingly by changing the way of looking at the problem and solving it.

606   Do not confuse holy intransigence with rude stubbornness.

"I'll break, but I won't give in", you said with a certain haughtiness.

Listen carefully: A broken instrument remains useless, and leaves the way open for those who, with apparent leniency, afterwards impose a *damaging* intransigence.

607   *Sancta Maria, Sedes Sapientae*—Holy Mary, Seat of Wisdom. Invoke Our Mother often in that way, so that she may fill her children, in their study, work, and social relations, with the Truth that Christ has brought to us.

AMBITION

608 Against those who reduce religion to a set of negative statements, or are happy to settle for a watered-down Catholicism; against those who wish to see the Lord with his face against the wall, or to put him in a corner of their souls, we have to affirm, with our words, and with our deeds, that we aspire to make Christ the King reign indeed over all hearts, theirs included.

609 When you work in apostolic enterprises, do not build for the present alone. Dedicate yourself to these tasks with the hope that others—brothers of yours sharing the same spirit as you—may reap what you are now sowing abroad, and may crown the buildings for which you are now laying the foundations.

610 When you truly become filled with the Christian spirit your ambitions will be put right. You will feel no longer a hankering after celebrity, but a desire for passing on your ideal.

611 It would not be worth giving oneself unless it were to build up a great work which is very much for God—your own sanctity.

That is why the Church when canonizing saints proclaims the heroism of their lives.

612 When you work in earnest for the Lord, your greatest satisfaction will be to discover that there are many others competing with you.

613 During the time that God has granted you in this world, make up your mind in earnest to do something worthwhile; time is pressing and the mission of men— and women—on earth is most noble, heroic, and glorious when it enkindles shrunken and dried-up hearts with the fire of Christ.

It is worthwhile taking peace and happiness to others through a strong and joyful crusade.

614 You are ready to give your life for your honor... Be ready to give up your honor for your soul.

615 Through the Communion of Saints you should feel very closely united to your brothers. Defend that holy unity without fear.

If you were alone, your noble ambitions would be
doomed to failure. A sheep on its own is nearly always
a lost sheep.

616 I was amused by your vehemence. Faced by the
lack of material resources to set to work, and with no one
to help you, you said: "I have only two arms, but I
sometimes feel impatient enough to become a monster
with fifty arms to sow and reap the harvest".

Ask the Holy Spirit for that effectiveness, for he will
grant it to you!

617 You found yourself with two books in Russian,
and you felt an enormous desire to learn that language.
You imagined the beauty of dying like a grain of wheat
in that nation, now so arid, which in time will yield
enormous crops of wheat.

I think that those ambitions are good. But, for now,
dedicate yourself to the small task and great mission of
every day, to your study, your work, your apostolate, and,
above all, to your formation. This, since you still need to
do so much pruning, is neither a less heroic nor a less
beautiful task.

618 What use is a student who does not study?

619   When you find studying is an awfully uphill task offer that effort to Jesus. Tell him that you continue poring over your books, so that you may use your knowledge as a weapon to fight the enemy and so gain many souls. You can then be sure that your study is well on its way to becoming prayer.

620   If you waste hours and days, if you kill time, you are opening doors of your soul to the devil. That way of behaving is equivalent to saying to him: "Make yourself at home".

621   I grant you it is difficult not to waste time. But notice that God's enemy, the *other side*, does not rest.

What is more, remember the truth that Paul, a champion of the love of God, proclaims, *Tempus breve est*! This life is slipping away through our fingers, and it is impossible to recover it.

622   Do you realize how much depends on whether you are soundly prepared or not? Many, many, souls!

And now will you cease to study or work with perfection?

623   There are two ways of reaching the top: one—the Christian way—by noble and gallant effort of serving others; the other—the pagan way—by the mean and ignoble effort of dragging down your neighbor.

624 Don't try to convince me that you live facing God, if you do not try always and in everything to face men, any man, with sincere and open fraternity.

625 Those who are "ambitious", with small, personal, miserable ambitions, cannot understand that the friends of God should seek to achieve something through a spirit of service and without such "ambition".

626 You are anxious for one thing: to hurry and soon be forged, molded, polished, and hammered into a useful implement which will fulfill effectively the work it has been designed to do. This work is the mission it has been assigned to, in the vast field of Christ.

I pray a great deal that this desire of yours may spur you on when you are tired, when you fail, and in the hour of darkness, for "the mission it has been assigned to in the vast field of Christ" cannot change.

627 Fight courageously against that false humility— you should call it spirit of comfort—which stops you from behaving like a good son of God. You have to grow out of it.

Are you not ashamed when you see that your elder brothers have spent years in dedicated work, and you are not yet able, or do not want to be able, to lift a finger to help them?

628 Allow your soul to be consumed by desires— desires for loving, for forgetting yourself, for sanctity, for Heaven. Do not stop to wonder whether the time will come to see them accomplished, as some pseudo-adviser might suggest. Make them more fervent every day, for the Holy Spirit says that he is pleased with *men of desires*.

Let your desires be operative and put them into practice in your daily tasks.

629 If the Lord has called you a *friend* you must respond to the call and walk with a hurried pace, with all the urgency needed, at God's pace. Otherwise, you run the risk of becoming a simple spectator.

630 Forget about yourself. May your ambition be to live for your brothers alone, for souls, for the Church; in one word, for God.

631 In the middle of rejoicing at the feast in Cana, only Mary notices that they are short of wine. A soul will notice even the smallest details of service if, like her, it is alive with a passion for helping its neighbor, for God.

HYPOCRISY

632 Hypocrisy always leads those who cultivate it to a life of bitter and grudging mortification.

633 Herod said: "Go and inquire carefully for the child, and when you have found him, bring me back word, so that I too may come and worship him". Faced by such a proposal, let us ask the Holy Spirit to keep us from the "protection" or the "promise of good things" of people who appear well-intentioned.

We will not lack the light of the Paraclete if, as the Wise Men did, we seek the truth and speak with sincerity.

634 Are there people who protest because you say things clearly?

Perhaps they live with a troubled conscience, and they need to cover it up in that way.

You should continue to behave in the same way, to help them to change.

635   While you continue to interpret in bad faith the intentions of your neighbor, you have no right to demand that people should be understanding with you.

636   You are constantly talking about the need to change and reform things. Good. Reform yourself, for you need it badly, and already you will have begun the great reform.

In the meantime, I shall not be putting too much faith in your proclamations of reform.

637   There are some who are so pharisaical that they are scandalized when others repeat precisely what their own lips have let fall.

638   You are such a busybody that it seems as if your only concern were to dive into the lives of your neighbors. And when, at last, you stumble upon an upright man of good will and energy who has stopped you in your tracks, you complain in public as if he had offended you.

Your shamelessness and deformed conscience..., have led you thus far. And that goes for many others.

639   In one move, you have tried to appropriate the "honesty" of the true opinion and the ignoble "advantages" of the opposite opinion...

In any language, that is called duplicity.

640 How good they are! They are ready to "excuse" what is only worthy of praise.

641 It is an old stratagem for the persecutor to say that he is being persecuted. Popular wisdom has seen right through this all along. In the words of the old Spanish saying: "They throw the stone and then bandage themselves up".

642 Is it not true, unfortunately, that many people spread calumnies unjustly and then make their appeal to charity and honesty so that their victims cannot defend themselves?

643 It is a sad ecumenism indeed when Catholics ill-treat other Catholics!

644 What a mistaken view of objectivity they have when they focus upon people or tasks through the deformed lenses of their own defects and then, with acid shame-lessness, criticize or dare to offer their advice.

Let us make a firm resolution: when we correct or give advice, let us speak in the presence of God, and apply our words to our own behavior.

645 Never have recourse to the always deplorable method of organizing slanderous attacks on anyone. It is even worse if it is done through allegedly moral motives, which can never justify an immoral action.

646 You can never give advice dispassionately or with the right intention, if you get upset or think people show a lack of confidence in you when they also listen to the advice of other people of proven formation and good doctrine.

If you are really interested, as you claim, in the good of souls and in stating the truth, why are you offended?

647 Not even to Joseph does Mary communicate the mystery that God has wrought in her. This lesson teaches us not to become accustomed to speaking lightly but to channel our joys and our sorrows correctly without seeking praise or sympathy. *Deo omnis gloria!*—all for God!

INTERIOR LIFE

648 Those who are nearest are the first to be heard. That is why you must get close to God and be intent on becoming a saint.

649 I like to compare the interior life to clothing, to the wedding garment the Gospel speaks about. The cloth is woven from all the habits or acts of piety which, like threads, together give strength to the cloth. And so, just as a torn dress is rejected even though the rest of the material is in good condition, if you pray and work but are not penitent (or the other way round) your interior life is not (so to speak) complete.

650 When will you realize that your only possible way is to seek sanctity seriously.

Make up your mind—don't be offended—to take God seriously. That levity of yours, if you do not fight against it, could end up by becoming a sad and blasphemous mockery.

651 You sometimes allow the bad side of your character to come out, and it has shown itself, on more than one occasion, in an absurd harshness. At other times, you do not bother to prepare your heart and your head so that they may be a worthy dwelling for the Most Holy Trinity. And you invariably end up by remaining rather distant from Jesus, whom you know so little.

Going on like this, you will never have interior life

652 *Iesus Christus, perfectus Deus, perfectus Homo—* Jesus Christ, perfect God and perfect Man.

There are many Christians who follow Christ and are astonished by his divinity, but forget him as Man. And they fail in the practice of supernatural virtues, despite all the external paraphernalia of piety, because they do nothing to acquire human virtues.

653 Personal sanctity is a remedy for everything. That is why the saints have been full of peace, of fortitude, of joy, of security.

654 Until now you had not understood the message that we Christians bring to the rest of men: the hidden marvel of the interior life.

What a wonderful new world you are placing in front of them.

655 How many things you have discovered! And yet you are sometimes rather naive and think you have seen everything, that you have found out everything already. As time goes by, you will be able to reach out and touch the unique and unfathomable treasures of the Lord, who will always show you *new things*, if you respond with love and sensitivity. Then you will realize that you are only beginning, because holiness consists in identifying oneself with God, with that God of ours who is infinite and inexhaustible.

656 It is through Love rather than study that one comes to understand the *things of God*.

That is why you have to work, you have to study, you have to accept illness, you have to be sober—lovingly.

657 Here is a point for your daily examination. Have I allowed an hour to pass, without talking with my Father God? Have I talked to him with the love of a son? You can!

658 We should make no mistake. God is no shadowy or distant being who created us, then abandoned us; nor is he a master who goes away and does not return. Though we do not perceive him with our senses, his existence is far more true than any of the realities which we touch and see. God is here with us, really present, living. He sees and hears us, he guides us, and knows our smallest deeds, our most hidden intentions.

We believe this—but we live as if God did not exist. For we do not have a thought or a word for him; for we do not obey him, nor try to control our passions; for we do not show that we love him, and we do not atone...

Are we going to continue living with a dead faith?

659 If you had presence of God you would remedy many things that have apparently "no remedy".

660 How are you going to live in God's presence if you are only looking around everywhere?—It is as if you were drunk with novelties and futilities.

661 It is possible that you might be frightened by this word: meditation. It makes you think of books with old black covers, the sound of sighs, and the irksome repetition of routine prayers. But that is not meditation.

To meditate is to consider, to contemplate God as your Father, and yourself as his son in need of help. And then to give him thanks for all that he has given you and for all that he will give you.

662 This is the only way to get to know Jesus: speak to him. You will always find in him a Father, a Friend, an Adviser, a Helper in all the noble deeds of your everyday life.

And getting to know him will give rise to Love.

663 You go on attending some classes daily, merely because in them you acquire a certain rather limited knowledge. How is it then that you are not constant in going to the Master, who is always ready to teach you the science of interior life, with its eternal content and savor?

664 What is a man or the greatest reward on earth worth compared with Jesus Christ, who is always ready to be with you?

665 To meditate for a while each day and be united in friendship with God is something that makes sense to people who know how to make good use of their lives. It befits conscientious Christians who live up to their convictions.

666 Those in love do not know how to say good-bye: they are with one another all the time.

Do you and I know how to love the Lord like this?

667 Haven't you noticed how people in love dress to please one another by their appearance? Well, that is how you should fit out and deck your soul.

668 Grace, like nature, normally acts gradually. We cannot, properly speaking, move ahead of grace. But in all that does depend on us we have to prepare the way and cooperate when God grants grace to us.

Souls have to be encouraged to aim very high; they have to be impelled towards Christ's ideal. Lead them to the highest goals which should not be reduced or made weaker in any way. But remember that sanctity is not primarily worked out with one's own hands. Grace normally takes its time, and is not inclined to act with violence.

Encourage your holy impatience, but do not lose your patience.

669 Is corresponding to divine grace, you ask, a matter of justice or generosity?

It is a matter of Love!

670 "My affairs buzz around in my head at the most inopportune moments", you say.

That is why I have recommended you to try to establish some times for interior silence, and to guard your external and internal senses.

671 "Stay with us, it is towards evening…" The prayer of Cleophas and his companion was effective.

How sad it would be if you and I were not able to *detain* Jesus who is passing by. What a shame not to ask him to stay!

672 I advised you to read the New Testament and to enter into each scene and take part in it, as one more of the characters. The minutes you spend in this way each day enable you to *incarnate* the Gospel, reflect it in your life, and help others to reflect it.

673 Once you used to "enjoy" yourself a lot. But now that you bear Christ within you, your whole life has been filled with a sincere and infectious joy. That is why you attract other people.

Get to know him better, so that you can reach all people.

674 Be careful you don't get it wrong. While you raise the temperature of the atmosphere around you make sure you do not cool down.

675 Get accustomed to referring everything to God.

676 Have you noticed how many of your companions know how to be very kind and considerate when dealing with the people they love, whether it is their girlfriend, their wife, their children, or their family?

Tell them that the Lord does not deserve less, and ask it of yourself too. May they treat him in that way. Tell them that if they continue being kind and considerate, but do it with him and for him, they will achieve, even here on earth, a happiness they had never dreamed of.

677 The Lord sowed good seed in your soul. And for that sowing of eternal life he used the powerful means of prayer. For you cannot deny that often while you were in front of the Tabernacle, face to face with him, he made you hear in the depths of your soul that he wanted you for himself, that you had to leave everything. If you denied it now you would be a miserable traitor. And if you have forgotten it you are ungrateful.

Do not doubt, for you have never doubted it up to now, that he has also used the supernatural advice and suggestions of your director, who has insistently repeated to you things that you cannot ignore. At the beginning, too, in order to deposit the good seed in your soul he used that noble, sincere friend, who told you some solid truths which were filled with the love of God.

But you have discovered with surprise that the enemy has sown cockle in your soul. And he will continue to sow it, as long as you are comfortably asleep and slacken off in your interior life. That, and no other, is the reason why you find clinging to your soul all sorts of worldly weeds, which sometimes seem as if they are going to choke the grain of the good wheat you have received.

Uproot them once and for all. The grace of God is enough for you. Do not be afraid of leaving an empty space, a wound. The Lord will plant new seed of his there: love of God, fraternal charity, apostolic zeal. And after a certain time not the slightest sign will remain of the cockle. That is if, while there is still time, you pull it out by the roots, and better still, if you do not fall asleep, and watch your field overnight.

678 Jesus speaks to us all the time, and happy are those blessed souls who, when they hear Jesus being spoken about, recognize him immediately as the Way, the Truth, and the Life.

You are well aware that when we do not enjoy that happiness it is because we have lacked the determination to follow him.

679 Once again you felt Christ was very near. And once again you realized that you have to do everything for him.

680 Come closer to the Lord. Closer! Until he becomes your Friend, your Guide, in whom you can trust.

681 Every day you notice that you are more rooted in God, you tell me. Every day, then, you will be closer to your brothers.

682 If until now, when you had not yet found him, you wanted to run through life with your eyes wide open, to find out about everything, from this moment onwards you can run with a clear vision, to see with him what is really of abiding interest to you.

683 When there is interior life, you can have recourse to God in any contradiction, with the spontaneity with which blood rushes to a wound.

684 "This is my Body...", and the immolation of Jesus took place, hidden under the appearances of the bread. He is now there, with his Flesh and with his Blood, with his Soul, and with his Divinity. He is the same as on the day that Thomas placed his fingers in his glorious Wounds.

And yet, on so many occasions, you saunter by, giving not even a hint of a greeting out of simple good manners that you would give to any person you knew when you met him.

You have much less faith than Thomas!

685 If, in order to gain for you your liberty, a close friend of yours had gone to prison, would you not try to visit him, to talk to him for a while, bring him some present, console him, and show him the warmth of your friendship? And, if that conversation with the prisoner were to save you from some evil and do you good, would you go without it? And if instead of a friend it were to be your own father or your brother, what then?

686 Jesus has remained in the Sacred Host for us so as to stay by our side, to sustain us, to guide us. And love can only be repaid with love.

How could we not turn to the Blessed Sacrament each day, even if it is only for a few minutes, to bring him our greetings and our love as children and as brothers?

687 Imagine the scene. An old sergeant or a young lieutenant sees coming towards him a fine-looking recruit, of an incomparably better quality than the officer, but the salute and its return are still given.

Meditate on the contrast. From the tabernacle of that Church, Christ, perfect God, perfect Man, who has died for you on the Cross and gives you everything that you need, approaches you. And you go by without paying any attention to him.

688 You have started to visit the Blessed Sacrament every day, and I am not surprised to hear you say, "I have come to love the sanctuary light madly".

689 Do not neglect to say, "Jesus, I love you", and make one spiritual communion, at least, each day, in atonement for all the profanations and sacrileges he suffers because he wants to be with us.

690 Do you not greet warmly all the people you love, and speak to them cordially? Well, you and I are going to greet Jesus, Mary, and Joseph, and our Guardian Angels, many times a day.

691 Develop a lively devotion for Our Mother. She knows how to respond in a most sensitive way to the presents we give her.

What is more, if you say the Holy Rosary every day, with a spirit of faith and love, Our Lady will make sure she leads you very far along her Son's path.

692 Without Our Mother's aid, how can we manage to keep up our daily struggle? Do you seek it constantly?

693 The Guardian Angel always accompanies us as our principal witness. It is he who, at your particular judgment, will remember the kind deeds you performed for Our Lord throughout your life. Furthermore, when you feel lost, before the terrible accusations of the enemy, your Angel will present those intimations of your heart—which perhaps you yourself might have forgotten—those proofs of love which you might have had for God the Father, God the Son, God the Holy Spirit.

That is why you must never forget your Guardian Angel, and that Prince of Heaven shall not abandon you now, or at that decisive moment.

694 Your Communions were very cold: you paid little attention to the Lord: you were distracted by the smallest trifle. But ever since you began to realize during an intimate dialogue with God that the angels are present, your attitude has changed. You say to yourself: "Let them not see me like this".

And see how, as a result of thinking, "What will they say?"—this time, for a good motive—you have advanced a little towards Love.

695 When you see yourself with a dry heart, without knowing what to say, go with confidence to the Virgin Mary. Say to her, "My Immaculate Mother, intercede for me".

If you invoke her with faith, she will make you taste in the midst of your dryness the proximity of God.

PRIDE

696 Pull self-love out by the roots and plant in its place love for Jesus Christ. That is the secret of effectiveness and happiness.

697 Although you say you follow him, in one way or another you always make sure that it is *you* who do things, according to *your* plans, relying on *your* strength alone. But the Lord said: *Sine me nihil!*—without me you can do nothing.

698 They ignored what you call your "rights", which I translated for you as your "right to be proud". What a grotesque figure you cut. Because your attacker was powerful you could not defend yourself and you felt the pain of a hundred blows. And despite it all, you have not learned to humble yourself.

Now your conscience accuses you, calling you proud and cowardly. Give thanks to God because you are beginning to catch a glimpse of your "duty to be humble".

699   All the time it is you, you, you. And you will never be effective until it is him, him, him, so that you act *in nomine Domini*—in the name and with the strength of God.

700   How can you pretend to follow Christ, if you only revolve around yourself?

701   An impatient and disordered anxiousness to climb up the professional ladder can mask self-love under the appearances of "serving souls". It is a lie—and I really mean that—when we seek to justify our actions by saying that we must not miss certain opportunities, certain favorable chances.

Turn your eyes back to Jesus; he is "the Way". During his hidden years, there were also "very favorable" chances to advance his public life—when he was twelve years old, for instance, and the doctors of the law were in amazement at his questions and at the answers he gave. But Jesus Christ fulfilled the Will of his Father, and he waited. He obeyed.

Do not lose that holy ambition of yours to lead the whole world to God, but when certain possibilities present

themselves (they might show perhaps a desire to desert)
remember that you too have to be obedient and work
away at that obscure job, which does not seem at all
brilliant, for as long as God asks nothing else of you. He
has his own times and paths.

702 Those who enjoy privilege thanks to money,
ancestry, rank, position or intelligence and abuse it by
humiliating those who are less fortunate, show that they
are fatuous and proud.

703 Pride sooner or later ends up humiliating a man
in front of others, however much of "a man" he is, for
he will have been acting like a vain and brainless puppet,
moved by satan's strings.

704 Through presumption or simply through vanity,
many people run a *black market* to raise their own personal
worth artificially.

705 Positions. Who's in, who's out? What does it
matter to you? You have come, you tell me, to be useful,
to serve, with complete availability. Behave accordingly.

706 You comment and criticize. Without you, it seems,
nothing is done properly.

Don't be angry if I tell you that you are behaving like an arrogant despot.

707 A friend of yours, loyally and charitably, points out to you, on your own, certain things which tend to mar your behavior. You are convinced that he is mistaken: he does not understand you. If that false conviction, born of your pride, remains, you will never change.

I pity you: you lack the decision to seek holiness.

708 Malicious, suspicious, devious, mistrustful, grudging... these are all adjectives which you deserve, even though they might annoy you.

You must put things right. Why is it others always have to be bad, and you good?

709 You feel lonely; everything annoys you, and you complain. That is because you are isolated from your brothers by your selfishness, and because you do not come closer to God.

710 You are always trying to be noticed publicly. Above all you want more notice to be taken of you than of others.

711 Why do you always think that everything they say has a hidden meaning? By being so touchy you are limiting the action of grace all the time. And do not doubt that grace comes to you by means of those who fight to match their deeds to Christ's ideal.

712 For as long as you are convinced that others should always live as if they depended on you, and for as long as you delay the decision to serve (to hide yourself and disappear from view), your dealings with your brothers, colleagues, and friends will be a constant source of disappointment, ill-humor, and pride.

713 Detest showing off. Reject vanity. Fight against pride, every day, at every moment.

714 The proud, poor creatures, have to suffer a thousand silly little things which their self-love makes out to be enormous but are unnoticed by others.

715 Do you think that no one else has ever been twenty years old? Do you think they were never restricted by their parents when they were under age? Do you think they avoided the problems, however great or small, that you come up against? No. They went through the same things that you are going through now, and they matured, with the help of grace. They trod down their selfishness with generous perseverance, gave in when they should, and remained loyal—with calm humility—without being arrogant or hurting anyone when they should not have done.

716 Ideologically you are very Catholic. You like the atmosphere of the hall of residence. A pity the Mass is not at twelve, and the classes are not in the afternoon, so you could study late in the evening after one or two drinks. That "Catholicism" of yours does not come up with the real thing: it remains simply *bourgeois*.

Don't you see that you can't think like that at your age? Leave behind your laziness and your self-worship, and adapt to the needs of others, to the reality around you, then you will be taking your Catholicism seriously.

717 A person who had donated a statue of a saint to a church said: "This saint owes everything that it is to me".

This is not just a caricature. You also think— at least that is how it looks from your behavior—that you fulfill your duties towards God just by wearing some medals or practicing certain pious customs, more or less as a routine.

718 "If only they could see the good things I do". But don't you realize that you are carrying them around like trinkets in a basket for people to see how fine they are?

Furthermore, you must not forget the second part of Jesus' command: "that they may glorify your Father who is in heaven".

719 "To me, with the admiration I owe myself", he wrote on the first page of a book. And many other miserable souls might easily print the same thing on the last page of their life.

How sad it would be if you and I were to live or end up like this. Let us make a serious examination of conscience.

720 Never adopt a superior air towards Church matters, or towards your fellow human beings—your brothers. On the other hand that attitude might be necessary in your social behavior, when it is a matter of defending the interests of God and those of souls, for then you would not be acting out of superiority, but out of faith and fortitude, which we practise with a calm and humble confidence.

721 It is indiscreet, childish, and silly to say nice things about others and praise their good qualities in front of them.

In this way vanity is encouraged, with the risk of *stealing* glory from God, to whom everything is due.

722 Make sure that your good intentions are always accompanied by humility. For good intentions often go together with harsh judgments, almost amounting to an incapacity to yield, and a certain personal, national or party pride.

723 Do not be disheartened when you become aware of your mistakes. React against them.

Sterility is not so much a consequence of one's faults, especially if one repents, as a consequence of pride.

724 If you fall, get up with greater hope. Self-love alone is incapable of understanding that an error, when put right, helps us to know and to humble ourselves.

725 "We are no use", is a pessimistic and false statement. If we want to, with the help of God, which is the first and fundamental requirement, we can become useful, as a good instrument, for many enterprises.

726 It made me think when I heard that hard but true saying from a man of God, when he observed the haughtiness of a miserable creature: "He wears the same skin as the devil—pride".

And there came to my mind, in contrast, a sincere desire to wrap myself in the virtue taught by Jesus Christ when he said, *Quia mitis sum et humilis corde*—I am meek and humble of heart. It was the virtue which attracted the gaze of the Most Holy Trinity to his Mother and our Mother: the humility of knowing and being aware of our nothingness.

FRIENDSHIP

727 When you find it difficult to do a favor or a service for someone, remember that he or she is a child of God, and that the Lord has asked us to love one another.

Furthermore, go deeper into that evangelical precept every day; do not remain on the surface. Draw the right conclusions from it—it is quite easy to do so. Then adapt your conduct, on every occasion, to those requirements.

728 "There is so much hurry in the way we live that Christian charity has become a rare phenomenon in this world of ours, even though, at least nominally, Christ is being preached".

I grant you that. But what are you doing about it? For, as a Catholic, you have to become united to him, and follow in his footsteps. For we have been told that we must go and teach his doctrine to all peoples—*all* peoples—throughout the ages.

729 Through all the course of history men have always sought to work together to accomplish a collective mission and destiny.

Is the *unique destiny* of eternal life worth less to the men and women of today?

730 You understood the meaning of friendship when you began to feel that you were like the shepherd of a little flock which you had left abandoned, but were now trying to gather together again, taking it upon yourself to serve each one of them.

731 You cannot just be passive. You have to become a real friend of your friends. You can help them first with the example of your behavior and then with your advice and with the influence that a close friendship provides.

732 The spirit of fraternity and companionship you discovered unexpectedly filled you with enthusiasm. That is natural, for it was something you had dreamed about longingly but had never experienced. You had not experienced it because men forget they are brothers of Christ, that lovable Brother of ours, who gave his life for us, for every single one of us, without reserve.

733 You have had the good fortune to find real teachers, authentic friends, who have taught you everything you wanted to know without holding back. You have had no need to employ any tricks to *steal* their knowledge, because they led you along the easiest path, even though it had cost them a lot of hard work and suffering to discover it. Now, it is your turn to do the same, with one person, and another—with everyone.

734 Meditate upon this carefully and act accordingly: people who think you are unpleasant will stop thinking that when they realize that you *really* like them. It is up to you.

735 It's not enough to be good; you need to show it. What would you say of a rose bush which produced only thorns?

736 To be warmed up, the tepid need to be surrounded by the fire of enthusiasm.

Many could say to us: "There is no point in your lamenting my situation. Teach me how to get out of this condition which saddens you so much".

737 Your duty to be a brother to all souls will lead you to practice the "apostolate of little things", without others noticing it. You will want to serve them so that their way becomes pleasant.

738 Those who zealously keep a list of grudges show themselves to be very narrow-minded souls. Such poor wretches are impossible to live with.

True charity neither keeps account of the necessary services it renders all the time, nor takes note of the effronteries it has to put up with. *Omnia suffert*—it endures all things.

739 You fulfill a demanding plan of life: you rise early, you pray, you frequent the sacraments, you work or study a lot, you are sober and mortified, but you are aware that something is missing.

Consider this in your conversation with God: since holiness, or the struggle to achieve it, is the fullness of charity, you must look again at your love of God and your love of others for his sake. Then you may discover, hidden in your soul, great defects that you have not even been fighting against. You may not be a good son, a good brother, a good companion, a good friend, a good colleague. And, if you love *your holiness* in a disordered manner, you are envious.

You *sacrifice* yourself in many small *personal* details, and so you are attached to yourself, to your own person. Deep down you do not live for God or for others, but only for yourself.

740 You consider yourself a friend because you say nothing bad. That is true, but I see in you no sign of giving good example or service.

This kind makes the worst friends.

741 For a start, you treat people badly. Then, before anybody has time to react, you say: "Now, we must all be charitable".

If you began with the second point you would never come to the first.

742 Don't be someone who sows discord, like the person whose mother would say of him: "Introduce him to your friends, and he will make sure those friends quarrel with you".

743 I can see no Christian fraternity in a friend who warns you: "I've been told some terrible things about you. You shouldn't trust some of your friends".

I think it is not Christian because that *brother* has not taken the honest approach of silencing the slanderer first, and then telling you his name out of loyalty.

If that *brother* does not have the strength of character to demand such behavior of himself, he will end up making you live on your own, driving you to distrust everyone and to be uncharitable towards everyone.

744 You don't have an ounce of supernatural vision and it is only their social standing that you notice. Souls mean nothing to you at all, nor do you serve them. That is why you are not generous but live far from God with your false piety, even though you may pray a lot.

The Master has said very clearly: "Depart from me... into that eternal fire...for I was hungry...I was thirsty...I was in prison...and you did not care for me".

745 It is impossible to love God with perfection, and at the same time to let yourself be ruled by selfishness— or by apathy—in your dealings with your neighbor.

746 True friendship also means making a heartfelt effort to understand the convictions of our friends, even though we may never come to share them or accept them.

747 Never allow weeds to grow on the path of friendship. Be loyal.

748 Let us make a firm resolution about our friendships. In my thoughts, words, and deeds towards my neighbor, whoever he may be, may I not behave as I have done up to now. That is to say, may I never cease to practice charity, or allow indifference to enter my soul.

749   Your charity must be adapted and tailored to the needs of others, not to yours.

750   Being children of God transforms us into something that goes far beyond our being people who merely put up with each other. Listen to what the Lord says: *Vos autem dixi amicos*! We are friends who, like him, give our lives for each other, when heroism is needed and throughout our ordinary lives.

751   How do we suppose that people who do not have our faith can come to the Holy Church if they see the unhandsome way in which those who call themselves followers of Christ treat each other?

752   Your agreeable behavior should become more attractive by improving in kind and intensity. Otherwise, your apostolate will die out in closed and lifeless rooms.

753   Through your friendship and doctrine—or rather through charity and the message of Christ—you will move many non-Catholics to help in earnest and to do good to all men.

754   Take note of the words of that working man who commented so enthusiastically after he had attended a gathering you had organized: "I had never heard people speak as they do here, about being noble, honest, kind, and generous". And he concluded in amazement: "Compared to the materialism of the Left or the Right, this is the true revolution".

Any soul can understand the fraternity Christ has established. Let us make a point of not adulterating that doctrine.

755 Sometimes you try to excuse yourself, saying that you are distracted or absent-minded, or that it is your character to be dry and reserved. That, you add, is why you don't even know very well the people you live with.

Listen, isn't it true that this excuse doesn't really satisfy you?

756 I advised you to inject a great deal of supernatural outlook into every detail of your ordinary life. And I added immediately that living with other people provided you with ample opportunity throughout the day.

757 Practicing charity means respecting other people's way of thinking. It means rejoicing at their road to God, without trying to make them think like you or joining you.

It occurred to me to put this consideration to you. These other ways are different, but parallel; each person will reach God by following his own way. Don't get sidetracked in comparisons, or in wanting to know who is higher. That does not matter; what does matter is that we should all attain the end.

758 You say that he is full of defects. Very well...but, apart from the fact that people who are perfect are found only in Heaven, you too have defects, yet others put up with you and, what is more, appreciate you. That is because they love you with the love Jesus Christ had for his own, and they had a fair number of shortcomings.

Learn from this.

759 You complain that he shows you no understanding. I am certain he does as much as he can to try to understand you. But what about you? When will you make a bit of an effort to understand him?

760 All right, I agree. That person has behaved badly; his behavior has been reprehensible and unworthy; he deserves no merit at all.

Humanly speaking he deserves to be utterly despised, you added.

I understand what you mean, I can assure you, but I do not share this concluding view of yours. That life which seems so mean is sacred. Christ has died to save it. If he did not despise it, how can you dare to?

761 If your friendship is brought down to such a level that you become an accomplice in the wretched behavior of others, it will have been reduced to a sad confederacy which deserves no esteem whatsoever.

762 It is true that life, which by its nature is already rather narrow and uncertain, sometimes becomes difficult. But that will help you to become more supernatural and to see the hand of God. Then you will be more human and understanding with those around you.

763 Forbearance is proportional to authority. A simple judge has to condemn—even if he takes into account extenuating circumstances—the convicted criminal who has admitted being guilty. The sovereign power of the country may sometimes grant a pardon or amnesty. God always forgives a contrite soul.

764 "Through you I have seen God, who has forgotten my follies and my offenses, and has welcomed me with the affection of a Father". This is what a contrite prodigal son of the twentieth century wrote to his family when he returned to his father's house.

765 It has cost you a lot to begin getting rid of those niggling worries and forgetting about those personal things you were looking forward to. They may have been few and not very splendid, but they were deeply rooted. In exchange, you are sure now that you are interested and concerned about your brothers, and not only about them, for you have learned to discover Jesus Christ in your neighbor.

766 "A hundredfold!" You remembered a few days ago that promise of the Lord.

In the fraternity that is lived among your companions in the apostolate, I assure you, you will find that hundredfold.

767 How many fears and dangers can be allayed by the true love among brothers which is not mentioned, for then it would seem to be profaned, but which shines in every little detail.

768 Have recourse to the Blessed Virgin every day with complete confidence. Your soul and your life will feel comforted at once. She will let you partake of the treasures she keeps in her heart, for "never has it been known that anyone who sought her protection was left unaided".

THE WILL

769 To advance in interior life and apostolate, you do not need devotion that you can feel, but a definite and generous disposition of the will to respond to what God asks of you.

770 Without the Lord you will not be able to take one sure step forward. This conviction that you need his help will lead you to be more united to him, with a strong, enduring confidence, accompanied by joy and peace, even though the road might become hard and steep.

771 Look at the great difference between the natural and supernatural way of acting. The first begins well, but later ends up slackening. The latter begins equally well, and later struggles to become even better.

772 It is not at all bad to behave well for upright human reasons. But what a difference it makes when the supernatural ones *rule*.

773 When he saw the happiness with which that hard work was being done, that friend asked: "Is it through enthusiasm that you get these tasks done?" And they answered him happily and calmly: "Through enthusiasm? That would be the day! *Per Dominum Nostrum Iesum Christum*!—through Our Lord Jesus Christ, who is constantly awaiting us".

774 The world is waiting for us to wake up those who are asleep, to encourage the timid, to guide those who have lost their way; in other words, for us to enrol them in the ranks of Christ, so that all their energy is not lost.

775 Perhaps you too might find it helpful to make use of this reminder of supernatural things which shows all the sensitivity of willing love. It was what a soul very much given to God used to repeat when he was faced by the various demands made on him. "It is high time to make up your mind in earnest to do something worthwhile".

776 What sort of Christian perfection do you expect to achieve if you are only following your whims and doing "what you like"? All your defects, unless you fight against them, will produce bad works as a natural consequence. And your will, untempered by a persevering fight, will be of no use to you when a difficult occasion arises.

777 The facade appears full of strength and resilience. But how much softness and lack of willpower there is within!

You must hold to your determination not to let your virtues become fancy dress but clothes which define your character.

778 "I know some men and women who do not even have the strength to ask for help", you tell me with sorrow and disappointment. Don't leave them in the lurch. Your desire to save yourself and them can be the starting point for their conversion. Furthermore, if you think about it carefully you will realize that someone also had to lend you a hand.

779 Soft people who complain about a thousand silly trivialities are the ones who do not know how to sacrifice themselves for Jesus in those daily trifles—let alone sacrifice themselves for others.

What a shame if your behavior, which is so hard and demanding with other people, should show the same softness in your daily life.

780 You suffer a lot because you realize that you don't make the grade. You would like to do more, and do it more effectively, but very often you do things in a complete daze, or you don't dare do them at all.

Contra spem, in spem!—live in certain hope, against all hope. Rely on that firm rock which will save you and help you on. It is a wonderful theological virtue, which will encourage you to press on, without being afraid of going too far, and will not let you stop.

Don't look so troubled. Yes, cultivating hope means strengthening the will.

781 Whenever your will weakens in your ordinary work, you must recall these thoughts: "Study, work, is an essential part of my way. If I were discredited professionally as a consequence of my laziness it would make my work as a Christian useless or impossible. To attract and to help others, I need the influence of my professional reputation, and that is what God wants".

Never doubt that if you abandon your task, you are going away from God's plans and leading others away from them.

782 You were scared of following the way of the children of God, for in the name of the Lord you were urged to undertake things, to deny yourself, and climb down from your ivory tower. You excused yourself from

taking part, and I admit that I do not find it at all strange
that you should now feel that weight which is oppressing
you: a set of complexes and hang-ups, of inhibitions and
scruples, which leaves you useless.

Don't be annoyed with me if I tell you that you have
behaved with less courage than depraved people, who
boldly propagate evil, as if you were worse or lower than
them.

Surge et ambula!—get up and walk. Make up your
mind; you can still get rid of that evil dead weight if you
listen with the grace of God to what he is asking, and,
above all, if you do it fully and wholeheartedly.

783 It is good that your soul should be eaten up by
that impatience. But don't be in a hurry. God wants you
to prepare yourself seriously, taking all the months or
years necessary, and is counting on your decision to do
so. With good reason did that emperor say: "Time is my
ally".

784 This is how a right-minded man summarized
jealousy or envy: "They must be very ill-intentioned to
want to stir up such clean waters".

785 You ask if you have to remain silent and inactive.
In the face of unjust aggression against a just law, the
answer is: *No*.

786   Every day you are becoming more exhilarated. It is noticeable in the wonderful self-assurance and confidence that knowing you are working for Christ has given you.

Sacred Scripture has already proclaimed it: *Vir fidelis multum laudabitur*—the faithful man merits praise from all.

787   You have never felt so absolutely free as you do now that your freedom is interwoven with love and detachment, with security and insecurity; for you do not trust yourself at all, but trust in God for everything.

788   Have you seen how water is stored in reservoirs against a time of drought? In the same way, to achieve the even character that you need in times of difficulty, you have to store up cheerfulness, clear insights, and the light which the Lord sends you.

789   As the flames of your first enthusiasm die down, it becomes difficult to advance in the dark. But that progress is the more reliable for being hard. And then, when you least expect it, the darkness vanishes, and the enthusiasm and light return. Persevere.

790   God wants his children to be on the offensive. We cannot stay on the defensive. Our business is to fight, wherever we may be, as an army in battle array.

791 It is not a matter of fulfilling your obligations in a hurry, but of bringing them to a finish without a pause, at God's pace.

792 You have the agreeable manner of an intelligent conversationalist. But you are also very apathetic. "Nobody has come to look for me" is your excuse.

I'll point out what I mean: if you don't change and seek out those who are waiting for you, you will never be an effective apostle.

793 There are three important things you need to do to draw people to God. Forget yourself, and think only of the glory of your Father God. Subject your will filially to the Will of Heaven, as Jesus Christ taught you. Follow with docility the lights of the Holy Spirit.

794 Mary spent three days and three nights looking for the son who was lost. May you and I also be able to say that our willingness to find Jesus knows no rest.

THE HEART

795 You need a heart which is in love, not an easy life, to achieve happiness.

796 After twenty centuries, we have to proclaim with complete conviction that the spirit of Christ has not lost its redemptive force, which alone can satisfy the desires of the human heart. Begin by feeding that truth into your own heart, which will be perpetually restless, as St Augustine wrote, until it rests entirely in God.

797 To love is to cherish one thought, to live for the person loved, not to belong to oneself, happily and freely with one's heart and soul to be subjected to another will… and at the same time to one's own.

798 You still do not love the Lord as a miser loves his riches, as a mother loves her child. You are still too concerned about yourself and about your petty affairs.

And yet you have noticed that Jesus has already become indispensable in your life.

Well, as soon as you correspond completely to his call, he will also be indispensable in each one of your actions.

799 Cry aloud—for that cry is the folly of one in love: "Lord, even though I love you, don't trust me. Bind me to yourself, more closely every day".

800 The heart has been created to love, do not doubt it. Let us therefore bring Our Lord Jesus Christ into the love that we feel. Otherwise, the empty heart takes revenge and fills itself up with the most despicable vileness.

801 There is no heart more human than that of a person overflowing with supernatural sense. Think of Holy Mary, who is full of grace, Daughter of God the Father, Mother of God the Son, Spouse of God the Holy Spirit. Her Heart has room for all humanity and makes no distinction or discrimination. Every person is her son or her daughter.

802 When someone has a very small heart, it seems as if he keeps his desires in a narrow, neglected drawer.

803 Each day you must behave to those around you with great understanding, with great affection, together, of course, with all the energy needed. Otherwise understanding and affection become complicity and selfishness.

804   That friend of ours with no false humility used to say: "I haven't needed to learn how to forgive, because the Lord has taught me how to love".

805   Forgiveness. To forgive with one's whole heart and with no trace of a grudge will always be a wonderfully fruitful disposition to have.

That was Christ's attitude on being nailed to the Cross: "Father, forgive them, they know not what they are doing". From this came your salvation and mine.

806   You were very sorry to hear that most un-Christian comment, "Forgive your enemies: you can't imagine how it angers them!"

You could not keep quiet, and you replied calmly, "I don't want to cheapen love by humiliating my neighbor. I forgive, because I love, and I am hungry to imitate the Master".

807   Carefully avoid anything that can hurt other people's hearts.

808   Out of ten ways of saying *No*, why must you always choose the most disagreeable? Virtue has no wish to hurt.

809 Look: we have to love God not only with our heart, but with *his*, and with the hearts of all humanity throughout time, Otherwise, we should fall short of corresponding to his Love.

810 It distresses me to see those who have given themselves to God giving the impression that they are old bachelors, or allowing themselves to be taken for such, since they possess the Love beyond all loves. They would be old bachelors indeed if they did not know how to love the One who loves so much.

811 Someone has compared the heart to a windmill, moved by the wind of love and passion.

Indeed, that windmill can grind wheat, barley or dried dung. It is up to us.

812 The devil, father of lies and victim of his own pride, tries to imitate the Lord even in the way he seeks converts. Have you noticed that in the same way as God makes use of men to save souls and lead them to holiness, so does satan use other people to impede that work and even to bring them to ruin. And—don't be frightened— in the same way as Jesus sought those who were nearest, relatives, friends or colleagues to be instruments, the devil also often attempts to get the people we love most to lead us into evil.

That is why, if the bonds of blood relationship tie us down and hinder us from following the ways of God, we should cut them promptly. And perhaps your resolve will also release others who were being caught up in the nets of Lucifer.

813 I give you thanks, my Jesus, for your decision to become perfect Man, with a Heart which loved and is most lovable; which loved unto death and suffered; which was filled with joy and sorrow; which delighted in the things of men and showed us the way to Heaven; which subjected itself heroically to duty and acted with mercy; which watched over the poor and the rich and cared for sinners and the just.

I give you thanks, my Jesus. Give us hearts to measure up to yours!

814 Ask Jesus to grant you a Love like a purifying furnace, where your poor flesh—your poor heart—may be consumed and cleansed of all earthly miseries. Pray that it may be emptied of self and filled with him. Ask him to grant you a deep-seated aversion to all that is worldly so that you may be sustained only by Love.

815 You have seen very clearly your vocation to love God, but only with your head. You assure me that you have put your heart into the way you are following. But you say that you are distracted at times, and even attempt to look back. That is a sign that you have not completely put your heart into it. You need to be more sensitive.

816 The master said: "I have come to set a man at variance with his father, and the daughter with her mother, and the daughter-in-law with her mother-in-law". If you fulfill what he demands of you, you will show you really love your parents. That is why you must not use the whole-hearted affection you should have for them as a shield when the moment comes for personal sacrifice. Otherwise, believe me, you will be putting love for your parents before the love of God. And you will be putting your own self-love before love for your parents.

Do you now understand more deeply the relevance of those words of the Gospel?

817 The heart! From time to time, without your being able to help it, your all too human memory casts a crude, unhappy, "uncouth" shadow on your mind.

Go to the tabernacle immediately, at least in spirit, and you will return to light, happiness, and Life.

818 The frequency of our visits to the Lord is in proportion to two factors: faith and the involvement of the heart; seeing the truth and loving it.

819 Love is strengthened by self-denial and mortification.

820 If you had a big heart and were a bit more sincere you would not be troubled by feelings of mortification over little things—nor would you use them to mortify other people.

821 Sometimes it is a duty to feel annoyed; sometimes it is a weakness. But let it last only for a few minutes. Moreover, make sure there is always charity and affection there.

822 You may often have to tell someone off. But you should be teaching him how to correct a defect, never merely demonstrating your bad temper.

823 When you need to correct someone, it should be done clearly and with kindness, even with a smile if that is suitable. It should never, or very seldom, be overpowering.

824 Do you feel as if goodness and absolute truth have been deposited with you, and therefore that you have been invested with a personal title or right to uproot evil at all costs?

You will never solve anything like that, but only through Love and with love, remembering that Love has forgiven you and still forgives you so much.

825 Love good people because they love Christ. Love those too who do not love him because of their misfortune, and especially because Christ loves both kinds of people.

826 The people of that land, so far away from God and lost, reminded you of the Master's words: "They are like sheep without a shepherd".

And you too were filled with a strong feeling of compassion deep within you. Make up your mind, where you are now, to give your life as a holocaust for all.

827 A friend of ours used to say: "The poor are my best spiritual book and the main motive of my prayers. It pains me to see them, and in each one of them, Christ. And because it hurts, I realize I love him and love them".

828 If the love of God is put into friendships, they are cleansed, reinforced, and spiritualized, because all the dross, all the selfish points of view, and excessively worldly considerations are burned away. Never forget that the love of God puts our affections in order, and purifies them without diminishing them.

829   The thought of what has happened to you burns within you. Christ came to you when you were only a miserable leper. Until then, you had developed only one good quality, a generous concern for others. After that encounter you were given the grace to see Jesus in them, you fell in love with him, and now you love him in them. Now the altruism that used to impel you to help your neighbor in certain ways seems very small. You are right to think so.

830   Get accustomed to entrusting your poor heart to the Sweet and Immaculate Heart of Mary, so that she may purify it from so much dross, and lead it to the Most Sacred and Most Merciful Heart of Jesus.

PURITY

831 For everyone, whatever his state—single, married, widowed or priest—chastity is a triumphant affirmation of love.

832 The *miracle* of purity has prayer and mortification as its two points of support.

833 A temptation against chastity is more dangerous the more concealed it is. When it comes insidiously, it is the more deceptive.

Do not give in, not even with the excuse of not wanting to "seem strange".

834 Holy Purity is the humility of the flesh. You asked the Lord for seven bolts on your heart. And I advised you to ask for seven bolts for your heart and eighty years of gravity as well, for your youth.

And be watchful, for a spark is much easier to extinguish than a fire. Take flight, for in this it is low cowardice to be "brave"; a roving eye does not mean a lively spirit, but turns out to be a snare of satan.

Yet human diligence with mortification, the cilice, disciplines and fasting are all worthless without you, my God.

835 This is how a confessor killed concupiscence in a sensitive soul who confessed to a certain curiosity: "Nonsense, it is just a question of male and female instincts".

836 As soon as you willfully allow a dialogue with temptation to begin, the soul is robbed of its peace, just as consent to impurity destroys grace.

837 He followed the way of impurity with all his body and soul. His faith became obscured even though he knew it is not a problem of faith.

838 "You told me, Father, that after my past life it is still possible to become *another* St Augustine. I do not doubt it, and today more than yesterday I want to try to prove it".

But you have to cut out sin courageously from the root, as the holy Bishop of Hippo did.

839 Yes, ask for pardon with contrition and do penance in abundance for the impure things that happened in your past life, but do not try to recall them.

840 That conversation was as dirty as a sewer.

It is not enough to take no part in it. You must show your repugnance for it strongly.

841 It seems as if your *spirit* were growing smaller, shrinking to a little point. And your body seems to grow and become gigantic, until it gains control. It was for you that St Paul wrote: "I buffet my own body, and make it my slave; or I, who have preached to others, may myself be rejected as worthless".

842 One feels sorry for people who say from their own sad experience that you cannot be chaste while living and working in the midst of the world.

If they accepted the consequences of their illogical reasoning, they ought not to feel hurt if others were to insult the memory of their parents, brothers or sisters, wife or husband.

843 That confessor was a bit rough, but he was experienced and managed to stop a soul talking nonsense. He brought him to his senses by saying: "The way you are now means you are acting like a goat; next you will be

happy to behave like a pig; and then what? You will
always be acting like an animal which doesn't know how
to look up to heaven".

844   Perhaps you are... just what you are, a little animal. But you must admit that there are people of integrity who are chaste. Well, don't get upset then, if they
leave you out of things. Those men and women include
in their human plans people with a body and a soul, not
animals.

845   Some people bring children into the world for
their own benefit, to serve their own purposes, out of
selfishness. They forget children are a wonderful gift
from God for which they will have to render a very
special account.

Do not be offended if I say that having offspring just
to continue the species is something that... animals can
do too.

846   No Christian married couple can want to block
the well-springs of life. For their love is based on the
Love of Christ, which entails dedication and sacrifice.
Moreover, as Tobias reminded Sara, a husband and wife
know that "we are children of saints, and we cannot come
together in the way of the Gentiles, who do not know
God".

847   When we were little, we kept close to our mother in a dark alley or if dogs barked at us.

Now, when we feel temptations of the flesh, we should run to the side of Our Mother in Heaven, by realizing how close she is to us, and by means of our aspirations.

She will defend us and lead us to the light.

848   No one is more of a man or more of a woman for leading a disordered life.

Obviously anyone who thinks so would find their ideal of a person in a prostitute, or someone who was perverted and corrupt—that is in those who have rotten hearts and cannot enter the Kingdom of Heaven.

849   May I give you some advice for you to put into practice daily? When your heart makes you feel those low cravings, say slowly to the Immaculate Virgin: "Look on me with compassion. Don't abandon me, my Mother". And recommend this prayer to others.

PEACE

850 In your heart and soul, in your intelligence and in your will, implant a spirit of trust and abandonment to the loving Will of your heavenly Father. From this will arise the interior peace you desire.

851 How can you be at peace if you allow passions you do not even attempt to control to drag you away from the *pull* of grace?

Heaven pulls you upwards; you drag yourself downwards. And don't seek excuses—that is what you are doing. If you go on like that you will tear yourself apart.

852 We have both peace and war within us.

Victory and peace cannot be attained if loyalty and resolve to win the combat are lacking.

853 There is a remedy for those anxieties of yours. Be patient, have rectitude of intention, and look at things with a supernatural perspective.

854 God is with you: so cast far away from you that fear and spiritual agitation. They are reactions to avoid in the first place, for they only serve to multiply temptations and increase the danger.

855 Everything may collapse and fail. Events may turn out contrary to what was expected and great adversity may come. But nothing is to be gained by being perturbed. Furthermore, remember the confident prayer of the prophet: "The Lord is our judge, the Lord gives us our laws, the Lord is our king; it is he who will save us".

Say it devoutly every day, so that your behavior may agree with the designs of Providence, which governs us for our own good.

856 If you fix your sight on God and thus know how to keep calm in the face of worries; if you can forget petty things, jealousies, and envies, you will save a lot of energy, which you need if you are to work effectively in the service of men.

857 Someone we know well told us sincerely, in confidence, that he had never been bored, for he had never been on his own, without our Friend.

It was late in the evening, and there was a great silence. You felt very intently the presence of God. And what peace there was in the knowledge of that reality.

858 One day when you were travelling, a hearty greeting from a brother reminded you that the honest ways of the world are open to Christ. It is just a matter of launching out on them with the spirit of conquerors.

If God has created the world for his children, for them to live in and sanctify, what are you waiting for?

859 You are extraordinarily happy. Sometimes you may find out that God has been abandoned by a son of his. Then, in the midst of the peace and joy deep within you, you feel a pang of grief and a sorrow which arises from affection, but you do not allow it really to disturb or upset you.

All right, but make sure you use all human and supernatural resources available to help him change his mind. And you must trust fully in Jesus Christ. If you do, the waters will return to their course.

860 As soon as you truly abandon yourself in the Lord, you will know how to be content with whatever happens. You will not lose your peace if your undertakings do not turn out the way you hoped, even if you have put everything into them, and used all the means necessary. For they will have *turned out* the way God wants them to.

861 Your forgetfulness and your faults are still there, and they hurt you. At the same time, you go on your way bursting with happiness.

Precisely because they cause you the pain of love, your failings no longer rob you of your peace.

862 When darkness surrounds us and our soul is blind and restless, we have to go to the Light, like Bartimaeus. Repeat, shout, cry out ever more strongly, *Domine ut videam*!—Lord, that I may see. And daylight will dawn upon you, and you will be able to enjoy the brightness he grants you.

863 Fight against your harshness of character, against your selfishness, your spirit of comfort, and your dislikes. We have to be co-redeemers; and, besides, consider carefully that the prize you receive will bear a very direct relation to the sowing you may have done.

864 The task for a Christian is to drown evil in an abundance of good. It is not a question of negative campaigns, or of being *anti* anything. On the contrary, we should live positively, full of optimism, with youthfulness, joy, and peace. We should be understanding with everybody, with the followers of Christ and with those who abandon him, or do not know him at all.

But understanding does not mean holding back, or remaining indifferent, but being active.

865 Through Christian charity and human good manners, you should make an effort not to create an unbridgeable distance between you and anybody else. You should leave a way out for others, so that they need go no further from the Truth.

866 Violence is not a good method for convincing anyone. Even less is it so in the apostolate.

867 A violent person always stands to lose, even though he may win the first battle, for he ends up isolated and hedged around by his lack of understanding.

868 The tactics of a tyrant towards those who could overthrow him if they were united are to make them quarrel among themselves. It is an old ploy of the enemy, the devil and his followers, to destroy many apostolic plans.

869 Those who see adversaries where there are only brothers deny with their works the Christianity they profess.

870   Matters can rarely be resolved by aggressive polemics which humiliate people. And things are certainly never cleared up when among those arguing the case there is a fanatic.

871   I can't understand why you are annoyed and disappointed. They paid you back in your own currency, delighting in insults by word and deeds.

Learn from the lesson and never forget from now on that the people who live with you have a heart too.

872   To help you keep your peace during those times of hard and unjust contradictions I used to say to you: "If they break our skulls, we shall not take it too seriously. We shall just have to put up with having them broken".

873   A paradox: I have had fewer worries on my mind every day since I decided to follow the advice of the psalm: "Cast your cares upon the Lord, and he will sustain you". And at the same time, once we have done whatever needs doing, everything can be solved more easily.

874   Holy Mary is the Queen of peace, and thus the Church invokes her. So when your soul or your family are troubled, or things go wrong at work, in society or between nations, cry out to her without ceasing. Call to her by this title: *Regina pacis, ora pro nobis*—"Queen of peace, pray for us". Have you at least tried it when you have lost your calm? You will be surprised at its .immediate effect.

BEYOND DEATH

875   A true Christian is always ready to appear before God. Because, if he is fighting to live as a man of Christ, he is ready at every moment to fulfill his duty.

876   When facing death, be calm. I do not want you to have the cold stoicism of the pagan, but the fervor of a child of God who knows that life is changed, not taken away. To die is to live!

877   He acquired a Doctorate in law and in philosophy, and was applying for a post as a professor at the University of Madrid. He had specialized in two demanding subjects and had done brilliantly in both. He sent word to me: he was ill, and wanted me to go and see him. I arrived at the lodgings where he was staying. He greeted me with the words: "Father, I am dying". I comforted him affectionately. He wished to make a general confession. That very same night, he died.

An architect friend and a doctor helped me dress the corpse. Seeing that young body, which soon began to decompose, the three of us agreed that two university qualifications were worth nothing compared to the definitive qualification which as a good Christian he had just obtained.

878 There is an answer to everything except death. And death is the answer to everything.

879 Death comes and cannot be avoided. What empty vanity it is, then, to center our existence on this life. See how much many men and women suffer. Some suffer because life is coming to an end and it pains them to leave it; others because it is going on, and they are sick of it. In neither case is there room for the mistaken view that makes our passage through this world an end in itself.

One must leave that way of thinking behind and anchor oneself to another, an eternal one. A total change is required, to empty oneself of self-centered motives, which pass away, and to be renewed in Christ, who is eternal.

880 When you think about death, do not be afraid, in spite of your sins. For he already knows that you love him and what stuff you are made of.

If you seek him, he will welcome you as the father welcomed the prodigal son; but you have to seek him.

881 *Non habemus hic manentem civitatem*—here we have no lasting city. And lest we forget it, at the hour of death this truth appears crudely at times, in lack of understanding, say, or in persecution or in being despised. But there is always a sense of loneliness, for even though we may be surrounded by affection, every person dies alone.

Now is the time to untie all the bonds that bind us. Let us prepare ourselves at all times for that step which will bring us into the eternal presence of the Most Holy Trinity.

882 Time is our treasure, the *money* with which to buy eternity.

883 You were consoled by the idea that life is to be spent, burned in the service of God. And spending ourselves entirely for him is how we shall be freed from death, which brings us the possession of Life.

884 That priest, a friend of ours, worked away while thinking of God, holding on to his paternal hand and helping others to make these fundamental ideas their own. That is why he said to himself: "When you die, all will be well, because he will continue to look after things".

885 Don't make a tragedy out of death, for it is not one. Only unloving children do not look forward to meeting their parents.

886 Everything down here is a handful of dust. Consider the millions of "important" people who have "recently" died and nobody remembers at all.

887 The great Christian revolution has been to convert pain into fruitful suffering and to turn a bad thing into something good. We have deprived the devil of this weapon; and with it we can conquer eternity.

888 The judgment will be dreadful for those who knew the way perfectly well, showed it to others or encouraged them to follow it, but would not go along it themselves.

God will judge and condemn them out of their own mouths.

889 Purgatory shows God's great mercy and washes away the defects of those who long to become one with him.

890 Hell alone is a punishment for sin. Death and judgment are only consequences, which those who are in the grace of God do not fear.

891 If at any time you feel uneasy at the thought of our sister death because you see yourself to be such a poor creature, take heart. Heaven awaits us and consider: what will it be like when all the infinite beauty and greatness, and happiness and Love of God will be poured into the poor clay vessel that the human being is, to satisfy it eternally with the freshness of an ever new joy?

892 When the honest soul is confronted with the cruel injustice of this life, how it rejoices when it remembers the eternal justice of its eternal God!

With the knowledge of its own wretchedness, it utters with a fruitful desire that Pauline exclamation: *Non vivo ego*—it is no longer I who live, but Christ who lives in me. And he will live forever.

893 How happy when they die must be those who have lived heroically every minute of their life! I can assure you it is so, because I have seen the joy of those who have prepared themselves for many years, with calm impatience, for this encounter.

894 Pray that none of us may fail the Lord. It will not be difficult, unless we play the fool. For Our Father God helps us in everything, even by making this our exile on earth last for only a while.

895 The thought of death will help you to grow in the virtue of charity, for it might be that this particular instant in which you are together with one person or another is the last one. They, or you, or I, could be gone at any moment.

896 A soul who was ambitious to be united with God used to say: "Fortunately, we men are not eternal".

897 That piece of information made me think: fifty-one million people die every year; ninety-seven every minute. The Master had already told us when he said: the fisherman throws his nets into the sea; the Kingdom of Heaven is like a drag-net..., and from the catch the good will be selected; the bad, those that are of no use, will be rejected forever. Fifty-one million people die every year, ninety-seven every minute. Tell other people as well.

898 Our Mother went up to Heaven, body and soul. Tell her often that we, her children, do not want to be separated from her. She will hear you!

THE TONGUE

899 Having the gift of tongues is knowing how to transmit the knowledge of God—an essential requisite for whoever is to be an apostle. That is why I ask God Our Lord each day to grant it to everyone of his sons and daughters.

900 Learn how to say *No*, without hurting people unnecessarily or having recourse to the kind of abrupt rejection which destroys charity.

Remember that you are always in the presence of God.

901 Do you object to my repeating in the same way the same essential things without taking into account the latest fashionable trends? Look, the straight line has been defined in the same way for centuries, because it is the clearest and briefest definition. Other definitions would be more obscure and complicated.

902   Acquire the habit of speaking about everyone and about everything they do in a friendly manner, especially when you are speaking of those who labor in God's service.

Whenever that is not possible, keep quiet. Sharp or irritated comment may border on gossip or slander.

903   A young man who had just given himself more fully to God said: "What I need to do now is speak less, visit the sick, and sleep on the floor".

Apply that to yourself.

904   One should speak about Christ's priests only in order to praise them.

I hope with all my heart that my brothers and I bear this in mind in our daily behavior.

905   There are many sides to lying: reticence, intrigue, slander... But it is always the coward's weapon.

906   You are wrong to let yourself be impressed by the first words someone says to you or by the last one.

Listen with respect and interest. Give due credit to people, but carefully ponder your judgment in the presence of God.

907 They spread slander and then make sure themselves that someone comes along immediately to tell you: *"It is said* that..." No doubt that is villainous, but don't lose your peace; the tongue can do you no harm, if you work honestly. Consider how silly they are, how tactless, humanly speaking, and what a lack of loyalty they show towards their brothers—and especially towards God!

And don't go and fall into slander yourself, through an ill-conceived idea of the right to reply. If you have to say anything, make use of fraternal correction as the Gospel advises us.

908 Don't be worried by those contradictions and all that talk. It is true that we are working in a divine undertaking, but we are men. And it is natural that as we walk we raise dust along the road.

If anything bothers you or hurts you, make use of it for your purification and, if necessary, to straighten out your own behavior.

909 Gossip is a very human thing, they say. And I reply: we have to live in a divine manner.

The evil or flippant word of only one man can create a climate of opinion, and even make it fashionable to speak badly about somebody. Then that thin mist of slander rises from below, reaches a high level, and perhaps condenses into black clouds.

But when the man persecuted in this way is a soul of God, the clouds shower down a beneficial rain, come what may; and the Lord ensures that he is exalted by the very means with which they tried to humiliate or defame him.

910   You didn't want to believe it, but you had to yield to the evidence, to your cost. Those statements you made simply and with a sound Catholic sense have been twisted maliciously by enemies of the faith.

It is true that "we have to be simple as doves and wise as serpents". Don't talk out of place or at the wrong time.

911   Because you don't know, or don't want to know, how to imitate that man's upright manner of acting, your secret envy makes you seek to ridicule him.

912   Speaking badly of others is the daughter of envy; and envy is where the sterile seek refuge.

So, now you are faced by sterility, examine the way you see things. If you carry on working and do not get annoyed at others who are also working and obtaining results, then the sterility of your effort will merely be an apparent one. In time you will gather the harvest.

913 Some people seem to think that when they are not causing harm or mortifying others they are at a loose end.

914 Sometimes I think slanderers are like men possessed. For the devil always insinuates himself and his evil spirit here, forever critical of God or God's followers.

915 "They are doing some pretty dreadful things", you say looking down on them.

Do you know them personally? You don't? Then, how can you speak of what you do not know?

916 This is how you should answer a backbiter: "I shall tell the person concerned" or "I shall speak to him about it".

917 A contemporary author has written: "Going around gossiping is always inhuman; it reveals a person of mediocre quality; it is a sign of being uneducated; it shows a lack of refinement of feeling; it is unworthy of a Christian".

918 You should always avoid complaining, criticizing, gossiping. You must avoid absolutely anything that could bring discord among brothers.

919   Having a position of high authority, you would be imprudent to interpret the silence of those who listen to you as a sign of acquiescence. Ask your self whether you allow them to make suggestions, or whether you take offense if they actually let you know what they think. You must change your ways.

920   This has to be your attitude when faced by defamation. First, forgive everyone from the very beginning and with all your heart. Then love. Never fall into a single uncharitable act. Always respond with love.

But if your Mother the Church is being attacked, defend her courageously. Keep calm, but be firm. Have the strength not to give in, and prevent anyone fouling up or blocking the way ahead for Christian souls when they in their turn are eager to forgive and respond with charity to personal insults.

921   Someone who was fed up with gossip once said that he wished the smallest town were the capital.

He didn't realize, poor man, that it would be exactly the same there.

For the love of God and your neighbor, don't fall into such a small-town defect. It is so un-Christian. It was said of the first followers of Christ: "See how they love one another". Can this be said of you, and of me, at all times?

922 Criticisms of apostolic enterprises are usually of two kinds: the work is presented by some people as a most complicated structure; others deem it to be a comfortable and easy task.

In the end, such "objectivity" boils down to narrow-mindedness, with a good dose of idle chatter thrown in. Don't get annoyed, but ask them: "What is it that *you* do?"

923 You might not be able to expect understanding for the demands of your faith, but you do have to ask for respect.

924 Those people you heard speak ill of that loyal friend of God will also speak ill of you when you decide to behave better.

925 Certain comments can hurt only those who consider themselves to be affected. That is why, once you are following the Lord with all your heart and soul, you can accept criticisms as purification, and as a goad to make you lengthen your stride.

926 The Most Holy Trinity has crowned Our Mother.

God the Father, God the Son, God the Holy Spirit, will ask us to render an account of every idle word. That is another reason for asking Holy Mary to teach us always to speak in the presence of the Lord.

SPREADING THE FAITH

927 Be convinced of this: your apostolate consists in spreading goodness, light, enthusiasm, generosity, a spirit of sacrifice, constancy in work, deep study, complete self-surrender, being up-to-date, cheerful and complete obedience to the Church, and perfect charity.

Nobody can give what he does not have.

928 This advice is for you, since you are still young and have just started along your way. As God deserves everything, try to be outstanding professionally, so that you will later be able to spread your ideas more effectively.

929 Don't forget that we will be more convincing the more convinced we are.

930 "Nor do men light a lamp and put it under a bushel, but on a stand, and it gives light to all in the house.

Let your light so shine before men, that they may see your good works, and give glory to your Father who is in heaven".

And at the end of his time upon earth, Christ commanded: *Euntes docete*—go out and teach. He wants his light to shine in the behavior and words of his disciples, and in yours too.

931 It is striking how often, even in the name of freedom, many people fear and oppose Catholics being simply good Catholics.

932 Be on guard against the propagators of scandal and innuendo, which some take in through lack of reflection while others do so through bad faith. They destroy a calm atmosphere and poison public opinion.

Sometimes true charity demands that such abuses and their promoters should be denounced. Otherwise, with their devious or badly-formed consciences, they or those who listen to them could think: "They keep quiet, so they must agree".

933 Sectarians protest loudly against what they call our *fanaticism* because the centuries go by and the Catholic Faith remains immutable.

On the other hand, the fanaticism of the sectarians, since it bears no relation to the truth, changes its coat at different times. They raise against the Holy Church a bogey of mere words lacking in any factual content. Their "freedom" enchains men; their "progress" leads humanity back to the jungle; their "science" conceals ignorance. Behind their stall are hidden only old damaged goods. May such *fanaticism* for the Faith as yours become stronger every day, for it is the sole defense of the one Truth.

934 Do not be afraid, or surprised, to see the resistance of some people's minds. There will always be stupid people who deck out the armor of their ignorance with a display of culture.

935 How sad it is to realize that those who hate the Lord march arm-in-arm with some who claim they are in his service. They follow different passions, but are united against Christians, the children of God.

936 In certain surroundings, especially in the intel-lectual sphere, one sees and feels a sort of conspiracy of "cliques", not infrequently assisted by Catholics. With cynical perseverance they maintain and spread slanders to cast a shadow over the Church, or over certain individuals and organizations within it. All this is done against all truth or reason.

Pray each day with faith: *"Ut inimicos Sanctae Ecclesiae"*—enemies, because that is what they proclaim themselves to be—"*humiliare digneris, te rogamus audi nos*". Confound, Lord, those who persecute you, with the clarity of your light, which we are ready to spread.

937 Is the idea of Catholicism old and therefore unacceptable? The sun is older and has not lost its light; water is more ancient, and it still quenches the thirst and refreshes us.

938 No one, even with a good intention, should be allowed to falsify historical or biographical facts. But it is a great mistake to put on a pedestal enemies of the Church who have spent their days doing precisely that. Be sure of this: historical truth does not suffer because a Christian does not wish to collaborate in the construction of a pedestal which should not exist. Since when is hatred to be set up as a model?

939 The spreading of Christian teaching need not provoke antagonism, or harm those who do not know our doctrine. *Caritas omnia suffert!*—love bears all things. If one proceeds with charity, anyone who might otherwise have been opposed to Christianity and been deceived by error may easily and honestly end up committing himself to it. However, there can be no giving ground in dogma in the name of a naive "breadth of belief", for if anyone acted in this way he would risk putting himself out of the

Church. Instead of winning a benefit for others he would harm himself.

940 Christianity is "unusual"; it does not sit easily with the things of this world. And that is perhaps its greatest *nuisance value* when it is used as a banner by the worldly.

941 Some people know nothing about God because no one has talked to them about him in terms they can understand.

942 Pray that your *holy ingenuity* may achieve what your intelligence can not, so that you may give more service of a better kind to everyone.

943 Believe me, the apostolate of giving doctrine usually has to be, as it were, capillary, spreading from one to another, from each believer to his immediate companion.

The children of God care about all souls, because every soul is important.

944 Seek refuge with the Blessed Virgin, Mother of Good Counsel, so that your lips may never utter any offense against God.

RESPONSIBILITY

945 If we Christians really lived in accordance with our faith, the greatest revolution of all times would take place. The effectiveness of our co-redemption depends on each one of us. You should meditate on this.

946 You will feel completely responsible when you realize that, before God, you have only duties. He already sees to it that you are granted rights.

947 May you acquire the custom of concerning yourself every day about others, and give yourself to the task so much that you forget you even exist.

948 Here is a thought to help you in difficult moments. "The more my faithfulness increases, the better will I be able to contribute to the growth of others in that virtue". How good it is to feel supported by each other.

949   Don't come to me with *theories*. Each day our lives have to convert those high ideals into ordinary, heroic, fruitful reality.

950   We should indeed respect things that are old, and be grateful for them. Learn from them by all means, and bear in mind those past experiences, too. But let us not exaggerate; everything has its own time and place. Do we now dress in doublet and hose or wear powdered wigs on our heads?

951   Don't get annoyed. Irresponsible behavior denotes poor formation or a lack of intelligence, rather than want of good spirit.

Teachers and directors should be expected to fill in those gaps with the responsible fulfillment of their duties.

You should examine yourself if you are in such a position.

952   You run the great risk of being satisfied with living, or thinking that you have to live, "like a good boy", who stays in a cosy and neat house, with no problems, and knowing only happiness.

That is a caricature of the home in Nazareth. Because Christ brought happiness and order, he went out to spread those treasures among men and women of all times.

953 I think it is very natural for you to want the whole world to know Christ. But start with the responsibility of saving the souls who live with you and sanctifying each one of your fellow workers or fellow students. That is the principal mission that the Lord has entrusted to you.

954 You should behave as if it all depended on you: whether the atmosphere in your place of work is to be one of hard work, cheerfulness, presence of God, and supernatural outlook.

Why are you so apathetic? If you come across a group at work who are a bit difficult, you lose interest in them. Perhaps they have become difficult because you have neglected them. Yet you throw in the towel and think of them as a dead weight which holds back your apostolic ideals because they do not understand you...

You may love and serve them with your prayer and mortification, but how do you expect them to listen to you if you never speak to them?

You will have many surprises in store the day you decide to talk to them one by one. What is more, if you do not change, they will one day be able to point the finger at you and say quite rightly: *Hominem non habeo*— I have no one to help me.

955 Understand that holy things, when they are looked at and done every day in a holy manner, do not become "everyday" things. Everything Jesus Christ did on this earth was human, and divine.

956 You say you cannot be happy to live like everyone else, with the faith of the crowd. Indeed, you have to have a personal faith joined to a sense of personal responsibility.

957 The Most Holy Trinity grants you grace and expects you to make use of it responsibly. Given such an endowment, there is no place for your adopting easy, slow, lazy attitudes, because, apart from everything else, souls await you.

958 You have a big problem; but if such things are approached properly, that is to say, with a calm and responsible supernatural vision, the solution is always to be found.

959 When they take their little children in their arms, mothers—good mothers—make sure they do not have any pins in their clothes which could hurt them. When we deal with souls, we should have the same gentleness, together with all the determination required.

960 *Custos, quid de nocte?*—Watchman, how goes the night?

May you acquire the habit of having a day on guard once a week, during which to increase your self-giving and loving vigilance over details, and to pray and mortify yourself a little more.

Realize that the Holy Church is like a great army in battle array. And you, within that army, are defending one *front* on which there are attacks, engagements with the enemy and counter-attacks. Do you see what I mean?

This readiness to grow closer to God will lead you to turn your days, one after the other, into days on guard.

961 As the obverse side to a *lost* vocation, or of a negative response to one of those constant calls of grace, we have to see God's will allowing it to happen. True, but if we are sincere, we know well enough that this does not mean the excuse or mitigation of whatever happened. For, looking at the reverse side, we can see a personal failure to fulfill the divine Will, which has sought us for himself and found no response.

962 If you really love your own country, and I am sure you do, you would not hesitate to enlist as a volunteer to defend it from imminent danger. As I wrote to you before, everyone can be useful in an emergency: men and women; the old, the middle-aged, the young and even adolescents. Only invalids and children are left out.

Every day there is a call, not just for volunteers to enlist—that is very little—but for a general mobilization of souls to defend Christ's Kingdom. And the King himself, Jesus, has called you expressly by your name. He asks you to fight in God's battles, and to put at his service the noblest powers of your soul: your heart, your will, your understanding, all your being.

You must know that the flesh, with your clean life and especially with the protection of the Virgin Mary, is no problem. Are you going to be such a coward as to try to get out of being enlisted with the excuse that your heart or will or intellect are weak? Are you going to pretend to claim some grounds for remaining in the ancillary services?

The Lord wants to make you an instrument for the front line—you are one already—and if you turn your back you deserve only pity, as a traitor.

963 If time were mere gold you could perhaps afford to squander it. But time is life, and you don't know how much you have left.

964 The Lord converted Peter, who had denied him three times, without even a reproach, with a look full of Love.

Jesus looks at us with those same eyes, after we have fallen. May we also be able to say to him, as Peter did:

"Lord, you know all things, you know that I love you", and amend our lives.

965 They argue that they act gently and with understanding, in the name of charity, towards those who throw their weight around.

I pray to God that this gentleness and understanding of theirs may not be a camouflage for human respect and for seeking their own comfort, while they allow evil to be committed. For if that were so, this gentleness and understanding would merely be complicity in the offense against God.

966 The conversion of a soul cannot be made easy at the risk of many others possibly falling away.

967 If someone thought that wolves could be reared among sheep, imagine what chance the sheep would have.

968 Mediocre men, mediocre in mind and in Christian spirit, surround themselves by stupid people when they are in power. They are falsely persuaded by their vanity that in this way they will never lose control.

Sensible men, however, surround themselves with learned people who live a clean life as well as possessing knowledge, and become, through their help, men who can really govern. They are not in this matter deceived by their humility, for in making others great they themselves are made great.

969 There is no prudence in appointing untried men to important posts of direction just to see how it works out. It would be like risking the common good on a lucky tip.

970 You must be quite foolish to go by what people say when you have been given a position of authority. First of all you should worry about what God will say; then, very much in the second place, and sometimes not at all, you may consider what others might think. "Whoever acknowledges me before men", says the Lord. "I too will acknowledge him before my Father who is in heaven. But whoever disowns me before men, I will disown him before my Father who is in heaven".

971 If you occupy a position of responsibility you should remember as you do your job that personal achievement perishes with the person who made himself indispensable.

972 A fundamental rule for good management is to give responsibility to others without this becoming for you a way of seeking anonymity or comfort. I repeat, delegate responsibility and ask each person to give an account of how his job is going, so that you can "render an account" to God; and to souls, if necessary.

973 When you are dealing with problems, try not to exaggerate justice to the point of forgetting charity.

974 The strength of a chain is the strength of its weakest link.

975 Never say of anybody under you: he is no good.

It is you who are no good, for you cannot find a place where he will be of use.

976 Reject any ambition for honors. Think instead about your duties, how to do them well and the instruments you need to accomplish them. In this way, you will not hanker for position, and if one comes you will see it just as it is: a burden to bear in the service of souls.

977 In the hour of rejection at the Cross, the Virgin Mary is there by her Son, willing to go through the same fate. Let us lose our fear of behaving like responsible Christians when the environment in which we move is not easy. She will help us.

PENANCE

978 This is what Our Lord wants, for we need it if we are to follow him closely. There is no other way. This is the work of the Holy Spirit in each soul—in yours. Be docile and present no obstacles to God, until he makes your poor flesh like that of Jesus on the Cross.

979 If the word love is often on your lips, without being backed by little sacrifices, it becomes tedious.

980 From every point of view, mortification has an extraordinary importance.

Considering it humanly, anyone who does not know how to control himself will never be able to have a positive influence on others. He will be overwhelmed by his surroundings as soon as he finds they appeal to his personal tastes. He will be a man without energy, incapable of any great effort when required.

Considering it before God, do you not think it appropriate for us to show, with these small acts, how much we love, obey, and respect the One who gave everything to us?

981 A spirit of mortification, rather than being just an outward show of Love, arises as one of its consequences. If you fail in one of these little proofs, acknowledge that your love for the Love is wavering.

982 Have you not noticed that mortified souls, because of their simplicity, have a greater enjoyment of good things, even in this world?

983 Without mortification there is no happiness on earth.

984 When you make up your mind to be more mortified, your interior life will improve and you will be much more fruitful.

985 Let us not forget that in all human activities there must be men and women who, in their lives and work, raise Christ's Cross aloft for all to see, as an act of reparation. It is a symbol of peace and of joy, a symbol of the Redemption and of the unity of the human race. It is a symbol of the love that the Most Holy Trinity, God the Father, God the Son, and God the Holy Spirit had, and continues to have, for mankind.

986 "You won't laugh, Father, will you, if I tell you that, a few days ago, I found myself spontaneously offering the Lord the sacrifice of time it meant for me to mend a broken toy for one of my little children?"

I am not laughing. I am delighted because with that Love, God sets about mending our faults.

987 Be mortified, but not careless or bitter. Be recollected, but not timid.

988 A day without mortification is a day lost, because if we have not denied ourselves, we have not lived the holocaust.

989 Haven't you gone against your own preference, your whims, some time, in something? You must realize that the One who asks you is nailed to a Cross, suffering in all his senses and faculties, with a crown of thorns on his head... for you.

990 You present yourself as a wonderful theoretician. But you don't give way to others even in the most insignificant trifles. I do not believe in that spirit of mortification of yours.

991 Care in little things requires constant mortification. It is a way to make life more pleasant for others.

992 I prefer virtue to austerity, Yahweh said, using different words, to the chosen people, who set too much store by certain external formalities.

That is why we must cultivate penance and mortification as a proof of our true love for God and for our neighbor.

993 In our meditation, the Passion of Christ comes out of its cold historical frame and stops being a pious consideration, presenting itself before our eyes, as terrible, brutal, savage, bloody... yet full of Love.

And we feel that sin cannot be regarded as just a trivial error: to sin is to crucify the Son of God, to tear his hands and feet with hammer blows, and to make his heart break.

994 If you really want to be a penitent soul—both penitent and cheerful—you must above all stick to your daily periods of prayer, which should be fervent, generous, and not cut short. And you must make sure that those minutes of prayer are not done only when you feel the need, but at fixed times, whenever it is possible. Don't neglect these details.

If you subject yourself to this daily worship of God, I can assure you that you will be always happy.

995 A Christian always triumphs through the Cross, through his self-renunciation, because he allows God's omnipotence to act.

996 When you look back on your life, which seems to have been marked by no great efforts or achievements, think how much time you have wasted, and how you can recover it with penance and greater self-giving.

997 When you think of all the things in your life which remain worthless for not having been offered to God, you should act like a miser, anxious to get hold of every opportunity you can and make use of each and every suffering. For if suffering is always there for us poor creatures, what can it be but stupidity to waste it?

998 Do you entertain a spirit of opposition, of contradiction? Very well, exercise it by opposing and contradicting yourself.

999 While the Holy Family was asleep, the angel appeared to Joseph so that they would be able to flee to

Egypt. Mary and Joseph took the Child and started out on the journey without delay. They did not rebel, they did not find excuses, they did not wait till the following morning. Tell our Holy Mother Mary and our Father and Lord St Joseph that we wish to be prompt in loving all passive penance.

1000 I write this number so that you and I can finish this book with a smile, and so that those blessed readers who out of simplicity or malice sought a cabalistic significance in the 999 points of *The Way* may rest easy.

THE FORGE

FOREWORD

On August 7, 1931, the day the diocese of Madrid celebrated the Feast of the Transfiguration of Our Lord, Monsignor Escrivá made a note of a mystical experience granted to him by God. While he was saying Holy Mass that day, God gave him to understand in a new way the words of the Gospel, *et ego, si exaltatus fuero a terra, omnia traham ad meipsum.*[1] "I understood that it would be men and women of God who would raise the Cross with the doctrines of Christ on the summit of all human activities... And I saw the Lord triumph, drawing all things to himself." Then, as if in response to those lights, he continued: "In spite of feeling myself devoid of all

---

[1]"Yes, if only I am lifted up from the earth, I will draw all things to myself" (John 12:32). This is how the sacred text then stood in the official Vulgate version.

virtue and knowledge (humility is the truth—this is no sham), I would like to write books of fire, which would run like wild-fire throughout the world, giving light and warmth to men, turning their poor hearts into burning coals, that can be offered to Jesus as rubies for his kingly crown."[2]

Those desires of his found expression in books like *The Way, Furrow,* and *The Forge.* Although *Furrow* and *The Forge* have been published posthumously, they were begun then, and I cannot imagine a more suitable description of them than the words of the author which I have just quoted. *The Forge* is a book of fire. Reading it and meditating on it can bring many souls to the forge of divine Love and enkindle within them a zeal for holiness and apostolate. That was the desire of Monsignor Escrivá, as is clearly reflected in the *Preface*: "How can I fail to take up your soul—pure gold—and place it in *the forge*, and fashion it with fire and hammer, until that gold nugget is turned into a splendid jewel to be offered to my God, to your God?"

The Forge contains 1055 points for meditation, arranged in thirteen chapters. Many of the points are clearly autobiographical. They come from notes written by the founder of Opus Dei in some spiritual copybooks, not

---

[2] J. Escrivá, 7 August 1931; manuscript notes kept in the Archive of the Prelature of the Holy Cross and Opus Dei.

exactly a diary, which he kept in the 1930s. In these personal jottings, he recorded incidents that showed the action of God in his soul, so that he could go over them and meditate on them in his personal prayer. He also recorded events and anecdotes from everyday life from which he always tried to draw some supernatural lesson. Monsignor Escrivá never liked drawing attention to himself, and so references to circumstances and events of an autobiographical nature are normally related in the third person.

Those of us who had the good fortune to be living by his side often heard him refer to this book, which had been taking shape gradually over the years. Apart from putting the book into its finished order, he had intended to read over each point carefully, so as to put all his priestly love at the service of his readers. He was not interested in *embellishing* these points. What he wanted was to enter into the intimate world of each person and while he waited for a suitable occasion to carry out this task... God himself called him into his own intimacy. These words are now published exactly as their author left them.

The central theme of *The Forge* can be summarized in these words: "If we are faithful to him, Jesus' own life will somehow be repeated in the life of each one of us, both in its internal development (the process of sanctification) and in our outward behavior" (418).

The progressive identification of the soul with Jesus Christ, which is the essence of the Christian life, is carried out in a hidden way through the Sacraments.[3] It also needs an effort from each one to correspond to grace: to know and love Our Lord, and to have the same dispositions as he had.[4] The aim is to reproduce his life in our daily conduct, until we can exclaim with the Apostle: *Vivo autem, iam non ego: vivit vero in me Christus,*[5] it is not I who live, it is Christ who lives in me. God's program for us—holiness—is thus explained to us. It is something which God asks of each of us without exception. "Just think, there are so many men and women on earth, and the Master does not fail to call every single one. He calls them to a Christian life, to a life of holiness, to a chosen life, to life eternal" (13).

This interior journey leading gradually to our identification with Christ is, as it were, the backdrop of *The Forge.* The book does not offer a rigid mold for the interior life. Nothing could be further from the intention of Monsignor Escrivá, who had the greatest respect for every person's interior freedom. For in the last analysis, each individual soul follows his own way under the

[3] Cf. Second Vatican Council, Dogmatic Constitution, *Lumen gentium,* 7.

[4] Cf. Phil (2:5).

[5] Gal (2:20).

guidance of the Holy Spirit. These points for meditation are in the nature of friendly suggestions, fatherly advice for souls who decide to take their Christian vocation seriously.

The Forge, as we shall see, follows the soul in its journey towards holiness, from the moment it perceives the light of a Christian vocation to the point when this earthly life opens out to eternity. The first chapter is about this very matter of vocation. The author called it *Dazzled*, because we are dazzled each time God makes us realize that we are his children, that we have cost the Blood, every drop of it, of his only-begotten Son and that—in spite of our nothingness and of our personal wretchedness—he wants us to be co-redeemers with Christ. "We are children of God, bearers of the only flame that can light up the paths of the earth for souls, of the only brightness which can never be darkened, dimmed, or overshadowed" (1).

Responding to our divine vocation demands a constant warfare. Our fight is not a noisy one as it takes place on the battlefield of our ordinary life, for to be "a saint (...) doesn't mean doing strange things. It means a daily struggle in the interior life and in heroically fulfilling your duty right through to the end" (60).

We must accept that there will be defeats in this interior fight, and we may be threatened with the danger of discouragement. That is why the Founder of Opus Dei constantly instilled in souls that cry of *Possumus!*—"We can!"—of the sons of Zebedee.[6] It is not a cry that arises from presumption but from a humble trust in God's Omnipotence.

Monsignor Escrivá loved to use the example of the donkey. It is not a very handsome animal, but a humble and hardworking one, which earned the honor of bearing Jesus Christ in triumph through the streets of Jerusalem. The example of a persevering and obedient donkey, aware of its unworthiness, leads the author to encourage his readers to acquire and practise a series of virtues which, with his keen powers of observation, he discovered in the donkey which pulls the waterwheel. "Donkeys are humble, hardworking, persevering—stubborn—and faithful, with a sure step, tough and—if they have a good master—also grateful and obedient" (380).

Obedience is closely linked, in fact, with the humble perseverance of the little donkey at the waterwheel. "Be convinced that if you do not learn to obey, you will never be effective" (626). For to obey the person who directs our souls and channels our apostolate in God's name, is to open ourselves to divine grace, and to let the Holy Spirit act in us. This requires humility. It is God, then, whom we obey. And the Church too, for God's sake. There is no other way: "Convince yourself, my child, that

[6]Mark (10:39).

lack of unity within the Church is death" (631). This is another of those *basic ideas* in Monsignor Escrivá's preaching: not to separate Christ from his Church, nor to separate the Christian from Christ, to whom he is united by grace. Only thus will victory be assured.

Men and women who seek sanctity in the world carry out their apostolic tasks in, and by means of, the fulfillment of their ordinary duties. The first of these will be their job or profession. "From St Paul's teaching we know we have to renew the world in the spirit of Jesus Christ, that we have to place Our Lord at the summit and at the heart of all things. Do you think you are carrying this out in your work, in your professional task?" (678).

Together with work, all the other noble endeavors of men need to be converted into instruments of personal sanctity and apostolate. "You should be full of wonder at the goodness of Our Father God. Are you not filled with joy to know that your home, your family, your country, which you love so much, are the raw material which you must sanctify?" (689). And so, a number of points make reference to marriage and the family, and to our civic duties, for "the Lord wants his children, those of us who have received the gift of faith, to proclaim the original optimistic view of creation, the *love for the world* which is at the heart of the Christian message" (703).

The author often reminds us that we need a deep interior life if we are to "divinize things human;" other-

wise we would run the risk of "humanizing things divine." Nor should we forget—as I often heard Monsignor
Escrivá say—that "every supernatural thing, when it refers
to men, is also very human." That is why, the more
complete one's identification with Christ becomes, the
more pressing does apostolic zeal become, for, "whenever sanctity is genuine it overflows from its vessel to
fill other hearts, other souls, with its superabundance"
(856).

The Christian ends up acquiring a big heart, like
Christ's, in which there is room for everybody. "Jesus
will enable you to have a great affection for everybody
you meet, without taking away any of the affection you
have for him. On the contrary, the more you love Jesus,
the more room there will be for other people in your
heart" (876). And so, we come to detest any type of
narrow-mindedness, any form of provincialism or exclu-
sivism. Two attitudes typical of a mature soul are thus
intertwined: an insatiable thirst for souls—"not a single
soul—not one—can be a matter of indifference to you"
(951)—and the equally insatiable desire to be united to
God (cf. 927).

Hunger for God can never be satisfied in this world,
and so we seek complete union in *eternity*. This is the
theme of the last chapter of *The Forge*. In the manner of
St Paul, and in an especially intense way in the last years
of his life, the Founder of Opus Dei felt both the desire

of embracing his Love in Heaven as soon as possible (how often he repeated those words of the psalm: *vultum tuum, Domine, requiram!*[7]), and the desire to serve God effectively and for many years upon this earth. "To die is a good thing. How can anyone with faith be, at the same time, afraid to die? But as long as the Lord wants to keep you here on earth, it would be cowardice for you to want to die. You must live, live and suffer, and work for Love: that is your task" (1037).

Thus, there is a perfect continuity in the lives of the children of God: "Happiness in Heaven is for those who know how to be happy on earth" (1005). Happiness is the reward Jesus Christ promised his followers:[8] to be happy here, with a relative happiness, and to rejoice fully hereafter in the eternal life.

I venture to assure you, my dear reader, that if you and I enter into this *forge* of the Love of God, our souls will become better, being cleansed of some of the dross that clings to them. Monsignor Escrivá will guide us along the ways of the interior life, with the firm steps of one who knows every inch of the terrain, having walked over it so many times. It we really do embark on this road, beginning and beginning again as often as necessary (cf. 384), we too shall reach the end of our journey full of peace

---

[7]"Lord, I long to see they face." Ps (26:8).
[8]Cf. Matt (19:29).

and happiness, assured of a welcome in the arms of our Heavenly Father.

And do not forget that we are under Our Lady's protection. Let us turn to her as these pages end, with words from *The Forge*, so that by reading and meditating on this book we may obtain, by God's grace, the goal Monsignor Escrivá had in view for us when he wrote it. "Mother, do not leave me! Let me seek your Son, let me find your Son, let me love your Son—with my whole being" (157).

ALVARO DEL PORTILLO
ROME, DECEMBER 26, 1986

PROLOGUE OF THE AUTHOR

There was a mother
who, like all mothers,
was passionately fond of her little child,
whom she called
her prince, her king,
her treasure, her very sun.
I thought of you.
And I understood
—for what father does not carry
deep inside some maternal feelings?—
that it was no exaggeration
for that good mother to say:
you are more than a treasure,
you are worth more than the sun itself:
you are worth all Christ's Blood!
How can I fail to take up your soul
—pure gold—
and place it in the forge,
and fashion it with fire and hammer,
until that gold nugget is turned
into a splendid jewel
to be offered to my God,
to your God?

DAZZLED

1 We are children of God, bearers of the only flame that can light up the paths of the earth for souls, of the only brightness which can never be darkened, dimmed, or overshadowed.

The Lord uses us as torches, to make that light shine out. Much depends on us; if we respond many people will remain in darkness no longer, but will walk instead along paths that lead to eternal life.

2 God is my Father! If you meditate on it, you will never let go of this consoling thought.

Jesus is my dear Friend (another thrilling discovery) who loves me with all the divine madness of his Heart.

The Holy Spirit is my Consoler, who guides my every step along the road.

Consider this often: you are God's—and God is yours.

3 My Father—talk to him like that, confidently—who art in Heaven, look upon me with compassionate Love, and make me respond to thy love.

Melt and enkindle my hardened heart, burn and purify my unmortified flesh, fill my mind with supernatural light, make my tongue proclaim the Love and Glory of Christ.

4 Christ ascended the Cross with his arms wide open, with the all-embracing gesture of the Eternal Priest. Now he counts on us—who are nothing!—to bring the fruits of his Redemption to *all* men.

5 Lord, we are glad to find ourselves in your wounded palm. Grasp us tight, squeeze us hard, make us lose all our earthly wretchedness, purify us, set us on fire, make us feel drenched in your Blood.

And then, cast us far, far away, hungry for the harvest, to sow the seed more fruitfully each day, for Love of you.

6 Do not be afraid. Do not be alarmed or surprised. Do not allow yourself to be overcome by false prudence.

The call to fulfill God's will—this goes for vocation too—is sudden, as it was for the Apostles: a meeting with Christ and his call is followed.

None of them doubted. Meeting Christ and following him was all one.

7 The day of salvation, of eternity, has come for us. Once again the call of the Divine Shepherd can be heard, those affectionate words: *Vocavi te nomine tuo*—I have called you by your name.

Just like our mother, he calls us by our name, by the name we're fondly called at home, by our nickname. There, in the depths of our soul, he calls us and we just have to answer: *Ecce ego quia vocasti me*—here I am, for you have called me, and this time I'm determined not to let time flow by like water over the pebbly bed of a stream, leaving no trace behind.

8 Live your life close to Christ. You should be another character in the Gospel, side by side with Peter, and John, and Andrew. For Christ is also living *now*: *Iesus Christus, heri et hodie, ipse et in saecula!*—Jesus Christ lives! Today, as yesterday, he is the same, forever and ever.

9 Lord, may your children be like red-hot coals, but without flames to be seen from afar. Let them be burning embers that will set alight each heart they come into contact with.

You will make that first spark turn into a burning fire, for your angels are very skilled at blowing on the embers in our hearts. I know, I have seen it. And a heart cleared of dead ashes cannot but be yours.

10   Think about what the Holy Spirit says, and let yourself be filled with awe and gratitude: *Elegit nos ante mundi constitutionem*—he chose us before the foundation of the world, *ut essemus sancti in conspectu eius!*—that we might be holy in his presence.

To be holy isn't easy, but it isn't difficult either. To be holy is to be a good Christian, to resemble Christ. The more closely a person resembles Christ, the more Christian he is, the more he belongs to Christ, the holier he is.

And what means do we have? The same means the early faithful had, when they saw Jesus directly or caught a glimpse of him in the accounts the Apostles and Evangelists gave of him.

11   You owe such a great debt to your Father-God! He has given you life, intelligence, will... He has given you his grace—the Holy Spirit; Jesus, in the Sacred Host; divine sonship; the Blessed Virgin, the Mother of God and our Mother. He has given you the possibility of taking part in the Holy Mass; and he grants you forgiveness for your sins. He forgives you so many times. He has given you countless gifts, some of them quite extraordinary...

Tell me, my son: how have you corresponded so far to this generosity? How are you corresponding now?

12   I do not know how it strikes you, but I feel I must tell you how moved I am whenever I read the words of the prophet Isaiah: *Ego vocavi te nomine tuo, meus es tu!*—I have called you, I have brought you into my Church, you are mine! God himself telling me I am his! It is enough to make one go mad with Love!

13 Just think, there are so many men and women on earth, and the Master does not fail to call every single one.

He calls them to a Christian life, to a life of holiness, to a chosen life, to life eternal.

14 Christ suffered in your place and for your benefit, to tear you away from the slavery of sin and imperfection.

15 In these times of violence and of brutal, savage sexuality, we have to be rebels: we refuse point blank to go with the tide, and become beasts.

We want to behave like children of God, like men and women who are on intimate terms with their Father, who is in Heaven and who wants to be very close to—in-side!—each one of us.

16 Meditate on this frequently: I am a Catholic, a child of Christ's Church. He brought me to birth in a home that is *his*, without my doing anything to deserve it.

My God, how much I owe you.

17   Remind everyone (and especially all those fathers and mothers, who call themselves Christians) that a *vocation*, a call from God, is a grace from the Lord, a choice made by the divine goodness, a motive for holy pride, a call to serve all joyously for the love of Jesus Christ.

18   Please echo these words for me: it is no "sacrifice" for parents when God asks them for their children. Neither, for those he calls, is it a sacrifice to follow him.

It is, on the contrary, an immense honor, a motive for a great and holy pride, a mark of predilection, a very special affection that God has shown at a particular time, but which has been in his mind from all eternity.

19   Be grateful to your parents for bringing you into this world, thus enabling you to become a child of God. And be all the more grateful if it was they who placed in your soul the first seeds of faith and piety, of your Christian way, or of your vocation.

20   There are many people around you, and you have no right to be an obstacle to their spiritual good, to their eternal happiness.

You are under an obligation to be a saint. You must not let God down for having chosen you. Neither must you let those around you down: they expect so much from your Christian life.

21   The commandment to love our parents belongs to both natural law and to divine positive law, and I have always called it a "most sweet precept."

Do not neglect your obligation to love your parents more each day, to mortify yourself for them, to pray for them, and to be grateful to them for all the good you owe them.

22   Following the Master's wishes, you are to be salt and light while being fully immersed in this world we were made to live in, sharing in all human activities. Light illumines the hearts and minds of men. Salt gives flavor and preserves from corruption.

That is why if you lack apostolic zeal you will become insipid and useless. You will be letting other people down and your life will be absurd.

23   A reddish-blue wave of filth and corruption has set out to overcome the world, throwing its vile spittle over the Cross of the Redeemer.

Now he wants another wave to issue forth from our souls—a wave that's white and powerful, like the Lord's right hand—to overcome with its purity all the rottenness of materialism and undo the corruption that has flooded the world. It is for this, and more, that the children of God have come.

24   Many people ask with an air of self-justification: Why should I get involved in the lives of others?

Because it is your Christian duty to get involved in their lives, in order to serve them.

Because Christ has gotten involved in your life and in mine.

25   If you are another Christ, if you behave as a son of God, you will set things alight no matter where you are. Christ enkindles all hearts, leaving none indifferent.

26   It is painful to see that after two thousand years there are so few people in the world who call themselves Christians and that of those who do call themselves Christians, so few practise the true teaching of Jesus Christ.

It is worth while putting our whole life at stake, working and suffering for Love, in order to accomplish God's plans and co-redeem with him.

27   I look at your Cross, my Jesus, and I rejoice in your grace, because your Calvary has won for us the reward of the Holy Spirit. And you give yourself to me, each day, lovingly, *madly*, in the Sacred Host. And you have made me a son of God, and have given me your Mother to be mine.

I can't be satisfied with just giving thanks. My thoughts take flight: Lord, Lord, there are so many souls who are so far from you!

Foster those yearnings for apostolate in your life, that many may get to know him and love him and come to feel loved by him.

28 Sometimes one hears love described (you'll have heard me mention this more than once) as if it were a movement towards self-satisfaction, or merely a means of selfishly fulfilling one's own personality.

And I have always told you that it isn't so. True love demands getting out of oneself, giving oneself. Genuine love brings joy in its wake, a joy that has its roots in the shape of the Cross.

29 My God, how is it that I do not cry out in sorrow and love whenever I see a Crucifix?

30 Marvel at God's magnanimity: he has become Man to redeem us, so that you and I—who are absolutely worthless, admit it!—may come to know him and trust him.

31 O Jesus, strengthen our souls, open out the way for us, and, above all, intoxicate us with your Love. Make us into blazing fires to enkindle the earth with the heavenly fire you brought us.

32 Coming closer to God means being ready to be converted anew, to change direction again, to listen attentively to his inspirations—those holy desires he places in our souls—and to put them into practice.

33 What are you so proud of? Every impulse that moves you comes from him. Act accordingly.

34 What respect, veneration, and affection we should feel for every single soul when we realize that God loves it as his very own.

35 An inspiration: May we spend the days the Lord grants us only in pleasing him.

36 I would like you to behave as Peter and John did—speaking to Jesus about the needs of your friends and colleagues as you pray. And then with your example you will be able to say to them: *Respice in nos!*—Look at me!

37 When you love somebody very much, you want to know everything about him.

Meditate on this: Do you feel a hunger to know Christ? Because that is the measure of your love for him.

38   People who say that we priests are lonely are either lying or have gotten it all wrong. We are far less lonely than anyone else, for we can count on the constant company of the Lord, with whom we should be conversing without interruption.

We are in love with Love, with the Author of Love!

39   I see myself like a poor little bird, accustomed only to making short flights from tree to tree, or, at most, up to a third floor balcony. One day in its life it succeeded in reaching the roof of a modest building that you could hardly call a sky-scraper.

Suddenly our little bird is snatched up by an eagle, who mistakes the bird for one of its own brood. In its powerful talons the bird is borne higher and higher, above the mountains of the earth and the snow-capped peaks, above the white, blue, and rose-pink clouds, and higher and higher until it can look right into the sun. And then the eagle lets go of the little bird and says: Off you go. Fly!

Lord, may I never flutter again close to the ground. May I always be enlightened by the rays of the divine sun—Christ—in the Eucharist. May my flight never be interrupted until I find repose in your Heart.

40   That friend of ours would finish his prayer in this way: "I love the Will of my God and that is why, abandoning myself completely into his hands, I pray that he may lead me however and wherever he likes."

41   Ask the Father, the Son, and the Holy Spirit, and your Mother, to make you know yourself and weep for all those foul things that have passed through you, and which, alas, have left such dregs behind... And at the same time, without wishing to stop considering all that, say to him: Jesus, give me a Love that will act like a purifying fire in which my miserable flesh, my miserable heart, my miserable soul, my miserable body may be consumed and cleansed of all earthly wretchedness. And when I have been emptied of myself, fill me with yourself. May I never become attached to anything here below. May Love always sustain me.

42   Desire nothing for yourself, either good or bad. For yourself, want only what God wants.

Whatever it may be, if it comes from his hand, from God, however bad it may appear in the eyes of men, with God's help it will appear good, yes, very good, to you. And with an ever-increasing conviction you will say: *Et in tribulatione mea dilatasti me...,et calix tuus inebrians, quam praeclarus est!*—I have rejoiced in tribulation..., how marvellous is your chalice. It inebriates my whole being!

43 We should offer the Lord the sacrifice of Abel. A sacrifice of young unblemished flesh, the best of the flock; of healthy and holy flesh; a sacrifice of hearts that have one love alone—you, my God. A sacrifice of minds, which have been shaped through deep study and will surrender to your Wisdom; of childlike souls who will think only of pleasing you.

Lord, receive even now this sweet and fragrant sacrifice.

44 We have to learn how to give ourselves, to burn before God like the light placed on a lampstand to give light to those who walk in darkness; like the sanctuary lamps that burn by the altar, giving off light till their last drop is consumed.

45 The Lord, the teacher of Love, is a jealous lover who asks for all we possess, for all our love. He expects us to offer him whatever we have, and to follow the path he has marked out for each one of us.

46 My God, I see I shall never accept you as my Savior unless I acknowledge you as my Model at the same time.

Since you yourself chose to be poor, make me love holy poverty. I resolve, with your grace, to live and die in poverty, even though I may have millions at my disposal.

47   You became very thoughtful when I told you: "The way I see it, everything seems too little when it is for the Lord."

48   It would be good if it could be said of you that the distinguishing feature of your life was "loving God's Will."

49   Any job, no matter how hidden, no matter how insignificant, when offered to the Lord, is charged with the strength of God's life!

50   Feel the responsibility of your mission: the whole of Heaven is looking down on you.

51   God awaits you. So, wherever you are, you must commit yourself to imitating him and uniting yourself to him, cheerfully, lovingly, keenly, though circumstances might require you—even permanently—to go against the grain.

God awaits you—and needs you to be faithful.

52   You wrote: "My King, I hear you proclaiming in a loud voice that still resounds: *Ignem veni mittere in terram, et quid volo nisi ut accendatur?*—I have come to cast fire upon the earth, and would that it were already kindled!"

Then you added: "Lord, I answer, with all my heart, with all my senses and faculties: *Ecce ego quia vocasti me!*—here I am because you have called me."

May this answer of yours be a daily reality.

53 You should show the moderation, fortitude, and sense of responsibility that many people acquire after many long years, in their old age. You will achieve all this, while you are still young, if you do not lose the supernatural outlook of a son of God. For he will give you, more than to the old, those qualities you need for your apostle's work.

54 You enjoy an interior happiness and peace that you would not exchange for anything in the world. God is here. There is no better way than telling him our woes for them to cease being such.

55 Is it possible, you asked me, that Christ should have spent so many years—twenty centuries—acting on earth, and the world should be now what it is? Is it possible, you went on, that there should still be people who do not know Our Lord?

And I answered you with conviction: It is our fault. For we have been called to be co-redeemers, and at times, perhaps often, we do not follow the Will of God.

56   How humble Jesus is. What a shame, in contrast, that I who am nothing but dust from a dungheap should so often have disguised my pride under the cloak of dignity, or justice. And as a result, how many opportunities to follow the Master I have missed or wasted, by failing to supernaturalize them.

57   Sweet Mother, lead us to that madness that will make others fall madly in love with our Christ.

Sweet Lady Mary, may Love not be in us a flash in the pan, or a will-ó-the-wisp, such as decomposing corpses sometimes produce. May it be a true devouring fire, which sets alight and burns everything it touches.

STRUGGLE

58 Being chosen by God means, and *demands*, personal holiness.

59 If you respond to the call the Lord has made to you, your life—your poor life—will leave a deep and wide furrow in the history of the human race, a clear and fertile furrow, eternal and godly.

60 Each day be conscious of your duty to be a saint. A saint! And that doesn't mean doing strange things. It means a daily struggle in the interior life and in heroically fulfilling your duty right through to the end.

61 Sanctity does not consist in great concerns. It consists in struggling to ensure that the flame of your supernatural life is never allowed to go out; it consists in letting yourself to be burned down to the last shred, serving God in the lowest place, or in the highest: wherever the Lord may call you.

62   Our Lord did not confine himself to *telling us* that he loved us. He showed it to us with deeds, with his whole life. What about you?

63   If you love the Lord, you will *necessarily* become aware of the blessed burden of souls that need to be brought to God.

64   For someone who wants to live for Love with a capital letter, the middle course is not good enough; that would be meanness, a wretched compromise.

65   Here is a recipe for your way as a Christian: pray, do penance, work without rest, fulfilling your duty lovingly.

66   My God, teach me how to love. My God, teach me how to pray.

67   We must ask God for faith, hope, and charity, with humility, with persevering prayer, with upright behavior and a clean life.

68   You told me that you did not know how to repay me for the holy zeal that flooded your soul.

I hastened to answer: It is not I who have given you any of those yearnings; it is the Holy Spirit.

Desire his company, get to know him. That way you will come to love him better and better, and you will come to thank him for taking up his abode in your soul so that you may have interior life.

69 Keep struggling, so that the Holy Sacrifice of the Altar really becomes the center and the root of your interior life, and so your whole day will turn into an act of worship—an extension of the Mass you have attended and a preparation for the next. Your whole day will then be an act of worship that overflows in aspirations, visits to the Blessed Sacrament and the offering up of your professional work and your family life.

70 Try to give thanks to Jesus in the Eucharist by singing the praises of Our Lady, the Virgin most pure, without stain, who brought forth the Lord into this world.

And with childlike daring, say to Jesus: My dearest Love, blessed be the Mother who brought you into this world!

I assure you it will please him, and he will put even greater love in your soul.

71 St Luke the Evangelist tells us that Jesus prayed. What must his prayer have been like!

Contemplate this fact slowly: the disciples had the opportunity of talking to Jesus and in their conversations with him the Lord taught them by his words, and deeds, how they should pray. And he taught them this amazing truth of God's mercy: that we are God's children and that we can address him as a child addresses his Father.

72 When you start out each day to work by Christ's side and to look after all those souls who seek him, remember that there is only one way of doing it: we must turn to the Lord.

Only in prayer, and through prayer, do we learn to serve others.

73 Remember that prayer does not consist in making pretty speeches, or high-sounding or consoling phrases.

Prayer, at times, will be a glance at a picture of Our Lord or of his Mother; sometimes a petition, expressed in words; or offering good works, and the fruits of faithfulness.

We have to be like a guard on sentry duty at the gate of God Our Lord: that's what prayer is. Or like a small dog that lies down at it's master's feet.

Do not mind telling him: Lord, here I am, like a faithful dog; or better still like a little donkey, which will not kick the one who loves him.

74 We all have to be *ipse Christus*—Christ himself. This is what St Paul commands in the name of God: *Induimini Dominum Iesum Christum*—put on the Lord Jesus Christ.

Each one of us—and that includes *you*—has to see how he puts on that clothing of which the apostle speaks. Each one personally has to sustain an uninterrupted dialogue with the Lord.

75 Your prayer cannot stop at mere words. It has to lead to deeds and practical consequences.

76 The way to cut short all the evils we suffer is to pray.

77 Here is a piece of advice I shall never tire of telling souls: Love the Mother of God madly, for she is our Mother too.

78 Heroism, sanctity, daring, require a constant spiritual preparation. You can only ever give to others what you already have. And in order to give God to them, you yourself need to get to know him, to live his Life, to serve him.

79 I will not stop repeating until it is deeply engraved in your soul: Piety, piety, piety! For if you lack charity it will be for want of interior life, not for any defect of character.

80   If you are a good son of God, your first and last thought each day will be for him, just as a little child needs to be assured of the presence of his parents when he gets up in the morning or goes to bed at night.

81   You must be constant and demanding with yourself in your regular practices of piety, even when you feel tired and arid. Persevere! Those moments are like the tall red-painted poles which serve as markers along the mountain roads when there are heavy snowfalls. They are always there to show where it is safe to go.

82   Make an effort to respond at each moment to what God is asking of you: have the will to love him with deeds. They may be little deeds, but do not leave any out.

83   Interior life is strengthened by a daily struggle in your practices of piety, which you should fulfill—or rather which you should *live*—lovingly, for the path we travel as children of God is a path of Love.

84   Seek God in the depths of your pure, clean heart; in the depths of your soul when you are faithful to him. And never lose that intimacy.

And if ever you do not know how to speak to him or what to say, or you do not dare to look for Jesus inside yourself, turn to Mary, *tota pulchra*, all pure and wonderful, and tell her: Our Lady and Mother, the Lord wanted you yourself to look after God and tend him with your own hands. Teach me, teach us all, how to treat your Son.

85   You must instill in all souls the heroism of doing the little things of each day perfectly, as if the salvation of the world depended on each one of those actions.

86   With your life of piety, you will learn how to practise the virtues befitting your condition as a son of God, as a Christian.

And together with those virtues you will acquire a whole range of spiritual values which seem small but are really very great. They are like shining precious stones, and we must gather them along the way and then take them up to the foot of God's Throne in the service of our fellow men: simplicity, cheerfulness, loyalty, peace, small renunciations, little services which pass unnoticed, the faithful fulfillment of duty, kindness.

87   Don't create more obligations for yourself than God's glory, his Love, his Apostolate.

88   Our Lord has made you see your way clearly as
a Christian in the middle of the world. Nevertheless, you
tell me that you have often thought, enviously (though in
the end you admitted it would be taking the easy way out)
of the happiness of being a nobody, of working away,
totally obscure, in the remotest corner—just God and
you!

Now, apart from the idea of missionary work in Japan,
the thought of just such a hidden and sacrificed life has
come to your mind. But if, free from other holy natural
obligations, you were to try to "hide away" in a religious
institution, assuming that was not your vocation, you
would not be happy. You would lack peace; because you
would have done your own will, not God's.

Your "vocation," in that case, would deserve another
name: it would be a defection. It would not be the result
of divine inspiration, but of sheer human reluctance to
face the coming struggle. And that would never do!

89   In living holy purity and a clean life, there is a great
difficulty to which we are all exposed. The danger is one
of becoming *bourgeois*, either in our spiritual life or in
our professional life; the danger—also a real one for those
called by God to marriage—of becoming dry old bachelors, selfish; people who do not love.

Fight that danger tooth and nail, without making
concessions of any kind.

90 Because we shall always have to put up with this little donkey which is our body, in order to conquer sensuality you have to practise daily and generously little mortifications—and sometimes big ones as well. And you must live in the presence of God, who never ceases to watch over you.

91 Your chastity cannot be confined to avoiding falls or occasions. In no way can it be a cold and mathematical negative.

Haven't you realized that chastity is a *virtue* and that as such it should grow and become more perfect?

It is not enough, then, to be continent according to your state. You have to be chaste, with a heroic virtue.

92 The *bonus odor Christi*, the fragrance of Christ, is also that of our clean life, of our chastity—the chastity of each one in his own state, I repeat—of our holy purity, which is a joyful affirmation. It is something solid and at the same time gentle; it is refined, avoiding even the use of unfitting words, since they cannot be pleasing to God.

93 Get used to thanking the guardian angels in advance, thus putting them under an obligation.

94 One ought to be able to apply to every Christian the name that was used in the early ages: *Bearer of God*.

Your actions should be such that you *really* deserve to be called by that wonderful name.

95 Think what would happen if we Christians chose not to behave as such... and then rectify your conduct.

96 Discover Our Lord behind each event and in every circumstance, and then, from everything that happens, you will be able to draw more love for God and a greater desire to respond to him. He is always waiting for us, offering us the possibility to fulfil at all times that resolution we made: *Serviam!* I will serve you.

97 Renew each day the effective desire to annihilate yourself, to deny yourself, to forget yourself, to walk *in novitate sensus*, with a new life, exchanging this misery of ours for all the hidden and eternal grandeur of God.

98 Lord, make me so much yours that not even the holiest affections may enter my heart except through your wounded Heart.

99 Try to be considerate, well-mannered. Don't be boorish!

Try to be polite always, which doesn't mean being affected.

100 Charity succeeds always. Without it, there's "nothing doing."

Love, then, is the secret of your life. Love. Suffer gladly. Toughen up your soul. Invigorate your will. And as for your self-surrender, link it tightly to the will of God, and with this your life will be effective.

101 Have the piety and simplicity of a child, and the strength and fortitude of a leader.

102 Peace, and the joy which comes with it, cannot be given by the world.

Men are forever "making peace" and forever getting entangled in wars. This is because they have forgotten the advice to struggle inside themselves and to go to God for help. Then he will conquer, and we will obtain peace for ourselves and for our own homes, for society, and for the world.

If we do things in this way, you and I will have joy, because it is the possession of those who conquer. And with the grace of God—who never loses battles—we will be able to count ourselves conquerors as long as we are humble.

103 Your life, your work, should never be negative, nor *anti* anything. It is—it must be—positive, optimistic, youthful, cheerful, and peaceful.

104 In national life there are two things which are really essential: the laws concerning marriage and the laws to do with education. In these areas God's sons have to stand firm and fight with toughness and fairness, for the sake of all mankind.

105 Joy is a Christian possession which we will have as long as we keep fighting, for it is a consequence of peace. Peace is the fruit of having conquered in war, and the life of man upon this earth—as we read in Sacred Scripture—is a warfare.

106 This divine warfare of ours is a marvellous sowing of peace.

107 The person who stops struggling causes harm to the Church, to his own supernatural undertaking, to his brothers, and to all souls.

Examine yourself. Could you not put a more lively love for God into your spiritual struggle? I am praying for you—and for everyone. You should do the same.

108 Jesus, if there is anything in me which is displeasing to you, tell me what it is so that we may uproot it.

109 There is an enemy of the interior life which is both little and silly. Unfortunately, it can be very effective. It is the neglect of effort in one's examination of conscience.

110 In Christian asceticism the examination of conscience meets a need of love, and of sensitivity.

111 If there is anything in you that is out of harmony with God's spirit, get rid of it straight away.

Think of the Apostles. They were not of much account, yet they could work miracles in the name of the Lord. Only Judas, who at one time may also have worked miracles, went astray by voluntarily separating himself from Christ, because he did not cut himself away violently and courageously from what was out of harmony with God's spirit.

112 My God, when am I really going to be converted?

113 Don't wait until you are old to start becoming a saint. That would be a great mistake.

Begin right now, in earnest, cheerfully and joyfully, by fulfilling the duties of your work and of your everyday life.

Don't wait until you are old to become a saint. Because—I insist—apart from its being a great mistake, you never know whether you will live as long as that.

114   Ask the Lord to grant you all the sensitivity you need to realize how evil venial sin is, so as to recognize it as an outright and fundamental enemy of your soul, and, with God's grace, to avoid it.

115   You need to think about your life calmly and without scruples, to ask for forgiveness, and make a firm, definite, and determined resolution to improve in one point and another, to improve in that particular small detail which you find hard, and in that other one which as a rule you do not carry out as you should, even though you well know you ought to be doing it.

116   To be full of good desires is indeed a holy thing, and God praises it. But don't leave it at that. You have to be a soul—a man, a woman—who deals in realities. To carry out those good desires, you have to form clear and precise resolutions.

And then, my child, you have to *fight* to put them into practice, with the grace of God.

117   "What do I have to do to maintain my love for God and make it increase?" you asked me, fired with enthusiasm.

Leave the "old man" behind, my son, and cheerfully give up things which are good in themselves but hinder your detachment from yourself. You have to repeat constantly and with deeds, "Here I am, Lord, ready to do whatever you want."

118   A saint! A son of God should exaggerate in practising virtue—if exaggeration is possible here. Because other people will see themselves reflected in him, as in a mirror, and it is only by our aiming very high that others will reach a middling level.

119   Do not be ashamed to discover in your heart the *fomes peccati*—the inclination to evil, which will be with you as long as you live, for nobody is free from this burden.

Do not be ashamed, for the all-powerful and merciful Lord has given us all the means we need for overcoming this inclination: the Sacraments, a life of piety, and sanctified work.

Persevere in using these means, ever ready to begin again and again without getting discouraged.

120   Lord, rescue me from myself!

121   An apostle who does not pray regularly and methodically will necessarily fall into lukewarmness... and he will then cease to be an apostle.

122   Lord, from now on let me be another: no longer "me," but that "other person" you would like me to be.

Let me not deny you anything you ask of me. Let me know how to pray. Let me know how to suffer. Let me not worry about anything except your glory. Let me feel your presence all the time.

May I love the Father. May I hunger for you, my Jesus, in a permanent Communion. May the Holy Spirit set me on fire.

123 The Lord has told you: *Meus es tu*—you are mine.

To think that God, who is all beauty and all wisdom, all splendor and all goodness, should say to you that you are his and then, after all this, you can't bring yourself to respond to him!

124 You should not be surprised to feel in your life that weight dragging you down which St Paul spoke of: "I see in my members another law at war with the law of my mind."

Remember then that you belong to Christ, and have recourse to the Mother of God, who is also your Mother. They will never abandon you.

125 Receive the advice you are given in spiritual guidance as though it came from Jesus Christ himself.

126 You asked me to suggest a way for winning through in your daily struggles, and I replied: When you lay your soul open, say first of all what you wouldn't like to be known. In this way the devil will always end up defeated.

Lay your soul wide open, clearly and simply, so that the rays of God's Love may reach and illuminate the last corner of it.

127 If that dumb devil mentioned in the Gospel gets into your soul, he will spoil everything. On the other hand, if you get rid of him immediately, everything will turn out well; you will carry on merrily, and all will be well.

Resolve firmly to be "savagely sincere" in spiritual direction (always keeping your good manners) and to be sincere *immediately*.

128 Love and seek help from the person who guides your soul. In spiritual direction lay your heart completely open—if it were rotten, show it as it is, rotten—with all sincerity, with the desire to be cured. If you don't, you will never get rid of that rottenness.

If you go to a person who only cleanses the wound in a superficial way, you are a coward, because you will be going along to hide the truth, and that can only do you harm.

129 Never be afraid of telling the truth. But don't forget that sometimes it is better to remain silent out of charity towards your neighbor. However, you should never be silent out of laziness, or love of comfort, or cowardice.

130 The world thrives on lies even twenty centuries after the Truth came among men.

We have to tell the truth! This is precisely what we have to do as children of God. When men get used to proclaiming and hearing the truth, there will be more understanding in this world of ours.

131 To give way in matters of faith would be a false charity. It would be a diabolical, deceitful charity. We must be *fortes in fide*—strong, firm in faith, as St Peter demands.

This is not fanaticism, but quite simply the practice of our faith. It does not entail disliking anyone. We can give way in all accidental matters, but in matters of faith we cannot give way. We cannot spare the oil from our lamps, otherwise when the Bridegroom comes he will find they have burned out.

132 Humility and obedience are the indispensable conditions for acquiring good doctrine.

133 Welcome the Pope's words with a religious, humble, internal and effective acceptance. And pass them on.

134 You must love, venerate, pray, and mortify yourself for the Pope, and do so with greater affection each day. For he is the foundation stone of the Church and, throughout the centuries, right to the end of time, he carries out among men that task of sanctifying and governing which Jesus entrusted to Peter.

135 Your deepest love, your greatest esteem, your most heartfelt veneration, your most complete obedience and your warmest affection have also to be shown towards the Vicar of Christ on earth, towards the Pope.

We Catholics should consider that after God and the most Holy Virgin, our Mother, the Holy Father comes next in the hierarchy of love and authority.

136 May the daily consideration of the heavy burden which weighs upon the Pope and the bishops move you to venerate and love them with real affection, and to help them with your prayers.

137 Your love for Our Lady should be more lively, more supernatural.

Don't just go to the Virgin Mary to ask her for things. You should also go to give: give her your affection; give her your love for her divine Son; and show her your affection with deeds of service to others, who are also her children.

138 Jesus is our model. Let us imitate him.

Let us imitate him by serving the Holy Church and all mankind.

139 When contemplating the scene of the Incarnation, strengthen in your soul the resolve to be "humble in practice." See how he lowered himself, taking on our poor nature.

That is why every day you need to react, right away, with God's grace, accepting—and wanting—the humiliations the Lord may offer you.

140 Live your Christian life with naturalness. Let me stress this: make Christ known through your behavior, just as an ordinary mirror reproduces an image without distorting it or turning it into a caricature. If, like the mirror, you are *normal*, you will reflect Christ's life, and show it to others.

141 If you are fatuous, if all you can think of is your own personal comfort, if you center everyone else and even the world itself on yourself, then you have no right to call yourself a Christian or to consider yourself a disciple of Christ. He set the level of what can be demanded of us when he offered, for each of us: *et animam suam*—his own soul, his whole life.

142 Try to make "intellectual humility" an axiom in your life.

Think about it carefully. Isn't it true that it just doesn't make sense to be "intellectually proud?" That saint and doctor of the Church put it very well when he said: "It is a detestable disorder for a man to see God become a little child, and yet still want to appear great in this world."

143 The moment you have anyone—whoever he may be—at your side, find a way, without doing anything strange, to pass on to him the joy you experience in being a son of God and living as such.

144 The mission to serve which the Divine Master has entrusted to us is a great and beautiful mission. That is why this good spirit—which entails great self-mastery—is perfectly compatible with the love of freedom that should pervade the work of all Christians.

145 You must never treat anyone unmercifully. If you think someone is not worthy of your mercy, you should realize that you don't deserve mercy either.

You do not deserve to have been created, or to be a Christian, or to be a son of God, or to have the family you have...

146 Don't neglect the practice of fraternal correction, which is a clear sign of the supernatural virtue of charity. You may find it hard, for it's easier to be inhibited. It's *easier* to behave that way, but it's not supernatural.

And you will have to render an account to God for such omissions.

147 When you have to make a fraternal correction, do it with great kindness—with charity—in what you say and in the way you say it, for at that moment you are God's instrument.

148 When you love other people and you spread that affection—Christ's kindly, gentle charity—all around you, you will be able to support one another, and if someone is about to stumble he will feel that he is being supported, and also encouraged, to be faithful to God through this fraternal strength.

149 Bring out your spirit of mortification in those nice touches of charity, eager to make the way of sanctity in the midst of the world attractive for everyone. Sometimes a smile can be the best proof of a spirit of penance.

150 May you know how to put yourself out cheerfully, discreetly, and generously each day, serving others and making their lives more pleasant.

To act in this way is to practise the true charity of Jesus Christ.

151 You should make sure that wherever you are, there is that *good humor*—that cheerfulness—which is born of an interior life.

152 Make sure you practise this very interesting mortification: that of not making your conversation revolve around yourself.

153 Here is a good way of doing an examination of conscience:

Have I accepted in a spirit of expiation the difficulties which have come to me this day from the hand of God, or those which came from the behavior of my colleagues, or from my own wretchedness?

Have I managed to offer Our Lord in expiation the very sorrow I feel for having offended him so many times? Have I offered him the shame of all my inner embarrassment and humiliation at seeing how little progress I make along the path of virtue?

154   Habitual and customary mortifications are a good thing, but don't become one-track minded about them.

They need not necessarily be the same ones all the time. What should be constant, habitual, and customary—without your getting accustomed to it—is to have a *spirit* of mortification.

155   You want to follow in Christ's footsteps, to wear his livery, to identify yourself with Jesus. Well then, make your faith a living faith, full of sacrifice and deeds of service, and get rid of everything that stands in the way.

156   Sanctity has the flexibility of supple muscles. Whoever wishes to be a saint should know how to behave so that while he does something that involves a mortification for him, he omits doing something else—as long as this does not offend God—which he would also find difficult, and thanks the Lord for this comfort. If we Christians were to act other-wise, we would run the risk of becoming stiff and lifeless, like a rag doll.

Sanctity is not rigid like cardboard; it knows how to smile, to give way to others, and to hope. It is life—a supernatural life.

157   Mother, do not leave me! Let me seek your Son, let me find your Son, let me love your Son—with my whole being. Remember me, my Lady, remember me.

DEFEAT

158 When our vision is clouded, when our eyes have lost their clarity, we need to go to the light. And Jesus Christ has told us that he is the Light of the world and that he has come to heal the sick.

That is why your weaknesses and your falls—when God allows them—should not separate you from Christ, but rather draw you closer to him.

159 In my wretchedness I complained to a friend of mine, saying that it seemed as if Jesus were passing me by, and leaving me on my own.

But immediately I thought better of it and was sorry. Full of confidence, I said: It is not true, my Love. Quite clearly it is I who have gone away from you. Never again!

160 Beg the Lord for his grace so that you may be purified by his Love—and by constant penance.

161   Turn to Our Lady and ask her—as a token of her love for you—for the gift of contrition. Ask that you may be sorry, with the sorrow of Love, for all your sins, and for the sins of all men and women throughout the ages.

And with that same disposition, be bold enough to add: "Mother, my life, my hope, lead me by the hand. And if there is anything in me which is displeasing to my Father God grant that I may see it, so that, between the two of us, we may uproot it."

Do not be afraid to continue, saying to her: "O clement, O loving, O sweet Virgin Mary, pray for me, that by fulfilling the most lovable Will of your Son, I may be worthy to obtain and enjoy what Our Lord Jesus has promised."

162   Heavenly Mother, let me regain once more fervor, dedication, self-denial—in one word, *Love.*

163   You shouldn't be so easy on yourself. Don't wait until the New Year to make your resolutions. Every day is a good day to make good decisions. *Hodie, nunc!*—Today, now!

It tends to be the poor defeatist types who leave it until the New Year before beginning afresh. And even then, they never really begin.

164 I agree. You acted badly, out of weakness. But what I fail to understand is how, with a clear conscience, you have not repented. You cannot do something wrong and then say, or think, that it is something holy, or that it is of no importance.

165 You must always remember that the spiritual faculties are fed by what they receive from the senses. Guard them well!

166 As you very well know, you lose your peace when you consent in matters which entail unfaithfulness to your way.

Make up your mind to be consistent and responsible in your behavior.

167 The indelible memory of the favors you have received from God should always be a compelling force within you; especially so in times of tribulation.

168 There is but one fatal illness, one deadly mistake you can make: to settle for defeat, not to know how to fight with the spirit of a child of God. If this personal effort is lacking, the soul becomes paralyzed and languishes alone, and is incapable of bearing fruit.

Such cowardice on man's part puts pressure on Our Lord to utter those words addressed to him by the paralytic at the pool of Bethsaida, *hominem non habeo!*—I have no man to help me.

What a pity if Jesus does not find in you the man or the woman he expects.

169   The ascetical struggle is not something negative and therefore hateful, but rather a joyful affirmation. It is a sport.

A good sportsman doesn't fight to gain just one victory, and that at the first attempt. He has to build himself up for it, training over a long period of time, calmly and confidently. He keeps trying again and again, and if he doesn't succeed at the first attempt, he keeps on trying with determination until the obstacle is overcome.

170   You are my hope in all things, dear Jesus. Convert me!

171   When that priest, our good friend, used to sign himself "the sinner," he did so convinced that what he wrote was true.

My God, purify me too!

172   If you have done something wrong, be it big or small, go running back to God.

Savor those words of the psalm, *cor contritum et humiliatum, Deus, non despicies*—the Lord will never despise or ignore a contrite and humbled heart.

173 Keep turning this over in your mind and in your soul: Lord, how many times you have lifted me up when I have fallen and once my sins have been forgiven, have held me close to your Heart.

Keep returning to the thought...and never separate yourself from God again.

174 You see yourself as a poor man whose master has stripped him of his livery. You are only a sinner! And you understand the nakedness felt by our first parents.

You should be weeping all the time. And you *have* wept. You have suffered a great deal. And yet you are very happy. You wouldn't change places with anyone. For many years now you have not lost your *gaudium cum pace*—your peaceful joy. You thank God for this and would like to let everyone into the secret of your happiness.

Yes, I can see why people have often said of you— though you couldn't care less about "what people say"— that you are "a man of peace."

175 Some people do only what lies within the capacity of poor human creatures to accomplish, and consequently waste their time. What Peter experienced is repeated once more, word for word: *Praeceptor, per totam noctem laborantes nihil cepimus*—Master, we have toiled all night and caught nothing.

If they work on their own, without being united with the Church, not reckoning with the Church, what possible effectiveness could their apostolate have? None at all!

They need to be convinced that *on their own* they can achieve nothing. You should help them to go on listening to the rest of that Gospel story: *in verbo autem tuo laxabo rete*—at your word I will let down the net. It is then that the catch will be plentiful and effective.

How beautiful it is to mend our ways when we find we have done, for whatever reason, "our" apostolate, not his.

176 It was you who wrote what I am now copying out: "*Domine, tu scis quia amo te!*—Lord, you know that I love you! How very often, Jesus, I repeat again and again those words your dear Cephas uttered, as a bittersweet litany. For I know that I love you, and yet I am so very unsure of myself that I cannot bring myself to say it to you clearly. There are so many denials in my wicked life. *Tu scis, Domine!*—*You know* that I love you. May my actions, Jesus, never go against these yearnings of my heart."

Keep up this prayer of yours and he will certainly hear you.

177   Repeat this with confidence: Lord, if only my tears had been contrite!

Ask him humbly to grant you the sorrow you desire.

178   How villainous has been my behavior and how unfaithful I have been to God's grace.

My Mother, Refuge of Sinners, pray for me. May I never again hinder God's work in my soul.

179   So close to Christ for so many years—and such a sinner!

Doesn't that intimate love of Jesus for you move you to tears?

180   It is not that I lack true joy; on the contrary. And yet, painfully aware of my unworthiness, it is only natural that I should cry out with St Paul, "wretched man that I am!"

It is at such a time that you should increase your desire to tear down once and for all the barriers you yourself have set up.

181   Do not become alarmed or discouraged to discover that you have failings—and such failings!

Struggle to uproot them. And as you do so, be convinced that it is even a good thing to be aware of all those weaknesses, for otherwise you would be proud. And pride separates us from God.

182 Be filled with wonder at God's goodness, for Christ wants to live in you. Be filled with wonder too when you are aware of all the weight of your poor flesh, of your wretched flesh, and all the vileness of the poor clay you are made of.

Yes, but then remember too that call from God: Jesus Christ, who is God and Man, understands me and looks after me, for he is my Brother and my Friend.

183 Your life is happy, very happy, though on occasions you feel a pang of sadness, and even experience almost constantly a real sense of weariness.

Joy and affliction can go hand in hand like this, each in its own "man:" the former in the new man, the latter in the old.

184 Humility is born of knowing God and knowing oneself.

185 Lord, I ask for a gift from you: Love, a Love that will cleanse me. And another gift as well: self-knowledge so that I may be filled with humility.

186 The saints are those who struggle right to the end of their lives, who always get up each time they stumble, each time they fall, and courageously embark on their way once more with humility, love, and hope.

187 If your mistakes make you more humble, if they make you reach out more urgently for God's helping hand—then they are a road to sanctity. *Felix culpa!*—O happy fault!, the Church sings.

188 Prayer—even my prayer—is all-powerful.

189 Humility teaches each soul not to lose heart in the face of its own blunders.

True humility leads us to ask for forgiveness.

190 If I were a leper, my mother would kiss me. She would kiss my wounds without fear or hesitation.

Well then, what would the Blessed Virgin Mary do? When we feel we are like lepers, all full of sores, we have to cry out: Mother! And the protection of our Mother will be like a kiss upon our wounds, which will then be healed.

191 In the Sacrament of Penance it is Jesus who forgives us.

Christ's merits are applied to us there. It is for love of us that he is on the Cross with his arms stretched out, stitched to the wood more by the Love he has for us than by the nails.

192   If ever you fall, my son, go quickly to Confession and seek spiritual guidance. Show your wound so that it gets properly healed and all possibility of infection is removed, even if doing this hurts you as much as having an operation.

193   Sincerity is indispensable if we are to achieve greater union with God.

If you have an ugly "toad" inside you, my son, let it out! As I have always advised you, the first thing you must mention is what you wouldn't like anybody to know. Once the "toad" has been let out in Confession—how well one feels.

194   *Nam, et si ambulavero in medio umbrae mortis, non timebo mala*—though I should walk through the valley of the shadow of death, no evil will I fear. Neither my wretchedness nor the temptations of the enemy will worry me, *quoniam tu mecum es*—for you, Lord, are with me.

195   Just now, Jesus, when I was considering my wretchedness, I said to you: allow yourself to be taken in by this son of yours, just like those good fathers, full of kindness, who put into the hands of their little children the presents they want to receive from them—knowing perfectly well that little children have nothing of their own.

And what joy father and son have together, even though they are both in on the secret.

196 Jesus, my Love, to think that I could offend you again! *Tuus ego sum... salvum me fac.*—I am yours, save me.

197 You, who see yourself so badly lacking in virtues, in talents, in abilities... Do you not feel the desire to cry out like the blind Bartimaeus, "Jesus, Son of David, have pity on me?"

What a beautiful aspiration for you to say very often, "Lord, have pity on me!"

He will hear you and come to your aid.

198 Foster a desire for atonement in your soul, so that you may acquire greater contrition each day.

199 If you are faithful you will be able to count yourself a conqueror.

Even though you may lose some battles in your life, you will not know defeat. You can be sure that there is no such thing as *failure* if you act with purity of intention and with a desire to fulfill the Will of God.

And then, whether you win or lose, you will always triumph in the end, because you will have carried out your work with Love.

200 I am sure that God has listened to your humble and heartfelt plea: My Lord, I am not worried about what "others" may say. Forgive me for my unworthy life. May I be a saint—but it's you alone I wish to please.

201 In a Christian's life *everything* has to be for God— even personal weaknesses, once they have been put right. The Lord understands and forgives them.

202 What have I done to you, Jesus, that you should love me so? I have offended you...and loved you.

Loving you—this is what my life is going to be all about.

203 Surely all those consolations I receive from the Master are given me so that I may think of him all the time and serve him in little things, and so be able to serve him in great things.

A resolution: to please my good Jesus in the tiniest details of my daily life.

204 We have to love God because our heart is made for love. That is why, if we don't give our heart to God, to Our Lady and Mother, to souls... with a pure affection, it will seek revenge—and will breed worms instead.

205 Tell Our Lord with your whole heart: In spite of all my wretchedness I am madly in Love—drunk with Love!

206 From now on, truly sorrowful for my many falls, I shall remain, with God's grace, always upon the Cross.

207 What has been lost through the flesh, the flesh should pay back: be generous in your penance.

208 Invoke the Lord, and beg him for the spirit of penance of one who conquers himself every day, and offers him this constant victory unassumingly and perseveringly.

209 In your personal prayer, whenever you experience the weakness of the flesh you should repeat: Lord, give the Cross to this poor body of mine, which gets tired and rebellious.

210 How right that priest was when he preached, saying, "Jesus has forgiven me the great multitude of my sins in spite of my ingratitude. How generous he is. If the many sins of Mary Magdalene were forgiven because she loved greatly, many more have been forgiven me. What a great debt of love still remains for me to pay."

Jesus, teach me to go to the point of madness and heroism. With the help of your grace, even if I have to die for you, Lord, I will never abandon you again.

211 Lazarus rose because he heard the voice of God and immediately wanted to get out of the situation he was in. If he hadn't *wanted* to move, he would just have died again.

A sincere resolution: to have faith in God always; to hope in God always; to love God always—he never abandons us, even if we are rotting away as Lazarus was.

212 Let us marvel at the lovable paradox of our Christian condition: it is our own wretchedness which leads us to seek refuge in God, to become "like unto God." With him we can do all things.

213 When you have fallen or when you find yourself overwhelmed by the weight of your wretchedness, repeat with a firm hope: Lord see how ill I am; come and heal me, Lord, you who died on the Cross for love of me.

Be full of confidence. Keep on calling out to his most loving Heart. He will cure you, as he cured the lepers we read about in the Gospel.

214 Trust fully in God and have a greater desire each day never to run away from him.

215 Virgin Immaculate, my Mother, do not abandon me. See how my poor heart is filled with tears. I do not want to offend my God!

I already know, and I trust I shall never forget, that I am worth nothing. My smallness and my loneliness weigh upon me so much! But... I am not alone. You, Sweet Lady, and my Father God will never leave me.

Faced with rebellion of my flesh and all manner of diabolical arguments against my Faith, I love Jesus and I believe—I do Love and do Believe.

PESSIMISM

216 With God's grace, you have to tackle and carry out the impossible, because anybody can do what is possible.

217 Reject your pessimism and don't allow those around you to be pessimistic. God should be served with cheerfulness and abandonment.

218 Get rid of that human prudence which makes you so very cautious, so—sorry to be so blunt!—cowardly.

Let us not be narrow-minded. Let us not be infantile men or women, who are nearsighted and lack a supernatural breadth of vision. Could we be working for ourselves? Of course, not!

Well then, let us say quite fearlessly: Dearest Jesus, we are working for you. Are you going to deny us the material means we need? You know full well how worthless we are; still, I would not treat a servant working for me in that way.

Therefore, we hope and are sure you will give us all we need to be able to serve you.

219 An act of faith: Nothing can prevail against God. Nothing can prevail against God's people.

Don't forget it.

220 Don't lose heart. Carry on! Carry on with that holy stubbornness which in spiritual terms is called *perseverance*.

221 My Lord, you always come to meet our real needs.

222 You are not getting worse. It is just that now you have more light to see yourself as you really are. You must avoid even the slightest hint of discouragement.

223 Along the road that leads to personal sanctity we can at times get the impression that we are going backwards instead of forwards, that we are getting worse instead of better.

As long as there is interior struggle this pessimistic thought is only an illusion, a deception to be rejected as false.

Persevere and don't worry. If you fight with tenacity you are making progress and are growing in sanctity.

224 Interior dryness is not lukewarmness. When a person is lukewarm the waters of grace slide over him without being soaked in. In contrast, there are dry lands which seem arid but which, with a few drops of rain at the right time, yield abundant flowers and delicious fruit.

That is why I ask: When are we going to be convinced? How important it is to be docile to the divine calls which come at each moment of the day, because it is precisely there that God is awaiting us!

225 Be clever, spiritually clever. Don't wait for the Lord to send you setbacks; go out to meet them with a spirit of voluntary atonement. Then you'll receive them not so much with resignation (an old-sounding word) as with Love—a word which is forever young.

226 Today, for the first time, you had the feeling that things were getting simpler, that everything was "sorting itself out". At last you see an end to the problems that were worrying you. And you understand that they are more thoroughly and better resolved the more you abandon yourself into the arms of your Father God.

What are you waiting for to start behaving always as a son of God? This should be the driving force in your life.

227 Turn to Our Lady—the Mother, Daughter, and Spouse of God, and our Mother—and ask her to obtain more graces for you from the Blessed Trinity: the grace of faith, of hope, of love, and of contrition. So that when it seems that a harsh dry wind is blowing in your life, threatening to wither those flowers of your soul, they will not wither—and neither will those of your brothers.

228 Be filled with faith and rest assured. The Lord tells us this through the prophet Jeremiah: *orabitis me, et ego exaudiam vos*—whenever you call upon me, whenever you pray, I will listen to you.

229 I refer everything to you, my God. Without you —who are my Father—what would become of me?

230 Allow me to give you the advice of an experienced soul: your prayer—and your whole life should be spent in prayer—ought to have the simplicity of a "child's prayer".

231 A sick man is brought to Jesus, who looks at him. Contemplate the scene closely and meditate upon his words: *confide, fili*—take heart, my son.

This is what Our Lord says to you when you feel the weight of your errors. Have faith. In the first place: faith. And then allow yourself to be carried like the paralytic did, with interior and submissive obedience.

232 My son, you can do nothing on the supernatural level through your own strength; whereas when you become God's instrument you can do everything. *Omnia possum in eo qui me confortat!*—I can do all things in him who strengthens me. For in his goodness he wishes to use inadequate instruments, like you and like me.

233 Whenever you pray, make the effort to have the kind of faith of those sick people we read about in the Gospel. You can be sure Jesus is listening to you.

234 My Mother! Mothers on earth look with greater love upon the weakest of their children, the one with the worst health, or who is least intelligent, or is a poor cripple.

Sweet Lady, I know that you are more of a Mother than all other mothers put together. And, since I am your son, since I am weak, and ill, and crippled, and ugly…

235 We lack faith. The day we practise this virtue, trusting in God and in his Mother, we will be daring and loyal. God, who is the same God as ever, will work miracles through our hands.

Grant me, dear Jesus, the faith I truly desire. My Mother, sweet Lady, Mary most holy, make me really believe.

236 A firm resolution: to abandon myself in Jesus Christ with all my wretchedness. Whatever he may want, at any moment, *Fiat*—let it be done.

237 Never lose heart, for Our Lord is always ready to give you the grace to bring about the new conversion you need, a real advance on the supernatural plane.

238 "Blessed be God," you said to yourself after having finished your sacramental Confession. And you thought: it is as if I had just been born again.

You then continued calmly: "*Domine, quid me vis facere?*—Lord, what would you have me do?"

And you yourself came up with the reply: "By the help of your grace I will let nothing and no one come between me and the fulfillment of your most Holy Will: *Serviam*—I will serve you unconditionally."

239 We read in the Gospel that the Magi were filled with great joy, *videntes stellam*—when they saw the star.

They rejoiced, my son, they were immensely glad, because they had done what they were supposed to do, and they rejoiced because they knew for certain they would reach the King who never abandons those who seek him.

240 When you really come to love God's Will you will never, even in the worst state of agitation, lose sight of the fact that our Father in Heaven is always close to you, very close, right next to you, with his everlasting Love and with his unbounded affection.

241 If the outlook in your interior life and in your soul is darkened, allow yourself to be led along by the hand, as a blind man would do.

In time the Lord will reward this humble surrendering of your own judgment by giving clarity of mind.

242 To be afraid of anything or anybody, but especially of the person who directs our soul, is unworthy of a son of God.

243 Are you not moved to hear some affectionate word addressed to your mother?

The same thing happens to Our Lord. We cannot separate Jesus from his Mother.

244 When you find yourself worn out or fed up, go and confide in Our Lord, as that good friend of ours did, and say: "Jesus, see what you can do about it. Even before I begin to struggle, I am already tired."

He will give you his strength.

245 A task which presents no difficulties lacks human appeal—and supernatural appeal too. If you find no resistance when hammering a nail into a wall, what can you expect to hang on it?

246 It seems incredible that a man like you—who say you know you're nothing—should dare to place obstacles in the way of God's grace.

Yet this is what you're doing with your false humility, your "objectivity," your pessimism.

247 Lord, grant me the grace to give up everything that has to do with myself. I should have no other concern than your Glory—in other words, your Love. Everything for Love!

248 "When Herod heard this," (that the King had come to this earth), "he was troubled, and all Jerusalem with him."

This is an everyday occurrence. We see the same thing happening now. In the face of God's greatness, which shows itself in a thousand ways, there are always some people—sometimes even in positions of authority—who are troubled. It's because they do not love God; because they have no real wish to meet him; because they don't want to follow his inspiration, and so they become obstacles in God's path.

Be forewarned; carry on working and don't worry. Seek the Lord and pray—he will triumph.

249 You are not alone. Neither you nor I can ever find ourselves alone. And even less if we go to Jesus through Mary, for she is a Mother who will never abandon us.

250 Don't give way to sadness when it feels as if the Lord has given up on you. Seek him with greater determination. He who is Love does not leave you on your own.

Be convinced that "he has left you on your own" out of Love, so that you may see clearly in your life what is his and what is yours.

251 You said to me: "I seem not only unable to go ahead along my way, but also unable to be saved without a miracle of grace. Oh, my poor soul! I remain cold and, what is worse, almost indifferent. It's as if I were an outsider looking at 'a case' (mine) which had nothing to do with him. Will these days turn out to be completely futile?

And nevertheless, my Mother is my Mother and Jesus is—dare I say it?—*my* Jesus. And there are good and saintly souls, at this very moment, praying for me."

Go on walking hand in hand with your Mother, I replied, and "dare" to say to Jesus that he is yours. In his goodness he will bring clear light to your soul.

252 Grant me, Jesus, the Cross with no Simon of Cyrene to help me. No, that's not right; I need your grace, I need your help here as in everything. *You* must be my Simon of Cyrene. With you, my God, no trial can daunt me.

But what if my Cross should consist in boredom or sadness? In that case I say to you, Lord, with you I would gladly be sad.

253 As long as I don't lose you, no sorrow will be a sorrow at all.

254 Jesus will refuse a word to no one, and his words bring healing, they console, they bring light.

This is what you and I have to remember at all times, especially when we find ourselves tired and weighed down by work or opposition.

255 Don't expect people's applause for your work.

What is more, sometimes you mustn't even expect other people and institutions, who like you are working for Christ, to understand you.

Seek only the glory of God and, while loving everyone, don't worry if there are some who don't understand you.

256 If there are mountains in the way, obstacles, misunderstandings, and backbiting, which Satan seeks and God allows, you must have faith, faith with deeds, faith with sacrifice, faith with humility.

257 Faced by apparent sterility in your apostolate you begin to detect the first waves of discouragement, which your faith rejects quite firmly. But you realize that you need a more humble, lively, and operative faith.

As someone who longs to bring health to souls, you should cry out like the father of that sick boy possessed by the devil: *Domine, adiuva incredulitatem meam!*— Lord, help my unbelief!

Have no doubt: the miracle will be performed again.

258 What a beautiful prayer for you to say frequently, that one of our good friend praying for a priest whom hatred for religion imprisoned: "My God, comfort him, since it is for you he suffers persecution. How many there are who suffer because they serve you!"

What a source of joy the Communion of Saints is.

259 The measures taken by some governments to ensure that the faith in their countries dies out reminds me of the seals set upon the tomb of Jesus by the Sanhedrin.

He was not subject to anybody or anything, and despite those seals, he rose again.

260 The solution is to love. St John the Apostle wrote some words which really move me: *qui autem timet, non est perfectus in caritate.* I like to translate them as follows, almost word for word—the fearful man doesn't know how to love.

You, therefore, who do love and know how to show it, you mustn't be afraid of anything. So, on you go!

261 God is with you. The Blessed Trinity dwells in your soul in grace.

That is why, inspite of your wretchedness, you can and should keep up a continuous conversation with the Lord.

262 You should pray at all times—always.

You should feel the need to go to God after every success and after every failure in your interior life.

263 May your prayer always be a real and sincere act of adoration of God.

264 When the Lord brought you into the Church he put an indelible mark upon your soul through Baptism: you are a son of God. Don't forget it.

265 Give thanks often to Jesus, for through him, with him, and in him you are able to call yourself a son of God.

266 If we feel we are beloved sons of our Heavenly Father, as indeed we are, how can we fail to be happy all the time? Think about it.

267 As he was giving out Holy Communion that priest felt like shouting out: this is Happiness I am giving to you!

268 Build up a gigantic faith in the Holy Eucharist. Be filled with wonder before this ineffable reality. We have God with us; we can receive him every day and, if we want to, we can speak intimately with him, just as we talk with a friend, as we talk with a brother, as we talk with a father, as we talk with Love itself.

269 How beautiful our Christian vocation is—to be sons of God! It brings joy and peace on earth which the world cannot give.

270 Lord, grant me the love with which you want me to love you.

271 To remove the dark shadow of pessimism which hung over you that morning, you again appealed to your Angel as you do every day—but this time you were more *thorough*. You said a few nice words to him and you asked him to teach you to love Jesus at least, at least as much as *he* loves him. And with that you recovered your calm.

272 Ask your Mother Mary, ask St Joseph and your Guardian Angel to speak to the Lord and tell him the things you can't manage to put into words because you are so dull.

273 Fill yourself with confidence. The Mother we have is the Mother of God, the Most Blessed Virgin, the Queen of Heaven and Earth.

274 Jesus was born in a cave in Bethlehem because, Sacred Scripture tells us, "there was no room for them in the inn."

I am not departing from theological truth when I say that Jesus is still looking for shelter in your heart.

275 Our Lord is upon the Cross saying, I am suffering so that men, who are my brothers, may be happy, not only in Heaven, but also—as far as possible—on earth, if they really embrace the most Holy Will of my heavenly Father.

276 It is true that your contribution is nil and that it is God who does everything in your soul.

However, let not this be the case as far as your correspondence to his grace is concerned.

277 Practise the virtue of hope and, with God as your motive, even when you find it hard, persevere at your work and try to finish it well, convinced that those efforts of yours are not useless in the Lord's sight.

278 When there is the desire and also the reality of pleasing God continually in your daily work, which is normally made up of many little things, I assure you that nothing is ever lost.

279 You would be right in thinking: how good the Lord is, who has sought me and has made known to me this holy path where I can be effective and where I can love all men, bringing them peace and happiness.

This thought has then to be turned into resolutions.

280 You know that you will never lack God's grace, because he has chosen you from all eternity. And if this is what he has done for you, he will grant you all the help you need to be faithful to him as his son.

Go forward, therefore, with a sure step and try to correspond at every moment to the promptings of God's grace.

281 I ask the Mother of God to smile upon us if she wishes, if she can... She will indeed do so.

Moreover, she will reward our generosity a thousandfold here on earth. A thousandfold that's what I am asking her for!

282 Practise a cheerful charity which is at once kindly and firm; human and at the same time supernatural. It should be an affectionate charity, knowing how to welcome everyone with a sincere and habitual smile, and how to understand the ideas and the feelings of others.

In this way, with gentleness and strength, and without concessions in matters of personal morals or in doctrine, the charity of Christ—when it is being well lived—will give you a spirit of conquest. Each day you will have a greater desire to work for souls.

283 My son, I said with assurance, in spreading our "madness" to other apostles I am not unaware of the "obstacles" we will find. Some of them may appear insurmountable... But *inter medium montium pertransibunt* *aquae*—the waters will pass through the midst of the mountains. Our supernatural spirit and the drive of our zeal will cut through the mountains and we shall overcome those obstacles.

284 "My God, my God. All of them were equally loved, through you, in you, and with you, and now they are all scattered." Thus you complained when you saw yourself once again all alone and lacking in human resources.

But Our Lord immediately made you feel sure in your soul that he would sort it out. And you said to him: "You will fix everything."

And so he did. God solved everything sooner, more fully, and better than you expected.

285 It is indeed just that the Father, the Son, and the Holy Spirit should crown the Blessed Virgin as Queen and Lady of all created things.

You have to make use of her power. With the daring of a child, join in this celebration in Heaven. For myself, since I have no precious stones or virtues to offer, I crown the Mother of God and my Mother with my failings, once they have been purified.

She is expecting something from you too.

YOU CAN!

286 I want to warn you against a difficulty that may arise: it is the temptation of weariness and discouragement.

Isn't it still fresh in your memory what life—your old life—used to be like, with no aim to it, no purpose, no sparkle, and then with God's light and your own dedication, a new direction was given to it and you were filled with joy?

Don't be so silly as to exchange your new life for that other one.

287 If you feel for whatever reason that you cannot manage to go on, abandon yourself in God telling him: Lord, I trust in you, I abandon myself in you, but do help me in my weakness!

And filled with confidence, repeat: See Jesus what a filthy rag I am. My life seems to me so miserable. I am not worthy to be a son of yours. Tell him all this—and tell him so over and over again.

It will not be long before you hear him say, *Ne timeas!* —do not be afraid; and also: *Surge et ambula!*—Rise up and walk!

288   You were still rather hesitant when you were telling me: "I am deeply aware of the occasions when the Lord is asking more of me."

All I could think of was to remind you how you used to assure me that the only thing you wanted was to identify yourself with him. What's keeping you back?

289   If only you could manage to fulfill that resolution you made: "to die a little to myself each day."

290   Cheerfulness, and supernatural and human optimism, can go hand in hand with physical tiredness, with sorrow, with tears (because we have a heart), and with difficulties in our interior life or our apostolic work.

He who is *perfectus Deus, perfectus Homo*—perfect God and perfect Man—and who enjoyed every happiness in Heaven, chose to experience fatigue and tiredness, tears and suffering... so that we might understand that if we are to be supernatural we must also be very human.

291 Jesus is asking you to pray more. You see this very clearly.

Nonetheless... how poor your response has been. Everything is a great effort for you: you are like a baby who is too lazy to learn to walk. But in your case it isn't just laziness. It is fear, too, and a lack of generosity.

292 You should repeat very often: Jesus, if ever a doubt creeps into my soul, setting up other noble ambitions in place of what you are asking of me, I tell you now that I prefer to follow you, no matter how much it costs. Do not leave me!

293 Seek union with God and buoy yourself up with hope—that *sure* virtue—because Jesus will illumine the way for you with the gentle light of his mercy, even in the darkest night.

294 Your prayer went like this: "My wretchedness weighs me down, but it doesn't overwhelm me because I am a son of God. I want to atone, to Love... And," you added, "like St Paul, I want to turn my weaknesses to good use, convinced that the Lord will not abandon those who place their trust in him."

Carry on like that. I assure you that—with God's grace—you will succeed, and you will overcome your wretchedness and your shortcomings.

295 Anytime is the right time to make an effective resolution, to say "I believe," to say "I hope," to say "I love."

296 Learn to praise the Father, the Son, and the Holy Spirit. Learn to have a special devotion to the Blessed Trinity: I believe in God the Father, I believe in God the Son, I believe in God the Holy Spirit; I hope in God the Father, I hope in God the Son, I hope in God the Holy Spirit; I love God the Father, I love God the Son, I love God the Holy Spirit. I believe, I hope, and I love the most Holy Trinity.

This devotion is much needed as a supernatural exercise for the soul, expressed by the movement of the heart, although not always in words.

297 The system, the method, the procedure, the only way to have a life abundant and fertile in supernatural fruits, is to follow the Holy Spirit's advice, which comes to us via the *Acts of the Apostles: omnes erant perseverantes unanimiter in oratione*—all these with one accord devoted themselves to prayer.

Nothing can be done without prayer!

298 My Lord Jesus has a Heart more tender than the hearts of all good men put together. If a good man (of average goodness) knew that a certain person loved him, without seeking personal satisfaction or reward of any kind (he loves for love's sake); and if he also knew that all this person wanted from him was that he should not object to being loved, even from afar... then it would not be long before he responded to such a disinterested love.

If the Loved One is so powerful that he can do all things, I am sure that, as well as surrendering in the end to the faithful love of a created being (in spite of the wretchedness of that poor soul) he will give this lover the supernatural beauty, knowledge, and power he needs so that the eyes of Jesus are not sullied when he gazes upon the poor heart that is adoring him.

Love, my child; love and await.

299 If there is sacrifice when you sow love, you will also reap Love.

300 My child, are you not aflame with the desire to bring all men to love him?

301 Jesus as a child and as an adolescent. I love to picture you like this, Lord, because I somehow pluck up more courage. I love to see you as a tiny, almost helpless babe. It makes me feel you need me.

302 Whenever I go into the oratory, having become a little child once more, I say to Our Lord that I love him more than anyone.

303 How wonderfully effective the Holy Eucharist is in the actions, and even before that in the souls, of those who receive it frequently and piously.

304 If all those people became so enthusiastic and were ready to acclaim you over a piece of bread, even granting that the multiplication of loaves was a very great miracle, shouldn't we be doing much more for all the many gifts you have granted us, and especially for giving us your very self unreserved in the Eucharist?

305 Good child: see how lovers on earth kiss the flowers, the letters, the mementos of those they love...

Then you, how could you ever forget that you have him always at your side—yes, *him*? How could you forget... that you can eat him?

306 Put your head frequently round the oratory door to say to Jesus: I abandon myself into your arms.

Leave everything you have—your wretchedness—at his feet.

In this way, in spite of the welter of things you carry along behind you, you will never lose your peace.

307   Pray resolutely using the words of the Psalmist: "Thou, Lord, art my refuge and my strength, I trust in thee."

I promise you that he will preserve you from the ambushes of the "noontide devil," when you are tempted and even when you fall, and when your age and virtues ought to have proved solid and you should have known by heart that he alone is your stronghold.

308   Do you think people are grateful for services rendered only reluctantly? Evidently not. You might even say it would have been better not to have bothered.

And yet you think you can serve God with sour looks? No, you can't! You have to serve him cheerfully, in spite of your wretchedness, which we will be able to get rid of with God's grace.

309   Doubts assail you, temptations, with that gloss of elegance about them.

I love to hear you say how this shows that the devil considers you his enemy, and that the grace of God will never leave you unprotected. Keep up the struggle!

310   The majority of people who have personal problems "have them" because they selfishly think about themselves.

311   Everything seems so peaceful. God's enemy, however, is not asleep...

The Heart of Jesus is also awake and watching! Herein lies my hope.

312   Sanctity consists in struggling, in knowing that we have defects, and in heroically trying to overcome them.

Sanctity, I insist, consists in overcoming those defects—although we will still have defects when we die; for if not, as I have told you, we would become proud.

313   Thank you, Lord, because—as well as allowing us to be tempted—you also give us the strength and beauty of your grace so that we can win through. Thank you, Lord, for the temptations you allow us to have so that we may be humble.

314   Do not abandon me, Lord. Don't you see the bottomless pit this poor son of yours would end up in?

My Mother: I am your son too.

315   Without God's help it is impossible to live a clean life. God wants us to be humble, and to ask him for his help through our Mother who is his Mother.

You should say to Our Lady, right now, speaking without the sound of words, from the accompanied solitude of your heart: "O, my Mother, sometimes this poor heart of mine rebels; but if you help me…" She will indeed help you to keep it clean and to follow the way God has called you to pursue. The Virgin Mary will always make it easier for you to fulfill the Will of God.

316 To preserve holy purity and live a clean life you have to love and practise daily mortification.

317 Whenever you feel the stirrings of your poor flesh, which sometimes attacks with violent assaults, kiss your crucifix, kiss it many times with firm resolve, even if it seems you are doing so without love.

318 Place yourself before the Lord each day and tell him slowly and in all earnestness, like the man in the Gospel who was in such great need, *Domine, ut videam!*—Lord, that I may see; that I may see what you expect from me, and struggle to be faithful to you.

319 My God, how easy it is to persevere when we know that you are the Good Shepherd, and that we—you and I—are sheep belonging to your flock!

For we know full well that the Good Shepherd gives his whole life for each one of his sheep.

320 Today in your prayer you confirmed your resolution to be a saint. I understand you when you make this more specific by adding, "I know I shall succeed, not because I am sure of myself, Jesus, but because I am sure of you."

321 By yourself, if you don't count on grace, you can do nothing worthwhile, for you would be cutting the link which connects you with God.

With grace, on the other hand, you can do all things.

322 Do you want to learn from Christ and follow the example of his life? Open the Holy Gospels and listen to God in dialogue with men—with you.

323 Jesus knows very well what is best—and I love his Will and will do so always. He it is who controls "the puppets" and so he will always give whatever I ask of him, provided it is a means to achieving our end—even if there are godless men who are determined to put obstacles in the way.

324 True faith shows itself in humility. *Dicebat enim intra se*—that poor woman said to herself: *Si tetigero tantum vestimentum eius, salva ero*—if I can but touch the hem of his garment, I shall be healed.

What humility she showed. It was both a result and a sign of her faith.

325 If it is God who lays the burden upon you, God will also give you the strength to bear it.

326 Invoke the Holy Spirit in your examination of conscience so that you may get to know God better, and yourself also. In this way you will be converted each day.

327 Spiritual direction. You must have that true supernatural sense and holy shamelessness to allow another to poke at your soul and determine how far you are able—and willing—to give glory to God.

328 *Quomodo fiet istud quoniam virum non cognosco?*—How can this marvel take place if I have no knowledge of man? Mary asks the angel in words which reflect the sincerity of her Heart.

Observing the Blessed Virgin has confirmed for me a clear rule of conduct: if we want to enjoy peace, and also to live in peace, we must be very sincere with God, with those who direct our souls and with ourselves.

329 A foolish child wails and stamps his feet when his loving mother puts a needle to his finger to get a splinter out. A sensible child, on the other hand, perhaps with his eyes full of tears—for the flesh is weak—looks

gratefully at his good mother who is making him suffer
a little in order to avoid much greater harm.

Jesus, may I be a sensible child.

330 My child, my little donkey: if the Lord, with
Love, has washed your grimy back, so accustomed to the
muck, and has laid a satin harness upon you, and covered
you with dazzling jewels, don't forget, poor donkey, that
with your faults you *could* throw that beautiful load on
to the ground... But on your own you *couldn't* put it back
on again.

331 Draw strength from your divine filiation. God is
a Father—your Father!—full of warmth and infinite love.

Call him Father frequently and tell him, when you are
alone, that you love him, that you love him very much,
and that you feel proud and strong because you are his
son.

332 Cheerfulness is a necessary consequence of our
divine filiation, of knowing that our Father God loves us
with a love of predilection, that he holds us up and helps
us and forgives us.

Remember this and never forget it: even if it should
seem at times that everything around you is collapsing,
in fact nothing is collapsing at all, because God doesn't
lose battles.

333 The best way of showing our gratitude to God is to be passionately in love with the fact that we are his children.

334 You are like the little pauper who suddenly finds out that he is the son of the King. That is why now the only thing that concerns you on this earth is the Glory of your Father God, his Glory in everything.

335 My little friend, say to him: Jesus, knowing that I love you and that you love me, nothing else matters—all is well.

336 "I have asked Our Lady for many things," you were telling me, and then you corrected yourself: "What I should say is that I have brought many things to Our Lady's attention."

337 "I can do all things in him who strengthens me." With him there is no possibility of failure, and this conviction gives rise to the holy "superiority complex" whereby we take on things with a spirit of victory, because God grants us his strength.

338 The artist stood before his canvas with a deep desire to surpass himself and cried out, "Lord, I want to paint for you thirty-eight hearts, thirty-eight angels bursting with continual love for you, thirty-eight marvels embroidered on your Heaven, thirty-eight suns upon your mantle, thirty-eight flames of fire, thirty-eight ardors, thirty-eight feats of madness, thirty-eight joys..."

Then, humbly, he had to admit that it was all in his imagination and desire. In reality what confronts him are thirty-eight figures which haven't come out properly and which mortify the sight rather than give pleasure.

339 We have no right to claim that the Angels should obey us—but we can be absolutely sure that the holy angels hear us always.

340 Allow God to lead you. He will lead you along "his path," making use of innumerable adversities—possibly including your own sluggishness—so that it may clearly be seen that your work is being carried out by him.

341 Ask him without any fear, and insist. Remember that scene of the multiplication of loaves we read about in the Gospel. Notice how magnanimously he says to the Apostles, How many loaves do you have? Five?... How many are you asking for? And he gives six, a hundred, thousands... Why?

Because Christ sees all our needs with divine wisdom, and with his almighty power he can and does go far beyond our desires.

Our Lord sees much farther than our poor minds can discern and he is infinitely generous!

342 When we're working for God we have to have a superiority complex, I told you.

But isn't that a sign of pride? you asked me. No. It is a consequence of humility; the humility which makes me say: Lord, you are who you are. I am nothingness itself. You have all the perfections: power, strength, love, glory, wisdom, authority, dignity... If I unite myself to you, like a child who goes to the strong embrace of his father or sits on his dear mother's knee, I will feel the warmth of your divinity, I will experience the light of your wisdom, I will sense your strength coursing through my veins.

343 If you live in the presence of God, high above the deafening storm, the sun will always be shining on you; and deep below the roaring and destructive waves, peace and calm will reign in your soul.

344 For a son of God each day should be an opportunity for renewal, knowing for sure that with the help of grace he will reach the end of the road, which is Love.

That is why if you begin and begin again, you are doing well. If you have a will to win, if you struggle, then with God's help you will conquer. There will be no difficulty you cannot overcome.

345 Make your way to Bethlehem, go up to the Child, rock him in your arms, say warm and tender things to him, press him close to your heart...

I am not talking childish nonsense, I am speaking of love! And love is shown with deeds. In the intimacy of your soul, you can indeed hug him tight.

346 We should let Jesus know that we are children. And when children are tiny and innocent, what a lot of effort it takes for them to go up one step. They look as though they are wasting their time, but eventually they manage to climb up. Now there is another step. Crawling on their hands and knees, and putting their whole body into it, they score another success—one more step. Then they start again. What an effort! There are only a few more steps to go now. But then the toddler stumbles, and—whoops!—down he goes. With bumps all over and in floods of tears, the poor child sets out and begins to try again.

We are just like that, Jesus, when we are on our own. Please take us up in your loving arms, like a big and good Friend of the simple child. Do not leave us until we have reached the top. And then—oh then!—we will know how to correspond to your Merciful Love, with the daring of young children, telling you, sweet Lord, that after Mary and Joseph, there never has been nor will there ever be a mortal soul—and there have been some who have been really crazy—who love you as much as I love you.

347 Don't be ashamed of doing little childlike things, I advised you. As long as they are not done out of routine, they will not be fruitless.

Here is an example. Imagine that a soul who is following the way of spiritual childhood is moved each night, during the hours of sleep, to adorn a wooden statue of the Blessed Virgin.

Our intelligence would reject such an action as quite useless. But humble souls, touched by grace, understand very well that a child would indeed act like this out of love.

And then the strong will, which all those who are little children spiritually have, insists and moves the intelligence to give way... And if that childlike soul were to continue each day dressing up the statue of Our Lady, there would be repeated each day a little act of childlike love which would be fruitful in the eyes of God.

348 When you are genuinely a child and you follow the ways of childhood—if you are moved by God to follow this path—you will be invincible.

349 The confident petition of a small child: Grant me, Lord, the sort of compunction which those who have pleased you most have had.

350 Small child, you would cease to be one if anyone or anything came between you and God.

351 I shouldn't ask Jesus for anything. I will concentrate on pleasing him in everything and telling him things as though he didn't know them already, just as a little child does with his father.

352 Little child, say to Jesus: I will not be satisfied with anything less than you.

353 In your prayer of spiritual childhood what childish things you say to your Lord! With the confidence of a child speaking to his great Friend of whose love he is utterly sure, you confided in him, saying, May I live only for your Glory!

Thinking things over you admit in all sincerity that everything you do turns out badly. "But," you add, "this can't surprise you, Jesus. It is impossible for me to do anything right. You have to help me. Please do it for me and you will see how well it turns out."

Then, with great daring, and without departing from the truth, you continue: "May your Spirit thoroughly penetrate me and intoxicate me so that I may be able to do your Will. I want to do it. And if I don't do it... it's because you are not helping me. But you *are* helping me!"

354 You have to feel the urgent necessity to see yourself as small, weak, and bereft of everything. You will then clamber on to the lap of our Mother in Heaven, with heartfelt aspirations and loving glances, Marian devotions... which are such a vital part of your filial spirit.

She will watch over you.

355 Persevere along your way no matter what happens; persevere, cheerfully and optimistically, because the Lord is bent on sweeping aside all obstacles.

Hear me well: I am quite certain that if you struggle, you will be a saint!

356 When Our Lord called the first Apostles they were busy mending their broken nets by the side of an old boat. Our Lord told them to follow him and *statim*—immediately—they left everything—*relictis omnibus*—everything! And followed him.

Sometimes, though we wish to imitate them, we find we don't manage to leave everything, and there remains some attachment in our heart, something wrong in our life which we're not willing to break with and offer it up to God.

Won't you examine your heart in depth? Nothing should remain there except what is his. If not, we aren't really loving him, neither you nor I.

357   Tell Our Lord constantly that you sincerely desire to be a saint and to do apostolate. Then the poor vessel of your soul will not get broken. And should it do so, it will be put together again and acquire an added attractiveness, and it will continue to be of use for your sanctity and the apostolate.

358   Your prayer should be that of a child of God, and not that of the hypocrites who will hear from Jesus' lips: "Not every one who says to me, Lord, Lord, shall enter into the Kingdom of Heaven."

Your prayer, your clamor of "Lord, Lord" should be linked in a thousand different ways throughout the day to a desire and an effective effort to fulfill the Will of God.

359   Little one, say to him: O Jesus, I don't want the devil to get hold of souls!

360 If God's Love has chosen you out and called you to follow him, you have a duty to respond to him... and it is also your duty, an equally serious duty, to lead and help your fellow men towards sanctity and the right path.

361 Cheer up! Not least when the going gets hard. Doesn't it make you happy to think that your faithfulness to your Christian commitments depends to a large extent on you?

Be full of joy and freely renew your decision: "Lord, I want it too. Count on the little I have to offer."

362 God is not removing you from your environment. He is not taking you away from the world, or from your condition in life, or from your noble human ambitions, or from your professional work... But he wants you to be a saint—right there!

363 Putting yourself in the presence of God, and with your forehead flat against the ground, consider how (for that's the way it is) you are more filthy and despicable than the sweepings swept up by a broom.

And in spite of this, the Lord has chosen you.

364 When are you going to make up your mind?

Many people around you live a life of sacrifice simply for human reasons. These poor people forget they are children of God and act the way they do perhaps only out of pride, or ostentation, or in order to be more comfortably off later on in life. They are willing to give up all kinds of things!

You instead have many motives for which to sacrifice yourself. You have the sweet burden of the Church, of your family, your colleagues, and friends. What are you doing about it? Are you ready to act with a proper sense of responsibility?

365 "O Lord, why did you come looking for me—who am nothing—when there are so many holy, wise, and rich people, so full of prestige?"

You are perfectly right. And so, thank God for having done just that. Thank him with deeds and with love.

366 Jesus, may all in your Holy Church persevere in their way, following their Christian vocation, like the Wise Men who followed the star, spurning Herod's advice—for that type of advice will not be lacking.

367 Let us ask Jesus Christ that the fruits of his Redemption may grow abundantly in men's hearts: more and more, ever more abundantly—divinely abundantly!

And for this to be so, may he make us good children of his Blessed Mother.

368 Would you like to know a secret to happiness? Give yourself to others and serve them, without waiting to be thanked.

369 Live and work for God, with a spirit of love and service, with a priestly soul, even though you may not be a priest. Then all your actions will take on a genuine supernatural meaning which will keep your whole life united to the source of all graces.

370 Looking on the immense panorama of souls who are awaiting us, and being struck by the wonderful and awesome responsibility before us, you may at times have asked yourself, as I have: "Can I contribute anything, when the task is so vast? I, who am so puny?"

It is then we have to open the Gospel and contemplate how Jesus cures the man born blind. He uses mud made from the dust of the earth and saliva. Yet this is the salve which brings light to those blind eyes!

That is what you and I are. Fully aware of our weaknesses and our worthlessness, but with the grace of God and our good will, we can be salve to give light and provide strength for others as well as for ourselves.

371 Said an apostolic soul: Jesus, you know what needs to be done... you know I am not working for myself.

372 If you persevere in your prayer, with "personal perseverance," God Our Lord will give you all the means you need to be more effective and to spread his kingdom in the world.

But you have to keep faithful: asking, asking, asking... Are you really behaving this way?

373 The Lord wants his children in all the honest pathways of this earth, sowing the seeds of understanding and forgiveness, of harmony, charity, and peace.

How about you? What are you doing?

374 The Redemption is still being accomplished, even now, and you are—you *have* to be—a co-redeemer.

375 To be a Christian in the world doesn't mean isolating oneself—on the contrary! It means loving all mankind and burning with a desire to enkindle in everyone the fire of the love of God.

376 Dear Lady, Mother of God and my Mother, not in the remotest way do I wish that you may ever be anything less than Mistress and Empress of the whole of creation.

TO FIGHT
ONCE MORE

377 Follow St Paul's advice: *hora est iam nos de somno surgere!*—it is time to get down to work. Both on the inside, building up your soul; and on the outside, building up the Kingdom of God, right where you are.

378 All contrite you told me: "How much wretchedness I see in myself! I am so stupid and I am carting around such a weight of concupiscence that it is as though I had never really done anything to get closer to God. Lord, here I am beginning, beginning, always just beginning! I will try, however, to push forward each day with all my heart."

May he bless those efforts of yours.

379 Father, you told me, I have committed many errors, I have made so many mistakes.

I know, I replied. But God Our Lord, who also knows all that and has taken it into account, only asks you to be humble enough to admit it and asks that you struggle to make amends, so as to serve him better each day with more interior life, with continual prayer and with piety, and making use of the proper means to sanctify your work.

380 Would that you could acquire, as I know you would like to, the virtues of the donkey. Donkeys are humble, hardworking, persevering—stubborn—and faithful, with a sure step, tough, and—if they have a good master—also grateful and obedient.

381 Continue thinking about the donkey's good qualities and notice how in order to do anything worthwhile, it has to allow itself to be ruled by the will of whoever is leading it. On its own the donkey would only...make an ass of itself. Probably the brightest thing that would occur to it to do would be to roll over on the ground, trot to the manger, and start braying.

Dear Jesus, you too should say to him, *ut iumentum factus sum apud te!*—you have made me be your little donkey. Please don't leave me: *et ego semper tecum!*—and I'll try to stay with you always. Lead me, tightly harnessed by your grace: *Tenuisti manum dexteram meam...* —you have led me by the halter; *et in voluntate tua deduxisti me...*—make me do your Will. And so I will love you forever and ever—*et cum gloria suscepisti me!*

382 You make a big tragedy out of the most insignificant mortification. Sometimes Jesus makes use of your *peculiarities* and silly little fads, to help you mortify yourself, by turning something you ought to be doing anyway into a virtue.

383 Dear Jesus, I do want to correspond to your Love, but I am so feeble.

With your grace, I will know how to.

384 Spiritual life is—and I repeat this again and again, on purpose—a constant beginning and beginning again.

Beginning again? Yes. Every time you make an act of contrition—and you should make many every day—you begin again, because you offer a new love to God.

385 We can never be content with what we are doing to serve our God, just as an artist is never satisfied with the painting or statue he is working on. Everyone tells him how marvellous it is, but he thinks: "No. It isn't quite right. I wanted it to be better." This is how *we* should feel.

Moreover, the Lord has given us so much. He has a right to the very best from us—and we must go at his pace.

386 You lack faith—and you lack love. Were it not so you would go immediately and much more often to Jesus, asking for this thing and that.

Don't delay any further; call out to him and you will hear Christ speaking to you: "What do you want me to do for you?" Just as when he stopped for that poor blind man by the roadside who kept on crying out, undeterred.

387 That good friend of ours wrote: "I have asked the Lord many times to forgive me my very great sins. Kissing the Crucifix, I have told him that I love him and I have thanked him for his fatherly providence during these days. I was rather surprised, as I had been years ago, when I found myself saying (I didn't realize it until later): *Dei perfecta sunt opera*—all the works of God are perfect. At the same time I was left with the complete certainty, without the slightest doubt, that this reply to his sinful yet loving creature came from my God. All my hope is in him. May he be blessed forever."

I hastened to reply: "The Lord always acts as the good Father he is, and gives us continual proofs of his Love. Place all your hope in him—and keep up your struggle."

388 O Jesus! If in spite of the poor way I have behaved, you have done for me what you have done, what would you do if I were to respond well?

This truth will lead you to be generous without measure.

Weep and show with sorrow and love how much it pains you, for Our Lord and his Blessed Mother deserve different treatment from you.

389 Even though at times you don't feel like praying and you think you are only saying things with your lips, nevertheless keep up your acts of faith and hope and love. Don't fall asleep. Otherwise, when things are going fine, an ill wind will come and it will drag you off.

390 This is how you should pray: If I am to do anything worthwhile, Jesus, *you* will have to do it for me. May your Will be done. I *do* love it, even if your Will should permit that I be always as I am now, falling dismally only to be lifted up by you!

391 Make me into a saint, my God, even if you have to beat me into it. I don't want to be a hindrance to your Will. I want to respond, I want to be generous... But what sort of a wanting is mine?

392 You are full of concern because you do not love as you ought. Everything annoys you. And the enemy does all he can to make you show your bad temper.

I realize you feel very humiliated. Precisely because of this you must take measures to react without delay.

393 The holiness which makes people say that "to put up with a saint you need two saints" is not true holiness. At best, it would only be its caricature.

394 The devil tries to draw us away from God, and if you allow him to dominate you, good people will *draw away* from you, because they *draw away* from the devil's friends and from those possessed by him.

395 When you speak to God, even if you think yours are just empty words, ask him for a greater dedication, for a more determined progress towards Christian perfection. Ask him to put more fire into you!

396 Renew your firm resolution to live your Christian life *right now*, at every moment, and in all circumstances.

397 Don't place obstacles in grace's way. You need to be convinced that in order to be leaven you must become a saint, and must struggle to identify yourself with him.

398 Say slowly and in all earnestness: *Nunc coepi*— Now I begin.

Don't get discouraged if, unfortunately, you don't see any great change in yourself brought about by the Lord's right hand. From your lowliness you can cry out: Help me, my Jesus, because I want to fulfill your Will—your most lovable Will.

399 Agreed: your concern ought to be for *them*. But your first concern must be yourself, your own interior life. Otherwise, you will not be able to serve them.

400 How difficult you find that mortification suggested to you by the Holy Spirit! Look at a Crucifix, steadily—and you will come to love that expiation.

401 "To be nailed to the Cross!" This aspiration kept coming again and again, as a new light, to the mind and heart and lips of a certain soul.

"To be nailed to the Cross?" he asked himself. "How hard it is!" And yet he knew full well the way he had to go, against himself, the way of self-denial: *agere contra*. This is why he earnestly implored, "Help me, Lord!"

402 When we look upon Calvary, where Jesus died, the realization of our own sins should move us to be sorry, to make a deeper and more mature decision not to offend him again.

403 We need to smooth off the rough edges a little more each day—just as if we were working in stone or wood—and get rid of the defects in our own lives with a spirit of penance. And with small mortifications, which are of two types: *active* mortifications—the ones we ourselves look for, like little flowers we gather up during the course of the day—and *passive* mortifications, which come from without and we find difficult to accept. Jesus Christ will later make up for whatever is lacking.

What a wonderful figure of the crucified Christ you will become if you give your all, generously and cheerfully.

404 Our Lord, with his arms outstretched, is continually begging for your love.

405 Draw close to Jesus who has died for you; draw close to that Cross, outlined against the sky on the summit of Golgotha.

But draw close sincerely and with interior recollection, which is the sign of Christian maturity. That way the divine and human events of the Passion will sink deep into your soul.

406 We should accept mortification with those same sentiments that Jesus Christ had in his Holy Passion.

407 Mortification is a necessary premise for every kind of apostolate, and for bringing each apostolate to perfection.

408 A spirit of penance is to be found first of all in taking advantage of the many little things—deeds, renunciations, sacrifices, services rendered, and so on—which we find daily along our way and we then convert into acts of love and contrition, into mortifications. In this way we shall be able to gather a bouquet at the end of each day— a fine display which we can offer to God.

409 The best spirit of sacrifice is to persevere in the work you have begun, both when you find it exciting and when it proves an uphill struggle.

410 Take your plan of mortifications to your spiritual director, for him to monitor them.

But to monitor will not always mean to diminish. It can also mean increasing them, if he thinks fit. Either way, accept his advice.

411 We can say with St Augustine that our evil passions tug at our garments, dragging us down. At the same time we are aware of great, noble, and pure ambitions within our hearts, and know that a struggle is going on.

If, with the grace of God, you make use of the ascetical means: if you seek to have presence of God, if you look for mortification and—don't be afraid—penance, then you will make progress, you will find peace, and victory will be yours.

412   Custody of the heart. That priest used to pray: "Jesus, may my poor heart be an enclosed garden; may my poor heart be a paradise wherein you dwell; may my Guardian Angel watch over it with a sword of fire and use it to purify every affection before it comes into me. Jesus, seal my poor heart with the divine seal of your Cross".

413   Each person in his own situation should lead a pure life, courageously lived. We have to learn to say *No* for the sake of that great Love, Love with a capital letter.

414   There is a Spanish saying which speaks clearly enough: *Entre santa y santo, pared de cal y canto* ("Twixt holy man and holy maid, a wall of solid stone be laid").
   We have to watch over our hearts and our senses, and pull ourselves away from all occasions of sin. No matter how holy it may appear, passion must not have its way.

415   Dear Lord, I find beauty and charm in everything I see! I will guard my sight at every moment, for the sake of Love.

416   You are a Christian and, as a Christian, a son of God. You should feel a grave responsibility for corresponding to the mercies you have received from the Lord, showing careful vigilance and loving firmness, so that nothing and nobody may disfigure the distinctive features of the Love he has imprinted upon your soul.

417 You have reached a level of real intimacy with this God of ours, who is so close to you, so deeply lodged in your soul. But what are you doing to increase and deepen this intimacy? Are you careful not to allow silly little hindrances to creep in which would upset this friendship?

Show courage! Don't refuse to break with every single thing, no matter how small, which could cause suffering to the One who loves you so much.

418 If we are faithful to him, Jesus' own life will somehow be repeated in the life of each one of us, both in its internal development (the process of sanctification) and in our outward behavior.

Give thanks to him for being so good.

419 It seems an excellent idea to me that you should tell the Lord often about your great and ardent desire to be a saint, even though you see yourself filled with wretchedness...

Tell him—precisely because of this!

420 You have seen very clearly that you are a child of God. Even if you were never again to see it—it won't happen!—you should continue along your way forever, out of a sense of faithfulness, without ever looking back.

421 A resolution: to be faithful to my timetable—heroically faithful and without excuses—on ordinary days and on extraordinary days.

422 You might have thought occasionally, with holy envy, about the adolescent Apostle John, *quem diligebat Iesus*—whom Jesus loved.

Wouldn't *you* like to deserve to be called "the one who loves the Will of God?" Then take the necessary steps, day after day.

423 You can be sure of the following: the desire—shown by deeds—to live like a good son of God brings permanent youthfulness and serenity, joy and peace.

424 If you abandon yourself once more in God's hands, the Holy Spirit will give light to your understanding and strength to your will.

425 Listen to that parable which comes to us from Jesus' own lips and is told us by St John in his Gospel: *Ego sum vitis, vos palmites*—I am the vine, you are the branches.

Picture the whole parable in your imagination and in your mind. You will see that a branch separated from the stock, from the vine, is useless, it cannot produce fruit. It will end up like a dry stick which men or animals trample underfoot, or will be thrown on the fire.

You are the branch; draw the necessary conclusions.

426 Today once again I prayed full of confidence. This was my petition: "Lord, may neither our past wretchedness which has been forgiven us, nor the possibility of future wretchedness cause us any disquiet. May we abandon ourselves into your merciful hands. May we bring before you our desires for sanctity and apostolate, which are hidden like embers under the ashes of an apparent coldness."

"Lord, I know you are listening to us." You should say this to him too.

427 Be sincere when you open up your soul. Speak out and don't try to gild the lily; that could be a very childish thing to do.

And then continue on your way, with docility. You will be holier, and happier.

428 Don't look for consolations apart from God. See what that priest wrote: There should be no unburdening of your heart to any other friend when there is no need to do so.

429 Holiness is attained with the help of the Holy Spirit, who comes to dwell in our souls, through grace given us by the sacraments and as a result of a constant ascetical struggle.

My son, let us not have any false illusions about this. You and I—I'll never tire of repeating it—will always have to struggle, always, until the end of our lives. We will thus come to love peace, and we will spread peace around us, and we will receive our everlasting reward.

430 Don't confine yourself to speaking to the Paraclete. Listen to him as well.

When you pray, consider how the life of childhood which enabled you to realize more deeply that you are a son of God filled you with a filial love for the Father. Think how, before that, you have gone through Mary to Jesus, whom you adore as his friend, as his brother, as his lover for that is what you are.

After receiving this advice you realized that until now you had known that Holy Spirit was dwelling in your soul, to sanctify it. But you hadn't really *grasped* this truth about his presence. You needed that advice. Now you feel his Love within you, and you want to talk to him, to be his friend, to confide in him. You want to facilitate his work of polishing, uprooting, and enkindling.

I wouldn't know how to set about it, you thought. Listen to him, I insist. He will give you strength. He will do everything, if you so want. And you *do* want!

Pray to him: Divine Guest, Master, Light, Guide, Love, may I make you truly welcome inside me and listen to the lessons you teach me. Make me burn with eagerness for you, make me follow you and love you.

431 To draw closer to God, to fly all the way to God, you need the strong and generous wings of Prayer and Expiation.

432 To avoid routine in your vocal prayers try to say them with the same ardor with which a person who has just fallen in love speaks...and as if it were the last chance you had to approach Our Lord.

433 If you feel proud to be a son of Our Lady, ask yourself: How often do I express my devotion to the Virgin Mary during the day, from morning to night?

434 That friend was saying to himself: Apart from other reasons, there are two good reasons why I should make reparation to my Immaculate Mother every Saturday and on the eve of her feasts.

The second is that on Sundays and on the feasts of Our Lady (which are often local feasts), instead of dedicating such days to prayer, so many people spend them offending Our Jesus with public sins and scandalous crimes— you have only to look around you and see.

The first reason is that, perhaps due to the devil's influence, those of us who want to be good sons are not taking proper care in the way we live these days dedicated to Our Lord and to his Mother.

You'll realize that unfortunately these reasons are still very valid. And so we too should make reparation.

435 I have always understood Christian prayer as being a loving conversation with Jesus, which shouldn't be interrupted even in the moments when we are physically far from the Tabernacle, because our whole life is a serenade of human love for our God... and we can love always.

436 God's love for his creatures is so boundless and our response to it should be so great that time ought to stand still when Holy Mass is being said.

437 When the branches are united to the vine they grow to maturity and bear fruit.

What then should you and I do? We should get right close to Jesus, through the Bread, and through the Word.

He is our vine. We should speak affectionate words to him throughout the day. That is what people in love do.

438 Love Our Lord very much. Maintain and foster in your soul a sense of urgency to love him better. Love God precisely now when perhaps a good many of those who hold him in their hands do not love him, but rather ill-treat and neglect him.

Be sure to take good care of the Lord for me, in the Holy Mass and throughout the whole day.

439 Prayer is the most powerful weapon a Christian has. Prayer makes us effective. Prayer makes us happy. Prayer gives us all the strength we need to fulfill God's commands.

Yes, indeed, your whole life can and should be prayer.

440 Personal sanctity is not an abstruse theory, but a specific reality, which is both divine and human. And it manifests itself constantly in daily acts of Love.

441 The spirit of prayer which fills the entire life of Jesus Christ among men teaches us that all our actions—great or small—ought to be preceded by prayer, accompanied by prayer, and followed by prayer.

442 Contemplate and live the Passion of Christ, with him. Proffer your own shoulders frequently, daily, when he is scourged; offer your own head to be crowned with thorns.

Where I come from they say: "Love is repaid with love."

443 A person in love doesn't miss the tiniest detail. I have seen it in so many souls. Those little things become something very great: Love!

444 Love God for those who do not love him. You should make this spirit of reparation and atonement flesh of your flesh.

445 If at any time the going gets harder in our interior struggle, that will be a good moment to show that our Love is in earnest.

446 You are certain it was God who made you see quite clearly that you must return to the more childlike *little things* of your earlier interior life, and persevere for months and even years in those heroic *trivialities*. (You needn't take into account your feelings here since they are so often slow to recognize the good). Your will may be cold but let it be ready to fulfill those little duties out of Love.

447 Persevere in your life of piety, willingly and with love, even if you feel arid. Don't worry if you find yourself counting the minutes or days still to go before you finish that act of piety or that job or work, with the turbid delight of the lazy schoolboy who in a similar situation is looking forward to the end of term; or of the petty criminal who can't wait to get back to his tricks once he is out of jail again.

Persevere, I insist, with a real and effective determination. Don't cease, not even for a moment, to want to fulfill and benefit from those means of piety.

448 Practise your faith cheerfully, keeping very close to Jesus Christ. Really love him—but really, really love him!—and you will take part in a great Adventure of Love, because you will be more in love each day.

449 Say slowly to the Master: Lord, all I want is to serve you. All I want is to fulfill my duties and love you with all my heart. Make me feel your firm step by my side. May you be my only support!

Say this to him slowly... and really mean it!

450 You need interior life and doctrinal formation. Be demanding on yourself! As a Christian man or woman, you have to be salt of the earth and the light of the world, for you are obliged to give good example with holy shamelessness.

The charity of Christ should compel you. Feeling and knowing yourself to be another Christ from the moment you told him that you would follow him, you must not separate yourself from your equals—your relatives, friends, and colleagues—any more than you would separate salt from the food it is seasoning.

Your interior life and your formation include the piety and the principles a child of God must have in order to give flavor to everything by his active presence there.

Ask the Lord that you may always be that good seasoning in the lives of others.

451 We Christians, with a spirit of youthfulness, have come to collect the treasures of the Gospels, which are always new, so that we can make them reach every corner of the earth.

452 You need to imitate Jesus Christ and make him known through your behavior. I want you not to forget that Christ assumed our human nature so as to raise all men to a divine way of life; and so that, united to him, we might live the commands of Heaven both individually and as members of society.

453   Because you are a Christian you cannot turn your back on any concern or any need of your fellowmen.

454   How very insistent the Apostle St John was in preaching the *mandatum novum*, the new commandment that we should love one another.

I would fall on my knees, without putting on any act—but this is what my heart dictates—and ask you, for the love of God, to love one another, to help one another, to lend one another a hand, to know how to forgive one another.

And so, reject all pride, be compassionate, show charity; help each other with prayer and sincere friendship.

455   You will only be good if you know how to see the good points and the virtues of the others.

That is why when you have to correct, you should do so with charity, at the opportune moment, without humiliating. And being ready yourself to learn and to improve in the very faults you are correcting.

456   Love and practise charity without setting any limits or discriminating between people, for it is the virtue which marks us out as disciples of the Master.

Nevertheless, this charity cannot lead you to dampen your faith—for it would then cease to be a virtue. Nor should it blur the clear outlines that define the faith, nor soften it to the point of changing it, as some people try to do, into something amorphous and lacking the strength and power of God.

457   You have to live in harmony with your fellow-men and understand them as a brother would. As the Spanish mystic says, you have to put love where there is no love to obtain love.

458   Whenever you need to criticize, your criticism must seek to be positive, helpful, and constructive. It should never be made behind the back of the person concerned.

To act otherwise would be treacherous, sneaky, defamatory, slanderous even, as well as being utterly ignoble.

459   Whenever you see that the glory of God and the good of the Church demand that you should speak out, you cannot remain silent.

Think about it. Who would lack courage before God and in the face of eternity? There is nothing to be lost and instead so much to be gained. Why do you hold back then?

460   We are not good brothers to our fellowmen if we are not ready to continue behaving correctly, even when those around us may interpret our actions badly or react in an unpleasant manner.

461 Your love for Mother Church and the service you render her should in no way be conditioned by the greater or lesser holiness of the individuals who make up the Church, even though we ardently desire that everyone will achieve Christian perfection.

You have to love the Spouse of Christ, your Mother. She is, and always will be, pure and spotless.

462 Our striving for our own sanctification has repercussions on the sanctity of so many souls and also on the sanctity of God's Church.

463 Be convinced of this: if only you wish it (and don't forget that God listens to you and loves you and promises you glory and you will be protected by the almighty hand of your Father in Heaven) you can be a person full of fortitude, ready to be a witness everywhere to the most lovable truth of his doctrine.

464 The Lord's field is fertile and the seed he sows of good quality. Therefore when weeds appear in this world of ours, never doubt that they spring up because of a lack of correspondence on the part of men, Christians especially, who have fallen asleep and have left the field open to the enemy.

Don't complain, for there's no point; examine your behavior, instead.

465 The following comment, which caused me great sorrow, will also make you reflect: "I see very clearly why there is a lack of resistance, and why what resistance there is to iniquitous laws is so ineffective, for above, below, and in the middle there are many people—so very many—who just follow the crowd."

466 The enemies of God and of his Church, manipulated by the devil's unremitting hatred, are relentless in their activities and organization.

With "exemplary" constancy they prepare their cadres, run schools, appoint leaders, and deploy agitators. In an undercover way—but very effectively—they spread their ideas and sow, in homes and places of work, a seed which is destructive of any religious ideology.

What is there that we Christians should not be ready to do in order to serve our God, of course always with the truth?

467 Don't confuse serenity with being lazy or careless, with putting off decisions or deferring the study of important matters.

Serenity always goes hand in hand with diligence, which is a virtue we need in order to consider and solve outstanding problems without delay.

468 My son, where do men find in you the Christ they are looking for? In your pride? In your desire to impose yourself on others? In those little character defects which you don't wish to overcome? In your stubbornness?... Is Christ to be found there? No, he is not!

You need to have your own personality, agreed. But you should try to make it conform exactly to Christ's.

469 I will suggest to you a good rule of conduct for living fraternity and a spirit of service. When you are not around, other people should be able to go ahead with the work you have in hand, thanks to the experience you have generously passed on to them, and to your not having made yourself indispensable.

470 The responsibility for the sanctity of others, for their Christian behavior, and for their effectiveness, lies with you. And this is so even though you have passions.

You are not on your own. If you stop, you could be holding up or harming so many people!

471 Think about your Mother the Holy Church and consider how, if one member suffers, the whole body suffers.

Your body needs each one of its members, but each member needs the whole body. What would happen if my hands were to stop doing their duty... or if my heart were to stop beating?

472 You saw it quite clearly: while so many people do not know God, he has looked to you. He wants you to form a part of the foundations, a firm stone upon which the life of the Church can rest.

Meditate upon this reality and you will draw many practical consequences for your ordinary behavior: the foundations, made of blocks of stone—hidden and possibly rather dull—have to be solid, not fragile. They have to serve as a support for the building. If not, they are useless.

473 Since you feel you have been chosen by God to support and co-redeem—without forgetting that you are... wretched and utterly so—your humility should lead you to place yourself under the feet—at the service—of all. This is what the supports of a building do.

But foundations need to be strong. Fortitude is an indispensable virtue for someone who has to sustain or encourage others.

Say this to Jesus and say it to him strongly: May I never through false humility stop practising the cardinal virtue of fortitude. Make me know how to separate, my God, the dross from the gold.

474 Our Mother, our Hope! How safe and sure we are when we keep close to you, even when everything around us is quivering and shaking.

RECOVERY

475 You feel the need of conversion: He is asking more of you... and you are giving him less each day!

476 For each one of us, as for Lazarus, it was really a *veni foras*—come out—which got us moving.

How sad it is to see those who are still dead and do not know the power of God's mercy!

Renew your holy joy, for opposite the man who is decomposing without Christ, there is another who has risen with him.

477 Earthly affections, even when they aren't just squalid concupiscence, usually involve some element of selfishness.

So, though you must not despise those affections— they can be very holy—always make sure you purify your intention.

478 Don't be anxious for people to sympathize with you. That is often a sign of pride or vanity.

479 Whenever you speak of the theological virtues, of faith, of hope, of love, remember that they are first of all virtues to be practised rather than to be speculated on.

480 Is there something in your life that does not suit your dignity as a Christian, something which makes you unwilling to be cleansed?

Examine your conscience, and change.

481 Take a good look at the way you behave. You will see that you are full of faults that harm you and perhaps also those around you.

Remember, my child, that microbes may be no less a menace than wild beasts. Just as bacteria are cultivated in a laboratory, so you are cultivating those faults and those errors, with your lack of humility, with your lack of prayer, with your failure to fulfill your duty, with your lack of self-knowledge. Those tiny germs then spread everywhere.

You need to make a good examination of conscience every day. It will lead you to make definite resolutions to improve, because it will have made you really sorry for your shortcomings, omissions, and sins.

482 Almighty God, Omnipotent and Infinitely Wise, had to choose his Mother.

What would you have done, if you had had to choose yours? I think that you and I would have chosen the mother we have, filling her with all graces. That is what God did: and that is why, after the Blessed Trinity, comes Mary.

Theologians have given a rational explanation for her fullness of grace and why she cannot be subject to the devil: it was fitting that it should be so, God could do it, therefore he did it. That is the great proof: the clearest proof that God endowed his Mother with every privilege, from the very first moment. That is how she is: beautiful, and pure, and spotless in soul and body!

483 Is this how it is? You are longing for the victory, the end of the struggle... but it doesn't come!

Thank God as if you had already gained what you are seeking, and offer him your feelings of impatience: *Vir fidelis loquetur victoriam*, the faithful man will sing the joys of victory.

484 There are moments in which you are deprived of that union with Our Lord which enabled you to pray continually, even when you were asleep. You seem almost to be wrestling with God's Will.

It is your weakness, as you well know. Love the Cross. Love the fact that you lack so many things which the world thinks of as necessary; love the obstacles that you find as you start or... as you continue on your way; love your very littleness and spiritual wretchedness.

Offer—with a desire that is effective—all you have, and all that belongs to those who are yours. Humanly speaking, it's quite a lot, but from a supernatural point of view, it's nothing.

485 At times, someone has told me: "Father, I feel tired and cold; when I pray or fulfill some other norm of piety, I seem to be acting out a farce."

To that friend, and to you, if you are in the same boat, I answer: A farce? What an excellent thing, my child! Act out that farce! The Lord is your audience—the Father, the Son, and the Holy Spirit. The Blessed Trinity is contemplating us in those moments when we are "acting out a farce."

Acting like that in front of God, out of love, in order to please him, when our whole life goes against the grain: how splendid, to be God's juggler! How marvellous it is to play one's part for Love, with sacrifice, without any personal satisfaction, just in order to please Our Lord!

That indeed is to live for Love.

486   A heart which loves the things of the earth beyond measure is like one fastened by a chain—or by a "tiny thread"—which stops it flying to God.

487   "Watch and pray, that you may not enter into temptation." It makes one shudder to see how someone can give up a divine undertaking for the sake of a fleeting delusion.

488   A lukewarm apostle: that's the great enemy of souls.

489   A clear sign of lukewarmness is a lack of supernatural "stubbornness," of fortitude to keep on working and not stop until you have laid "the last stone."

490   Some hearts are hard, but noble. When they come close to the warmth of Christ's Heart, they melt like bronze into tears of love, of reparation. They catch fire.

But lukewarm people have hearts of clay, of mean flesh. They crack and turn to dust. A sorry sight.

Say with me: "Our Jesus, keep us from being lukewarm. We do not want to be lukewarm."

491   All goodness, all beauty, all majesty, all loveliness, all grace adorn our Mother. Doesn't it make you fall in love, to have a Mother like that?

492 We are in love with Love. That is why Our Lord doesn't want us to be dry, stiff, lifeless. He wants us to be steeped in his tenderness!

493 See if you can understand this apparent contradiction. At thirty years of age, that man wrote in his diary: "I'm not young any more." When he was over forty, he wrote again: "I will stay young till I'm eighty: if I die before that, I'll think I haven't done my stint."

Wherever he went he took with him, in spite of the passing years, the mature youthfulness of Love.

494 How well I understand that question put by a soul in love with God: "Have I made any grimace of distaste, has there been anything in me which could have hurt you, my Lord, my Love?"

Ask your Father-God to grant us the grace to be constantly demanding in that way.

495 Have you seen the affection and the confidence with which Christ's friends treat him? In a completely natural way the sisters of Lazarus "blame" Jesus for being away: "We told you! If only you'd been here!"

Speak to him with calm confidence: "Teach me to treat you with the loving friendliness of Martha, Mary, and Lazarus and as the first Twelve treated you, even though at first they followed you perhaps for not very supernatural reasons."

496 How I like to think of John, leaning his head on Christ's breast! It is like giving up one's intelligence lovingly, difficult though this is, to let it be set on fire by the flame of the Heart of Jesus.

497 God loves me. And John the Apostle writes: "Let us love God, then, since God loved us first." As if this were not enough, Jesus comes to each one of us, in spite of our patent wretchedness, to ask us, as he asked Peter: "Simon, son of John, do you love me more than these others?"

This is the moment to reply: "Lord, you know all things, you know that I love you!" adding, with humility, "Help me to love you more. Increase my love!"

498 "Love means deeds and not sweet words." Deeds, deeds! And a resolution: I will continue to tell you often, Lord, that I love you. How often I have repeated this today! But, with your grace, it will be my conduct above all that shows it. It will be the little things of each day which, with silent eloquence, will cry out before you, showing you my Love.

499 We men don't know how to show Jesus the gentle refinements of love that some poor, rough fellows— Christians all the same—show daily to some pitiful little creature—their wife, their child, their friend—who is as poor as they are.

This truth should help us react.

500 The Love of God is so attractive, and so fascinating, that there are no limits to its growth in the life of a Christian.

501 You cannot behave like a naughty child, or like a madman.

You have to be strong, a child of God. You have to be calm in your professional work and in your dealings with others, with a presence of God which makes you give perfect attention to even the smallest details.

502 If bare justice is done, people may feel hurt.

Always act, therefore, for the love of God, which will add to that justice the balm of a neighborly love, and will purify and cleanse all earthly love.

When you bring God in, everything becomes supernatural.

503 Love Our Lord passionately. Love him madly. Because if there is love—when there is love— I would dare to say that resolutions are not needed. My parents—think of yours—did not need to make any resolutions to love me: and what an effusion of tenderness they showed me, in little details every day.

With that same human heart we can and should love God.

504 Love is sacrifice; and sacrifice for Love's sake is a joy.

505 Answer this question in your heart: How often each day does your will ask you to set your heart on God, to give him your expressions of love and your actions?

This is a good way to measure the intensity and quality of your love.

506 Be convinced, my child, that God has a right to ask us: Are you thinking about me? Are you aware of me? Do you look to me as your support? Do you seek me as the Light of your life, as your shield..., as your all?

Renew, then, this resolution: In times the world calls good, I will cry out: "Lord!" In times it calls bad, again I will cry: "Lord!"

507 I don't want you ever to lose your supernatural outlook. Even though you see your own meannesses, your evil inclinations—the clay of which you are made—in all their raw shamefulness, God is counting on you.

508 Live as the others around you live, with naturalness, but "supernaturalizing" every moment of your day.

509 In order to be able to judge with rectitude of intention, we need a pure heart, zeal for the things of God and love of souls, free from prejudices.

Think about it.

510 I heard some people I knew talking about their radio sets. Almost without realizing it, I brought the subject round to the spiritual area: we have got a strong earth, too strong, and we have forgotten to put up the aerial of the interior life.

That is why there are so few souls who keep in touch with God. May we never be without our supernatural aerial.

511 Is it true that I pay more attention to trifles and trivialities, that bring me nothing and from which I expect nothing, than I do to my God? Who am I with, when I am not with God?

512 Tell him: Lord, I want nothing other than what you want. Even those things I am asking you for at

present, if they take me an inch away from your Will,
don't give them to me.

513 The secret of being effective, at root, lies in your
piety, a sincere piety. This way you will pass the whole
day with him.

514 A resolution: to "keep up", without interruption
as far as you can, a loving and docile friendship and
conversation with the Holy Spirit. *Veni, Sancte Spiritus...!*
—Come, O Holy Spirit, and dwell in my soul!

515 Repeat to yourself, with all your heart, and with
ever-increasing love, and more when you are in front of
the tabernacle or have the Lord within your breast: *Non
est qui se abscondat a calore eius*—"No one can hide
from his warmth." May I not flee from you, may I be
filled with the fire of your Holy Spirit.

516 *Ure igne Sancti Spiritus!*—Burn me with the fire
of your Spirit, you cried. You then added: "My poor soul
needs to fly again as soon as possible, and not stop flying
until it rests in God!"

I think your desires are admirable. I will pray for you
often to the Paraclete. I will invoke him continually, so
that he may nestle in the center of your being, presiding

and giving a supernatural tone to all your actions and words, thoughts and desires.

517 When you celebrated the feast of the Exaltation of the Holy Cross you asked Our Lord, with the most earnest desire of your heart, to grant you his grace so as to "exalt" the Holy Cross in the powers of your soul and in your senses. You asked for a new life; for the Cross to set a seal on it, to confirm the truth of your mission; for the whole of your being to rest on the Cross!

We shall see...

518 Mortification has to be constant, like the beating of the heart. In this way we will have dominion over ourselves and the charity of Christ for others.

519 To love the Cross means being able to put oneself out, gladly, for the love of Christ, though it's hard—and because it's hard. You have enough experience to know that this is not a contradiction.

520 Christian cheerfulness is not something physiological. Its foundation is supernatural, and it goes deeper than illness or difficulties.

Cheerfulness does not mean the jingling of bells, or the gaiety of a dance at the local hall.

True cheerfulness is something deeper, something within: something that keeps us peaceful and brimming over with joy, though at times our face may be stern.

521 I wrote to you: Though I can understand that it's not an uncommon way of talking, I'm not happy when I hear people describe the difficulties born of pride as "crosses." These burdens are not the Cross, the true Cross, because they are not Christ's Cross.

So struggle against those invented obstacles, which have nothing to do with the seal Christ has set on you. Get rid of all the disguises of self!

522 Even on those days when you seem to be wasting time, in the prose of the thousand details of the day there is more than enough poetry for you to feel that you are on the Cross: on a Cross which no one notices.

523 Do not fix your heart on anything that passes away. Imitate Christ, who became poor for us, and had nowhere to lay his head.

Ask him to give you, in the midst of the world, a real detachment, a detachment that has nothing to soften it.

524 One clear sign of detachment is genuinely not to consider anything as one's own.

525 Whoever really lives his faith knows that the goods of the world are means, and uses them generously, heroically.

526 The risen Christ, Christ in glory, has divested himself of the things of this earth, so that we men, his brothers, should ask ourselves what things we need to get rid of.

527 We have to love the Blessed Virgin Mary more. We will never love her enough.

Love her a lot! It shouldn't be enough for you to put up pictures of her, and greet them, and say aspirations. You should learn to offer her, in your strenuous life, some small sacrifice each day, to show her your love, and to show her the kind of love that we want the whole human race to proclaim for her.

528 The truth of a Christian's life is this: self-giving and love—founded on sacrifice. Love for God, that is, and, for God's sake, love for one's neighbor.

529 Jesus, I put myself trustingly in your arms, hiding my head on your loving breast, my heart touching yours: I want what you want, in everything.

530 Nowadays the world we live in is full of disobedience and gossip, of intrigue and conspiracy. So, more than ever we have to love obedience, sincerity, loyalty, and simplicity: and our love of all these will have a supernatural significance, which will make us more human.

531 You say yes, you are determined to follow Christ.

All right. Then you should walk at his pace, not at your own.

532 You want to know on what our faithfulness is founded?

I would say, in broad outline, that it is based on loving God, which makes us overcome all kinds of obstacles: selfishness, pride, tiredness, impatience...

A man in love tramples on his own self. He is aware that when he is loving with all his soul, he isn't yet loving enough.

533 I heard—and I write it down, because it's very beautiful—something that was said by a goodly nun from Aragon, in her gratitude for God's fatherly goodness: "How 'smart' he is! He's got his eye on everything."

534 Like all God's children, you too need personal prayer. You need to be intimate with him, to talk directly with Our Lord. You need a two-way conversation, face to face, without hiding yourself in anonymity.

535 The first thing needed as far as prayer is concerned is to keep at it; the second thing is to be humble.

Have a holy stubbornness, be trusting. Remember that when we ask the Lord for something important, he may want to be asked for many years. Keep on! But keep on with ever increasing trust.

536 Persevere in prayer, as the Master told us. This point of departure will be your source of peace, of cheerfulness, of serenity, and so it will make you humanly and supernaturally effective.

537 You were in a place where they were talking and listening to music. Prayer welled up in your soul, bringing an unspeakable solace. In the end you said: "Jesus, I don't want consolation; I want you."

538 Your life must be a constant prayer, a never-ceasing conversation with Our Lord: when things are pleasant or unpleasant, easy or difficult, usual or unusual.

In every situation, your conversation with your Father God should immediately come to life. You should seek him right within your soul.

539 To recollect oneself in prayer, in meditation, is so easy! Jesus doesn't make us wait. He doesn't leave us in the waiting-room. It is he who does the waiting.

You only have to say "Lord, I want to pray, I want to talk to you!" and you are at once in God's presence, talking to him.

And as if this were not enough, he doesn't begrudge you his time. He leaves it up to you, just as you please. And not just for ten minutes or a quarter of an hour, but for hours and hours! For the whole day! And he is who he is: the Almighty, the Most Wise.

540 In the interior life, as in human love, we have to persevere.

You have to meditate often on the same themes, keeping on until you *re-discover* an old discovery.

"How could I not have seen this so clearly before?" you'll ask in surprise. Simply because sometimes we're like stones, that let the water flow over them, without absorbing a drop.

That's why we have to go over the same things again and again—because they aren't the same things—if we want to soak up God's blessings.

541 In the Holy Sacrifice of the altar, the priest takes up the Body of our God, and the Chalice containing his Blood, and raises them above all the things of the earth, saying: *Per Ipsum, et cum Ipso, et in Ipso*—through my Love, with my Love, in my Love!

Unite yourself to the action of the priest. Or rather, make that act of the priest a part of your life.

542 The Gospel tells us that Jesus hid himself when they wanted to make him king after he had worked the miracle.

Lord, you make us share in the miracle of the Eucharist. We beg you not to hide away. Live with us. May we see you, may we touch you, may we feel you. May we want to be beside you all the time, and have you as the King of our lives and of our work.

543 Talk to the Three Persons, to God the Father, to God the Son, to God the Holy Spirit. And so as to reach the Blessed Trinity, go through Mary.

544 You don't have *living* faith if you aren't giving yourself to Jesus here and now.

545 All Christians should seek Christ and get to know him, so as to love him better and better. It's like courting. A couple need to get to know each other well, for if they don't, they will not really love each other. And our life is a life of Love.

546 Pause to consider the holy wrath of the Master, when he sees his Father's honor abused in the temple at Jerusalem.

What a lesson for you! You should never be indifferent, or play the coward, when the things of God are treated without respect.

547 Fall in love with the Sacred Humanity of Jesus Christ.

Aren't you glad that he should have wanted to be like us? Thank Jesus for this wonderful expression of his goodness.

548 Advent is here. What a marvellous time in which to renew your desire, your nostalgia, your real longing for Christ to come—for him to come every day to your soul in the Eucharist. The Church encourages us: *Ecce veniet!*— He is about to arrive!

549 Christmas. The carols sing *Venite, venite,* "O come ye, O come ye." Let us go to him. He has just been born.

After contemplating how Mary and Joseph care for the Child, I now dare to hint to you: Look at him again, gaze at him without ceasing.

550 Although it pains us to admit it—and I ask God to increase that sorrow in us—you and I have our share in the death of Christ. For the sins of men were the hammer-blows which stitched him to the Cross with nails.

551   St Joseph. One cannot love Jesus and Mary without loving the Holy Patriarch.

552   There are many good reasons to honor St Joseph, and to learn from his life. He was a man of strong faith. He earned a living for his family—Jesus and Mary—with his own hard work. He guarded the purity of the Blessed Virgin, who was his Spouse. And he respected—he loved!—God's freedom, when God made his choice: not only his choice of Our Lady the Virgin as his Mother, but also his choice of St Joseph as the Husband of Holy Mary.

553   St Joseph, our father and lord: most chaste, most pure. You were found worthy to carry the Child Jesus in your arms, to wash him, to hug him. Teach us to get to know God, and to be pure, worthy of being other Christs.

And help us to do and to teach, as Christ did. Help us to open up the divine paths of the earth, which are both hidden and bright; and help us to show them to mankind, telling our fellowmen that their lives on earth can have an extraordinary and constant supernatural effectiveness.

554   Love St Joseph a lot. Love him with all your soul, because he, together with Jesus, is the person who has most loved our Blessed Lady and been closest to God. He is the person who has most loved God, after our Mother.

He deserves your affection, and it will do you good to get to know him, because he is the Master of the interior life, and has great power before the Lord and before the Mother of God.

555 Our Lady. Who could be a better Teacher of the love of God than this Queen, this Lady, this Mother, who has the closest bond with the Trinity: Daughter of God the Father, Mother of God the Son, Spouse of God the Holy Spirit? And at the same time she is our Mother!

Go and pray personally for her intercession.

556 You will become a saint if you have charity, if you manage to do the things which please others and do not offend God, though you find them hard to do.

557 St Paul has given us a wonderful recipe for charity: *alter alterius onera portate et sic adimplebitis legem Christi*—bear one another's burdens, and so you will fulfill the law of Christ.

Is this what happens in your life?

558 Jesus Our Lord loved men so much that he became incarnate, took to himself our nature, and lived in daily contact with the poor and the rich, with the just and with sinners, with young and old, with Gentiles and Jews.

He spoke to everyone: to those who showed goodwill towards him, and to those who were only looking for a way to twist his words and condemn him.

You should try to act as Our Lord did.

559 Loving souls for God's sake will make us love everyone: understanding, excusing, forgiving all.

We should have a love that can cover the multitude of failings contrived by human wretchedness. We have to have a wonderful charity, *veritatem facientes in caritate*, defending the truth, without hurting anyone.

560 When I speak to you of *good example*, I mean to tell you, too, that you have to understand and excuse, that you have to fill the world with peace and love.

561 Ask yourself often: am I making a real effort to be more refined in my charity towards the people I live with?

562 When I preached that we have to make ourselves a carpet so that the others may tread softly, I am not simply being poetic: it has to be a reality!

It's hard, as sanctity is hard; but it's also easy, because, I insist, sanctity is within everyone's reach.

563 In the midst of so much selfishness, so much coldness—everyone out for what he can get—I call to mind those little wooden donkeys. They were trotting on a desk-top, strong, and sturdy. One had lost a leg, but it carried on forward, supported by the others.

564 When we Catholics defend and uphold the truth, without making concessions, we have to strive to create an atmosphere of charity, of harmony, to drown all hatred and resentment.

565 In a Christian, in a child of God, friendship and charity are one and the same thing. They are a divine light which spreads warmth.

566 To practise fraternal correction—which is so deeply rooted in the Gospel—is a proof of supernatural trust and affection.

Be thankful for it when you receive it, and don't neglect to practise it with those you live with.

567 When you correct someone—because it has to be done and you want to do your duty—you must expect to hurt others and to get hurt yourself.

But you should never let this fact be an excuse for holding back.

568 Get very close to your Mother, the Virgin Mary. You ought to be united to God always: seek that union with him by staying near his Blessed Mother.

569 Listen to me: being in the world and belonging to the world does not mean being worldly.

570 You have to act like a burning coal, spreading fire wherever it happens to be; or at least, striving to raise the spiritual temperature of the people around you, leading them to live a truly Christian life.

571 God wants the works he entrusts to men to go ahead on the basis of prayer and mortification.

572 The foundation of all we do as citizens—as Catholic citizens—lies in an intense interior life. It lies in being really and truly men and women who turn their day into an uninterrupted conversation with God.

573 When you are with someone, you have to see a soul: a soul who has to be helped, who has to be understood, with whom you have to live in harmony, and who has to be saved.

574 You insist on trying to walk on your own, doing you own will, guided solely by your own judgment. And you can see for yourself that the fruit of this is *fruitlessness*.

My child, if you don't give up your own judgment, if you are proud, if you devote yourself to "your" apostolate, you will work all night—your whole life will be one long night—and at the end of it, all the dawn will find you with your nets empty.

575 To think of Christ's Death means to be invited to face up to our everyday tasks with complete sincerity, and to take the faith that we profess seriously.

It has to be an opportunity to go deeper into the depths of God's Love, so as to be able to show that Love to men with our words and deeds.

576 Make sure that your lips, the lips of a Christian— for that is what you are and should be at all times—speak those *compelling* supernatural words which will move and encourage, and will show your committed attitude to life.

577 There is a great love of comfort, and at times a great irresponsibility, hidden behind the attitude of those in authority who flee from the sorrow of correcting, making the excuse that they want to avoid the suffering of others.

They may perhaps save themselves some discomfort in this life. But they are gambling with eternal happiness—the eternal happiness of others as well as their own—by these omissions of theirs. These omissions are real sins.

578 For many people a saint is an "uncomfortable" person to live with. But this doesn't mean that he has to be unbearable.

A saint's zeal should never be bitter. When he corrects he should never be wounding. His example should never be an arrogant moral slap in his neighbor's face.

579 There was a young priest who used to address Jesus with the words of the Apostles: *Edissere nobis parabolam*, explain the parable to us. He would add: Master, put into our souls the clarity of your teaching, so that it may never be absent from our lives and our works. And so that we can give it to others.

You too should say this to Our Lord.

580 Always have the courage—the humility, the desire to serve God—to put forward the truths of faith as they are, without watering them down, without ambiguity.

581 There is no other possible attitude for a Catholic: we have to defend the authority of the Pope *always*, and to be ready *always* to correct our own views with docility, in line with the teaching authority of the Church.

582 A long time ago someone asked me, tactlessly, whether those of us whose career is the priesthood are able to retire when we get old. And since I gave him no answer, he persisted with his impertinent question.

Then an answer came to me which, I thought, put it in a nutshell. "The priesthood," I told him, "is not a career: it is an apostolate."

That's how I feel about it. And I wanted to put it down in these notes so that—with God's help—none of us may ever forget the difference.

583 To have a Catholic spirit means that we should feel on our shoulders the weight of our concern for the entire Church—not just of this or that particular part of it. It means that our prayer should spread out north and south, east and west, in a generous act of petition.

If you do this you will understand the cry—the aspiration—of that friend of ours, when he considered how unloving so many people are towards our Holy Mother: "The Church: it hurts me to see her treated so!"

584 "And, apart from other things, there is the daily pressure upon me of my anxiety for all the churches", St Paul wrote. This sigh of the apostle is a reminder for all Christians—for you, too—of our duty to place at the feet of the Spouse of Christ, of the Holy Church, all that we are and all that we can be; loving her faithfully, even at the cost of livelihood, of honor, of life itself.

585 Don't be scared by it. In so far as you can you should fight against the conspiracy of silence they want to muzzle the Church with. Some people stop her voice being heard; others will not let the good example of those who preach with their deeds be seen; others wipe out every trace of good doctrine..., and so very many cannot bear to hear her.

Don't be scared, I say again. But don't get tired, either, of your task of being a loudspeaker for the teachings of the Magisterium.

586 Become more *Roman* day by day. Love that blessed quality which is the ornament of the children of the one true Church, for Jesus wanted it to be so.

587 Devotion to Our Lady in Christian souls awakens the supernatural stimulus we need in order to act like *domestici Dei,* as members of God's family.

VICTORY

588 Imitate the Blessed Virgin. Only by openly admitting that we are nothing can we become precious in the eyes of our Creator.

589 I am convinced that John, the young Apostle, is at the side of Christ on the Cross because our Mother draws him there. The Love of Our Lady is so powerful!

590 We will never achieve true supernatural and human cheerfulness, *real* good humor, if we don't *really* imitate Jesus: if we aren't humble, as he was.

591 To give oneself sincerely to others is so effective that God rewards it with a humility filled with cheerfulness.

592 Our humiliation, our self-effacement, our disappearing and passing unnoticed, should be complete, entire, total.

593 Sincere humility. What can upset a person who delights in being insulted because he knows that he deserves nothing better?

594 My Jesus: what's mine is yours, because what's yours is mine, and what's mine I abandon in you.

595 Are you able to undergo those humiliations which God asks of you, in matters of no importance, matters where the truth is not obscured? You are not? Then you don't love the virtue of humility.

596 Pride dulls the edge of charity. Ask Our Lord each day for the virtue of humility, for you and for everyone. Because as the years go by, pride increases if it is not corrected in time.

597 Is there anything more displeasing than a child acting the grown-up? How can a poor man—a child—be pleasing to God if he "acts grown-up", puffed up by pride, sure that he's worth something and trusting only in himself?

598 Certainly you can go to Hell. You are convinced it could happen, for in your heart you find the seeds of all kinds of evil.

But if you become a child in front of God, that fact will bring you close to your Father God, and to your Mother, Holy Mary. And St Joseph and your angel will not leave you unprotected when they see you are a child.

Have faith. Do as much as you can. Be penitent, and be loving. They will supply whatever else you need.

599 How difficult it is to live humility! As the popular wisdom of Christianity says, "Pride dies twenty-four hours after its owner."

So when you think you're right, against what you are being told by someone who has been given a special grace from God to guide your soul, be sure that you are *completely wrong*.

600 Serving and forming children, caring lovingly for the sick.

To make ourselves understood by simple souls, we have to humble our intellect; to understand poor sick people we have to humble our heart. In this way, on our knees in both body and mind, it is easy to reach Jesus along that sure way of human wretchedness, of our own wretchedness. It will lead us to make "a nothing" of ourselves in order to let God build on our nothingness.

601 A resolution: unless I really have to, never to speak of my personal affairs.

602 Thank Jesus for the confidence he gives you. It's not stubbornness, but God's light that makes you firm as a rock. Meanwhile, others, good as they are, present a sorry picture. They seem to be sinking in the sand. They lack the foundation of the faith.

Ask Our Lord to grant that the demands of the virtue of faith may be met both in your life and in the lives of others.

603 If I behaved differently, if I were more in control of my character, if I were more faithful to you, Lord, how marvelously would you help us!

604 Your Father God puts a longing for atonement in your soul. That longing will be satisfied if you unite your own poor expiation to the infinite merits of Jesus.

Rectify your intention, and love suffering in him, with him, and through him.

605 You have no idea whether you are making progress, or, if you are, how much. But what use is such a reckoning to you?

What is important is that you should persevere, that your heart should be on fire, that you should be more enlightened and descry farther horizons; that you should strive for our intentions, that you should feel them as your

own—even though you don't know what they are—and
that you should pray for all of them.

606 Tell him: Jesus, I cannot see a single perfect
flower in my garden, all are blighted. It seems that all
have lost their color and their scent. Poor me! Face downwards in the muck, on the ground: that's my place.

That's the way, humble yourself. He will conquer in
you, and you will attain the victory.

607 I understood you very well when you ended up
saying: "Quite honestly, I haven't even made the grade
of being a donkey—the donkey that was the throne of
Jesus when he entered Jerusalem. I'm just part of a
disgusting heap of dirty tatters that the poorest rag picker
would ignore."

But I told you: all the same, God has chosen you and
wants you to be his instrument. So your wretchedness—
which is a genuine fact—should turn into one more reason
for you to be thankful to God for calling you.

608 Mary's humble song of joy, the *Magnificat*, re-
calls to our minds the infinite generosity of the Lord
towards those who become like children, towards those
who abase themselves and are sincerely aware that they
are nothing.

609   God is very pleased with those who recognize his goodness by reciting the *Te Deum* in thanksgiving whenever something out of the ordinary happens, without caring whether it may have been good or bad, as the world reckons these things. For everything comes from the hands of our Father: so though the blow of the chisel may hurt our flesh, it is a sign of Love, as he smooths off our rough edges and brings us closer to perfection.

610   When human beings have work to do, they try to use the right tools for the job.

If I had lived in another century, I would have written with a quill pen: now I use a fountain pen.

But when God wants to carry out some piece of work, he uses unsuitable means, so that it can be seen that the work is his. You have heard me say this very often.

So you and I, who are aware of the massive weight of our failings, should tell him: "Lord, wretched as I am, I still understand that in your hands I am a divine instrument."

611   We will dedicate all the exertions of our life, great and small, to the honor of God the Father, God the Son, and God the Holy Spirit.

I am moved when I recall the work of those brilliant professionals—two engineers and two architects—cheerfully moving furniture into a student residence. When they had put a blackboard into a classroom, the first thing those four artists wrote was: *Deo omnis gloria!*—all the glory to God.

Jesus, I know that this pleased you greatly.

612 Wherever you may happen to be, remember that the Son of Man did not come to be served, but to serve. Be sure that anyone who wants to follow him cannot attempt to act in any other way.

613 God has a special right over us, his children: it is the right to our response to his love, in spite of our failings. This inescapable truth puts us under an obligation which we cannot shirk. But it also gives us complete confidence: we are instruments in the hands of God, instruments that he relies on every day. That is why, every day, we struggle to serve him.

614 God expects his instruments to do what they can to be fit and ready: you should strive to make sure you are always fit and ready.

615 I have come to see that every Hail Mary, every greeting to Our Lady, is a new beat of a heart in love.

616 Our life—a Christian's life—has to be as ordinary as this: trying every day to do well those very things it is our duty to do; carrying out our divine mission in the world by fulfilling the little duty of each moment.

Or rather, struggling to fulfill it. Sometimes we don't manage, and when night comes, in our examination, we'll have to tell Our Lord, "I am not offering you virtues; today I can only offer you defects. But with your grace I will be able to count myself a victor."

617   I wish with all my heart that God, in his mercy, in spite of your sins (may you never offend Jesus again!), may make you constantly live that blessed life which is to love his Will.

618   In God's service there are no unimportant posts: all are of great importance.

The importance of the post depends on the spiritual level reached by the person filling it.

619   Aren't you glad to have the sure confidence that God is interested in even the tiniest details of his creatures?

620   Show him again that you really want to be his. "Jesus, help me. Make me really yours; may I burn and be consumed, by dint of little things that no one notices."

621 The Holy Rosary: the joys, the sorrows, and the glories of the life of Our Lady weave a crown of praises, repeated ceaselessly by the angels and the saints in Heaven—and by those who love our Mother here on earth.

Practise this holy devotion every day, and spread it.

622 Baptism makes us *fideles*, faithful. This is a word that was used—like *sancti*, the saints—by the first followers of Jesus to refer to one another. These words are still used today: we speak of *the faithful* of the Church.

Think about this.

623 God does not let himself be outdone in generosity. Be sure that he grants faithfulness to those who give themselves to him.

624 Don't be afraid to be demanding on yourself. Many souls do so in their hidden inner life, so that only Jesus may shine out.

I wish you and I would react as that person did who wanted to be very close to God, on the feast of the Holy Family. In those days it was celebrated within the octave of the Epiphany.

"I have had a number of little crosses. There was one yesterday that hurt so much it made me weep. Today it made me think that my father and lord, St Joseph, and my Mother, Holy Mary, won't have left this child of theirs without its Christmas present. The present was the light that made me see my thanklessness to Jesus in my failing to correspond to his grace; and to see how mistaken I was to resist, by my boorish behavior, the most Holy Will of God, who wants me as his instrument."

625 When the holy women reached the tomb they found that the stone had been rolled aside.

This is what always happens: when we make up our minds to do what we should, the difficulties are easily overcome.

626 Be convinced that if you do not learn to obey, you will never be effective.

627 When you are told what to do, let no one show more alacrity than you in obeying; whether it is hot or cold, whether you feel keen or are tired, whether you are young or less so, it makes no odds.

Someone who "does not know how to obey" will never learn to command.

628 It's remarkably stupid for a director to be content with a soul rendering four when it could be rendering twelve.

629   You have to obey—and you have to command—always with great love.

630   Help me with your prayer. I want all of us within Holy Church to feel that we are members of the same body, as the apostle asks of us. I want us to be vividly and profoundly aware, without any lack of interest, of the joys, the troubles, the progress of our Mother who is one, holy, catholic, apostolic, Roman.

I want us to live as one, each of us identified with the cares of the others, and all identified with Christ.

631   Convince yourself, my child, that lack of unity within the Church is death.

632   Pray to God that in the Holy Church, our Mother, the hearts of all may be one heart, as they were in the earliest times of Christianity; so that the words of Scripture may be truly fulfilled until the end of the ages: *Multitudinis autem credentium erat cor unum et anima una*—the company of the faithful were of one heart and one soul.

I am saying this to you in all seriousness: may this holy unity not come to any harm through you. Take it to your prayer.

633 Faithfulness to the Pope includes a clear and definite duty: that of knowing his thought, which he tells us in encyclicals or other documents. We have to do our part to help all Catholics pay attention to the teaching of the Holy Father, and bring their everyday behavior into line with it.

634 I pray every day with all my heart that God may give us the gift of tongues. Such a gift of tongues does not mean knowing a number of languages, but knowing how to adapt oneself to the capacities of one's hearers.

It's not a question of "simplifying the message to get through to the masses", but of speaking words of wisdom in clear Christian speech that all can understand.

This is the gift of tongues that I ask of Our Lord and of his Holy Mother for all their children.

635 A few are wicked, and many are ignorant: that is how the enemy of God and of the Church reigns.

Let us confound the wicked, and enlighten the minds of the ignorant. With the help of God, and with our effort, we will save the world.

636 We have to try to ensure that in all fields of intellectual activity there are up-right people, people with a true Christian conscience, who are consistent in their lives, who can use the weapons of knowledge in the service of humanity and of the Church.

Their presence will be necessary because in the world there will always be, as there were when Jesus came on earth, new Herods who try to make use of knowledge— even if they have to falsify it—to persecute Christ and those who belong to him.

What a great task we have ahead of us!

637 In your work with souls—and all your activity should be work with souls—be filled with faith, with hope, with love, because all the difficulties will be overcome.

To confirm this truth for us, the psalmist wrote: *Et tu, Domine, deridebis eos: ad nihilum deduces omnes gentes*—You, O Lord, will laugh at them: You will bring them to nothing.

These words confirm those other words: *Non praevalebunt*; the enemies of God shall not prevail. They will not have any power against the Church, nor against those who serve the Church as instruments of God.

638 Our Holy Mother the Church, in a magnificent outpouring of love, is scattering the seed of the Gospel throughout the world; from Rome to the outposts of the earth.

As you help in this work of expansion throughout the whole world, bring those in the outposts to the Pope, so that the earth may be one flock and one Shepherd: one apostolate!

639 *Regnare Christum volumus!*: we want Christ to reign. *Deo omnis gloria!*: all the glory to God.

This ideal of warring, and winning, with Christ's weapons will only become a reality through prayer and sacrifice, through faith and Love.

Well, then: pray, believe, suffer, Love!

640 The work of the Church, each day, is like the weaving of a great fabric which *we* offer to God: because all of us who are baptized make up the Church.

If we carry out our tasks faithfully and selflessly, this great fabric will be beautiful and flawless. But if we loosen a thread here, a thread there, another over there... instead of a beautiful fabric we will have a tattered rag.

641 Why don't you make up your mind to make that fraternal correction? Receiving one hurts, because it is hard to humble oneself, at least to begin with. But making a fraternal correction is always hard. Everyone knows this.

Making fraternal corrections is the best way you can help, after prayer and good example.

642 He has shown that he trusts you, by bringing you to the Church. So you have to have the balance, the calm, the strength, the human and supernatural prudence of a mature person, those qualities that it takes many people many years to acquire.

Don't forget what you learned in your Catechism: that "a Christian" means a man or woman who has faith in Jesus Christ.

643 You want to be strong? Then first realize that you are very weak. After that, trust in Christ, your Father, your Brother, your Teacher. He makes us strong, entrusting to us the means with which to conquer—the sacraments. Live them!

644 I understood you very well when you confessed to me: I want to steep myself in the liturgy of the Holy Mass.

645 How great is the value of piety in the Holy Liturgy! I was not at all surprised when someone said to me a few days ago, talking about a model priest who had died recently: "What a saint he was!"

"Did you know him well?" I asked.

"No," he said, "but I once saw him saying the Mass."

646   Since you call yourself a Christian, you have to live the Sacred Liturgy of the Church, putting genuine care into your prayer and mortification for priests—especially for new priests—on the days marked out for this intention, and when you know that they are to receive the Sacrament of Order.

647   Offer your prayer, your atonement, and your action for this end: *ut sint unum!*—that all of us Christians may share one will, one heart, one spirit. This is so that *omnes cum Petro ad Iesum per Mariam*—that we may all go to Jesus, closely united to the Pope, through Mary.

648   You ask me, my child, what you can do to make me very pleased with you.

If Our Lord is satisfied with you, then I am too. And you can know that he is happy with you, by the peace and joy in your heart.

649   A clear mark of the man of God, of the woman of God, is the peace in their souls: they have *peace* and they give *peace* to the people they have dealings with.

650   Get used to replying to those poor "haters," when they pelt you with stones, by pelting them with Hail Marys.

651 Don't worry if your work seems barren just now. When it is holiness that is being sown, it is not lost: others will gather in the harvest.

652 Even though you gain little light in your prayer, even though it seems dry and irksome, you should consider, with a sure, ever-new insight, that you need to persevere in every detail of your life of piety.

653 You grew in the face of difficulties in the apostolate when you prayed: "Lord, you are the same as ever. Give me the faith of those men who knew how to correspond to your grace, who worked great miracles, real marvels, in your Name..." And you finished off: "I know that you will do it: but I also know that you want to be asked. You want to be sought out. You want us to knock hard at the door of your Heart."

At the end you renewed your resolve to persevere in humble and trusting prayer.

654 When you are troubled... and also in the hour of success, say again and again, "Lord, don't let go of me, don't leave me, help me as you would a clumsy child; always lead me by the hand!"

655 *Aquae multae non potuerunt exstinguere caritatem!*—the great turmoil of waters could not quench the fire of charity. I offer you two interpretations of these words of Holy Scripture. First: the throng of your past sins, now that you have fully repented of them, will not take you away from the Love of our God; and a second one: the waters of misunderstanding, the difficulties that you are perhaps encountering, should not interrupt your apostolic work.

656 Work on to the end, to the very end! My child, *qui perseveraverit usque in finem, hic salvus erit*—it is the one who perseveres right to the end who will be saved.

We children of God have the means we need: you too! We will finish, we will top out our building, for we can do all things in him who strengthens us.

With God there are no *impossibles*. They are overcome always.

657 Sometimes the immediate future is full of worries, if we stop seeing things in a supernatural way.

So, faith, my child, faith—and more deeds. In that way it is certain that our Father-God will continue to solve your problems.

658 God's ordinary providence is a continual miracle; but he will use extraordinary means when they are required.

659 Christian optimism is not a sugary optimism; nor is it a mere human confidence that everything will turn out all right.

It is an optimism that sinks its roots in an awareness of our freedom, and in the sure knowledge of the power of grace. It is an optimism which leads us to make demands on ourselves, to struggle to respond at every moment to God's calls.

660 The Lord's triumph, on the day of the Resurrection, is final. Where are the soldiers the rulers posted there? Where are the seals that were fixed to the stone of the tomb? Where are those who condemned the Master? Where are those who crucified Jesus? He is victorious, and faced with his victory those poor wretches have all taken flight.

Be filled with hope: Jesus Christ is always victorious.

661 If you look for Mary you will *necessarily* find Jesus; and you will learn, in greater and greater depth, what there is in the Heart of God.

662 When you are preparing for a work of apostolate, make your own these words of a man who was seeking God: "Today I start to preach a retreat for priests. God grant we may draw profit from it—and, first of all, myself!"

And later: "I have been on this retreat for several days now. There are a hundred and twenty on it. I hope that Our Lord will do good work in our souls."

663 My child, it's worth your while being humble, obedient, loyal. Drench yourself in the spirit of God, so as to be able to carry it from where you are, from your place of work, to all the peoples that fill the earth!

664 During a war, the courage of the soldiers facing the enemy would be of little use if there were not others who seem to take no part in the struggle but who supply the fighting men with armament and food and medicines...

Without the prayer and sacrifice of many souls there would be no genuine apostolate of action.

665 The power of working miracles! How many dead —and even rotting—souls you will raise, if you let Christ act in you.

In those days, the Gospel tells us, the Lord was passing by; and they, the sick, called to him and sought him out. Now, too, Christ is passing by, in your Christian life. If you help him, many will come to know him, will call to him, will ask him for help: and their eyes will be opened to the marvellous light of grace.

666 You insist on doing your own thing, and so your work is barren.

Obey: be docile. Each cog in a machine must be put in its place. If not, the machine stops, or the parts get damaged. It will surely not produce anything, or if it does, then very little. In the same way, a man or a woman outside his or her proper field of action will be more of a hindrance than an instrument of apostolate.

667 The apostle has no aim other than letting God work, making himself available.

668 The first Twelve, too, were strangers in the lands where they taught the Gospel. They came up against the people whose world was built on foundations completely opposed to Christ's doctrine.

Look: despite these adverse circumstances, they knew that they had been entrusted with the divine message of the Redemption. And so the apostle cries, "Woe to me if I do not preach the Gospel!"

669 Our lives can effectively co-redeem, in an eternal way, only if we act with humility, passing unnoticed, so that others can discover him.

670 When the children of God act in their apostolate, they have to be like those great lighting systems which fill the world with light, but the lamp is not seen.

671 Jesus says: "He who hears you hears me."

Do you still think it is your words that convince people? Don't forget either that the Holy Spirit can carry out his plans with the most useless instrument.

672 St Ambrose has some words that fit the children of God marvelously well. He is speaking of the ass' colt, tethered to its dam, which Jesus needed for his triumph: "Only an order of the Lord could untie it," he says. "It was set loose by the hands of the apostles. To do such a deed, one needs a special way of living and a special grace. You too must be an apostle, to set free those who are captive."

Let me comment on this text for you once more. How often, upon a word from Jesus, will we have to loosen souls from their bonds, because he needs them for his triumph! May our hands be apostles' hands, and our actions, and our lives also. Then God will give us an apostle's grace, too, to break the fetters of those who are enchained.

673 We can never attribute to ourselves the power of Jesus who is passing by amongst us. Our Lord is passing by: and he transforms souls when we come close to him with one heart, one feeling, one desire: to be good Christians. But it is he who does it: not you nor I. It is Christ who is passing by!

And then he stays in our hearts—in yours and in mine —and in our tabernacles.

Jesus is passing by, and Jesus comes to stay. He stays in you, in each one of you, and in me.

674 Our Lord wants to make us co-redeemers with him.

That is why to help us understand this marvel, he moves the evangelists to tell us of so many great wonders. He could have produced bread from anything... but he doesn't! He looks for human cooperation: he "needs" a child, a boy, a few pieces of bread, and some fish.

He needs you and me: and he is God! This should move us to be generous in our corresponding with his grace.

675 If you help him, even with a trifle, as the Apostles did, he is ready to work miracles; to multiply the bread, to reform wills, to give light to the most benighted minds, to enable those who have never been upright to be so, with an extraordinary grace.

All this he will do...and more, if you will help him with what you have.

676 Jesus has died. He is a corpse. Those holy women had no expectations. They had seen how he had been abused, and how he had been crucified. How vivid in their minds was the violence of the Passion he had undergone!

They knew, too, that the soldiers were keeping watch over the place. They knew that the tomb was sealed shut. "Who will roll away the stone for us from the door?" they asked themselves, for it was a massive slab. But all the same, in spite of everything, they went to be with him.

Look: difficulties, large and small, can be seen at once. But if there is love, one pays no heed to those obstacles: one goes ahead with daring, with conviction, with courage. Don't you have to confess your shame when you contemplate the drive, the daring, and the courage of these women?

677 Mary, your Mother, will bring you to the Love of Jesus. There you will be *cum gaudio et pace*, with joy and peace. And you will be always "brought", because on your own you would fall and get covered with mud: you will be brought onward, brought to believe, to love, and to suffer.

WORK

678 From St Paul's teaching we know that we have to renew the world in the spirit of Jesus Christ, that we have to place Our Lord at the summit and at the heart of all things.

Do you think you are carrying this out in your work, in your professional task?

679 Why don't you try converting your whole life into the service of God—your work and your rest, your tears and your smiles?

You can... and you must!

680 Each and every creature, each and every event of this life, without exception, must be steps which take you to God, which move you to know him and love him, to give him thanks, and to strive to make everyone else know and love him.

681 We`are under an obligation to work, and to work conscientiously, with a sense of responsibility, with love and perseverance, without any shirking or frivolity. Because work is a command from God, and God is to be obeyed, as the psalmist says, *in laetitia*, joyfully!

682 We have to conquer for Christ every noble human value.

683 When a person really lives charity, there is no time left for self-seeking. There is no room left for pride. We will not find occasion for anything but service!

684 Every activity—be it of great human importance or not—must become for you a means to serve Our Lord and your fellowmen. That is the true measure of its importance.

685 Work always and in everything with sacrifice, in order to put Christ at the summit of all human activities.

686 Correspondence to grace is to be found also in the ordinary little things of each day, which seem unimportant and yet have the over-riding importance of Love.

687 You cannot forget that any worthy, noble and honest work at the human level can—and should!—be raised to the supernatural level, becoming a divine task.

688 As Jesus, who is our Lord and Model, grows in and lives as one of us, he reveals to us that human life—your life—and its humdrum, ordinary business, have a meaning which is divine, which belongs to eternity.

689 You should be full of wonder at the goodness of our Father God. Are you not filled with joy to know that your home, your family, your country, which you love so much, are the raw material which you must sanctify?

690 My daughter, you have set up a home. I like to remind you that you women—as you well know—have a great strength, which you know how to enfold within a special gentleness, so that it is not noticed. With that strength, you can make your husband and children instruments of God, or demons.

You will always make them instruments of God: he is counting on your help.

691 I am moved that the Apostle should call Christian marriage *sacramentum magnum*—a great sacrament. From this, too, I deduce the enormous importance of the task of parents.

You share in the creative power of God: that is why human love is holy, good, and noble. It is a gladness of heart which God—in his loving providence—wants others freely to give up.

Each child that God grants you is a wonderful blessing from him: don't be afraid of children!

692 In conversations I have had with so many married couples, I tell them often that while both they and their children are alive, they should help them to be saints, while being well aware that none of us will be a saint on earth. All we will do is struggle, struggle, struggle.

And I also tell them: you Christian mothers and fathers are a great spiritual motor, sending the strength of God to your loved ones, strength for that struggle, strength to win, strength to be saints. Don't let them down!

693 Don't be afraid of loving others, for his sake: and don't worry about loving your own people even more, provided that no matter how much you love them, you love him a million times more.

694 *Coepit facere et docere*—Jesus began to do and then to teach. You and I have to bear witness with our example, because we cannot live a double life. We cannot preach what we do not practise. In other words, we have to teach what we are at least struggling to put into practice.

695 Christian, you have the obligation of being an example in everything you do: including being an example as a citizen, in your fulfillment of the laws directed to the common good.

696 You are very demanding. You want everyone else, including those who work in the public service, to carry out their obligations. "It is their duty!" you say. Have you then ever thought about whether you respect your own timetable, whether you carry it out conscientiously?

697 Carry out all your duties as a citizen. Do not try to get out of any of your obligations. Exercise all your rights, too, for the good of society, without making any rash exceptions.

You must give Christian witness in that also.

698 If we really want to sanctify our work, we have inescapably to fulfill the first condition: that of working, and working well, with human and supernatural seriousness.

699 Your charity should be likeable. Without neglecting prudence and naturalness, try to have a smile on your lips for everyone at all times, though you may be weeping inside. The service you give to others should be unstinting too.

700 That half-finished work of yours is a caricature of the holocaust, the total offering God is asking of you.

701 If you say that you want to imitate Christ... and yet have time on your hands, then you are on the road to lukewarmness.

702 Professional work—and the work of a housewife is one of the greatest of professions—is a witness to the worth of the human creature. It provides a chance to develop one's own personality; it creates a bond of union with others; it constitutes a fund of resources; it is a way of helping in the improvement of the society we live in, and of promoting the progress of the whole human race...

For a Christian, these grand views become even deeper and wider. For work, which Christ took up as something both redeemed and redeeming, becomes a means, a way of holiness, a specific task which sanctifies and can be sanctified.

703 The Lord wants his children, those of us who have received the gift of faith, to proclaim the original optimistic view of creation, the *love for the world* which is at the heart of the Christian message.

So there should always be enthusiasm in your professional work, and in your effort to build up the earthly city.

704 You must be careful: don't let your professional success or failure—which will certainly come—make you forget, even for a moment, what the true aim of your work is: the glory of God!

705 Christian responsibility in work cannot be limited to just putting in the hours. It means carrying out the task with technical and professional competence... and, above all, with love of God.

706 What a pity to be killing time when time is a treasure from God!

707 All honest professions can and must be sanctified. No child of God, then, has a right to say: I cannot do apostolate.

708 You must draw from the hidden life of Jesus this further consequence: you must not be in a hurry... even though you are!

First and foremost, that is, comes the interior life. Everything else—the apostolate, any apostolate—is a corollary.

709 Face up to the problems of this world with a sense of the supernatural, and following the principles of ethics. They do not threaten or undermine your personality: they provide a framework for it.

In this way you will bring to your behavior a living strength which will win people over; and you will be confirmed in your progress along the right path.

710 God Our Lord wants you to be holy, so that you can make others holy. For this to be possible you need to look at yourself with courage and frankness; you need to look at the Lord Our God; then, and only then, you need to look at the world.

711 Encourage your noble human qualities. They can be the beginning of the building of your sanctification. At the same time, remember what I have already told you before, that when serving God, you have to burn everything, even "what people will say", and if necessary even what they call reputation.

712 You need formation, because you need a profound sense of responsibility, if you are to encourage and direct the activity of Catholics in public life and do so with the respect that everyone's freedom deserves, reminding each and every one that he has to be consistent with his faith.

713 Through your professional work, which you bring to completion with all the human and supernatural perfection that is possible, you can and should give Christian standards in the places where you carry out your profession or job.

714 As a Christian you have a duty to act and not stand aloof, making your contribution to serve the common good loyally and with personal freedom.

715 We children of God, who are citizens with the same standing as any others, have to take part *fearlessly* in all honest human activities and organizations, so that Christ may be present in them.

Our Lord will ask a strict account of each one of us if through neglect or love of comfort we do not freely strive to play a part in the human developments and decisions on which the present and future of society depend.

716 With a sense of profound humility—strong in the name of our God, and, as the psalmist says, not "in numbers of our chariots and of our horses"—we have to make sure, without regard for human considerations, that there are no corners of society where Christ is not known.

717 Freely, according to your own interests and talents, you have to take an active, effective part in the wholesome public or private associations of your country, in a way that is full of the Christian spirit. Such organizations never fail to make some difference to people's temporal or eternal good.

718 Struggle to make sure that those human institutions and structures in which you work and move with the full rights of a citizen, are in accordance with the principles which govern a Christian view of life.

In this way you can be sure that you are giving people the means to live according to their real worth; and you will enable many souls, with the grace of God, to respond personally to their Christian vocation.

719 It is a Christian's duty, and a citizen's duty, to defend and promote, out of piety and general culture, those monuments that are found along streets and highways—the wayside crosses, the images of Our Lady, and the like. We should restore those which vandalism or the weather have damaged or destroyed.

720 We have to stand out boldly against those "damning freedoms"—those daughters of license, granddaughters of evil passions, great granddaughters of original sin—which come down, as you can see, in a direct line from the devil.

721 For the sake of the objective truth, and to put a stop to the damage they do, I have to insist that we should give neither publicity nor *hosannas* to the enemies of God; not even after they are dead.

722 Nowadays our Mother the Church is being attacked in the social field and by the governments of nations. That is why God is sending his children—is sending you!—to struggle, and to spread the truth in those areas.

723 You are an ordinary citizen. It is precisely because of that *secularity* of yours, which is the same as, and neither more nor less than, that of your colleagues, that you have to be sufficiently brave—which may sometimes mean being very brave—to make your faith *felt*. They should see your good works and the motive that drives you to do them.

724 Children of God—like yourself—cannot be afraid of living in the professional or social surroundings which are proper to them. They are never alone!

God Our Lord, who always goes with you, grants you the means to be faithful to him, and to bring others to him.

725 All for Love! This is the way of holiness, the way of happiness.

Face up to your intellectual tasks, the highest things of the spirit and also those things that are most down to earth, the things we all of necessity have to do, with this in mind; and you will live joyfully and with peace.

726 As a Christian, you can give way, within the limits of faith and morals, in everything that is your own; you can give way with all your heart. But in what belongs to Jesus Christ, you cannot give way!

727 When you have to give orders, do not humiliate anyone. Go gently. Respect the intelligence and the will of the one who is obeying.

728 Naturally, you have to use earthly means. But put a lot of effort into being detached from everything of the earth, so that you can deal with it with your mind always fixed on the service of God and of your fellowmen.

729 Plan everything? Everything! you told me. All right: we need to use our prudence. But bear in mind that human undertakings, whether they are hard or simple, always have to count on a margin of the unforeseen; and that a Christian should never shut off the road of hope, or be forgetful of God's Providence.

730   You have to work with such supernatural vision that you let yourself be absorbed by your activity only in order to make it divine. In this way the earthly becomes divine, the temporal eternal.

731   Things done in the service of God never fail through lack of money: they fail through lack of spirit.

732   Aren't you glad to feel the poverty of Jesus so close to you? How splendid it is to be lacking even what is necessary! But in our case, as in his, it should pass silently and unnoticed.

733   Sincere devotion—true love of God—leads us to work hard, to fulfill the duty of each day, even though it is far from easy.

734   People have often drawn attention to the danger of deeds performed without any interior life to inspire them; but we should also stress the danger of an interior life—if such a thing is possible—without deeds to show for it.

735   The interior struggle doesn't take us away from our temporal business—it makes us finish it off better!

736 Your life cannot be the repetition of actions which are monotonously all the same, because the next one should be more upright, more effective, more full of love than the last. Each day should mean new light, new enthusiasm—for him!

737 Every single day, do what you can to know God better, to *get acquainted* with him, to fall more in love with him each moment, and to think of nothing but of his Love and his glory.

You will carry out this plan, my child, if you never, for any reason whatever, give up your times of prayer, your presence of God, with the aspirations and spiritual communions that set you on fire, your unhurried Holy Mass, and your work, finished off well for him.

738 I will never share the opinion—though I respect it—of those who separate prayer from active life, as if they were incompatible.

We children of God have to be contemplatives: people who, in the midst of the din of the throng, know how to find silence of soul in a lasting conversation with Our Lord, people who know how to look at him as they look at a Father, as they look at a Friend, as they look at someone with whom they are madly in love.

739 Those who are pious, with a piety devoid of affectation, carry out their professional duty perfectly, since they know that their work is a prayer raised to God.

740 Our being children of God, I insist, leads us to have a contemplative spirit in the midst of all human activities; to be light, salt, and leaven through our prayer, through our mortification, through our knowledge of religion and of our profession. We will carry out this aim: the more within the world we are, the more we must be God's.

741 Good gold and diamonds lie far down in the depths of the earth, not within everyone's reach.

Your task of holiness—your holiness and that of others—depends on your fervor, your cheerfulness, your everyday, obscure, normal, ordinary work.

742 In our ordinary behavior we need a power far greater than that of the legendary King Midas, who changed all he touched to gold.

We have to change, through love, the human work of our usual working day into the work of God: something that will last forever.

743 If you put your mind to it, everything in your life can be offered to the Lord, can provide an opportunity to talk with your Father in Heaven, who is always keeping new illumination for you, and granting it to you.

744 Work with cheerfulness, with peace, with presence of God.

In this way you will also carry out your task with common sense. You will carry it through to the end. Though tiredness is beating you down, you will finish it off well; and your works will be pleasing to God.

745 You should maintain throughout the day a constant conversation with Our Lord, a conversation fed even by the things that happen in your professional work.

Go in spirit to the tabernacle...and offer to God the work that is in your hands.

746 From there, where you are working, let your heart escape to the Lord, right close to the tabernacle, to tell him, without doing anything odd, "My Jesus, I love you."

Don't be afraid to call him so—my Jesus—and to say it to him often.

747 A priest who was saying the Divine Office prepared himself for prayer in this way: "I will follow the rule of saying, when I start: 'I want to pray as the saints pray,' and then I will invite my Guardian Angel to sing the Lord's praises with me."

Try this in your own vocal prayer, and also as a way of increasing your presence of God in your work.

748 You have received God's call to a specific way: it is to be at all the crossroads of the world, while remaining all the while, and as you carry out your professional work, in God.

749 Don't ever lose the supernatural point of view. Correct your intention as the course of a ship is corrected on the high seas: by looking at the star, by looking at Mary. Then you will always be sure of reaching harbor.

CRUCIBLE

750 I don't ask you to take away my feelings, Lord, because I can use them to serve you with: but I ask you to put them through the crucible.

751 Faced with the marvels of God, and with all our human failures, we have to make this admission: "You are everything to me. Use me as you wish!" Then, for you—for us—there will be no more loneliness.

752 The great secret of sanctity comes down to becoming more and more like him, the only and most lovable Model.

753 When you pray, but see nothing, and feel flustered and dry, then the way is this: don't think of yourself. Instead, turn your eyes to the Passion of Jesus Christ, our Redeemer.

Be convinced that he is asking each one of us, as he asked those three most intimate Apostles of his in the Garden of Olives, to "Watch and pray."

754 When you open the Holy Gospel, think that what is written there—the words and deeds of Christ—is something that you should not only know, but live. Everything, every point that is told there, has been gathered, detail by detail, for you to make it come alive in the individual circumstances of your life.

God has called us Catholics to follow him closely. In that holy Writing you will find the Life of Jesus, but you should also find your own life there.

You too, like the Apostle, will learn to ask, full of love, "Lord, what would you have me do?" And in your soul you will hear the conclusive answer, "The Will of God!"

Take up the Gospel every day, then, and read it and live it as a definite rule. This is what the saints have done.

755 If you really want your heart to respond in a genuine way, I would recommend you to enter one of the Wounds of Our Lord. In this way you will get to know him closely, you will cleave to him, you will feel his Heart beating...and you will follow him in everything that he asks of you.

756 There can be no doubt that for us who love Jesus, prayer is the great *pain-reliever*.

757 The Cross symbolizes the life of an apostle of Christ. It brings a strength and a truth that delight both soul and body, though sometimes it is hard, and one can feel its weight.

758 I understand. Through Love, you want to suffer with Christ: you want to put your back between him and the butchers who are flogging him; to offer your head instead of his for the thorns, and your hands and feet for the nails. Or at least you want to accompany our Mother, Holy Mary, on Calvary, and to plead guilty to deicide on account of your sins... and to suffer and to love.

759 You tell me: I have made up my mind to go more often to the Paraclete, to ask him for his light.

Good. But remember, my child, that the Holy Spirit comes as a result of the Cross.

760 The cheerful love that fills the soul with happiness is founded on suffering. There is no love without renunciation.

761 Christ is nailed to the Cross. And you? Still taken up with your whims and fancies—or rather, nailed by them!

762   We cannot, must not, be easy-going Christians: on earth there must be sorrow and the Cross.

763   In this life of ours we must expect the Cross. Those who do not expect the Cross are not Christians, and they will be unable to avoid their own "cross," which will drive them to despair.

764   Now, when the Cross has become a serious and weighty matter, Jesus will see to it that we are filled with peace. He will become our Simon of Cyrene, to lighten the load for us.

Then say to him, trustingly: "Lord, what kind of a Cross is this? A Cross which is no cross. Now I know the trick. It is to abandon myself in you; and from now on, with your help, all my crosses will always be like this."

765   Renew in your own soul the resolution that friend of ours made long ago: "Lord, what I want is suffering, not exhibitionism."

766   To have found the Cross is to have found happiness: it is to have found you, Lord!

767   What really makes a person—or a whole sector of society—unhappy, is the anxiety-ridden, selfish search for well-being, that desire to get rid of whatever is upsetting.

768 The way of Love has a name: it is *Sacrifice*.

769 The Cross, the Holy Cross, is heavy.

First there are my sins. Then the sad truth of our Mother the Church's suffering. For so many Catholics are apathetic: they want, without really wanting. And those we love are separated from us, for all kinds of reasons. And other people or we ourselves are suffering illness and trials.

The Cross, the Holy Cross, is heavy. *Fiat, adimpleatur...!* "May the most just, the most lovable Will of God be done, be fulfilled, be praised and exalted above all things forever! Amen. Amen."

770 When you walk where Christ walked; when you are no longer just resigned to the Cross, but your whole soul takes on its form—takes on its very shape; when you love the Will of God; when you actually love the Cross... then, only then, is it he who carries it.

771 Join your suffering, your Cross that comes from within or without, to the Will of God, by saying a generous *Fiat!* And you will be filled with joy and with peace.

772   These are the unmistakable signs of the true Cross of Christ: serenity, a deep feeling of peace, a love which is ready for any sacrifice, a great effectiveness which wells from Christ's own wounded Side. And always— and very evidently—cheerfulness: a cheerfulness which comes from knowing that those who truly give themselves are beside the Cross, and therefore beside Our Lord.

773   You must always be aware of and thankful for that favor of the King which throughout your life marks your flesh and your spirit with the royal seal of the Holy Cross.

774   That friend of ours wrote: "I carry a little Crucifix. Its Crucified is worn by use and by the kisses it receives. It was left to my father when his mother, who had used it, died.

It's a poor thing and much the worse for wear, so I would not have the nerve to give it away to anyone. That's why when I see it, my love for the Cross will grow."

775   There was a priest who prayed in a moment of affliction: "Jesus, let whatever Cross You want come to me. I resolve here and now to receive it joyfully, and I bless it with all the richness of my blessing as a priest."

776 When you receive a hard knock, a Cross, you should not be downcast. Rather the reverse: with a happy face you should give thanks to God.

777 Yesterday I saw a picture which moved me profoundly, a picture of Jesus lying dead. An angel was kissing his left hand with an inexpressible devotion. Another, at the Savior's feet, was holding a nail torn out of the Cross. In the foreground with his back to us there was a tubby little angel weeping as he gazed at Christ.

I prayed to God that they would let me have the picture. It is beautiful. It breathes devotion. I was saddened to hear that they had shown it to a prospective buyer who had refused to take it, saying, "It's a corpse!" To me, you will always be Life.

778 Lord, I have no qualms in repeating this thousands of times: I want to keep you company, suffering with you, in the humiliations and cruelties of your Passion and Cross.

779 To find the Cross is to find Christ.

780 Jesus, may your Divine Blood enter my veins, to make me live the generosity of the Cross at every moment.

781   Look at Jesus hanging dead on the Cross, and pray. In this way the Life and Death of Christ can become the model and the spur of your life, and for your answer to the Will of God.

782   At the moment of sorrow or expiation, remember this: the Cross is the symbol of the redeeming Christ. It has ceased to be the symbol of evil, becoming instead the sign of victory.

783   Among the ingredients of your meal include that *most delicious* of ingredients, mortification.

784   To do great mortifications some days, and nothing on others, is not the spirit of penance.

   The spirit of penance means knowing how to overcome yourself every single day, offering up both great and small things for love, without being noticed.

785   If we join our own little things, those insignificant or big difficulties of ours, to the great sufferings of Our Lord, the Victim (he is the only Victim!), their value will increase. They will become a treasure, and then we will take up the Cross of Christ gladly and with style.

   And then every suffering will soon be overcome: nobody, nothing at all, will be able to take away our peace and our cheerfulness.

786 To be an apostle you have to bear within you Christ crucified, as St Paul teaches us.

787 It's true: when the Holy Cross comes into our lives it unmistakably confirms that we are his, Christ's.

788 The Cross is not pain, or annoyance, or bitterness. It is the holy wood on which Jesus Christ triumphs... and where we triumph too, when we receive what he sends us with cheerful and generous hearts.

789 You have come to see that, after the Holy Sacrifice, it is on your Faith and your Love, on your penance, your prayer, and your activity, that the perseverance, and even the life on earth of your people to a great extent depend.

Bless the Cross: the Cross that he—my Lord Jesus— and you and I bear.

790 Jesus, I want to be a blazing fire of Love— madness. I want it to be sufficient for me just to be present in order to set the world on fire for miles around, with an unquenchable flame. I want to know that I am yours. Then, let the Cross come...

This is the marvelous way: to suffer, to love, and to believe.

791 When you are ill, offer up your sufferings with love, and they will turn into incense rising up in God's honor, and making you holy.

792 As a child of God, with his grace in you, you have to be a strong person, a man or woman of desires and achievements.

We are not hothouse plants. We live in the middle of the world, and we have to be able to face up to all the winds that blow, to the heat and the cold, to rain and storms, but always faithful to God and to his Church.

793 Insults hurt so much, even though you want to love them.

Don't be surprised: offer them to God.

794 You were very hurt at being slighted. That means you are forgetting too easily who you are.

795 When we think we have been accused of something unjustly, we should examine our behavior, in God's presence, *cum gaudio et pace*—calmly and cheerfully; and we should change our ways if charity bids us, even if our actions were harmless.

We have to struggle to be saints, more and more each day. Then let people say what they like so long as we can apply the words of the beatitude to their utterances: *Beati estis cum...dixerint omne malum adversus vos mentientes propter me*—Blessed are you when they slander you for my sake.

796 Someone—I don't remember who, or when— once said that the hurricane of slander always rages against those who are outstanding, just as the wind beats most furiously on the tallest pines.

797 Plots, wretched misinterpretations, cut to the measure of the base hearts that will read them, cowardly insinuations... It is a picture that, sadly, we see over and over again, in different fields. They neither work themselves, nor let others work.

Meditate slowly on those verses of the Psalm: "My God, I have become a stranger to my brothers, an alien to my mother's sons. Because zeal for thy house has consumed me, and the insults of those who insult thee have fallen on me." And keep on working.

798 It is not possible to do good, even among good people, without running into the holy Cross of gossip.

799 *In silentio et in spe erit fortitudo vestra*—in quietness and in trust shall be your strength. This is what the Lord assures to those who are his own. Keep quiet, and trust in him. These are two essential weapons in moments of difficulty, when there doesn't seem to be any human solution.

Look at Jesus in his Holy Passion and Death: suffering borne without complaint is also a measure of love.

800 This is the prayer of a soul who wanted to belong wholly to God, and, for his sake, to all mankind: "Lord, I beg you to work on this sinner, to rectify and purify my intentions, to pass them through the crucible."

801 I was deeply impressed by the disarming frankness of that holy and learned man, by his willingness to yield as well as by his refusal to give way, when he said "I can come to terms with anything except an offense against God."

802 Think of the good that has been done you throughout your lifetime by those who have injured or attempted to injure you.

Others call such people their enemies. Not so you. You should imitate the saints, even in this. You are nothing so special that you should have enemies; so call them "benefactors." Pray to God for them: as a result, you will come to like them.

803 Listen to me, my child: you must be happy when people treat you badly and dishonor you, when many come out against you and it becomes the done thing to spit on you, because you are *omnium peripsema*, like the refuse of the world.

It's hard, it's very hard. It is hard, until at last one goes to the tabernacle, seeing oneself thought of as the scum of the earth, like a wretched worm, and says with all one's heart "Lord, if you don't need my good name, what do I want it for?"

Up to then even a child of God does not know what happiness is—up to that point of nakedness and self-giving. It is a self-giving of love, but it is founded on mortification, on sorrow.

804 Opposition from good people? It's the devil's doing.

805 When you lose your peace and get nervous, it's like not listening to reason.

At such times, one hears again the Master's words to Peter as he sank among the waves of his own nerves and lack of peace: "Why did you doubt?"

806 Order will bring harmony to your life, and lead you to perseverance. Order will give peace to your heart, and weight to your behavior.

807 I copy these words for you because they can bring peace to your soul. "My financial situation is as tight as it ever has been. But I don't lose my peace. I'm quite sure that God, my Father, will settle the world business once and for all.

I want, Lord, to abandon the care of all my affairs into your generous hands. Our Mother—your Mother—will have let you hear those words, now as in Cana: 'They have none!' I believe in you, I hope in you, I love you, Jesus. I want nothing for myself: it's for them."

808 I love your Will. I love holy poverty, my own great lady.

And, now and forever, I detest and abominate anything that might mean the slightest lack of attachment to your most just, most lovable, and most fatherly Will.

809 The spirit of poverty, of detachment from the goods of the earth, results in effectiveness in the apostolate.

810 Nazareth: a way of faith, of detachment: a way in which the Creator subjects himself to his creatures as he does to his Heavenly Father.

811 Jesus always speaks with love... even when he corrects us or allows us to undergo trials.

812 Identify yourself with the Will of God. Then no trouble will be any trouble.

813 God loves us infinitely more than you love yourself. So let him make demands on you.

814 Accept the Will of God fearlessly. Resolve unhesitatingly to work all your life, with the material which the teachings and the demands of our Faith provide.

If you do, you can be sure that along with the sufferings, and even along with slander, you will be happy, with a happiness that will move you to love others and give them a share in your supernatural joy.

815 If troubles come, you can be sure they are a proof of the Fatherly love God has for you.

816 All those who love find that their life is a forge, a forging in the fire of sorrow. There, in that forge, Our Lord teaches us that those who tread fearlessly where the Master treads, hard though the going is, find joy.

817 Strengthen your spirit with penance, so that when difficulty comes you may never lose heart.

818 When will you make up your mind, once and for all, to identify yourself with Christ, with Life!

819 In order to persevere in following in the footsteps of Jesus, you need always to be free, always to want, and always to make use of your own freedom.

820 You are amazed to find there are many different goals that can be pursued within each field in which improvement is possible.

They are other ways within *the way*, and they help you to avoid possible routine and bring you closer to Our Lord.

Be generous: aim for the highest.

821 Work with humility. I mean, count first on God's blessings, which will not fail you. Then, on your good desires, on the plans you have for working—and on your difficulties! Do not forget that among those difficulties you must always include your own lack of holiness.

You will be a good instrument if every day you struggle to be better.

822 You told me, in confidence, that in your prayer you would open your heart to God with these words: "I think of my wretchedness, which seems to be on the increase despite the graces you give me. It must be due to my failure to correspond. I know that I am completely unprepared for the enterprise you are asking of me. And when I read in the newspapers of so very many highly qualified and respected men, with formidable talents, and no lack of financial resources, speaking, writing, organizing in defense of your kingdom... I look at myself, and see that I'm a nobody: ignorant, poor: so little, in a word. This would fill me with shame if I did not know that you want me to be so. But Lord Jesus, you know how gladly I have put my ambition at your feet... To have Faith and Love, to be loving, believing, suffering. In these things I *do* want to be rich and learned: but no more rich or learned than you, in your limitless Mercy, have wanted me to be. I desire to put all my prestige and honor into fulfilling your most just and most lovable Will."

I then said to you: don't leave this merely as a good desire.

823 Love for God invites us to shoulder the Cross squarely: to feel on our back the weight of the whole human race, and to fulfill, in the circumstances of our own situation in life and the job we have, the clear and at the same time loving designs of the Will of the Father.

824 He was the greatest madman of all times. What greater madness could there be than to give oneself as he did, and for such people?

It would have been mad enough to have chosen to become a helpless Child. But even then, many wicked men might have been softened, and would not have dared

to harm him. So this was not enough for him. He wanted
to make himself even less, to give himself more lavishly.
He made himself food, he became Bread.

Divine Madman! How do men treat you? How do I
treat you?

825   Jesus, the madness of your Love has stolen my
heart. You are small and helpless, so that those who eat
you can become great.

826   You have to make your life essentially, totally
eucharistic.

827   I like to call the tabernacle a prison—a prison of
Love.

For twenty centuries he has been waiting there, willingly locked up, for me, and for everyone.

828   Have you ever thought how you would prepare
yourself to receive Our Lord if you could go to Communion only once in your life?

We must be thankful to God that he makes it so easy
for us to come to him: but we should show our gratitude
by preparing ourselves to receive him very well.

829   Tell Our Lord that from now on, every time you
celebrate Mass or attend it, and every time you administer
or receive the Sacrament of the Eucharist, you will do so

with a great faith, with a burning love, just as if it were to be the last time in your life.

And be sorry for the carelessness of your past life.

830 I can understand your keenness to receive the Holy Eucharist each day. Those who feel they are children of God have an overpowering need of Christ.

831 While you are at Mass, think that you are sharing in a divine Sacrifice. For that is how it is: on the altar, Christ is offering himself again for you.

832 When you receive him, tell him: Lord, I hope in you: I adore you, I love you, increase my faith. Be the support of my weakness: You, who have remained defenseless in the Eucharist so as to be the remedy for the weakness of your creatures.

833 We should dwell on those words of Jesus, and make them our own: *Desiderio desideravi hoc Pascha manducare vobiscum:* I have longed and longed to eat this Passover with you. There is no better way to show how great is our concern and love for the Holy Sacrifice than by taking great care with the least detail of the ceremonies the wisdom of the Church has laid down.

This is for Love: but we should also feel the *need* to become like Christ, not only inside ourselves but also in what is external. We should act, on the wide spaciousness of the Christian altar, with the rhythm and harmony which holy obedience provides, the holy obedience that unites us to the will of the Spouse of Christ, to the Will of Christ himself.

834 We should receive Our Lord in the Eucharist as we would prepare to receive the great ones of the earth, or even better: with decorations, with lights, with new clothes...

And if you ask me what sort of cleanliness I mean, what decorations and what lights you should bring, I will answer you: cleanliness in each one of your senses, decoration in each of your powers, light in all your soul.

835 Be a eucharistic soul!

If the center around which your thoughts and hopes turn is the Tabernacle, then, my child, how abundant the fruits of your sanctity and apostolate will be!

836 The objects used in divine worship should have artistic merit, but bearing in mind that worship is not for the sake of art: art is for the sake of worship.

837 Go perseveringly to the Tabernacle, either bodily or in your heart, so as to feel safe and calm: but also in order to feel loved... and to love.

838 I copy some words which a priest wrote for those who followed him in an apostolic enterprise: "When you contemplate the Sacred Host exposed on the altar in the monstrance, think how great is the love, the tenderness of Christ. My way to understand it is by thinking of the love I have for you: if I could be far away, working, and at the same time at the side of each one of you, how gladly I would do it!

But Christ really can do it! He loves us with a love that is infinitely greater than the love that all the hearts of the world could hold; and he has stayed with us so that we can join ourselves at any time to his most Sacred Humanity, and so that he can help us, console us, strengthen us, so that we may be faithful."

839 Don't think that turning your life into service is easy. This good desire needs to be translated into deeds, for "the Kingdom of God does not consist in talk, but in power," as the apostle teaches us. Moreover, the practice of constantly helping other people is not possible without sacrifice.

840 You must always have, in everything, the same "instinct" as the Church. For this, you must acquire the spiritual and doctrinal training that you need, which will make you a person of sound judgment in temporal matters, humble, and quick to correct yourself when you realize you have made a mistake.

Correcting your own mistakes, nobly, is a very human and very supernatural way of using your freedom.

841   There is an urgent need for spreading the doctrine of Christ.

Store up your training, fill yourself with clear ideas, with the fullness of the Christian message, so that afterwards you can pass it on to others.

Do not expect God to illuminate you, for he has no reason to when you have definite human means available to you: study and work.

842   Error does not only darken the understanding: it also sunders wills.

But *veritas liberabit vos*: the truth will set you free from the partisan spirit that dries up charity.

843   You spend your time with that companion of yours who is scarcely even civil to you: and it's hard.

Keep at it, and don't judge him. He'll have his "reasons," just as you have yours, which you strengthen so as to pray for him more each day.

844   You make such a mess of your own life—how can you be surprised if other people are not angels?

845 Be lovingly on your guard in order to live holy purity, because a spark is more easily put out than a roaring blaze.

But all human care, and mortification, and the cilice, and fasting, which are essential weapons, and how little all these are worth without you, my God!

846 Constantly call to mind that at every moment you are cooperating in the human and spiritual formation of those around you, and of all souls—for the blessed Communion of Saints reaches as far as that. At every moment: when you work and when you rest; when people see you happy or when they see you worried; when at your job, or out in the street, you pray as does a child of God and the peace of your soul shows through; when people see that you have suffered, that you have wept, and you smile.

847 Holy coercion is one thing; blind violence or revenge is quite another.

848 The Master has said it already: if only we children of the light were to put at least as much effort and obstinacy into doing good as the children of darkness put into their activities!

Don't complain. Work instead to drown evil in an abundance of good.

849 The charity that harms the supernatural effectiveness of the apostolate is a false charity.

850 God needs men and women who are sure and strong, on whom he can lean.

851 We do not live for the world, or for our own honor, but for the honor of God, for the glory of God, for the service of God. It is this that should be our motive!

852 Ever since Jesus Christ Our Lord founded the Church, this Mother of ours has suffered continual persecution. Perhaps in other times persecution was carried out openly, while nowadays it is often done surreptitiously: but today as yesterday the Church continues to be attacked.

How great is our obligation to live every day as responsible Catholics!

853 Use this prescription for your life: "I don't remember my own existence. I don't think of my own affairs, because I haven't the time."

Work and service!

854 These are the characteristics that define the incomparable goodness of our holy Mother, Mary: a love taken to the extreme, fulfilling the Will of God with tender care; a complete forgetfulness of herself, for she is happy to be where God wants her to be.

For this reason, not even the slightest gesture of hers is trivial. Learn from her.

SELECTION

855 Committed. How much I like that word! We children of God freely put ourselves under an obligation to live a life of dedication to God, striving that he may have complete and absolute sovereignty over our lives.

856 Whenever sanctity is genuine, it overflows from its vessel to fill other hearts, other souls, with its super-abundance.

We, the children of God sanctify ourselves by sanctifying others. Is Christianity spreading to those around you? Consider this every day.

857 The Kingdom of Jesus Christ: that is our task. So, my child, be generous: do not be anxious to know any of the many reasons he has to want to reign in you.

If you look at him, it will be enough for you to consider how much he loves you. You will feel a hunger to correspond to his love, crying aloud that you really love him here and now; and you will understand that if you don't leave him, he won't leave you.

858   The first step towards bringing others to the ways of Christ is for them to see you happy and serene, sure in your advance towards God.

859   A Catholic man or woman can never forget this key idea: we have to imitate Jesus Christ in every sphere of society, without rejecting anyone.

860   Our Lord Jesus wants it: we have to follow him closely. There is no other way.

This is the task of the Holy Spirit in each soul, in yours too. You have to be docile, so as not to put obstacles in the way of your God.

861   A clear sign that you are seeking holiness is what I might call "the healthy psychological prejudice" of thinking usually about others (while forgetting yourself) so as to bring them closer to God.

862   It should be engraved deeply on your soul that God doesn't need you. His calling is a most loving mercy of his Heart.

863   Treat those who are in error with loving kindness, with Christian charity. But do not compromise with anything that goes against our holy Faith.

864   Have recourse to the sweet Lady Mary, Mother of God and our Mother also, entrusting to her care the cleanliness of soul and body of all mankind.

Tell her that you want to call upon her, and want others to call upon her continually. And that you want to conquer always, in the bad moments—or the good, very good moments—of your struggle against those who are hostile to our being children of God.

865   He came on earth because *omnes homines vult salvos fieri*, he wants to redeem the whole world.

While you are at your work, shoulder to shoulder with so many others, never forget that there is no soul that does not matter to Christ!

866   "Lord," you were telling him, "I like to say thank you. I want to be grateful to everyone, always."

Well, look: you aren't a stone, or a speechless tree, or a mule. You are not one of those created things whose life is completed here on this earth. This is because God chose to make you a man or woman, a child of his. And he loves you *in caritate perpetua*, with an eternal love.

So you like to be grateful? And are you going to make an exception of your Lord? Make sure that your thanksgiving comes pouring out from your heart every day.

867 Understanding is real charity. When you really achieve it, you will have a great heart which is open to all without discrimination. Even with those who have treated you badly, you will put into living practice that advice of Jesus: "Come to me all you that... are heavy laden, and I will give you rest."

868 Be loving towards those who are ignorant of the things of God. And with all the more reason treat those who do know him in the same way. If not, you cannot do the former either.

869 If you really loved God with all your heart, then that love for your neighbor, which you sometimes find so hard to have, would come as a necessary consequence of your Great Love. You would never feel hostility towards anyone, nor would you discriminate between people.

870 Have you that urge, that divine madness, to bring souls to know the Love of God? In your ordinary life, then, offer up mortifications, pray, carry out your duty, and conquer yourself in all kinds of tiny details.

871 Tell him slowly: Good Jesus, if I am to be an apostle, and an apostle of apostles, you have to make me very humble.

May I know myself. May I know myself and know you.

Then I will never lose sight of my nothingness.

872 *Per Jesum Christum Dominum nostrum*: through Jesus Christ, Our Lord. That is the way you should do things: through and for Jesus Christ!

It's good that you have a human heart. But if you act merely because it's a particular person, that's bad. You should certainly also do it for that brother of yours, for that friend of yours: but above all do it for Jesus Christ!

873 The Church expects a lot from you, as do other people—people of all lands, and of all times, present and to come. But you should have it very firmly fixed in your head and in your heart that you will be fruitless if you are not a saint or, let me put it better, if you don't struggle to be a saint.

874 Let yourself be formed by the rough or gentle strokes of grace. Strive to be an instrument rather than an obstacle. And, if you are willing, your most Holy Mother will help you; and you will be a channel for the

waters of God, rather than a boulder which diverts their
flow.

875 Lord, help me to be faithful and docile towards
you, *sicut lutum in manu figuli*, like clay in the potter's
hands. In this way it will not be I that live, but you, my
Love, who will live and work in me.

876 Jesus will enable you to have a great affection for
everybody you meet, without taking away any of the
affection you have for him. On the contrary, the more you
love Jesus, the more room there will be for other people
in your heart.

877 The closer a creature comes to God, the more
universal it feels. Its heart expands, making room for
everything and everybody in its single great desire to
place the whole universe at the feet of Jesus.

878 When Jesus died on the Cross he was only thirty-
three years old. Youthfulness can be no excuse!

Anyway, with each day that passes you are ceasing to
be young... though with him you will possess his eternal
youth.

879 You must reject that form of nationalism which
hinders understanding and harmony. In many moments
of history it has been one of the most evil of barriers.

You must reject it yet more strongly, since it would be all the more harmful, when it tries to set foot within the Body of the Church, where the unity of everyone and everything in the love of Jesus Christ ought to shine out most clearly.

880   Child of God, what have you done up to now to help the souls around you?

You cannot be content with that passiveness, with that idleness of yours. He wants to reach others through your example, through your words, through your friendship, through your service.

881   Sacrifice yourself, give yourself, and work at souls one by one, as the jeweller works on precious stones: one by one.

Indeed you should exercise even more care, because you are dealing with something of incomparable value. The purpose of that spiritual attention you give is to prepare good instruments for the service of God: and they, each one of them, have cost Christ all of his Blood.

882   To be a Christian, and in particular to be a priest —bearing in mind, too, that all of us who are baptized share in Christ's priesthood—is to be at all times on the Cross.

883 If you are consistent, now that you have seen his light you would want to be as great a saint as you were once a sinner: and you would struggle to make those desires a reality.

884 It is not pride, but fortitude, when you make your authority felt, cutting out what needs to be cut out, when the fulfillment of the Holy Will of God demands it.

885 Hands must sometimes be tied, with respect and with temperateness, without insult or discourtesy. Not out of revenge, but as a remedy; not as a punishment, but as a medicine.

886 You looked at me very seriously. But at last you understood, when I told you: "I want to reproduce the life of Christ in the children of God, by getting them to meditate on it, so that they may act like him and speak only of him."

887 Jesus has remained within the Eucharist for love... of you.

He has remained, knowing how men would treat him... and how you would treat him.

He has remained so that you could eat him, so that you could visit him and tell him what's happening to you; and so that you could talk to him as you pray beside the tabernacle, and as you receive him sacramentally; and so that you could fall in love more and more each day, and make other souls, many souls, follow the same path.

888 You tell me that you want to live the virtue of holy poverty. You want to be detached from the things you use. Ask yourself this question: have I got the same affections and the same feelings as Jesus Christ has, with regard to riches and poverty?

I told you: as well as resting in the arms of your Father-God, with all the confident abandonment of one who is his child, you should fix your eyes particularly on this virtue in order to love it as Jesus does. Then, instead of seeing it as a cross to bear, you will see it as a sign of God's special love for you.

889 At times some Christians do not give the commandment of charity its full scope and value in their actions. In that last wonderful discourse of his, we find Christ surrounded by his chosen ones and leaving them these words as a form of testament: *Mandatum novum do vobis, ut diligatis invicem*—a new commandment I give to you, that you love one another.

Then he went further: *In hoc cognoscent omnes quia discipuli mei estis*—by this all men will know that you are my disciples, if you have love for one another.

If only we would make up our minds to live as he wants!

890 Piety is the bond which ties us close to God and, for his sake, to others too since we see Christ in them. Without it, disunity comes inevitably, and with disunity the loss of all Christian spirit.

891 Be grateful to God from the bottom of your heart for those wonderful and awesome faculties he chose to give you when he made you—your intellect and your will. They are wonderful, because they make you like him; and awesome because there are human beings who turn their faculties against their Creator.

It seems to me we could sum up the thankfulness that we owe as children of God by saying to this Father of ours, now and always, *serviam!* I will serve you.

892 Without interior life, and without formation, there is no true apostolate and no work that is fruitful. Whatever work is done will be fragile, fictitious even.

How great, then, is our responsibility as children of God! We have to hunger and thirst for him and for his doctrine.

893 Someone told that good friend of ours, seeking to humiliate him, that his was a second or third-rate soul.

As he was convinced of his nothingness, he was not upset. Instead he reasoned this way: "Each man has just one soul. I have mine, just this one. So for each one his own soul is first rate. I'm not going to lower my sights. So, my soul, is of the very, very best: and with God's help, I want to purify it and whiten it and set it on fire, to please my Beloved."

You must not forget this: you cannot "lower your sights" either, despite the fact that you see yourself full of wretchedness.

894 You complain that you are alone, and that your surroundings militate against you. Think of this, then: Jesus, the Good Sower, takes each of us, his children, and holds us tight in his wounded hand, like wheat. He soaks us in his Blood. He purifies and cleanses us. He fills us with his "wine"! And then, he scatters us generously throughout the world, one by one, for wheat is not sown by the sackful, but grain by grain.

895 I insist: ask God to grant us, his children, the "gift of tongues," the gift of making ourselves understood by all.

You can find the reason why I want this "gift of tongues," in the pages of the Gospel, which abounds in parables, in examples which materialize the doctrine and illustrate spiritual truths, without debasing or degrading the word of God.

Everyone, both the learned and the less learned, finds it easier to reflect on and understand God's message through these human images.

896 God wants us, now and always, to spread his seed, a divine sowing in all surroundings. But he also wants it to maintain its quality while it gains in quantity.

You, very clearly, have a supernatural mission of helping to ensure that this quality is not lost.

897 Yes, you're right: how base your wretchedness is! By your own efforts, where would you be now, where would you have gotten to?

You admitted: "Only a Love that was full of mercy could keep on loving me."

Cheer up. He will not deny you his Love or his Mercy, if you go to him.

898 Your aim should be that there be many souls in the midst of the world who love God with all their hearts.

It's time to do your sums: how many souls have you helped to discover that Love?

899 The children of God are present and give witness in the world to draw others, not to be drawn by them.

They should spread their own atmosphere, the atmosphere of Christ, not let themselves be won over by a different atmosphere.

900 You have a duty to reach those around you, to shake them out of their drowsiness, to open wide new horizons for their selfish, comfortable lives, to make their lives more *complicated* (in a holy way, that is), to make them forget about themselves and show understanding for the problems of others.

If you do not, you are not a good brother to your brothers in the human race. They need that *gaudium cum pace*, that joy and that peace, which maybe they do not know or have forgotten.

901 No son or daughter of Holy Church can lead a quiet life, without concern for the anonymous masses— a mob, a herd, a flock, as I once wrote. How many noble passions they have within their apparent listlessness! How much potential!

We must serve all, laying our hands on each and every one, as Jesus did, *singulis manus imponens*, to bring them back to life, to enlighten their minds and strengthen their wills: so that they can become useful!

902 I didn't think God would get hold of me the way he did either. But, let me tell you once again, God doesn't ask our permission to *complicate our lives*. He just gets in: and that's that!

903 Lord, I will trust in you alone. Help me to be faithful to you. I know that I can look forward to everything as a result of being faithful in your service, abandoning all my cares and worries in your hands.

904 Let us thank God deeply and often for the wonderful calling we have had from him. May our gratitude be deep and genuine, closely joined to humility.

905 The privilege of being numbered among the children of God is the greatest happiness there can be: and it is always undeserved.

906 That cry of the Son of God, lamenting that the harvest is plentiful but the laborers are few, is always relevant. How it tears at our heartstrings.

That cry came from Christ's mouth for you to hear too. How have you responded to it up to now? Do you pray at least daily for that intention of his?

907 To follow Our Lord you need to give yourself once and for all, stoutheartedly and without holding anything back. You need to burn your boats once and for all, so that there is no chance of going back.

908 Don't be scared when Jesus asks you for more, even the happiness of your own family. You must be convinced that from the supernatural point of view he has the right to override all your people, for the sake of his Glory.

909 You say that you want to be an apostle of Christ.

I'm very glad to hear it. I pray that God may give you perseverance. Remember that from our mouths, from our thoughts, from our hearts, no single thing should issue that is not of God, of hunger for souls, of themes that lead us one way or another to God—or at least, that do not take us away from him.

910 The Church needs priests, and always will. Ask the Blessed Trinity for them each day, through Holy Mary.

And pray that they may be cheerful, hardworking, effective; that they may be well trained: and that they may sacrifice themselves joyfully for their brothers, without feeling that they are victims.

911 Turn constantly to the most Holy Virgin, the Mother of God, and Mother of the human race; and she, with a Mother's gentleness, will draw down the love of God on the souls you deal with, so that they may make up their minds to be witnesses for Jesus Christ, in their profession, in their ordinary work.

FRUITFULNESS

912 You should correspond to God's love by being faithful, very faithful! And this faithfulness should lead you to transmit the Love you have received to other people, so that they too may rejoice at meeting God.

913 My Lord Jesus, grant that I may feel your grace and second it in such a way that I empty my heart, so that you, my Friend, my Brother, my King, my God, my Love... may fill it!

914 If your prayers, your sacrifices, and your actions do not show a constant concern for the apostolate, it is a sure sign that you are not happy, and that you have to be more faithful.

The man who possesses happiness, and the good, will always seek to give it to others.

915 When you really trample on yourself and live for others you will become a good instrument in God's hands.

He called—and is calling—his disciples, commanding them *ut eatis!*—"Go and seek all men."

916 Make up your mind to set the world ablaze—you really can do it—with a love that is pure, and so you will make all mankind happy by bringing them really closer to God.

917 *In modico fidelis!*—faithful in little things. My son, your job is not just to save souls but to bring them to holiness, day after day, giving to each moment—even to apparently ordinary moments—the dynamic echo of eternity.

918 We cannot separate the seed of doctrine from the seed of piety.

The only way to inoculate your work of sowing doctrine against the germs of ineffectiveness is by being sincerely devout.

919 Just as all the powerful machinery in dozens of factories is brought to a standstill and rendered useless when the electricity fails, so does apostolate cease to bear fruit when prayer and mortification fail, for they are what move the Sacred Heart of Christ.

920 If you follow faithfully the promptings of grace, you will yield good fruit, lasting fruit for the glory of God.

To be a saint necessarily entails being effective, even though the saint may not see or be aware of the results.

921 Rectitude of intention consists in seeking "only and in all things" the glory of God.

922 The apostolate—which is a sure sign of spiritual life—means being constantly on the lookout so as to supernaturalize each detail of the day, whether big or small, by putting the love of God into everything one does.

923 As a bookmark for whatever book he happened to be reading, he always used a strip of paper with the following phrase written on it in a bold and energetic hand: *Ure igne Sancti Spiritus!*—Inflame with the fire of the Holy Spirit! You could almost say that, rather than writing the words, he had engraved them.

O Christian, I wish I could leave this divine fire emblazoned upon your soul, burning on your lips and setting ablaze everything you do.

924 You should try to have the holy shamelessness of a child who *knows* that his Father God always sends him what is best.

That is why he doesn't worry when even the apparently most essential things are lacking; and with complete serenity he says: At least I still have the Holy Spirit with me.

925 Please say a prayer each day for the following intention: that all of us Catholics may be faithful and determined to struggle to be saints.

It is so obviously reasonable. What else are we to desire for those we love, for those who are bound to us by the strong ties of the faith?

926 When I am told that there are people dedicated to God who are no longer striving with fervor for sanctity, I think that—if there is any truth in this—their lives are heading towards great failure.

927 *Qui sunt isti, qui ut nubes volant, et quasi columbae ad fenestras suas?*—"Who are these that fly like clouds, and like doves to their nesting places?" asks the Prophet. And a certain author comments: "Clouds come up from the sea and from rivers, and after circling about or following their course for a certain length of time, return once more to their source."

And I say to you that this is what you have to be: a cloud which makes the world fertile, making it live the life of Christ. Those divine waters will bathe and drench the very depths of the earth, and filter out the many impurities without themselves being dirtied. They shall give forth sparkling springs which will later become streams and mighty rivers able to slake the thirst of mankind. Afterwards you shall return to your shelter, to your boundless Sea, to your God, knowing that the fruits will continue to ripen, thanks to the supernatural watering done by your apostolate, and to the fruitfulness of the water of God which will last until the end of time.

928 My child, offer him even the sorrows and sufferings of other people.

929 Woes? Setbacks deriving from one thing or another? Can't you see that this is the will of your Father-God, who is good and who loves you—loves *you* personally—more than all the mothers in the world can possibly love their children?

930 Sincerely examine the way you are following the Master. Ask yourself if your self-surrender is of a dry, officious type, with a faith that has no sparkle to it; if there is no humility or sacrifice, or any good works throughout your day; if you are all show and pay no attention to the details of each moment... In a word, if you lack Love.

If this is the case, your ineffectiveness should come as no surprise to you. React right away, and be led by the hand of Our Lady.

931 Whenever you are in need of anything, or are facing difficulties, whether great or small, invoke your Guardian Angel, asking him to sort the matter out with Jesus, or to carry out the particular service you may require.

932 God is right there in the center of your soul, and mine, and in the soul of everyone who is in a state of grace. He is there for a purpose, that our salt may increase, that we may acquire more light and that from the place we each find ourselves in, we may be able to share out these gifts from God to others.

And how can we share out these gifts from God? With humility and piety, and by being very united to our Mother the Church.

Do you not recall the vine and the branches? How fruitful is each branch when united to the vine! What large bunches of grapes! And how sterile the broken-off branch that dries up and becomes lifeless!

933 Jesus, may my poor heart be filled from the ocean of your love, with waves which can cleanse me and expel all my wretchedness. Pour those most pure and ardent waters of your Heart into mine, until my desires for loving you are fully satisfied and I can no longer hold back my response to your divine ardor. My heart shall surely break then, dying for Love, and pour out that Love of yours which, in irresistible and most fertile, life-giving torrents, will reach other hearts that will beat through contact with these living waters, with the pulsating force of Faith and Charity.

934 Practise and *live* the Holy Mass!

You may be helped by a consideration which that priest, in love, used to repeat to himself: "Is it possible, my God, to take part in the Holy Mass and not be a saint?"

And he would continue, "Each day, in fulfillment of an old promise, I will remain hidden in the Wound of Our Lord's Side!"

Shouldn't you do the same?

935 You can do so much good, and yet also so much harm!

You will do good if you are humble and you give yourself cheerfully, with a spirit of sacrifice: good for yourself and for your fellowmen, and for that good Mother of yours, the Church.

But how much harm you will do if you allow yourself
to be led by your pride.

936   Please don't let yourself become *bourgeois*, for
if you do, you will be a hindrance. You will become a
dead weight for others in the apostolate and, above all,
a source of suffering for the Heart of Christ.

You must not stop doing apostolate, nor must you
abandon your effort to do your work as best you can, or
neglect your life of piety.

God will do the rest.

937   From time to time you have to deal with souls
as you would with a fire in the hearth, giving it a good
poke to get rid of the embers, which are what shine most
but are causing the fire of the love of God to die down.

938   Let us go to Jesus in the tabernacle where we can
get to know him and assimilate his teaching, and then be
able to hand out this food to souls.

939   When you hold Our Lord in your breast and you
taste the delights of his Love, promise him that you will
strive to change the course of your life in whatever way
is necessary, so that you can bring him to the masses of
people who do not know him, who live without ideals and
who, unfortunately, go on behaving like animals.

940 "Where charity and love are found, there is God" we sing in the liturgical hymn. Here is what a certain soul noted down: "Fraternal love is a great and marvellous treasure. It is not simply a consolation—which it certainly often has to be—but it really brings home the certainty of having God close to us, and shows itself in the charity our neighbors have for us and in the charity which we have for them."

941 Shun public display. May your life be known to God, for holiness passes unnoticed even though it is most effective.

942 Try to ensure that people don't notice when you lend a helping hand; try not to be praised or seen by anyone... so that, being hidden like salt, you may give flavor to your normal surroundings. And thus, as a result of your Christian outlook, you will be helping to give to everything about you a natural, loving, and attractive tone.

943 For this world of ours to set its course in a Christian direction—which is the only one worthwhile—we have to exercise a loyal friendship with all men, based on a prior loyal friendship with God.

944 You have heard me speak many times about the apostolate *ad fidem*.

I still think the same way. What a marvellous field of work awaits us throughout the world with those who do not know the true faith and who, nonetheless, are noble, generous, and cheerful.

945 I often feel like crying out to so many men and women in offices and shops, in the world of the media and in the law courts, in schools, on the factory floor, in mines and on farms and telling them that, with the backing of an interior life and by means of the Communion of Saints, they ought to be bringing God into all these different environments, according to that teaching of the Apostle: "Glorify God by making your bodies the shrines of his presence."

946 Those of us who bear in our hearts the truth of Christ have to put this truth into the hearts and minds and lives of others. Not to do so would show a love of comfort and bad tactics too.

Think it over once again: Did Christ ask you permission before coming into your soul? He left you free to follow him, but he was the one who sought you out, because he chose to.

947 With our acts of service we can prepare an even greater triumph for the Lord than that of his entry into Jerusalem. For there will be no repetition of the Judas episode, or that of the Garden of Gethsemane, or of that dark night. We will succeed in setting the world alight with the flames of that fire which he came to cast upon the earth. And the light of Truth—which is our Jesus—will enlighten men's minds with a brightness that never fades.

948 Don't look so alarmed. As a Christian you have the right and the duty to provoke a wholesome crisis in souls so that they live their lives with their eyes on God.

949 Pray for everyone, for people of every race and tongue and of every creed, for those who have only a vague idea about religion and for those who do not know the faith at all.

This zeal for souls, which is a sure and a clear sign that we love Jesus, will make Jesus come.

950 When they heard of work with souls in far-off lands, how their eyes sparkled! They seemed ready to cross the ocean in one leap. And indeed the world is very small when Love is great.

951 Not a single soul—not one—can be a matter of indifference to you.

952 A disciple of Christ can never think as follows:
"I try to be good; as for others, if that's what they want...
let them go to hell."

Such an attitude is not human. Nor is it in keeping
with the love of God, or with charity we owe our neighbor.

953 When a Christian understands what catholicity
means and practises it, and he realizes the urgent need to
proclaim the Good News of salvation to all creatures, he
knows that as the Apostle teaches, he has to make himself
"all things to all men, that all may be saved."

954 You have to love your fellowmen to the point
where even their defects, as long as they do not constitute
an offense against God, hardly seem to you to be defects
at all. If you love only the good qualities you see in
others—if you do not know how to be understanding, to
make allowances for them and forgive them—you are an
egoist.

955 You must not destroy the souls of your fellow
human beings through your neglect or your bad example.

In spite of your passions, you have a responsibility for
the Christian life of your neighbor, for the spiritual
effectiveness of everyone, indeed for their very sanctity.

956 Physically far away and yet feeling very close to them all, "very close to them all" you cheerfully repeated.

You were happy thanks to that communion of charity which I spoke to you about, and which you must not get tired of keeping alive.

957 You asked me what you could do to prevent the loneliness of that friend of yours.

I will tell you what I always say, because we have at our disposal a marvellous weapon which is the answer to everything: prayer. In the first place, you must pray. And then you must do for him what you would like others to do for you if you were in similar circumstances.

Without humiliating him, you must help him in such a way that the things he finds difficult can be made easy for him.

958 Put yourself always in your neighbor's shoes. You will then see the various issues or problems calmly. You will not get annoyed. You will be more understanding. You will be able to make allowances and will correct people when and as required. And you will fill the world with charity.

959 We cannot give way in matters of faith. But don't forget that in order to speak the truth there is no need to ill-treat anyone.

960   When the good of your neighbor is at stake you cannot remain silent. But speak in a kindly way, with due moderation, and without losing your temper.

961   It's not possible to comment on events or doctrines without making personal references..., although you are not judging anyone: *qui judicat Dominus est*—it is God who has to judge.

Don't worry, then, if now and again you come across someone who lacks an upright conscience and—either in bad faith or through lack of discernment—takes your words for gossip.

962   Some poor people seem to get annoyed by the good works you are doing, as if a thing ceases to be good when it is not being carried out or organized by themselves.

This lack of understanding cannot be an excuse for you to slacken off in what you are doing. Try to do it even better, right now. When you get no applause on earth, your work will be all the more welcome in Heaven.

963   At times, fifty per cent of the work is lost because of in-fighting stemming from a lack of charity, and from tales and backbiting among brothers. Furthermore, yet another twenty-five per cent of the work is lost by constructing buildings which are unnecessary for the apostolate. Gossip should never be allowed and we shouldn't waste our time building so many houses. People will then be apostles, one hundred per cent.

964 Pray for the priests of today, and for those who are to come, that they may really love their fellowmen, every day more and without distinction, and that they may know also how to make themselves loved by them.

965 I have been thinking of all the priests throughout the world. Help me to pray for the fruitfulness of their apostolates.

"My brother in the priesthood, please speak always about God and, when you really do belong to him, your conversations will never be monotonous."

966 Preaching—the preaching of Christ *crucified*—is the word of God.

Priests need to prepare themselves as best they can before carrying out such a divine ministry, the aim of which is the salvation of souls.

Lay people should listen with very special respect.

967 It made me very happy to hear what they said about that priest: "He preaches with all his soul... and with his body too."

968 Let this be your prayer, apostolic soul: Lord, may I know how to *lean on* people and get them all to burn like fires of Love, which will then become the driving force of all our undertakings.

969 We Catholics have to go through life being apostles, with God's light and God's salt. We should have no fear, and we should be quite natural; but with so deep an interior life and such close union with Our Lord that we may shine out, preserving ourselves from corruption and from darkness, and spread around us the fruits of serenity and the effectiveness of Christian doctrine.

970 The sower went out to sow, to scatter the seed at all the crossroads of this earth. What a blessed task we have. We have the job of making sure that in all the circumstances of time and place the word of God takes root, springs up, and bears fruit.

971 *Dominus dabit benignitatem suam et terra nostra dabit fructum suum*—the Lord will grant his blessing and the earth will bring forth its fruit.

That blessing is indeed the source of all good fruit, the necessary climate for producing saints, men and women of God, for this world of ours.

Dominus dabit benignitatem—the Lord will grant his blessing. Notice, however, that he goes on to point out that he awaits our fruit—yours and mine. Nor is this crop to be meager or blighted because we have not really given ourselves completely. He expects abundant fruit since he fills us with his blessings.

972 You saw your vocation like one of those pods that contain the seeds. The moment to expand will come and then the seeds will spread out and take root all at once.

973 You are to be yeast within the great multitudes that make up humanity—remember we are interested in all souls. In this way, with God's grace and your own correspondence to it, you will act as leaven throughout the world, adding quality, flavor, and volume to the bread of Christ so that it can nourish the souls of others.

974 The enemies of Jesus—and even some who call themselves his friends—come decked out in the armor of human knowledge and wielding the sword of power. They laugh at us Christians, just as the Philistine laughed at David and despised him.

In our own days too, the Goliath of hatred, the Goliath of falsehood, of dominating power, of secularism and indifferentism, will also come crashing to the ground. And then, once the giant of those false ideologies has been struck down by the apparently feeble weapons of the

Christian spirit—prayer, expiation, and action—we shall strip him of his armor of erroneous doctrines, equipping our fellowmen instead with true knowledge, with Christian culture and the Christian way of life.

975 In the campaigns against the Church there are many organizations which conspire together, sometimes going hand in hand with those who call themselves good. They influence people through newspapers, leaflets, satire, calumnies, and spoken propaganda. They then take people where they wish—to hell itself. They try to turn people into an amorphous mass, as if they had no souls. They are a pitiful sight.

However, since people do have souls, we have to snatch them out of the claws of these organizations of evil and place them at the service of God.

976 Quite a considerable proportion of the people who go to Church read bad publications...

Calmly and with love of God we need to pray and teach them sound doctrine so that they don't go on reading that diabolical stuff, which they claim their families buy— for they are ashamed of it—though perhaps it is they themselves who do so.

977 Defend the truth with charity and firmness when the things of God are at stake. Practise holy shameless-

ness in denouncing errors, even though at times they are
no more than insinuations; at other times they will be
odious utterances of the most blatant ignorance, and
normally, a sign of man's frustration at not being able to
endure the fruitfulness of the word of God.

978 In times of general confusion it may seem as
though God is not listening to your pleading with him on
behalf of *his* souls, and is turning a deaf ear to your calls.
You even reach the point of thinking that all your apostolic labors have been in vain.

Don't worry! Carry on working with the same cheerfulness, the same energy, the same zeal. Allow me to
insist: when you work for God, *nothing* is unfruitful.

979 My child, all the seas of this world are ours and
the places where it is harder to fish are the places where
it is all the more necessary.

980 Through your Christian doctrine, your upright
life, and your work well done, you have to give good
example to the people around you—relatives, friends,
colleagues, neighbors, pupils—in the way you carry out
your profession and fulfill the duties your job entails. You
cannot be a shoddy worker.

981   That close intimacy you have with Christ means that you have a duty to bear fruit.

And yours will be a fruit that will satisfy the hunger of men who come up to you in your work, in your day-to-day life and in your family environment.

982   When you carry out your duties in a cheerful and generous way you obtain abundant grace from God for other souls also.

983   Make an effort to spread your Christian spirit to the world about you, so that there may be many friends of the Cross.

984   As well as having given you abundant and effective grace, the Lord has given you a brain, a pair of hands, and intellectual powers so that your talents may yield fruit.

God wants to work miracles all the time—to raise the dead, make the deaf hear, restore sight to the blind, enable the lame to walk... —through your sanctified professional work, which you will have turned into a holocaust that is both pleasing to God and useful to souls.

985   The day you no longer strive to draw others closer to God—since you ought to be a burning coal all the time—you will become a contemptible piece of charcoal, or a handful of ashes to be scattered by the slightest puff of wind.

You have to be on fire; you need to be a thing that burns, producing flames of the love of God, of faithfulness and apostolate.

986 Invoke the Blessed Virgin. Keep asking her to show herself a Mother to you—*monstra te esse Matrem!* As well as drawing down her Son's grace, may she bring the clarity of sound doctrine to your mind, and love, and purity to your heart, so that you may know the way to God and take many souls to him.

ETERNITY

987 A son of God fears neither life nor death, because his spiritual life is founded on a sense of divine filiation. So he says to himself: God is my Father and he is the Author of all good; he is all Goodness.

But, you and I, do we really act as sons of God?

988 I was delighted to see that you understood what I had said to you: you and I have to work and live and die like people in love, and we will *live* in this way for all eternity.

989 God always wins. If you are his instrument, you too will win, because your battles will be his battles.

990 Sanctity consists precisely in this: in struggling to be faithful throughout your life and in accepting joyfully the Will of God at the hour of death.

991   When you receive Our Lord in the Holy Eucharist, thank him from the bottom of your heart for being so good as to be with you.

Have you ever stopped to consider that it took centuries and centuries before the Messiah came? All those patriarchs and prophets praying together with the whole people of Israel: Come, Lord, the land is parched!

If only your loving expectation were like this.

992   Even in our times, despite those who deny God, earth is very close to Heaven.

993   You wrote: "*Simile est regnum caelorum*—the Kingdom of God is like a treasure... This passage from the Gospel has taken root in my soul. I had read it so many times before, without grasping its meaning, its divine flavor."

Yes, *everything*. The prudent man has to sell everything to obtain the treasure—the precious pearl of Glory.

994   Talk with Our Lady and tell her trustingly, O Mary, in order to live the ideal which God has set in my heart I need to fly very high—ever so high!

It is not sufficient to detach yourself, with God's help from the things of this world, recognizing them as the merest clay. More is needed: even if you were to put the whole universe in a pile under your feet to get closer to Heaven... it wouldn't suffice!

You have to fly, without the support of anything here on earth, relying on the voice and the inspiration of the Spirit. And you will tell me: But my wings are stained and smeared with the clinging mud of many years.

And I repeat: Turn to Our Lady. Mary, you should say to her again, I can hardly get off the ground. The earth draws me like an accursed magnet. Mary, you can make my soul take off on that glorious and definitive flight which has as its destination the very Heart of God.

Trust in her, for she is listening to you.

995 Think how pleasing to Our Lord is the incense burnt in his honor. Think also how little the things of this earth are worth; even as they begin they are already ending.

In Heaven, instead, a great Love awaits you, with no betrayals and no deceptions. The fullness of love, the fullness of beauty and greatness and knowledge... And it will never cloy: it will satiate, yet still you will want more.

996 With a supernatural outlook, with serenity and peace. That is the way to see things, people and events— from the viewpoint of eternity.

And then, whatever barrier blocks your way—even if it is, humanly speaking, enormous—when you really raise your eyes to Heaven, how tiny it becomes!

997   If we are close to Christ and are following in his footsteps, we will wholeheartedly love poverty, privation, and detachment from earthly things.

998   In our spiritual life we often have to be ready to lose on earth so as to win in Heaven. This way we always end up winning.

999   Men lie when they say "forever" in temporal matters. The only true "forever," in the complete sense, is the *forever* of eternity.

And that is the way you have to live, with a faith that brings a foretaste of the sweet honey of Heaven whenever you think about that eternity which is truly everlasting.

1000   If this were the only life we had, life would be a cruel joke. It would be hypocrisy, evil, selfishness, betrayal.

1001   Keep going forward cheerfully and trying hard, even though you are so little—nothing at all!

When you are with him nobody in the world can stop you. Consider, moreover, how everything is good for those who love God. Every problem in this world has a solution, except death, and for us death is Life.

1002 Lord, you died on the Cross to save mankind. And yet for *one* mortal sin you condemn a man to a hapless eternity of suffering. How much sin must offend you, and how much I ought to hate it!

1003 St Teresa assures us that "anyone who doesn't pray doesn't need any devil to tempt him; while whoever prays, even if only for a quarter of an hour each day, will necessarily be saved." This is because our conversation with Our Lord—who is so loving, even in times of difficulty or dryness of soul—enables us to see things in their proper perspective and discover the true proportions of life.

Be a soul of prayer.

1004 "So you are a king?" ...Yes, Christ is the King, the King who not only grants you an audience whenever you like, but even in the madness of his love "gives up"— you know what I mean—his magnificent palace in Heaven, which you cannot yet reach, and waits for you in the tabernacle.

Don't you think it is absurd not to hurry to speak to him, and not to do so more assiduously?

1005   I am every day more convinced that happiness in Heaven is for those who know how to be happy on earth.

1006   With crystal clarity I see the formula, the secret of happiness, both earthly and eternal. It is not just a matter of accepting the Will of God but of embracing it, of identifying oneself with it—in a word, of loving the Divine Will with a positive act of our own will.

   This, I repeat, is the infallible secret of joy and peace.

1007   How often you will find yourself inundated, intoxicated with God's grace—and what a sin if you do not respond!

1008   In the hour of temptation, practise the virtue of Hope, saying: For my rest and enjoyment I have the whole of eternity ahead of me. Here and now, full of Faith, I will earn my rest through work and win my joy through suffering. What will Love be like in Heaven!

   Better still, you should practise your Love by saying: What I want is to please my God, my Love, by doing his Will in all things, as though there were neither reward nor punishment—simply to please him.

1009   Whenever the worrying thought enters your head that you lack rectitude of intention—sometimes it

may come like a flash of lightning, at other times like a
filthy pestering fly which you brush off but which keeps
coming back—always make acts of right intention straight
away, and carry on working calmly for him and with him.

At the same time, even though you might feel you are
only pronouncing the words mechanically, say slowly:
Lord, I want nothing for myself. May everything be for
your glory and for your Love.

1010   It is all the same to you, you tell me, to be here
or in China.

Well then, try to be always where you are fulfilling
the Holy Will of God.

1011   Much depends on you too. If you respond many
will remain in darkness no longer, but will walk instead
along paths that lead to everlasting life.

1012   Get into the habit of praying to the Guardian
Angel of each person you are following up. Their Angel
will help them to be good and faithful and cheerful, so
that when the time comes they will be able to receive the
eternal embrace of Love from God the Father, God the
Son, God the Holy Spirit, and from the Blessed Virgin.

1013   Like the grain of wheat, we too have to die in
order to become fruitful.

You and I, with the help of God's grace, want to open up a deep furrow, to blaze a trail. That is why we have to leave behind our poor animal man and launch out into the sphere of the spirit, giving a supernatural meaning to every human undertaking and, at the same time, to all those engaged in them.

1014 Jesus, let my distractions be the other way round. Instead of recalling the world when I am engaged in conversation with you, let me rather recall you when I am engaged in the things of this world.

1015 You became a bit frightened when you saw such dazzling light, so bright that you thought it would be difficult to look, or even to see.

Disregard your obvious weaknesses, and open the eyes of your soul to faith, to hope, and to love. Carry on, allowing yourself to be guided by God through whoever directs your soul.

1016 Be generous. Don't ask Jesus for even one consolation!

You ask me why. And I reply, because you know very well that even though this God of ours seems to be far away, he really is seated in the very center of your soul, imparting a divine character to your whole life.

1017 I was telling you that even people who had not received baptism had been moved to say, "I can well understand that saintly souls must be happy, for they look at events with a vision that is above the things of this world. They see things with the eyes of eternity."

May you not lack that same vision, I added afterwards, so that you can respond to the special love with which the Blessed Trinity has treated you.

1018 I assure you that if we want to, as children of God, we can make a powerful contribution towards lighting up the work and the lives of men with the divine and eternal splendor which it has pleased the Lord to place in our souls.

But "he who says he abides in Jesus ought to walk the same way he walked" as St John teaches. It is a path which always leads to glory. But it also always passes through sacrifice.

1019 What a disappointment awaited those who saw the light of the pseudo-apostle and wishing to come out of their darkness were drawn to his light. They raced to get there. They may have left shreds of their skin along the way. Some in their eagerness for that light may also have left behind some shreds of their very souls. And now, having reached the pseudo-apostle, they find cold and darkness. Cold and darkness which will eventually congeal the broken hearts of those who for a while have believed in that ideal.

It is an evil deed the pseudo-apostle has done. Those disappointed men who had been ready to give their very flesh in exchange for those glowing fires, for that gleaming ruby of charity, drop once more, instead, back to the earth from which they had come. Down they go, with a saddened heart, with a heart that is a heart no longer— just a chunk of ice shrouded in a darkness that will eventually cloud their minds.

You, false paradoxical apostle, see what you have done: because Christ is on your lips but not in your deeds; because you attract with a light which you yourself lack; because there is no warmth of charity in you, and you claim to be concerned about outsiders while all the time you are neglecting your own; because you are a liar, and lying is the daughter of the devil. And so, you are working for the devil, causing bewilderment to those who follow the Master, and even though you may triumph frequently here on earth, woe to you on that day which is approaching when our friend Death will come, and you shall see the anger of the Judge whom you have never deceived. Paradoxes, no, Lord: paradoxes? Never!

1020 This is the sure way: through humiliation to the Cross; then, from the Cross, with Christ, to the immortal Glory of the Father.

1021   How much I savored the epistle of that day! The Holy Spirit through St Paul teaches us the secret of immortality and of Glory. All of us human beings yearn to live on.

We would wish to make those moments in our lives when we are happy last forever. We would wish the memory of our deeds to be glorified. We would like our cherished ideals to become immortal. And so it is that when we seem to be happy, when something consoles us in our distress, we all naturally say and desire that it should last forever, forever.

Oh the wisdom of the devil! How well he knew the human heart. You will be like gods, he said to our first parents. That was a cruel deception. St Paul, in his *Epistle to the Philippians,* teaches us a divine secret by which to attain immortality and Glory: Jesus...emptied himself, taking the form of a slave... He humbled himself and became obedient unto death, even death on the Cross. Therefore God has highly exalted him and bestowed on him a name which is above every other name, that at the name of Jesus every knee should bow, in Heaven, and on earth, and under the earth...

1022   If we are to accompany Christ in his Glory, in his final triumph, we have first of all to share in his holocaust, becoming identified with him, who died on Calvary.

1023   Don't let yourself be distracted, don't give free rein to your imagination. Live the life within you and you will be closer to God.

1024   Help me repeat in the ear of this person and of that other one... and of everyone: a sinner who has faith, even if he were to obtain all the blessings of this earth, will necessarily be unhappy and wretched.

It is true that the motive that leads us (and should lead everyone) to hate sin, even venial sin ought to be a supernatural one: that God abhors sin from the depth of his infiniteness, with a supreme, eternal, and necessary hatred, as an evil opposed to the infinite good. But the first reason I mentioned to you can lead us to this other one.

1025   You will have as much sanctity, as you have mortification done for Love.

1026   Violent persecution had broken out. And that priest prayed: Jesus, may every sacrilegious fire increase in me the fire of Love and Reparation.

1027   When you consider the beauty, the greatness, and the effectiveness of apostolic work, you say that your head aches thinking of the amount of ground that still has to be covered—there are so many souls who are waiting!

But you feel so happy offering yourself as a slave to Jesus. You have a great desire for his Cross and for suffering, for Love and for souls. Without thinking about it, in an instinctive gesture—which was one of Love— you stretched out your arms and opened the palms of your hands, ready for him to nail you to this Holy Cross. You were ready to be his slave—*serviam*—which is to reign.

1028 I was moved by the heartfelt petition that came from your lips: "My God, my only desire is to be pleasing in your sight; nothing else matters to me. My Mother Immaculate, may I be motivated exclusively by Love."

1029 With your whole heart ask for death, and a thousand deaths, rather than offend your God.

And not because of the punishment due to sin, which we deserve so much, but because Jesus has been and is so good to you.

1030 My God, when will I love you for yourself? Although when we think about it, Lord, to desire an ever-lasting reward is to desire you, for you give yourself as our reward.

1031 Taste and see that the Lord is good, the psalm-ist says.

Spiritual conquest, which is Love, has to be a desire for the Infinite, a desire for eternity—in big things and small.

1032 Jesus, I don't want to think of what "tomorrow" will be like, for I don't want to put limits on your generosity.

1033 Make those reflections of your friend your own. He wrote: "I was considering how good God was to me and, full of interior joy, I was ready to shout out loud, there in the street, for everyone to know about my filial gratitude: 'Father! Father!' And though not in fact shouting out loud, I kept calling him so—'Father!'—in a low voice, many times, quite certain that it pleased him.

I seek nothing else. I only want to please him and give him Glory. Everything for him. If I desire my salvation and my sanctification it is because I know that he desires it. If in my Christian life I hunger for souls, it is because I know that he has this great hunger. I say this in all truth: I will never set my sights on the prize. I don't desire a reward: everything for Love!"

1034 How that sick woman whom I tended spiritually loved the Will of God! She saw her many, long-lasting and painful illnesses (not a single part of her body was healthy), as a blessing from Jesus and a sign of his special love. Although in her humility she used to say that she deserved punishment, the terrible sufferings that she felt all over her were not a punishment, but a mercy.

We spoke of death. And of Heaven. And of what she was going to say to Jesus and to Our Lady. And how she would be *working* much more from up there than she could down here. She was ready to die whenever God wanted... but, she exclaimed, full of joy, "If only it could be today!" She looked forward to death with the same joy as one who knows that when we die we go to meet our Father.

1035   Do not fear death. She is your friend!

Try to get used to the fact of death: peer into your grave often, looking at and touching, and smelling your own rotting corpse there, a week, no more, after your death.

Remember this especially when you are troubled by the impulses of your flesh.

1036   When he bared his soul to me he said, "These days I have been thinking about death as a rest, in spite of my crimes. And I thought that if I was told: 'The time has come for you to die', I would gladly reply: 'The time has come for me to Live'."

1037   To die is a good thing. How can anyone with faith be, at the same time, afraid to die? But as long as the Lord wants to keep you here on earth, it would be cowardice for you to want to die. You must live, live and suffer, and work for Love: that is your task.

1038   At least once daily, cast your mind ahead to the moment of death so that you can consider the events of each day in this light.

I can assure you that you will have a good experience of the peace this consideration brings.

1039   You became very serious when you heard me say: I accept death whenever God wants it, the way he wants it, where he wants it; and at the same time I think it is *too easy* to die early, because we should want to work many years for him, and because of him, in the service of others.

1040   To die?... That's too easy, I say once more.

Say, just as that holy bishop did when he was old and sick, *non recuso laborem*—Lord, as long as I can be useful, I do not refuse to keep on living and working for you.

1041   You shouldn't want to do things to gain merit, nor out of fear of the punishments of purgatory. From now on, and always, you should make the effort to do everything, even the smallest thing, to please Jesus.

1042   Desire ardently that, when that unavoidable good sister of yours, death, comes to render you the service of taking you to God, she will not find you attached to anything on this earth!

1043   If you long to have life—eternal life and happiness—you must not leave the barque of Holy Mother Church. Look, if you go beyond the confines of the ship you end up in the waves of the sea, heading for death, drowned in the ocean. You cease to be with Christ. You lose that friendship of his which you freely chose when you realized that it was he who was offering it to you.

1044   Jesus came down to this earth to suffer... and so that others might avoid sufferings, even earthly ones.

1045   There is no greater self-mastery than to make oneself a servant, the willing servant of all souls!

This is how to gain the greatest honors, both on earth and in Heaven.

1046   In the face of suffering and persecution, a certain soul with supernatural sense said, "I prefer to take a beating down here rather than get it in purgatory."

1047   If I love, there will be no hell for me.

1048   How good it is to live on God's bounty! How good it is to desire nothing other than his Glory.

1049   If you really want to attain eternal life and honor you must learn in many cases to put aside your own noble ambitions.

1050   Don't keep on talking about *your* health, *your* family name, *your* career, *your* work, or *your* next step... How annoying this can be! It would seem you have forgotten that *you* don't have anything, that everything is *his*.

When you feel sometimes—perhaps without reason— that you have been humiliated; when you think your opinion should prevail; when you notice that at every moment your "self" keeps cropping up: your this, your that, your something else...convince yourself that you are wasting, killing time, and that what you should be doing is *killing* your selfishness.

1051   I advise you not to look for praise, even when you deserve it. It is better to pass unnoticed, and to let the most beautiful and noble aspects of our actions, of our lives, remain hidden. What a great thing it is to become little! *Deo omnis gloria!*—All the glory to God.

1052 In moments of disappointment that soul said to Our Lord: "My Jesus, what else could I give you apart from my honor, if I had nothing else? If I had had a fortune I would have given it to you. If I'd had virtues, I would have built up each one to serve you better. The only thing I had was my honor and I have given it to you. May you be blessed! It's clear that it was safe in your hands!"

1053 It is from clay I come and the earth is the inheritance of all my lineage.

Who but God deserves praise?

1054 When you feel self-love—pride!—stirring within you, making you out to be a superman, it is time to cry out: *No!* In this way you will savor the joy of the good son of God who goes through life with not a few faults, but doing good.

1055 *Sancta Maria, Stella Maris*—Holy Mary, Star of the Sea, be our guide.

Make this firm request, because there is no storm which can shipwreck the most Sweet Heart of Mary. When you see the storm coming, if you seek safety in that firm Refuge which is Mary, there will be no danger of your wavering or going down.

INDEX

SUBJECT INDEX

585, 649, 695; charity, unity, 192, 550, 830, 847, 940, 955, 957, 962; obedience, 315, 488, 614, 616, 619, 629, 915, 941, 949-954; universality, 7, 812, 928, 947, 963-966, 980, 981; results, 28, 129, 199, 473, 697, 794, 916, 968; supernatural means, 82, 89, 105, 108, 470, 546-549, 837, 960, 969, 982; help of the guardian angels, 563-566, 570; apostolate of friendship, 846, 850, 971-975; naturalness in the apostolate, 380, 643, 835, 842, 970; through work, 347, 353, 799, 832, 979; through study, 335, 336, 340, 346, 782, 978; apostolate of giving doctrine, 338, 344, 349, 467, 582, 836, 849; letter-writing apostolate, 312, 546, 976, 977; Our Lady, 494, 505, 515, 982.

Furrow

181-232, 927-944; false apostolates, 966.

Apostolate and mortification, 182, 190, 206, 992.

Apostolate and work, 424, 471, 483, 504, 518, 522-523, 525, 530, 581, 617.

Apostolate ad fidem, 24, 64, 753. see ECUMENISM.

Apostolate of doctrine. see DOCTRINE.

Apostolate of example, 735, 930. see WITNESS.

Apostolate of friendship and trust, 191-193, 223, 471, 501, 730-731, 733-734, 753, 943.

Apostolic effectiveness, fruits, 64, 110, 186, 207-208, 217, 377, 418, 595, 609, 766, 884, 912. see EFFECTIVENESS.

Apostolic goals, 85, 927.

Forge

355. see EXAMINATION OF CONSCIENCE, LUKEWARMNESS, SANCTITY.

ASPIRATIONS

Furrow

53, 161, 180, 258, 344, 516, 847, 862, 874, 936, 964.

Forge

35, 66, 69, 117, 120, 176-177, 197, 306-307, 354, 401, 497, 506, 515, 527, 654, 746; *cor contritum et humiliatum...*, 172; *Deo omnis gloria*, 611, 639, 1051; *Domine adiuva incredulitatem meam!*, 257; *Domine, tu scis quia amo te*, 176; *Domine, quid me vis facere?*, 238; *Domine ut videam!*, 318; *ecce ego quia vocasti me*, 7, 52; *Fiat!*, 236, 769, 771; *hodie, nunc*, 381; *monstra te esse Matrem*, 986; *nunc coepi*, 398; *omnia in bonum*, 1001; *omnes cum Petro ad Iesum per Mariam*, 647; *omnia possum...*, 232, 337; *serviam!*, 96, 238, 891, 1027; *Tuus ego sum...*, 196; *ure igne Sancti Spiritus!*, 516, 923; *ut iumentum*, 381; *Veni, Sancte Spiritus...*, 514.

ATONEMENT

The Way

246, 269, 272, 288, 402, 436, 532, 897; reparation, 112, 182, 413, 527, 690, 861, 886; expiation, 210, 215, 216, 219, 222, 234, 242; Our Lady, 503, 506.

Furrow

258, 480, 518, 689, 996. see CONTRITION, PENANCE, SIN.

BLESSINGS
Furrow
250, 257, 482.

BLESSED TRINITY
Forge
2, 122, 430, 543, 611; dwelling in the soul, 261, 932, 1015; Our Lady, and the, 285, 482, 543, 555.

BLESSED VIRGIN
The Way
see OUR LADY.

BOOKS
The Way
339, 467.

BOURGEOIS ATTITUDES
Furrow
12, 206, 210, 716, 952. see LUKEWARMNESS.

CARICATURE
Furrow
58, 386, 595, 717, 952.

CAUTION
Furrow
26, 108, 306.

CERTAINTY
Furrow
174, 284, 663, 677, 762.

848; the means for preserving it, 132, 814, 832-841, 847, 849; in marriage, 846. see HEART, HEDON-ISM.

Forge

89, 315, 413, 553, 691; a joyful affirmation, 91-92; the means for living it, 90, 317, 414-415, 845, 864. see HEART (guard of the heart), HEDONISM.

CHEERFULNESS AND JOY

Furrow

52-95, 399, 519, 795, 861, 994; cheerfulness and apostolate, 63-64, 117, 188, 321; cheerfulness and fraternity, 55-57, 66; cheerfulness and illness, 254; cheerfulness and interior life, 52-54, 72-73, 94-95, 132, 296, 306, 411, 673, 773, 788, 857, 987, 994; joy of life and death, 83, 891, 893; joy of the children of God, 58-62, 305, 859; joy in the Cross, 70-71, 238, 249, 982-983; result of self-surrender, 2, 6-8, 18, 79-81, 85-88, 93, 98; sowing joy, 92, 185; sense of humor, 1000. see ASCETICAL STRUGGLE (cheerful and sporting), OPTIMISM.

Forge

180, 183, 520, 699, 858, 914, 1005-1006, 1021, 1024; good humor, 151, 392, 590; joy and peace, 648, 677; joy of the children of God, 105, 266, 269, 332, 423, 1054; joy in the Cross, 28, 174, 504; result of self-surrender, 54, 239, 275, 308, 368, 591, 814, 816; smiling asceticism, 149. see ASCETICAL

STRUGGLE (cheerful and sporting), MORTIFI-
CATION, OPTIMISM, SELF-SURRENDER.

CHILDHOOD, SPIRITUAL

The Way

from 852 to 901; divine filiation and abandonment,
852, 860, 863, 864, 867; humility, 862, 865, 868, 869,
871, 872, 880, 882; strength and maturity, 55, 697,
853-856, 858, 877, 899; Love, 875, 878, 881, 883,
885, 901; piety, 557, 859, 866, 876, 898; prayer, 153,
888-897; compunction, 861, 870, 873, 879, 884,
886, 887; daring, 389, 390, 402, 403, 857, 874; Our
Lady, 498, 516, 900.

CHINA

Forge

1010.

CHRISTIAN MORALS

Furrow

48, 267, 275, 295, 307, 357, 842. see CONSCIENCE.

Forge

709. see CONSCIENCE, HUMAN PERSON.

CHRISTIAN VOCATION

Furrow

407, 428, 757; apostolic vocation, 75, 211, 361, 930;
call to holiness, 167, 182, 728; living as Christians,
14, 48, 116, 295, 716-717, 931. see APOSTOLATE,
SANCTITY.

gether in harmony, 457. see AUTHORITY, LAW, SECULARITY, TEMPORAL ACTIVITIES, WORLD.

COMFORT

Furrow

158, 162, 167, 204, 265, 505, 509, 521, 525, 541, 558, 581, 627, 768, 863, 922, 965.

COMMITMENT

Furrow

9, 114, 184, 529, 539, 939.

COMMUNION OF SAINTS

The Way

from 544 to 550; communication of supernatural life, 315, 544, 547, 960; mutual help, 464, 545, 546, 549, 997; charity, 363, 469, 548, 550, 847, 977.

Furrow

56, 472, 479, 615, 689, 948.

Forge

107, 251, 258, 462, 470-471, 846; communication of supernatural life, 583, 640, 651, 692, 925, 955-957, 982; unity, 471, 630-632, 956.

CONDUCT

Furrow

23, 82, 130, 153, 156-157, 267, 322, 329, 339, 382, 521, 534, 543, 571, 627, 705, 707, 717, 731, 760, 772, 779, 803, 911, 951, 954; Christian, 4, 306, 317, 393, 504, 584, 644, 720, 727, 748, 855, 904, 930,

481, 883; with the help of Our Lady, 162.

CO-REDEEMERS

Furrow

1, 181, 211, 255, 291, 466, 826, 858, 945. see APOS-
TOLATE, CROSS, MORTIFICATION.

Forge

4, 5, 23, 26, 52, 55, 232, 374, 377, 669, 674, 970. see
APOSTOLATE, CROSS, MORTIFICATION.

COURAGE

The Way

12, 169, 387-391, 401, 479, 482, 487; in the ascetical
struggle and in the apostolate, 18, 132, 237, 251, 393,
497, 792, 841, 982; in defense of the truth, 33-35, 54,
353, 393, 394, 836, 849.

Furrow

36, 41, 46, 92-124, 166, 236, 362, 407, 785, 834, 920,
962; daring, 37, 39, 96-98, 112, 118, 124; fear, 102-103.

Forge

6, 466, 546, 884; in the defense of truth, 129, 459,
580. see DARING, FORTITUDE.

COWARDICE

The Way

18, 33-36, 54, 251, 603; in the interior life, 65, 169,
348, 714, 828, 985; in the apostolate, 792, 841, 903.

Furrow

11, 25, 51, 101, 121, 370, 505, 593, 698, 905. see
COURAGE.

EFFECTIVENESS

Furrow

557, 699.

Forge

425, 513, 536. see APOSTOLATE (apostolic effectiveness, fruits).

EGOISM

The Way

see SELFISHNESS.

ENVIRONMENT

The Way

having a Christian influence on it, 376, 566, 805, 850, 986; naturalness, 379, 380, 982.

Furrow

674, 954; going against the current, 361, 416, 840, 980; having recourse to Our Lady, 977. see WORLD.

Forge

570, 717, 720, 724, 792, 797, 848, 859, 899. see WORLD.

ETERNAL LIFE

Forge

987-1055; hope of Heaven, 992-996, 1031-1032; yearning for happiness, 1005-1006, 1021, 1030; eternal happiness, 577.

ETHICS

Forge

709.

EUCHARIST

see DOCILITY, DOCTRINE.

Forge

840-846; different aspects of formation, 603, 892; doctrinal formation, 450, 840-842; need for it, its aim and means, 468, 712; work of formation, 599, 628. see DOCILITY, DOCTRINE.

FORMATION, DOCTRINAL

The Way

from 360 to 386; necessity, 26, 344, 367, 376, 377, 382, 756; criterion, 305, 384, 400, 407, 603; for the apostolate, 346, 347, 349, 370, 371, 379, 380, 921.

FORMATION, PROFESSIONAL

The Way

332-334, 336, 339, 344, 372, 467; human virtues, 350-352, 877, 947; for the apostolate, 338, 340, 342, 345-347.

FORTITUDE

The Way

5, 11, 12, 361, 460, 696; strength, 20, 33, 44, 48, 54, 193, 295, 519, 615; humble, 314, 462, 603, 604, 610, 728, 729; in the ascetical struggle, 4, 19, 22, 167, 325, 853; the help of Our Lady, 508, 515, 982.

Furrow

26, 66, 97, 441, 653, 720, 803, 974; in governance, 822, 967; to overcome the environment, 416, 840, 980. see CONSTANCY, COURAGE, DARING, INTERIOR STRUGGLE, MAGNANIMITY, PA-

GOD'S WILL

Furrow

33, 53, 106, 146, 235, 252, 872; abandonment, 850, 855, 860; acceptance of, 67, 250, 656, 980; love, identification, 34, 273, 352, 793. see ABANDON-MENT, RECTITUDE OF INTENTION.

GOOD USE OF TIME

The Way

6, 13, 14, 251, 253, 254, 354, 355, 420; in our work, 15, 356-358; a plan of life, order, 17, 80, 530, 616.

GOSPEL, THE

The Way

2, 416, 470, 583, 586.

Furrow

reading of, 26, 671-672.

Forge

451, 495, 676; parables, 425, 895; reading of, 8, 322, 546, 754.

GOSSIP

Furrow

410, 902, 917.

GOVERNANCE

Furrow

383, 406, 967-976; mismanagement, tyranny, 386-387, 390, 397-398, 400, 919.

Characteristics of good governance, collegiate, 392;

delegating responsibilities, 972; demanding with affection, 405-406; how to govern, 968; not becoming indispensable, 971; not relying only on organization, 403; positive outlook, 399; teaching others, 402.

The virtues of those who govern, 968-970; fortitude, 383, 581, 967; good manners, 386; humility, 388, 392, 976; justice and charity, 404, 973; not being attached to the job, 705, 976; objectivity, 399; order, 387; prudence, 391, 396, 975; respect for freedom, 401; sense of responsibility, 951, 968-976; understanding, 395.

see AUTHORITY, SERVICE.

Forge

577, 627, 727, 884, 885. see AUTHORITY, SERVICE, SPIRITUAL DIRECTION.

GOVERNMENT

The Way

352, 407, 457; practicing virtues, 10, 53, 424, 463, 488; giving example, 371, 372, 383, 411, 621.

GRACE

The Way

56, 286, 324, 707, 719, 756, 897, 913; docility and correspondence to grace, 152, 242, 255, 362, 761, 784, 992; filial spirit and perseverance, 308, 318, 856, 990; corresponding fully, 670, 807, 829, 901, 965, 985; its action in the soul, 294, 313, 483, 599,

burning coal, 194; burning glance, 297; call to arms, 962; catching butterflies, 537; Christian revolution, 887; clinical history, 173; cutting diamonds, 235; divine adventure, 86, 184; drawbridge, 467; drowning evil in good, 864; fifth column, 112; first appointment, 450; following the banner, 211; gift and its wrapping, 288; gold and copper, 286; guerilla fighter on his own, 409; interior life like a dress, 649; lamps in the dark, 318; let each wayfarer follow his way, 231; links of the chain, 974; Machiavelli, 437; metal alloy, 358; needle to draw the thread, 348; open up the furrow, 215; peeling potatoes, 498; playing chess, 562; professionalitis, 502; return to catacombs, 301; salt of the earth, 342; Sara and Tobias, 846; sentry on guard, 463; seven locks, 834; soldier's wounds, 240; sooner, more and better, 462; spoilt child, 431; study-a-warhorse, 523; thorns and roses, 237; Utopia, 23; wind and the hurricane, 411; windmill, 811; wings to fly with, 414.

GRAPHIC EXAMPLES AND PHRASES

Forge

a double life, 694; accursed magnet, 994; aerial (supernatural), 510; armor of knowledge, 974; artist's dissatisfaction with his work, 385; at Christ's pace, 531; baby too lazy to learn to walk, 291; bacteria and wild beasts, 481; barque of Holy Mother Church, 1043; beating of the heart, 518; become a

HAPPINESS

Furrow

    2, 6, 7, 18, 52, 54, 61, 65, 67, 69-72, 74-76, 79, 81-
88, 146, 153, 167, 185, 249, 296, 305, 321, 340, 347,
471, 507, 517, 528, 613, 676, 678, 696, 795, 797,
817, 859, 861, 891, 893; eternal, 52, 305, 482, 507,
663, 729, 881, 882, 887, 891, 892.

HEART

The Way

    from 145 to 171; an upright heart, 130, 148, 162, 432,
687, 769; freedom and surrender of self, 145, 146,
163, 166, 167, 170, 434, 477, 666; detachment, 149,
151, 152, 636, 678, 726; guarding one's heart, 147,
150, 158-160, 188; big hearted, 525, 764, 912; to
love Jesus Christ, 102, 153-157, 161, 164, 165, 171,
402, 421, 422, 917; Our Lady, 504, 506.

Furrow

    98, 795-830; demands, 796, 800; family ties, 214,
812, 816; guard of the heart, 811-817, 834, 849; Our
Lady's example, 801; purity and the heart, 811, 814,
828, 830; sentimentality, 166; surrender of the heart,
41, 810, 815, 817; to have a heart, 183, 795, 802, 809,
820, 829; to the measure of the Christ's Heart, 813.
see CHARITY, CHASTITY.

Forge

    Guard of the heart, 98, 204, 315-316, 412, 414, 428,
477, 486, 598, 872. see CHASTITY.

HUMILITY

The Way

from 589 to 613; a fundamental virtue, 590, 592, 602, 604, 832; the humility of Our Lord, 432, 533, 538, 606, 607, 671; knowledge of God, 212, 252, 591, 597, 729, 780; self-knowledge, 45, 593, 595, 608, 609, 882; the struggle against pride, 200, 599-601, 611-613, 620, 674, 727; forgetting about ourselves, 177, 204, 207, 625, 676, 677, 726; deification in the good sense, 16, 274, 473, 592, 731; service, 185, 293, 484, 485; humility in the face of our weaknesses, 197, 211, 433, 475, 596, 605, 711, 712; value of humiliations, 165, 589, 594, 698, 771; humility and charity, 118, 430, 446; humility and human virtues, 43, 51, 351, 352, 365, 603, 610; Our Lady, 507, 509, 598, 653.

Furrow

259-289.

Its nature and need for it, 259, 289, 919; its results, 282, 995; and charity, 328, 422, 722, 824; and Our Lady, 124, 289; humiliations, 35, 45, 268, 281; signs of lack of humility, 263; true and false humility, 40, 45, 261-269, 627, 804. see SANCTITY.

Humility and God's glory, 95, 555, 675, 718, 721, 976. see RECTITUDE OF INTENTION.

Humility and self-effacement, 74, 279, 510-511, 515, 533, 630, 631, 697-700, 709-712, 739, 755, 765,

INTEGRITY

Furrow

306, 322, 356.

INTENTION

The Way

see RIGHT INTENTION.

INTERIOR LIFE

Furrow

648-695; characteristics, 79, 81, 154, 426, 649, 651, 655, 679, 682, 769; difficulties in the interior life, 463, 651, 677, 780; dryness, 459, 464, 695, 862; Eucharistic souls, 684-689; getting to know Jesus Christ, 662-683, 794; has to be shown with deeds, 197, 223, 683; need for it, 86, 122, 445, 447, 654, 697, 788-789, 798, 984; prayer, presence of God, 657-665; recourse to Our Lady and to the Saints, 690-695; sanctity and virtues, 648-656; workings of grace, 668-669, 677. see APOSTOLATE (foundation), ASCETICAL STRUGGLE, GRACE, JESUS CHRIST (becoming identified with Christ).

Forge

and Mary, 84, 157, 161-162, 543; and St Joseph, 553; difficulties, 109, 224, 290, 389, 477; foundation of the apostolate, 399, 572, 708, 890, 892, 936, 969; getting to know God, 78, 84, 417, 510, 1003, 1015; has to be shown in deeds, 734, 981; not a matter of feelings, 446, 484-485, 1015; perseverance, 540. see

JOY

The Way

from 657 to 666; a fruit of faith, 203, 297, 657, 770, 906; of abandonment, 659, 758, 766, 768; and of generosity, 237, 255, 308, 696, 704, 807, 992; its roots in the form of a cross, 217, 626, 658, 660, 671, 672, 692, 758; an always norm, 29, 260, 298, 662-666, 879; sowing joy in the world, 548, 661, 965.

JUDGMENT

The Way

168, 431, 745-748, 930.

Furrow

final, 358, 369, 693, 855, 875, 888, 890, 897; in human affairs, 135, 259, 329, 372, 396, 583, 722, 763, 906.

JUSTICE

The Way

36, 46, 400, 407, 603, 686, 702; and charity, 449-451, 454, 457.

Furrow

601, 763, 785, 827, 892, 973; social justice, 16, 227-228, 303, 466, 502, 528, 624, 702, 754.

Forge

502. see CHARITY, FIDELITY, RIGHTS AND DUTIES, TRUTHFULNESS.

Forge

anti-Christian laws, 259, 466, 722; civil laws, 104. see AUTHORITY, CIVIL SOCIETY, GOVERNANCE.

LAZARUS

Forge

211, 476, 495.

LAZINESS

The Way

11, 13, 21, 23, 354-358, 935; in the interior life, 325-331; in work, 15, 337, 343, 348; heroic minutes, 17, 78, 191, 206, 253.

Furrow

68, 165, 265, 377, 505, 509, 581, 716, 957.

LIFE, HUMAN

The Way

135, 224, 297, 306, 420, 692, 703, 752, 753; the meaning of life, 279, 280, 575, 582, 737, 738, 766, 783, 832.

LIFE, SUPERNATURAL

The Way

see SUPERNATURAL LIFE.

LITANY OF OUR LADY

Furrow

180.

LITTLE THINGS

LITURGY

MATURITY

The Way

seriousness, 2, 3, 43, 49-51, 55, 42; frivolity, 17, 18, 41, 42, 374, 939; remedies for frivolity, 13, 333, 343, 375, 564, 590.

Furrow

553, 627, 715; frivolity, 532-553. see CHARACTER, PERSONALITY, VIRTUES.

Forge

53, 307, 493, 642, 806, 850. see CHARACTER, CRITERIA, VIRTUES.

MEANS

The Way

from 470 to 491; don't spare them, 82, 317, 324, 345-347, 404, 471-473, 480; faith in the supernatural means, 365, 433, 470, 474-483, 489, 577, 585, 586; good will, 350, 362, 484-486, 488, 490, 491, 716, 990.

Furrow

material and financial means, 24, 616, 974. see DETACHMENT, POVERTY.

supernatural means, 3, 190, 403, 834, 936, 995; effectiveness, 123, 147, 873. see APOSTOLATE (the foundation).

Forge

material and financial, 218, 284, 525, 731, 807, 809, 963; supernatural, 72, 372, 407, 429, 431, 571, 664,

MISUNDERSTANDING

The Way

491, 643, 647, 650, 688, 697, 964.

MODESTY

Furrow

false, 266.

MORTIFICATION

The Way

from 172 to 207; the point of mortification, 169, 179, 182, 187, 194, 195, 299; fruits of mortification, 172, 180, 198, 199, 701, 929, 946; spirit of penance, 5, 208, 210, 214, 215, 218, 227, 231, 696; the Holy Cross, 163, 175, 178, 193, 203, 277, 647, 775; sacrifice, 186, 189, 306, 635, 683, 763, 834, 881; interior mortification, 13, 43, 173, 174, 177, 181, 188, 201, 631, 689; mortification of the senses, 181-184, 193, 196, 222, 368, 677, 679-682; penances, 200, 202, 221, 224, 232, 233; in ordinary things, 17, 20, 44, 85, 205, 373; small mortifications, 191, 204, 206, 223, 885, 899; Our Lady, 508, 509.

Furrow

Its nature and need for it, 255, 467, 632, 841, 978-984, 988, 992; and charity, 779, 819, 981, 990; and cheerfulness, 59, 982-983, 987.

Corporal mortification, 834, 903, 985; of the senses, 132, 660, 670, 682, 832.

NATURALNESS

The Way

from 639 to 656; spontaneity, 351, 352, 379, 380, 743, 840, 843, 858; discretion, 51, 55, 639-642, 645, 652, 655; humility, simplicity, 410, 440, 647-649, 651, 654, 656, 848, 877, 952; prudence, 643, 644, 646, 650, 674; in the apostolate, 347, 839, 846, 958, 970, 972, 986; Our Lady, 499, 510, 653.

Furrow

554-566; and effectiveness, 557; discretion, 647, 910; humility, simplicity, 203, 561-562, 564, 565; in Christian life, 558-560, 566, 833; in doing mortifications, 985-987; in the apostolate, 188, 320, 321, 555, 563; naturalness of Jesus, 554, 556. see ORDINARY LIFE.

Forge

140, 143, 508. see ORDINARY LIFE.

NOBILITY

Furrow

12, 26, 307, 441, 613, 615, 623, 639, 662, 677, 743, 754, 772, 911.

NORMS OF PIETY

Forge

81, 83, 485. see PLAN OF LIFE.

OBEDIENCE

The Way

from 614 to 629; trust in obedience, 617, 621-623, 625, 628, 629, 727; docility, 56, 62, 156, 362, 624, 761, 777; humble obedience, 63, 190, 618, 620, 626, 706, 715; intelligent obedience, 333, 615, 619, 627; in the interior life, 59, 60, 64, 377; in the apostolate, 315, 383, 614, 616, 936, 941, 952.

Furrow

13, 151, 372-382, 398, 408-415; its nature and need for it, 259, 376, 381; characteristics, 372-376, 378-380, 382, 415, 435, 999; discipline, 376, 409, 410, 412, 415; in the apostolate, 373, 377. see DOCIL-ITY, FAITH, FORMATION, GOVERNANCE, SPIRITUAL DIRECTION.

Forge

its nature and need for it, 132, 231, 241, 327, 530, 599; characteristics, 627, 629, 727; effectiveness, 574, 626; in the apostolate, 133, 175, 581, 666. see DOCILITY, FAITH (operative), FORMATION, SPIRITUAL DIRECTION.

OBSCURITY

Furrow

273, 485, 701.

OBSTINACY AND STUBBORNNESS

Furrow

65, 263, 274, 574, 606.

OFFERING UP OUR ACTIONS

Furrow

499, 675, 997.

OPTIMISM

The Way

40, 415, 472, 476, 482, 988; all for the best, 378, 404-406, 473, 879; consequence of faith, 474, 483, 487, 717, 719, 792, 875.

Furrow

faith, hope, 56, 78, 80, 90, 118, 127, 426, 864; in the struggle, 68, 80; *omnia in bonum*, 127; positive outlook in governing, 398-399. see CHEERFUL-NESS AND JOY, DIVINE FILIATION, HOPE, TRUST (in God).

Forge

assurance of victory, 283, 337, 344; Christian optimism, 220, 222, 237, 321, 659; in the interior struggle and in the apostolate, 217, 223, 637; not to fear anybody or anything, 260. see CHEERFULNESS AND JOY, DIVINE FILIATION, HOPE, PESSI-MISM, TRUST (in God).

ORDER

The Way

15, 76, 78-80.

Furrow

384, 448, 506, 509, 511-512, 584, 739, 828, 952-953. see TIME.

PERSEVERANCE

718, 772, 815, 884, 894; unity of life, 266, 271, 273, 275, 287, 359, 416, 882; the means, 268-270, 272, 288, 302, 312, 540, 564, 567, 986; through Our Lady, 276, 495, 900.

Furrow

334, 447-450, 473, 478, 657-660, 681, 856-857, 900, 906, 926. see ASPIRATIONS, CONTEMPLATIVES, MEDITATION, PRAYER.

Forge

as children of God, 80, 501; at work, 744-747; contemplatives in the midst of the world, 343, 506, 738, 740; human devices, 510, 923; in ordinary life, 90, 505-506, 511, 538, 743, 1014; we are never alone, 250, 724, 751. see ASPIRATIONS, CONTEMPLATIVES, PRAYER, PIETY.

PRESUMPTION

Furrow

704. see HOPE.

PRIDE

The Way

413, 485, 599-601, 611, 683, 780-783; manifestations, 25, 31, 48, 119, 200, 260, 351, 620, 698; struggle against pride, 177, 589, 602, 612, 613, 677, 709, 784, 949.

Furrow

65, 74, 135, 162, 261, 274, 383, 474, 695-726. see HUMILITY.

SELF-EFFACEMENT

Furrow

see HUMILITY (and self-effacement).

Forge

forgetting about oneself, 97, 141, 150, 217, 247, 592, 601, 683, 803, 853, 861, 915, 1049-1052; giving oneself to God, 43-44, 61, 162; giving oneself to others, 368, 591; sacrifice of Love, 208, 364, 532, 839. see CROSS, GENEROSITY, HUMILITY (and forgetting about oneself), MORTIFICATION, SELF-SURRENDER, SERVICE.

SELF-KNOWLEDGE

The Way

18, 50, 225, 686; a condition for humility, 591-597, 604-609, 690, 698, 729, 780, 882-884; spiritual direction, 33, 59, 63, 65, 932.

Forge

180-181, 185, 222, 314, 326, 363, 710, 794.

SELF-MASTERY

The Way

19, 295.

SELF-SACRIFICE

Furrow

71, 249, 793, 814, 819, 826, 998. see CROSS, GEN-EROSITY, HUMILITY (and self-effacement), MORTIFICATION, SELF-SURRENDER.

SIN

The Way

141, 296, 386, 662, 708, 880; hatred for sin, 286, 357, 435, 437, 734, 749; temptation, struggle, 127, 132-142, 167, 307, 713-716, 879, 992; venial sins, 327-331, 828; penance, 197, 211, 402, 532, 596, 671, 861, 886; pardon, 211, 267, 309, 310, 452, 686, 884, 887, 985; humility, confidence, 200, 260-264, 536, 711, 712, 719, 865, 870, 991; help of Our Lady, 493, 495, 498, 503, 506, 516.

Furrow

134, 139, 171, 315, 407, 836, 837, 839, 890, 944, 993; aversion from sin, 258, 814; its effects, 843-844, 848, 851; repentance, 65, 324, 838; struggle against sin, 143-144. see CONTRITION, REPARATION.

Forge

394, 464, 550, 1002, 1024, 1029; of omission, 146, 577; original sin, 183, 187, 720; sorrow, reparation, 207, 402, 417, 655, 1026; temptations, struggle, 119, 124, 158, 166, 411; venial sin, 114. see ATONEMENT, CONTRITION.

SINCERITY

The Way

with God, 47, 865, 868, 870, 880, 884, 887; with oneself, 18, 33, 34, 37, 236, 662, 700, 788; in spiritual direction, 64, 65, 259, 444, 596, 862, 932;

STUDY

The Way

> from 332 to 359; a grave obligation, 332, 334, 336, 348; good use of time, 354-358; sanctifying study, 333, 335, 337, 341, 343, 345, 359; apostolate, 338, 340, 344, 347, 602, 978.

Furrow

> 190, 229, 381, 396, 447-448, 471, 474, 483, 522-526, 572, 604, 617-619, 622, 656, 716, 739, 781, 927. see CULTURE, FORMATION, READING.

Forge

> 43, 467, 841. see CULTURE, FORMATION, READING, WORK.

SUFFERING

The Way

> 194, 208, 209, 215, 217, 419, 439, 699, 969; the will of God, 213, 294, 691, 718, 722; spirit of penance, 169, 182, 219, 224, 234, 436, 548, 690, 885; faith and hope, 199, 229, 230, 256, 692, 717, 726, 727; Our Lady of Sorrows, 506-509, 982.

Furrow

> 2, 52, 82, 139, 149, 204, 233, 236, 248, 268, 466, 567, 591, 593, 698, 714, 733, 780, 813, 861, 879, 887, 920, 989, 997.

SUPERFICIALITY

Furrow

> 542.

19, 27, 279, 773, 776, 904; reciting the *Te Deum*, 609.

THEOLOGY

Furrow

293, 353, 572.

TIME

Furrow

and eternal life, 613, 882-883, 893, 963; and God's glory, 508-509, 552, 997; in self-surrender, 167; in study, 523; in the apostolate, 194, 224; in the plan of life, 381; making good use of 19, 155, 510, 620-621, 996. see ORDER.

Forge

making good use of, 163, 522, 701, 705-706, 962-963.

TIMIDITY

Furrow

100, 118, 267, 306, 774.

TOUGHNESS

Furrow

92, 416, 418, 432, 777, 779, 781-782.

TRIBULATIONS

The Way

from 685 to 706; taking advantage of them, 201, 208, 219, 230, 308, 696, 701, 716, 727; contradictions, 14, 165, 485, 687-689, 693-695, 717, 955, 956; difficulties, 12, 317, 476, 480, 482, 487, 697, 700,

humility, hope in God, 158, 181, 187, 212, 606;
leaving them in the hands of God, 201, 426, 484. see
DEFECTS, HUMILITY (and weaknesses).

WILL, THE

The Way

316-318, 324, 490, 718, 756, 777; fortitude, 5, 11,
12, 21-25, 36, 44, 615; struggle, 4, 19, 42, 222, 295,
320, 714; actual willingness, 293, 382, 413, 757-
759, 762, 763, 766.

Furrow

154, 166, 523, 769-794, 798, 852. see CHARAC-
TER, PERSONALITY.

WILL OF GOD

The Way

from 754 to 778; identification with it, love, 213,
756, 757, 579, 762, 765, 773, 774; abandonment to
it, 718, 729, 731, 739, 758, 760, 766-768, 864;
fulfilling it, 413, 480, 691, 754, 755, 761, 763, 776,
912; docility, obedience, 156, 617, 628, 629, 775,
777; right intention, 287, 293, 490, 709, 772, 778,
787-789; the faithfulness of Our Lady, 497, 508,
510, 512.

Forge

love, identifying oneself with the will of God, 40, 42,
48, 100, 122, 240, 292, 323, 390, 398, 422, 484, 512,
529, 617, 769, 771, 775, 788, 803, 812-814, 822,
1006, 1034, 1039; Our Lady's example, 854; struggle

INDEX TO
SCRIPTURAL REFERENCES

OLD TESTAMENT

NEW TESTAMENT